Tracking the Jews

Manchester University Press

Tracking the Jews

Ecumenical Protestants, Conversion, and the Holocaust

Carolyn Sanzenbacher

MANCHESTER UNIVERSITY PRESS

Copyright © Carolyn Sanzenbacher 2024

The right of Carolyn Sanzenbacher to be identified as the author of this work has been asserted in accordance with the Copyright, Designs and Patents Act 1988.

Published by Manchester University Press
Oxford Road, Manchester, M13 9PL

www.manchesteruniversitypress.co.uk

British Library Cataloguing-in-Publication Data
A catalogue record for this book is available from the British Library

ISBN 978 1 5261 6129 1 hardback

First published 2024

The publisher has no responsibility for the persistence or accuracy of URLs for any external or third-party internet websites referred to in this book, and does not guarantee that any content on such websites is, or will remain, accurate or appropriate.

Typeset
by Cheshire Typesetting Ltd, Cuddington, Cheshire

*In honour of Professor Karl A. Schleunes (1937–2021),
pioneer scholar in Holocaust Studies, exemplary teacher,
friend and colleague for more than thirty years*

Contents

List of figures	*page* viii
Acknowledgements	ix
Abbreviations	xii
About the cover	xv
Introduction	1
1 Conversion and the Jewish problem: 1925–1932	25
2 In the shadows of response: 1933–1936	67
3 Antisemitism, refugees and war: 1937–1939	116
4 Voices and silences in war: 1940–1944	165
5 More than one guilt in the embers: 1945–1948	218
6 The Jews as a problem	270
Select bibliography	297
Index	327

Figures

0.1	Ecumenical movement, early to mid-twentieth century	10
1.1	Mission planning map for world distribution of Jews, 1928	37
1.2	European mission agencies associated with ICCAJ by 1932	48
2.1	Facsimile of 'Disappearance of Jew' illustration chart, 1933	79
2.2	ICCAJ Director European itineraries by nation, 1931–1936	84
3.1	From West to East: European 'sending' and 'receiving' missionary nations	132
3.2	ICCAJ Director European itineraries in the wake of the *Anschluss*	134
3.3	ICCAJ Director European itineraries after German occupation of Czechoslovakia	140
4.1	ICCAJ estimated 'Distribution of Jewish Population', December 1942	201
5.1	WCCIF itineraries in 1945 Allied occupied Germany before the Stuttgart Declaration of Guilt	227

Acknowledgements

This study began in 2005 with microfiche from Yale University Divinity Library, which led among other paths to the vast archives of the World Council of Churches in Geneva. The paper trail back and forth from Geneva to repositories in Britain, the United States and Continental Europe provided access to hundreds of World War II era archival boxes, as well as hundreds more of primary source printed materials. My appreciation for all who have encouraged, supported and informed the path of research which yielded more than 20,000 pages of archival documents could be a book in itself. All of the archivists from repositories listed in the bibliography aided the research immensely, but some must be mentioned for their help beyond any call of duty.

The expert aid of Karen Robson, Jenny Ruthven, Emily Rawlings and Sabrina Kett, as well as the breadth and depth of holdings in the University of Southampton Special Collections and Parkes Library, have been indispensable. Martha Smiley and Joan Duffy made weeks in Yale Divinity Library Special Collections not only productive but delightful. Anne-Emmanuelle Tankam, Hans von Reutte and Denyse Léger of the WCC archives provided support and work space for weeks at a time over many years with unlimited access to its web of archives, including unsorted World War II boxes still seemingly heavy with the dust of the period. Nancy Taylor and Jennifer Barr provided access to unprocessed period materials at the Presbyterian Historical Society in addition to innumerable catalogued boxes. Marc Schumacher at UNCG Jackson Library was invaluable for translation of French documents and acquisition of elusive articles in microfilm collections. Beth Rowe at UNC Chapel

Hill Davis Library helped with rare microfilm holdings over several years. Colin Harris in Special Collections at Oxford Bodleian Library was key to gaining access to restricted materials. Laurie Austin at the Harry S. Truman Presidential Library and Katie Small at Lambeth Palace Library were essential in the last stages of the book.

Simon De Montfalcon at University of Southampton Hartley Library literally saved the day on two critical occasions. Others who cannot go unmentioned are Laurel Wolfson, Hebrew Union Jewish Institute of Religion Library; Sandra Stelts, Rare Books and Manuscripts at Pennsylvania State University Libraries; Matthew Park, Anderson Library, University of Minnesota; Amanda Lawrence and Linda Stepp, University of Illinois at Urbana-Champaign Special Collections; Brian Keough and Jodi Boyle, University of Albany Special Collections; Sandra Costlich, Phi Beta Kappa Archives; Megan O'Connell, Rubenstein Rare Book and Manuscript Library at Duke University; Dexter McCrea, Duke Library Service Center, whose everyday smile was a pleasure to behold. In a category of their own, enough cannot be said about the excellence of work and ease of collaboration with cartographers Kelly Sandefer and Jonathan Wyss of Beehive Mapping. That is equally true of production editor Katie Evans, copyeditor Doreen Kruger, proofreader Kathrin Luddecke and indexer Louise Chapman, whose thoughtful consideration and attentiveness to detail have been of inestimable worth.

First among the many long-term investors without whom this book could not have been written is my husband, Dr Larry James Sanzenbacher, who in addition to his own professional work, kept our home fires burning during many long periods of absence. Without his sustaining investment and love over many years this project could not have been undertaken. I acknowledge with gratitude the encouragement of the Roger Swirk Award for Excellence in Philosophy, the Josephine Hege Phi Beta Kappa Award, the University of Southampton Humanities Archival Award, and Vice Chancellor's Research Scholarship, which provided funding to follow evidence and present research at international conferences in Germany, Poland, Italy, the Netherlands, US, UK and South Africa. The engaging comments from international colleagues have been profoundly valuable. I am especially grateful to Tom Lawson and Joachim Schloer for incisive critiques at a mid-stage version of this project, as well as the invaluable critical perspectives, questions and encouragements of anonymous reviewers.

My appreciation for the counsel and patience of Alun Richards at Manchester University Press through delays due to family illness and death can never be sufficiently expressed. My intellectual debts run equally deep, beginning with Gary Rosenkrantz, Joshua Hoffmann, Terry McConnell and Robert Rosthal of the UNCG Department of Philosophy for years of thinking on questions that matter. I thank Gary in particular for his unequalled help in thinking about theories of hatred and universalised ideas, particularly those with metaphysical cores. I am deeply grateful to Tony Kushner at the Parkes Institute, whose wealth of insightful questions, intellectual acumen and untiring efforts on behalf of scholarship cannot be adequately told. Working with him over the past decade has left an indelible mark I am proud to bear. Last, I am permanently indebted to Karl Schleunes for years of thinking on the 'Jewish question', for investment and prodding at every stage of this study until shortly before his death in 2021. There is no doubt in my mind, had he lived to see its publishing, he would have asked, as he often did, 'what about this? is there anything else that can be said to make more clear what is happening?' In a very real sense, this book, with full ownership of inadequacies or errors, is my attempt to frame an answer to that question.

Abbreviations

AFSC	American Friends Service Committee.
AJC	American Jewish Committee
BICCAJ	British Sector of ICCAJ
CC	*Christian Century*
CCAR	Central Conference of American Rabbis
CCJ	Council of Christians and Jews (British)
CCR	Christian Council for Refugees from Germany and Central Europe
CEFR	Church of England Council on Foreign Relations
CEMC	Church of England Missionary Council
CBMS	Conference of British Missionary Societies (formally, Conference of Missionary Societies in Great Britain and Ireland)
CIJS	Christian Institute for Jewish Studies
CMJ	Church Mission to Jews
CMJa	Church Mission to Jews Archives
CEMS	Church of England Missionary Council
DHL	Donald and Helen Lowrie Papers
ECB	European Central Bureau for Inter-Church Aid
ECCO	Emergency Committee of Christian Organizations
ECR	Ecumenical Commission for Refugees
EUICCAJ	European Sector of ICCAJ
ESR	European Student Relief
FCC	Federal Council of Churches
FCCGW	FCC Committee of Goodwill Between Christians and Jews
FFPC	French Federation of Protestant Churches

FMC	Foreign Missions Conference of North America
HCA	Hebrew Christian Alliance
HCR	High Commission for Refugees
HEM	*The History of the Ecumenical Movement, 1517–1948*
HMC	Home Missions Council
HSL	Henry Smith Leiper Papers
ICCAJ	International Committee on the Christian Approach to the Jews
ICCR	International Christian Committee for German Refugees
ICPIS	*International Christian Press and Information Service*
ICRC	International Committee of the Red Cross
IMC	International Missionary Council
IRM	*International Review of Missions*
ISS	International Student Service
JDB	*Jewish Daily Bulletin*
JDC	Jewish Joint Distribution Committee
JTA	*Jewish Telegraphic Agency*
LPL	Lambeth Palace Library
NAICCAJ	North American Sector of ICCAJ
NSDAP	National Socialist German Workers' Party
OCOR	*The Oxford Conference Official Report*
PC	WCCIF Provisional Committee
PP	James Parkes Papers
PRO	Public Records Office
RIIA	Royal Institute of International Affairs
SJC	Society of Jews and Christians
SCM	Student Christian Movement
SFPC	Swiss Federation of Protestant Churches
SVM	Student Volunteer Movement
UCCLW	Universal Christian Council for Life and Work
UNCHR	United Nation Commission on Human Rights
UNECOSOC	United Nations Economic and Social Council
UNRRA	United Nations Relief and Rehabilitation Administration
USGCC	United States Group Control Council Germany

WA	World Alliance for Promoting International Friendship through the Churches
WCC	World Council of Churches
WCCIF	World Council of Churches in Formation
WCFO	World Conference on Faith and Order
WJC	World Jewish Congress
WPA	War Prisoners Aid
WSCF	World Student Christian Federation
WYMCA	World Alliance of YMCAs
WYWCA	World Alliance of YWCAs
YDL	Yale Divinity Library

About the cover

In April and May of 1945, ordinary citizens of historically Christian towns in Germany were ordered by Allied troops to bury the corpses of concentration-camp inmates who were murdered on the notorious Nazi death marches in the last days of the war. A photographic record of those grim burial events has been preserved as proof that the human eye had indeed set on the unimaginable. British and American soldiers stand with shouldered guns as German citizens are forced to enter the world of Nazi extremes within the proximity of their own homes. Men, women and children walk slowly through the outposts of hatred and violence, between rows of emaciated corpses, through meadows of sloping hills scarred on both sides by the clothed and unclothed, the burnt and unburnt, the recent and rotting. Here and there like living props among stacks and lines of the dead a woman in a pinafore buries her mouth in a lace handkerchief, a child stares limply at the ground, a man in a suit clutches his briefcase as if it were a child. The young hold on to the old, the older lead the oldest, and the lame lean on the fit. Many have their hands clasped before them, higher or lower as in prayer, reverence or despair. In other captured scenes grim-faced men with shovels unearth bodies that were hastily buried by retreating SS troops. Some, both men and women, move bodies from pits and stacks to coffins that are placed on pyres, raised by groups of four, then carried through cobbled streets to places of burial. The cover image of a forced and sombre caravan confronting the evidence of Nazi atrocities they denied knowing anything about is representative of the hundreds captured. A copy of the original photograph has been dissected and reassembled on an indefinite background to emphasise that the lines of bystanders being confronted with the inconvenient evidence of what we now call the Holocaust reach far beyond the cobbled streets of German towns, far beyond the boundaries of Germany, beyond the killing fields of occupied Europe, beyond the spring of 1945.

Introduction

On Sunday 22 August 1948, three years after the near extermination of European Jewry, some 351 ecclesiastically attired delegates from 147 international churches in 44 countries marched in solemn procession through the stately Nieuwe Kerk of Amsterdam to celebrate the founding of the World Council of Churches (WCC). It was an occasion of long anticipated development, driven through two world wars by the idea of a unified ecumenical voice in a world in need of the truths of Christianity. Over the course of fourteen days, and through the theme of 'Man's Disorder and God's Design', the international delegates pondered what could be said together with spiritual authority about the universal Church and world disorder. The theme and content of the resulting statements reflected not only concern for the plight of postwar society, of which surviving Jews were a part, but also the belief that God's design for healing the world's disorder required its Christianisation. As formulated in an official statement recognising 'the extermination of six million Jews', while calling attention to 'the continued existence of a Jewish people which does not acknowledge Christ', that included Jewish acquiescence to Christianity.[1] Built into the official statement by way of title, committee name and opening words was 'the Christian Approach to the Jews'. Appearing first as a theme for International Missionary Council conferences in 1927 and then as a subsidiary organisation in 1929, the International Committee on the Christian Approach to the Jews (ICCAJ) had so stamped itself on Protestant thinking by the founding assembly of the WCC in 1948 that its views were described as representative of 'the official concern of the Protestant Churches about the Jewish Question'.[2]

What those views were, why they were held, and how this fledgling body achieved status as expert on the 'Jewish Question' in the same years its 'Final Solution' was being sought by Nazi Germany are categorical questions at the core of this book. The unfolding story in its broadest dimensions, from the rubbles of World War I to the ashes of World War II, is a multilayered history of relations between a Protestant framework for the global evangelisation of Jews, the network of bodies that made up the ecumenical Protestant movement of the early twentieth century, and the streams of thought on antisemitism and the Jewish question that flowed through its networking channels during the Hitler years. Under a more close-up lens, it is a story of metaphysical vision, beliefs, ideas and words: what they were, how they were used, and the ends to which they served.

In the fall of 1925 a neoteric theory on relations between the Jewish problem and Christianity's historical failure to convert the people it claimed to supersede began to emerge from the pages of the *International Review of Missions*. By spring 1927 a unanimity of delegates from mainstream Protestant bodies in twenty-six countries had given rise to a series of conference findings on relations between a universal Jewish problem and the societal need for Jewish conversion. ICCAJ, whose theoretical base was grounded in the claims of those findings, was brought into existence as a lobbying and planning body for international expansion and adoption of church policy on Jews and Jewish missions. By the eve of Hitler's rise, with regional sectors in Britain, Continental Europe and North America, the mandated enterprise had become a fully constituted body, a brand name programme of Jewish evangelisation recognised in thirty-six countries, and the self-christened agent for educating international Protestant churches on the right Christian attitude toward Jews, Jewish missions and antisemitism.

The conversionary theory derived from this ternary role was architecturally complex with theological-metaphysical, theoretical-sociological and geographical-political structures. Each was predicated on the belief that Christianity was the solution to societal ills (in general) and the Jewish problem (in particular). That a universal Jewish problem existed, that the problem arose wherever Jews were populated densely enough to manifest

'Jewish' traits, that Jews worsened societal conditions by refusing conversion were mainstay tenets of this transnationally shared understanding. Loving the Jews enough to help bring them to their 'spiritual destiny' was seen as the highest mark of Christian benevolence. It was also understood as a method of reparation for historical Christian injustices to Jews, and the two combined constituted the salvation aspect of an emerging benevolence vision. The other was comprised of a socio-political awareness of the Jewish problem and the Christian duty to solve it, involving two modes of defence: defence of Christendom against increasing Jewish influence and defence of Jews against racial discrimination, which was antithetical to Christian universalism. Both were critical to the vision of Christian benevolence, even though the former dealt with the realm of metaphysical salvation and the latter with earthly defence.

The primary objective of the mandated initiative was to plan, unify and educate all Protestant forces so that missions to Jews would become an everyday responsibility of every church in every nation of the world. The main strategies were global expansion of Jewish evangelisation and concomitant rallying and education of Protestants to the cause of Jewish missions. The combined work was to spread horizontally and vertically from regional cores in Continental Europe, Britain and North America.

Demographics were central to all aims and strategies. Knowing where Jews were on the geographic landscape was crucial to all stages of planning. With the outbreak of war, the destruction of European mission fields, and increasing numbers of Jewish refugees moving across the Continent, the use of data shifted accordingly. Conversionary theorists understood that postwar 'reoccupation' of European mission fields would depend upon wartime monitoring of shifting Jewish populations. By summer 1940 data were being requested from the League of Nations High Commission for Refugees about 'where the Jews were and how much the numbers... had been affected by emigration and forced removal'. By the end of 1942 more than five million European Jews were thought to be accounted for. As Jewish populations were tracked during the remainder of the war, postwar planning was contoured to fit the constitutional founding of the WCC, with the mutual goal of evangelising surviving European Jewry in WCC constituency countries.

This book analyses the beliefs, ideas, concepts, arguments and policies of the people who tracked the Jews. It reconstructs from primary sources the vision and motives of architects, builders, spokesmen and supporters of this unprecedented conversionary initiative, as well as its opposers. The narrative moves in chronological time with unfolding events, back and forth between London, Budapest, Warsaw, New York, Geneva, Berlin, Vienna and other European cities on a landscape of rapidly accelerating Nazi aggressions. In charting the path on which the initiative was becoming expert on the Jewish problem, it locates and follows a second social-issue trajectory as the two intermittently intersect on a refugee-laden landscape. It analyses the presences and absences of official Protestant voices on behalf of Jews from both trajectories, placing under the spotlight the backroom dynamics and politics of arriving at official responses. With Nobel Peace laureates of 1930 and 1946 on either end of a richly populated field of involvements, it marks the path taken from a 1925 call for Christian experts on the Jewish problem to the 1948 WCC statement calling attention to the 'continuing presence of a people which did not acknowledge Christ'. In so doing, it brings into focus on each end of its chronological structure the socio-theological conception of the ongoing existence of the 'Jewish people' as an unsolved problem for the Christian Church.

Overarching questions

There are two overarching and interconnecting sets of questions linked to the broader chronology and sources of this study. The first is concerned with what was being done by the initiative, to whom and why, which forces from the shadows a 1900-year history of metaphysical borders between the Christian 'saved' and Jewish 'unsaved'. By the early second century the emerging Church held that the inception of Christianity signified the end of Judaism and that conversion was necessary if Jews were to be other than an abandoned deicidal people. Jewish refusal to acquiesce to the Christian death knell of Judaism created manifold problems for the Church, not least of which was explaining how it marked the end of Judaism when Judaism continued to exist. Supersessionism required conversion, and failure to convert required apologia for conversionary failure. As seen in the *Adversus Judaeos* canon that passed from generation to generation as part of Christianity's theological heritage, that included a centuries long discourse on how, why and where the 'dissident' Jewish people fit into the metaphysical schemata governing Christian theology. The portrait of two identity-bearing groups – divinely established Christians bearing salvation to the world and divinely condemned Jews bearing witness to deicidal sin – remained unchanged throughout nineteen centuries of Jewish refusal to validate Christianity's death knell of Judaism.

The conversionary theory emerging in the postwar milieu of 1925 did so against this background of belief, asserting the failure of the Church to convert 'the Jews' as a central tenet of its platform. In trying to conceptualise what was happening as this played out in archival documents, neither 'proselytisation' nor 'evangelisation' sufficed to capture the urgency of proclaimed purpose. The concept of 'tracking' that arose from years of immersion in the archives is based on ideas and language embedded with geographical elements in the documents. First, divinely dispersed Jews were cast as the only people necessarily related to Christian and world destiny, the only ones with no country, the only ones for whom the world itself was providentially the field of mission operations. Second, because aspirations for global conversion required interaction with geographic landscapes, demographic data of Jewish populations, maps and the language of territorial 'occupation' were regular features of the discourse. Third, a universal Jewish problem transcending all geographic boundaries was theoretically incorporated into the discourse as warrant for the societal need of global expansion of Jewish missions. The permeation of all these elements, along with a repeatedly stated urgency and certitude of divine purpose for finding and following Jews, is what I am conceptualising as 'tracking'.

The second set of overarching questions has to do with when and how the 'tracking' was being done. By virtue of the fact that it was during the Hitler years, it also has to do with whether or not what was being done was in any way related to the question of how six million Jews could have been systematically murdered in twentieth-century Christian Europe. In asking this requisite historiographic question, I am calling attention to the 'Christian Church' as part of the bystander category in Holocaust research.[3] This artificially constructed category that no one loves, or wants to be put into, is at present the best we have to *begin* the differentiation that is necessary to a historical understanding of the Holocaust. As currently used, contemporaries who were neither perpetrators nor victims were bystanders, even if, as framed by Tony Kushner, they were co-present 'only through the media'.[4] The inclusive effect is that bystanders were not only more numerous than the six million Jewish victims or hundreds of thousands of perpetrators, they are the most disparate and least understood of the three basic research groups in Holocaust studies.

One of the major problems created by such grouping is that protectors, aiders and rescuers of Jews are in the same category as millions who did nothing to oppose Nazi atrocities against Jews or in varying ways aided, enabled, supported or legitimised perpetrator actions. This holds true across the bystander spectrum, whether within the immediate proximities of the killing fields, as depicted in the cover image of this book, or in cases as far removed as neutral Sweden, the Vatican in Rome, or the offices of a Church agency in Geneva, New York or London. The problem is common to all major divisions of the bystander category: democratic governments, Allied and neutral European states, German-occupied, Axis and satellite countries, the world press, international humanitarian alliances, world and national Jewish organisations, and the Christian Church.

Some issues, however, are specific only to the Church. After nearly eight decades of research and debate, scholars generally agree that, while there were no sufficient causes of the Holocaust, there were multiple necessary causes, one of which was the 1900-year history of negative Church teachings on Jews. It is also the case that the largest division of bystanders was the Christian Church, which means that the agent of a claimed necessary cause of the Holocaust was also a predominant bystander, appearing in every geographical schematic, overlapping in time and place in all Axis, occupied, neutral and Allied countries. This becomes all the more salient, and solemn, when placed with the additional fact that scholars have also indicted 'the Church' with a general unexplained silence during the twelve years of Nazi persecution and extermination of Jews. The problem of explaining the conversionary subject of this book is thus part of the larger problem of explaining *or* refuting the silence, indifference or complicity of the Church as it responded in widely diverse geographic conditions to escalating Nazi persecution of European Jewry.

The scope of sources for this study, as well as their conspicuous blending of the Jewish problem and Jewish conversion, place it in one of the most Church-sensitive and thorny areas of Holocaust research. Conversion and baptism are issues in perpetrator, victim and bystander research by virtue of their centrality to the Nazi Aryan legislation that became archetype to all disfranchisements of Jews in Nazi Europe. The first racial laws in 1933 defined as non-Aryan anyone with at least one Jewish grandparent. Non-Aryans were further defined in the 1935 Nuremberg Laws according to a complexly constructed definition of inherited 'Jewishness', based on the birth religion of forebears. Any Jew or Christian who had at least one Jewish grandparent was classified and marginalised as 'Jew' or first and second degree *'Mischling'* (half-Jew), to use period racial terms. Christian churches were pulled into the classifying system by way of their roles as keepers of baptismal records, conveyors of baptismal sacraments and dispensers of baptismal certificates. Possession or absence of the documents was the basis on which 'Jews' were defined and incrementally removed from the civil protections of their societies to a 'stateless' status under Nazi control. While Nazi and Nazi-inspired legislation made clear that baptism would not affect classification, numbers of Jews across Europe nonetheless sought conversion and baptism as an uncertain means of escaping the dangers of being classified as 'Jew'. Church responses to the defining laws, as well as clerical willingness or refusal to baptise or forge baptismal records and certificates, remain relevant to all three areas of Holocaust research.

This book brings to the literature the case of a sustained twelve-year international discourse on Jewish conversion and baptism taking place at the same time that Jews were being excised from European societies on the basis of insufficient conversionary evidence. In bringing the discourse to light, however, it resists a caution found in the broader literature on the Church and the

Holocaust. The multidisciplinary post-Holocaust research that gave rise to scholarly indictments of the Church also led to critical theological changes and impetus for the repair of Christian–Jewish relations. Because all three areas are linked to the triggering events of the Holocaust, it is not unusual to find historical, theological and dialogical concerns discussed in the same broad post-Holocaust literature. It is also not rare to find direct or inferential caution about continual emphasis on historical anti-Judaism, on the grounds that it will bear negatively on advancement of Christian–Jewish relations.[5]

While granting the importance of improved Christian–Jewish relations, this study yet argues that it is historiographically unproductive to view the dialogical work of the present as having precedence over the work of investigating the Holocaust past. Scholarship is still burdened with unsolved issues for which answers cannot be found without studying more closely the anti-Judaic traditions indicted by post-Holocaust research. The depth and degree of anti-Judaism in the discourse of this conversionary initiative in fact requires that a cohering theme is ideo-theological, with roots in both traditional anti-Judaic teachings of the Church and the modern construct of the Jewish problem.

The primary sources on which this book is based hold in common with Christopher Clark's study of late nineteenth and early twentieth-century missions to the Jews of Prussia that 'no other body of texts' provides such a 'sustained and considered appraisal of the Jewish Question'.[6] As with Clark, the sources here provide arguably the most inclusive and substantive preserve of non-Nazi Protestant discourse on the Jewish problem during the twelve years of Hitler's rule. The 'Jewish problem', or 'Jewish question', like the related term 'antisemitism', was a terminological and conceptual construct of mid-to-late nineteenth-century origin.[7] Although coined by non-Jews to describe what was said to be a societal problem, and claimed by those who from 1879 called themselves 'antisemitic', the historically familiar conceptual furnishings of the 'Jewish problem' had an appeal that extended far beyond those willing to accept that 'antisemitism' was its solution. As such, it was used by both professed antisemitic adherents and those who on varying grounds were not. The Protestant conversionists in Clark's study, as well as those here, were among latter countless groups who eschewed racial antisemitism while drawing from an expanding cache of western ideas to describe, explain and defend solutions to what was commonly understood to be a universal 'Jewish problem'. My use of these terms without encapsulating marks throughout this study is a stylistic choice to keep uncluttered an already complex topic, and does not in any way imply validation of the artificial and harmful constructs.

The broader ecumenical context

Any attempt to understand the origins, development and multidirectional influences of the conversionary initiative emerging in 1925 must begin with a wide-angle view. To think of this conceptually, structurally and historically, ICCAJ was part of the subcategory of western church agencies delineated as 'Protestant' and 'ecumenical', as opposed to the conciliar sense of ecumenical that stems from Catholicism or of Protestants who were not 'ecumenical'. The Greek word *oikoumene*, with a geographic meaning of the inhabited earth, is found in early Church history but it was not until the second half of the nineteenth century that perception of its breadth and outreach began to manifest in world missions and social relief programmes.

By 1910 a vision of unified Christian forces evangelising the globe had drawn some 1200 Protestant delegates to a World Missionary Conference in Edinburgh to explore ways and means of unifying missionary expansion. The use of 'World', 'International' and 'Universal' in the names of the bodies that evolved from the historic conference – International Missionary Council (1921), Universal Christian Council for Life and Work (1925), World Conference on Faith and Order (1927), World Council of Churches in Formation (1938), World Council of Churches (1948) – signified the breadth and depth of the burgeoning vision for a unified field of world Christian outreach. But the movement was more than the lines of organisations that evolved from the 1910 World Missionary Conference. As depicted upper left in Figure 0.1, a set of 'sister' organisations was internationally active prior to Edinburgh:

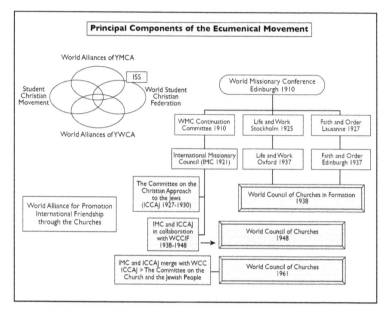

Figure 0.1 Ecumenical movement, early to mid-twentieth century

the two World Alliances of YMCA and YWCA (c.1844–1855); Student Christian Movement (c.1870s); World Student Christian Federation (WSCF, 1895), which was founded as a central coordinating body for national student movements. A third component, centre left, was the World Alliance for Promotion of International Friendship through the Churches, founded on the eve of World War I with the aim of advancing international relations through the peace-making principles of Christianity. The creation of ICCAJ within this structure of related aims and goals was purpose-driven by its mandate for unified world evangelisation of Jews.

While the overall network was understood spiritually as a manifestation of Christian unity, it was, concretely, an international collective of bodies working toward the manifestation of a Christian world through supranational missions and socio-political involvements. Crossover within the inter-connected structure was such that personnel developed in one part took up leadership roles in another, often simultaneously or consecutively. Nowhere was that more visible than in the work of American John Mott, a figure of world esteem whose influence on the movement was unequalled. Beyond founding the 1895 World Student Christian Federation and occupying the highest posts of the YMCA, he was prime mover of the 1910 World Missionary Conference (WMC), chairman of the Continuation Committee that evolved into the International Missionary Council (IMC), founder and *ex officio* of ICCAJ, first honorary president of the WCC, and Nobel Peace Laureate in 1946 for his role in the creation and advancement of 'peace-promoting religious brotherhood across national boundaries'.[8] His influence was felt in other ways as well. By virtue of his leadership in both the 'sister' organisations and central bodies emerging from the 1910 World Missionary Conference, many of the leaders of the central organisations made their way through years of training and service under the missionary emphasis of John Mott.

The war guilt debacle[9]

As a first critical point, not just ICCAJ and its parent IMC but *all* of the central bodies emerging from the World Missionary Conference in the 1920s – IMC (1921), UCCLW (1925), WCFO (1927) – were founded under the intensity of a bitter war guilt debacle that nearly severed the movement. It began with the outbreak of World War I and continued over the next twelve years, pushing, straining and threatening ecumenism as a whole. While affecting all aspects, it played out most intensely in the areas of missions and social-moral issues, which makes it a requisite background for understanding the motivations and concerns that informed the interwar and wartime development of the movement and ICCAJ's place within it. Some detail is necessary in order to grasp the intensity of issues and bitterness that the official history describes as 'almost impossible for those who did not live through the period to realize ...'.[10]

The first of the two major issues involved the supranationality at the heart of ecumenicity. When Germany declared war on Russia and France in the first days of August 1914, Britain declared war on Germany, and moved quickly with allies to capture German territories in Africa and the Pacific. The decision to seize German mission properties and intern or expel missionaries from Allied territories became one of the most bitter German contentions against churchmen of Allied nations.[11] The rancour went from general accusations in 1914 to specific charges in 1917 against John Mott and the mission arm of the movement. More plainly, after Mott served as religious adviser to President Wilson's diplomatic mission to Russia two months after America's entry into the war, his German vice-chairman of the 1910 WMC Continuation Committee, along with other German members, repudiated his leadership of WSCF and IMC as 'no longer recognised', on the grounds that he had violated the 'supranationality of Christian missions and the Church of Christ in general'.[12]

The second issue was closely related. Before the first month of war was out, twenty-nine German leaders in world missions published an 'Appeal to Protestant Christians Abroad', arguing that an 'incurable rent' was imminent if non-German churchmen fuelled 'a war in ecumenical relations' by participating in lies about Germany's blame for the war.[13] The archbishops of Canterbury, York and Armagh, with the support of forty ecclesiastics, responded in late September with a scathing public statement on Germany's violation of Belgian neutrality. Germany hit back on 4 October with a widely broadcast 'Appeal to the Civilised World', signed by ninety-three scholars, insisting that Germany's misunderstood actions were pre-emptively defensive and justified. Churchmen from Belgium and France soon responded with claims of German aggressions and civilian brutalities.[14] By the time Germany sank the *Lusitania* off the coast of Ireland on 7 May 1915, and Britain released its infamous Bryce Report in thirty languages five days later, claims and beliefs about German war guilt were pervasive in western ecclesiastic and ecumenical circles.[15]

The combined claims of German aggressions, violations of Belgian neutrality and contraventions in the supranationality of missions festered and inflamed throughout the war. Repeated attempts by Archbishop of Sweden Nathan Söderblom to broker peace between churchmen of belligerent nations were met by the same entrenched arguments. The armistice of November 1918 brought no relief, and the Treaty of Versailles in June 1919, which assigned blame to Germany and allies for 'all loss and damage' of the war, intensified the bitterness.[16] The following month another 'holy protest' was issued by the German churches, this time insisting that Protestant leaders of victor nations protest the Versailles Treaty and its 'scar' on Germany as unjust. In return, churchmen in France and Belgium demanded that German churchmen recognise the 'severities' of Versailles 'as justified', stressing again that there could be no ecumenical engagement until they openly recognised Germany's guilt.[17]

All of these tensions were present at the first postwar conference of the World Alliance for Promoting International Friendship through the Churches at Oud Wassenaar (Netherlands) in fall 1919. The 'most burning of all the problems debated' by the sixty delegates from fourteen nations was the war guilt issue. Both French and Belgians insisted that they would not engage ecumenically with Germany until her churches admitted Germany's guilt, the French going so far as to impose a condition that German delegates 'at least condemn the violation of Belgian neutrality as morally wrong and indefensible'. Some progress was made when delegates unilaterally agreed that supranationality in missions was 'essential' and that each nation had to have unimpeded freedom to carry God's word. British delegates nudged progress further by conceding that ecumenical engagement should not be conditioned on admission of guilt. In turn, five 'unofficial' German delegates, one of whom was Mott's vice-chair of the WMC Committee, registered a change in belief. They now declared that they 'personally considered Germany's violation of Belgian neutrality an act of moral transgression'. French and Belgian delegates followed by agreeing to engage with all German Christians 'who could subscribe to this declaration'.[18]

Yet instead of appeasement, the Oud Wassenaar declaration exacerbated the war guilt issue. German churchmen who were not there saw it as 'national self-abasement', while churchmen in France saw it as a model for stronger admission of German guilt. Within a month the French Federation of Protestant Churches demanded 'that German churches confess their nation's war guilt publicly as prerequisite to participation at ecumenical meetings'. Tension was so high by the following August (1920) that it disrupted even a conference brokered by Söderblom for the restoration of ecumenical unity. The French Federation, with the support of Belgians, issued a positional statement to the ninety delegates from fifteen countries, which stressed unity as a necessary condition of ecumenism while insisting that it could not be realised so long as the 'unresolved moral problem' about Germany's guilt 'stood as a barrier'.[19]

By mutual agreement the war guilt issue was not on the agenda of the 1925 Stockholm conference brokered by Söderblom, which effectually launched the social issue arm of the ecumenical movement. Yet the historic gathering of six hundred delegates from thirty-seven countries nevertheless became the watershed moment of the war guilt debacle. The more it appeared that conference consensus was moving toward a position that condemned war, the more the eighty German delegates argued that wars of defence and patriotism should always be valid. When Dr Hermann Kapler, head of the German delegation, raised objections to any unified resolution on war, corresponding doubts were raised about any moral commitment from Germany against war. But behind the scenes there was also recognition that resolution of the war guilt issue was imperative if the ecumenical movement was to go forward. That need became more immediate on the last day of the conference when Kapler introduced a letter calling for clarification of 'the War Guilt Question' as a moral 'task of importance ... for future ecumenical cooperative work'.[20]

Any doubt about what that meant was made clear in his follow-up letter to Söderblom, in which he reiterated the 'German threat of withdrawal ... unless satisfactory solution was found'. What was being sought through Kapler's strategy was a formalised distinction between the political and moral aspects of the war guilt issue, one that would exculpate German consciences while freeing the ecumenical movement of political stain.[21] What was being required by way of German threat of withdrawal was some form of ecumenical agreement that the Versailles 'war guilt confession, imposed without previous investigation and out of purely political motives, should not be recognised as *"res judicata"*'.[22]

The conciliatory solution was not found until a 1926 joint conference of the Stockholm Continuation Committee and the World Alliance in Bern (Switzerland).[23] The solutionary document neither removed nor assigned German blame by formulating the moral claims that 'right' could not be determined by war, that final moral judgment could not be imposed by political instruments, and that confessions imposed by force 'in any domain' had no 'moral value'.[24] A similar solution was brought to bear on the sensitive issue of supranationality by formalising 'the duty of every Communion ... to emphasize the supranational character of the Church and ... do all in its power to cultivate international fellowship on a Christian basis'.[25]

With all of this as legacy the Stockholm Continuation Committee created in 1928 the International Christian Social Institute in Geneva, whose aims were the study and promotion of Christian ethics, social justice and the supranational unity of the Church. In 1930 the Institute was reorganised into the Universal Christian Council for Life and Work (UCCLW), with four regional sectors in Continental Europe, Britain, America and Constantinople. Later that year UCCLW captured world attention when Archbishop Nathan Söderblom received the Nobel Peace Prize for his leading role in the creation of an international platform that promoted Christian unity and peace between nations through 'the light of the Word, the truth of the spirit, the courage of the will'. In his Nobel Lecture, Söderblom went on to describe UCCLW as 'an Ecumenical Council ... as magnificent an achievement as the League of Nations', hailing it as 'a mouthpiece for Christianity' and 'the Christian conscience', listing among its earliest achievements the resolution of the war guilt crisis through the 1926 Bern solutionary agreement 'about the cause of the World War'.[26]

The war guilt context in this study

This UCCLW, which was forged in the fires of divisiveness and then recognised by the Nobel Committee for the advancement of Christian unity, was the first stage of the social issue trajectory that merged into the World Council of Churches in Formation (WCCIF) in 1938 and the World Council of Churches (WCC) in 1948. The Bern declaration that formalised emphasis on supranationality as a 'duty' was central to that development. While the idea of supranational cooperation was intrinsic to earlier understanding, it was not until after the bitter war guilt period that the term and concept began to be systematically studied as a theological and theoretical banner of ecumenicity, one held 'higher and with unflinching fortitude', according to the official history, 'as the international barometer set towards "stormy" in the 1930s'.[27]

The Bern solution, however, did not mark the end of concern about the unity of the newly formed Council. Twenty-six months after Söderblom's Nobel Lecture the supranational structure of UCCLW was threatened again by German withdrawal. The issue reigniting the threat in March 1933, sixty days after Hitler's rise to power, was no longer Germany's war guilt but ecumenical protest against Germany's handling of its 'Jewish problem'. The reigniting issue not only challenged Söderblom's ideal of a Christian 'mouthpiece' for social justice, the memory and legacy of the war guilt divisiveness, settling first on UCCLW and then WCCIF as a hovering informant to the consequences of ecumenical division, put leaders on a twelve-year course of caution about what could and could not be said officially about Nazi Germany and its policies.

To place ICCAJ squarely within this historical development, the Stockholm conference that created the committee that evolved into UCCLW also produced a mandate on social concerns. The six hundred delegates from thirty-seven nations unanimously affirmed the need to marshal Christian forces in the area of 'burning' social problems.[28] Two months later the IMC missionary thrust so central to ecumenical aims issued a call for Christian experts to take up the study of the 'Jewish problem'. The 1927 mandate for creation of a global Jewish evangelisation programme was the initial result. The longer-term result was a confluence of three lines of transnational Protestant thinking: the metaphysical construct of the Jew in Christian theology, the theoretical construct of the Jewish problem in world society, and geographical planning for a conversionary solution.

This book is concerned with both of these parallel developments *in so far* as they are part of the processes that led to ICCAJ becoming the architect of the WCC founding statement on Jews in 1948. It must be stated clearly, however, that this is *not* a study of the multifaceted 'ecumenical movement' nor is it an attempt to sketch any kind of 'ecumenical' portrait, including that of the WCC. The idea that there may have been a particular 'ecumenical' attitude toward Jews, or for that matter toward anything including conversion, has no correspondence to the reality of the sprawling structure of organisations and diverse people, or the sheer impossibility of ever substantiating such a claim. The use of 'ecumenical' and 'ecumenical movement' as general descriptors can tell us much about the inclusiveness of the term and its broad interconnectedness of bodies and people,[29] but the same generic use in historical analyses of acts and actors can obscure differences, imply categorical similarities and thereby invite misinterpretations and inappropriate generalisations. That becomes all the more critical when approaching the sensitive area of analysing and explaining acts and actors during the period of the Holocaust.

This study navigates the ecumenical category by extensive differentiation and contextualisation. It is primarily concerned with relations between ICCAJ's origins in the burgeoning interwar movement, its developing discourse, and its culminating status with the more powerful and endowed WCC in 1948. The reconstruction of the conversionary initiative within these relational contexts is one part of the complex story of how and why it came to be seen as expert on the Jewish question at the same time that a 'Final Solution' was being sought by Nazi Germany. The other part is how and why it came to incrementally intersect with the social issue arm of the movement that evolved into the WCC. In tracing that development, UCCLW (1930 to 1938) was the central social-action arm of the movement until WCCIF (1938 to 1948) was brought into existence. The two-part story is thus a juxtaposition of two different trajectories carrying out different but congruent aspects of the same project of bringing about a predominantly Christian world.

The term 'ecumenical', when used in a non-generic way here, is a self-descriptive employed primarily but not exclusively by the period visionaries and builders of the UCCLW-WCCIF trajectory to define and discuss its theological and theoretical basis. Wherever the term was consciously applied in that sense, the underlying context was always that of an undivided supranational *Una Sancta* bound together in the higher purpose of advancing a Christianised world and worldview. While UCCLW and WCCIF each included a small constituency of Orthodox churches, the period organisations were yet predominately Protestant, and the core principles weighing in on the Jewish issues addressed here were exclusively so.[30] Those discussed from both trajectories are identified organisationally and individually, and every attempt is made to use 'ecumenical Protestant' and its cognates in ways that are appropriately descriptive of the period.

ICCAJ, which began functioning in 1930 and included as associates seven from Christopher Clark's study, has until now evaded critical analysis, even though it was period-distinguished as representative of the Protestant churches on the Jewish question.[31] That it was subsumed by the WCC and then incrementally buried under a series of name changes may help to explain why. When ICCAJ was integrated into WCC in 1961 its name was changed to the Committee on the Church and the Jewish People in the Division of World Mission and Evangelism. The name was changed again in 1973 to Consultation on the Church and the Jewish People in the complexly titled Sub-Unit of Dialogue with People of Living Faiths and Ideologies, under the WCC Program Unit on Faith and Witness.

What is known about the original body is sparse and scattered, but it illustrates a critical point about images created by evaluating from limited sources a single perspective of people and groups with multifaceted agendas. Three different impressions can be gleaned from the literature. The first is comprised of decontextualised excerpts or references to ICCAJ protests against Nazi antisemitism, advocacy for non-Aryan Christian refugees, or reports to mission advocates on the plight of European Jews.[32] The second, a PhD thesis by a former WCC secretary in the renamed Consultation on the Church and the Jewish People, whose stated aim was to non-critically record its theological history, credits ICCAJ with refining mission methodology, paving the way to post-Holocaust dialogue between the Church and the Jewish people.[33] The third, reflecting contemporary opposition, challenges its theory and motives,[34] charges its discourse with feeding 'flames of prejudice, hatred and persecution',[35] questioning if its position against antisemitism was even 'ethical or Christian'.[36]

What we have is thus three different glimpses into an initiative with the dual aims of advancing Jewish salvation and defending

Jews against racial persecution, while defending Christendom against proclaimed Jewish influence and incursions. It is what Christopher Clark calls in his work on Prussian conversionists the difficult to reconcile 'twin missionary tasks'.[37] It is what I find here as the two faces of a Protestant conversionary vision revealing itself in different ways and in different places throughout the Hitler years. How to present this complex duality of proclaimed benevolence in a way that is justly reflective of its global aims, discourse and interactions during the lethal years of Nazi persecutions has been one of the major challenges of this book.

Notes

* Note on variations in spelling: the primary sources of the period varied in spellings of 'antisemitism', including the hyphened forms: 'anti-semitism', anti-Semitism', 'Anti-semitism' and 'Anti-Semitism'. Discussion here will be limited to non-hyphened 'antisemitism' except when quoting directly. Capitalisation of 'Church' will be limited to the universal Church, except where indicated in quotations or titles, while 'church' will be used for all individual churches.

1 Report of WCC Committee IV on the Christian Approach to the Jews, *The First Assembly of the World Council of Churches held at Amsterdam 22 August–4 September 1948*, ed. W.A. Visser 't Hooft (New York: Harper & Brothers, 1948), 160–6.

2 W.W. Simpson and Ruth Weyl, *The Story of the International Council of Christians and Jews* (London: ICCJ, 1987), 16; Marcus Braybrooke, *Children of One God* (London: Vallentine Mitchell, 1991), 4.

3 The bystander category is discussed in more detail in Chapter 6.

4 Tony Kushner, 'Britain, the United States and the Holocaust: In Search of a Historiography', *The Historiography of the Holocaust*, ed. Dan Stone (New York: Palgrave Macmillan, 2004), 253–75, quot. 257.

5 For example, Marc Saperstein, 'Christian Doctrine and the Final Solution: The State of the Question', *Remembering for the Future: The Holocaust in an Age of Genocide*, ed. John Roth (London: Palgrave Macmillan, 2001), 814–41; 'A Jewish Response to John T. Pawlikowski and Mary C. Boys', *Christ Jesus and the Jewish People Today*, ed. Philip Cunningham et al. (Grand Rapids: Eerdmans, 2011), 64–76.

6 Christopher Clark, *The Politics of Conversion: Missionary Protestantism and the Jews in Prussia, 1728–1947* (Oxford: Clarendon, 1995); quot. 'Protestant Missions to the Jews in Prussia', *Leo Baeck Yearbook* (London: Secker & Warburg, 1993), 33.

7 Seven publications with titles on *die Judenfrage* appeared in the German language between 1938 and 1943. For transformation into a common 'household word' in western languages, Jacob Toury, 'The Jewish Question: A Semantic Approach', *Leo Baeck Institute Year Book XI* (Oxford Academic, 1966), 85–106; for etymology, Alex Bein, *The Jewish Question: Biography of a World Problem* (New York: Herzl, 1990). For texts unveiling the term *Antisemitismus*, Wilhelm Marr, *The Victory of Judenthum over Germandom* (1879), excerpts in Richard Levy, *Antisemitism in the Modern World* (Lexington: D.C. Heath, 1990), 74–93, and 'Statutes of the Anti-Semitic League' (1879), in Peter Pulzer, *The Rise of Political Anti-Semitism in Germany and Austria*, Revised (Cambridge University Press, 1988), 49.

8 Nobel Presentation by Herman Smitt Ingebretsen, 10 Dec. 1946, *Nobel Lectures, Peace 1926–1950*, F. W. Haberman, ed. (Amsterdam: Elsevier, 1972).

9 This account is derived from Söderblom's 1930 Nobel Lecture, *Nobel Lectures, Peace 1926–1950*, Haberman, ed. (1972); W.A. Brown, *Toward A United Church: Three Decades of Ecumenical Christianity* (New York: Charles Scribner's Sons, 1946); W. R. Hogg, *Ecumenical Foundations* (Eugene: Wipf and Stock, 1952); Nils Karlström, 'Movements of International Friendship and Life and Work, 1910–1925', *A History of the Ecumenical Movement, 1517–1948* (1954), 509–44, hereafter *HEM*; Ehrenström, 'Movements of International Friendship and Life and Work, 1925–1948', *HEM*, 545–98; Daniel Borg, 'German Protestants and the Ecumenical Movements: The War Guilt Imbroglio, 1919–1926', *A Journal of Church and State*, 10:1 (1968), 51–71; R.V. Pierard, 'John R. Mott and the Rift in the Ecumenical Movement During World War I', *Journal of Ecumenical Studies*, 23:4 (1986), 601–20, and 'Julius Richter and the Scientific Study of Christian Missions in Germany', *Missiology* (1978), 485–506; Charles Bailey, 'The British Protestant Theologians in the First World War: Germanophobia Unleashed', *Harvard Theological Review*, 77:2 (1984), 195–221, and 'The Verdict of French Protestantism against Germany in the First World War', *Church History*, 58:1 (1989), 66–82; Julian Jenkins, 'A Forgotten Challenge to German Nationalism: The World Alliance for International Friendship through the Churches', *Australian Journal of Politics and History* (1991), 286–301.

10 Nils Karlström, 'Movements of International Friendship and Life and Work, 1910–1925', *HEM*, ed. Ruth Rouse and S. C. Neill (Geneva, WCC, 1954), 549.
11 Pierard, 'John R. Mott and the Rift', 604–5. Hogg, *Ecumenical Foundations*, 186.
12 Hogg, *Ecumenical Foundations*, 174–5.
13 Bailey, 'Germanophobia Unleashed', 201–2; Bailey, 'The Verdict', 66, 70.
14 Bailey, 'The Verdict', 71; Bailey, 'Germanophobia Unleashed', 202.
15 *The Bryce Report*, 12 May 1915, held that German atrocities in the early months were 'unparalleled in any war between civilized nations [in] the last three centuries'.
16 Treaty of Versailles, Part VIII, Section 1, Article 231.
17 Pastoral letter of the Prussian General Superintendents, 20 Jul. 1919, Borg, 'War Guilt Imbroglio', 51; Karlström, 'Movements', 531.
18 Bailey, 'The Verdict', 75; Karlström, 'Movements', 532.
19 Karlström, 'Movements', 537; Borg, 'War Guilt Imbroglio', 55–57; Bailey, 'The Verdict', 75.
20 Borg, 'War Guilt Imbroglio', 59–69; Brown, 'Toward a United Church', 74–89; Ehrenström, 'Movements', 565.
21 Borg, 'War Guilt Imbroglio', 68.
22 Ibid., *res judicata*, a matter already judged that cannot be pursued further.
23 L&W Continuation Committee Min., Bern, 1926, 21. The Bern document was not approved by the Prussian General Synod until 1927.
24 Borg, 'War Guilt Imbroglio', 68; Ehrenström, 'Movements', 565–6.
25 Ehrenström, 'Movements', 577.
26 Nobel Presentation, 10 Dec. 1930; Söderblom, 'The Role of the Church', 11 Dec. 1930, *Nobel Lectures*, ed. Haberman.
27 Ehrenström, 'Movements', 577–8.
28 Karlström, 'Movements', 540–2. For full discussion of 'The Church and Moral and Social Problems', G.K.A. Bell, *The Stockholm Conference: The Official Report of the Universal Christian Conference on Life and Work held in Stockholm on 19–30 August 1925* (London: Oxford University Press, 1926), 359–412.
29 Victoria Barnett, who has uniquely published major translations of works dealing with the *Kirchenkampf* (Eberhardt Bethge's *Bonhoeffer* and Wolfgang Gerlach's *And the Witnesses Were Silent*) in addition to her own work on Protestant protests in Germany as well as British, American and general ecumenical responses to Nazi persecution of Jews, has perhaps gone furthest in trying to separate 'ecumenical' from the more generalised category of church protests. In important attempts to show that 'ecumenical' can be profitably examined by looking at its

many parts, she has sought statements on behalf of Jews that can be attributed to the ecumenical movement, but has been unable to find more than a few that can be attributed to the UCCLW–WCCIF trajectory. See 'The Role of the Churches: Compliance and Confrontation', *Dimensions*, 12 (1998), 37–9; 'Barmen, the Ecumenical Movement, and the Jews: the Missing Thesis', *Ecumenical Review*, 61:1, March 2009, 17–23; 'Christian and Jewish Interfaith Efforts During the Holocaust: The Ecumenical Context', *American Responses to Kristallnacht*, ed. Maria Mazzenga (Palgrave Macmillan, 2009), 13–29; 'Track Two Diplomacy, 1933–1939: International Responses from Catholics, Jews, and Ecumenical Protestants to Events in Nazi Germany', *Kirchliche Zeitgeschichte*, 27:1 (2014), 76–86; 'Ecumenical Protestant Response to the Rise of Nazism, Fascism and Antisemitism during the 1920s and 1930s', *Religion, Ethnonationalism, and Antisemitism in the Era of the Two World Wars*, ed. Kevin Spicer and Rebecca Carter Chand (Montreal: McGill-Queens University Press, 2022), 356–78.
30 Orthodox members of UCCLW and WCCIF Administrative Committees do not appear in recorded documents on Jewish matters, but there were times when one or more Orthodox members voted on an organisational resolution relating to Jewish issues.
31 Seven in Clark's study were delegates to the 1927 conferences that mandated the creation of ICCAJ, and one became a Continental European member.
32 As example, John Conway, 'Protestant Missions to the Jews', *HGS* 1:1 (1986), 134–6, quoting from an ICCAJ protest against antisemitism, suggests that ICCAJ was founded in response to antisemitism. Yaakov Ariel, *Evangelizing the Chosen People: Missions to Jews in America* (Chapel Hill: University of North Carolina Press, 2000), 128–9, 175–9, and Robert Ross, 'Perverse Witness to the Holocaust: Christian Missions and Missionaries', *Holocaust Studies Annual II* (1986), 127–9, cite passages from 1939 and 1941 pamphlets as evidence of concern about the plight of European Jews. Ariel importantly notes from research on other mission advocates that, while concern for the 'plight of converted Jews' was directly related to a mission position, conversionists 'felt responsible' for evangelised Jews.
33 Rev. Allan Brockway, 'For the Love of Jews: A Theological Approach to the International Missionary Council's Committee on the Christian Approach to the Jews' (PhD, University of Birmingham, 1992), was a secretary in the WCC Sub-Unit between 1979 and 1988. His stated aim was to 'record but largely refrain from commenting upon, much less arguing with' ICCAJ theological history. He non-critically assumed

that the hindsight of knowing what ICCAJ had become by the 1980s – a professed platform of dialogue instead of conversion – would be invaluable in documenting the positive theological changes that must have taken place.
34 Opposition to ICCAJ by British Anglican theologian and historian James Parkes is discussed in detail throughout this book. Many of the references to ICCAJ appear to stem from his autobiography where he noted briefly his opposition in *Voyage of Discoveries* (London: Victor Gollancz, 1969). Biographies and monographs in turn cited Parkes's opposition, as for example, Eleanor Jackson, *Red Tape and the Gospel* (Birmingham: Phlogiston, 1980); Robert Everett, *Christianity Without Antisemitism* (Oxford: Pergamon Press, 1993); Colin Richmond, *Campaigner Against Antisemitism* (London: Vallentine Mitchell, 2005); Haim Chertok, *He Also Spoke as a Jew* (London: Vallentine Mitchell, 2006); Tom Lawson, *The Church of England and the Holocaust* (Suffolk: Boydell Press, 2006).
35 Rabbi Samuel Cohon is representative of early Jewish opposition in 'The Jew and Christian Evangelisation', *IRM* 22:4 (1933), 470–80, quot. 474.
36 Max Eisen, who criticised the same elements as Cohon, illustrates postwar Jewish opposition in 'Christian Missions to the Jews in North America and Great Britain', *Jewish Social Studies* 10:1 (1948), 31–66.
37 Clark, *The Politics of Conversion*, 282, 286.

You and I somehow have got to win the Jew to Christ to save the Jew from becoming a problem and even a menace to the Christian faith. The more he becomes a menace, the more likely are we to have anti-Semitism: it is a vicious circle. The only way out is Christ. And we must save the Jews for Christ and by Christ and through Christ. The need was never greater than today in view of the geographical dispersion of the Jews to the ends of the earth, his racial pride, his aggressiveness.

– Dr Conrad Hoffmann, ICCAJ Director, July 1935

1

Conversion and the Jewish problem: 1925–1932

The call for Christian experts

In October 1925 a call was made from the pages of the *International Review of Missions* for 'experts and men of vision' to take up the study of the Jewish problem at a world conference on Jewish missions. The opening words – 'the challenge of the Jew is perennial and has in our time become all but universal' – set the tone of urgency that permeated the article. Citing pre-war Romania and Russia as countries in which outbreaks of antisemitic violence reminded the world that 'Jews living in them presented some particular problem', 'The Jewish Problem: Some Newer Aspects' went on to argue that all postwar nations had since discovered that 'a Jewish question exists'. This was said to be but one of the postwar changes in world Jewry that required immediate Christian thought and action. Others included universal attainment of political and social rights for Jews, the movement of Jews into all critical domains of society, and the concomitant increase in Jewish influence. Simultaneously occurring was the disintegration of Judaism, surging Jewish racial consciousness, and increasing movements of Jews toward Zionism, Bolshevism, nationalism and atheism. The overarching concern was that none of the postwar changes would serve 'Christian ends', or 'any religious end', and that Jews adrift from Judaism would become a more 'disintegrating element' in society. The problem, which had entered 'a new phase', was said to present 'a special, direct and urgent challenge to the whole Christian Church'. If left unrestrained 'non-Christian elements and forces' would proliferate within Christian nations.[1] With respect to what was being done:

> Despite much antipathy among church members towards the Jews and apathy towards the cause of their evangelization, increasing numbers of churchmen and missionary leaders throughout the world are .... [beginning] to understand that if the Church had thought aright and applied what is her sole possession, there would have been no Jewish problem at all.[2]

The author of this article on relations between the emergence of the Jewish problem and Christianity's failure to convert the people it claimed to supersede was Dr Macdonald Webster, an officer of the Conference of British Missionary Societies writing on behalf of the IMC. His framing of the Jewish problem as a universal societal issue just two months after the 1925 Stockholm conference mandated the study of 'burning' social problems was strategically timed but it was not a direct result of the mandate. As Christopher Clark has shown in his study of conversionary theory in late nineteenth-century Prussia, the 'Jewish problem' became part of mission discourse soon after *Die Judenfrage* was coined in 1843.[3] Before the end of the century the Jewish question was being asserted as a societal reality in German, English and Danish mission literature, with claims in English as early as 1894 that it was 'forcing itself ... on nearly every government on the face of the earth'.[4]

Macdonald Webster became a voice in the discourse near the end of World War I by singling out as two critical junctures in world history the 1917 Russian Revolution that emancipated half of the world Jewish population *and* the Balfour Declaration that was seeking a national Jewish home in Palestine. His main concerns in 1918, as in 1925, were the movements of eastern European Jews into western society and a build-up in Palestine of the 'same' anti-Christian 'tyrannical exclusiveness' that existed in the time of Christ. This alone was seen as sufficient reason for Christian experts to take up the study of the Jewish problem, for wherever emancipated eastern European Jews settled, whether 'orthodox or infidel', the Church would be faced with 'a non-Christian or anti-Christian influence exerted in ever-increasing strength and with ever-widening ramifications'.[5]

The institutional decision to study the Jewish problem as Webster framed it in 1918 was made by the IMC in the summer of 1923, two years after its constitutional founding.[6] IMC chairman John Mott utilised Webster's skills and experience by placing him at the centre of planning for the world conference. With more than thirty years in Jewish evangelisation, sixteen of which had been as assistant or director of the Church of Scotland Jewish mission enterprise in Budapest, Webster had become a revered expert on Jews in eastern Europe. No other in Protestant mission circles knew better that part of the world where some 70 per cent of the world Jewish population lived, and none doubted his assessment that it was the fountain of communism and atheism flowing to the west. It would be there, he often preached, that the Christian cause would 'be lost or won'.[7]

It was thus agreed, for those 'weighty and sufficient reasons', that the world conference should be located in eastern Europe.[8] As part of the extensive planning a questionnaire was distributed to world Protestant churches and agencies in the same month that the 1925 call for Christian experts appeared in *IRM*. The data were analysed into a forty-page summary on world Jewry as part of a pre-conference package that included demographic studies on size, density and distribution of world Jewry; Jewish types, beliefs and movements; intellectual, social and moral hindrances to Jewish conversion; and keynote papers on Christian–Jewish enmity and the history of antisemitism.

When the historic conference convened for two weeks of back-to-back meetings in Budapest and Warsaw in April 1927, some 175 delegates from mainstream Protestant bodies in twenty-six countries deliberated under the chairmanship of John Mott. Delegates included both ecclesiastics (58%) and lay (42%), more than a quarter of which held doctorates, and of those some 19 per cent carried the title of bishop or cathedral canon. Side by side with church and mission delegates were appointees from the Swiss Protestant Federation of Churches, French Federation of Protestant Churches, World Student Christian Federation, Student Christian Movement, World YMCA Committee, British and Foreign Bible Society, IMC, International Hebrew Christian Alliance, professors of theology and religion from universities in Budapest, Vienna, Leipzig, Jena, Copenhagen and Oslo. Geographically, delegates from eastern Europe and Asia (39%) outnumbered those from both central and northern Europe (31.5%) *and* the United Kingdom and North America (29.5%).[9] The countries most represented were Poland (25), Hungary (17), Germany (16), England (16), United States (12), Scotland (11), with the other nineteen having between one and seven delegates. Roughly 36% of the conference was Lutheran, 31% Reform, 22.7% Anglican, with all others (including Methodist, Baptist and Quaker) comprising 13.6%.

From the vantage of the multidenominational, multinational, multilingual assembly that deliberated like the League of Nations, speaking and pausing for interpretation into German and English, two achievements stood out from an array of attainments. The first, orchestrated by IMC chairman John Mott, was that all 147 points and subpoints of the conference findings were hammered across language and denominational lines until unanimous transnational agreement was achieved.[10]

The second, evolving from the first, was a vision of Christian benevolence which made clear that supersessionism – the words, beliefs and implications of Christianity's primacy – was not a thing of the past. As framed in a conference 'Message to the Jews', the highest welfare of the Jewish people would be secured when Christianity was embraced and Israel was brought to 'her destiny'. Embracing the duty to carry that message, to be the bearer of Christ, and to do so with humility, goodwill and self-sacrifice, was seen as the highest level of Christian benefaction.[11] The conference itself was seen as concrete evidence of an envisioned beneficence that held Jewish evangelisation as a divinely appointed Christian duty. Sincerity and purity of motive, sympathetic conveyance of God's message, and repentance for past failure to love the Jews enough to want them converted were to be part of this new mission impulse.[12] Evangelisation was also understood as a method of reparation for Christianity's historical ill-treatment of Jews. Both Budapest and Warsaw stressed the need for Christianity to repent 'the long record of injustice and ill-usage of Jews on the part of professedly Christian people', and both called on churches to oppose injustices to Jews wherever they arose.[13]

Closely related to the beneficent duty of evangelisation was a strong socio-political awareness of a universal Jewish problem and

Christianity's duty to solve it. The 200-page conference volume, acclaimed as 'the most up to date material [on] the Jewish problem', broadened this aspect of the vision to defending Christendom against the incursions of Jewish thought and influence.[14] It argued as a whole that the changing situation in postwar Jewry demanded missionary 'occupation' of all European and North American areas that were densely populated by Jews.[15]

The situation eliciting such concern, like that in Webster's *IRM* call for Christian experts, was the break-up of the 'old ghetto world' in eastern Europe and the concomitant attainment of social and political rights for Jews. Movement in every sense of the word – physical, intellectual, spiritual – was invoked to characterise the new stage of untethered Jewish freedoms. Redistribution of six million Russian Jews by way of postwar ceded territories to Poland, Estonia, Latvia, Lithuania and Romania was of noted concern, as was western immigration in large numbers from eastern outposts, but it was the general movement of Jews into all spheres of society that constituted the main issue of concern. The increasing movement of Jews *away* from the moral constraints of Judaism, increasing movement of Jews *toward* new ways of thinking in Zionism, nationalism and Bolshevism, increasing movement of Jews *into* the influential political, economic and intellectual domains of society were all seen as developments 'fraught with great danger to the world, unless ... directed into Christian channels'. Of no less concern was the belief that beneath widespread dispersion of world Jewry was an underlying Jewish unity that superseded national boundaries and differences.[16]

These transnational concerns were unpacked in the conference volume by way of parallel discussions on the old/new Jewish situation and the old/new Church attitude toward Jews. Each theme was central to delegates' understanding of the Jewish problem, and central to both was the theme of repentance for Christendom's past attitude toward Jews. 'Old' Church attitudes were seen as cause for 'aroused conscience' while 'new' attitudes of love and goodwill were to be embraced as a 'more excellent way' of offering amends for the past sins of Christendom.[17] The 'old' anti-Judaic attitudes called to repentance, however, were simultaneously posited as barriers to Jewish conversion. Warsaw delegates deplored past

Christian 'injustice and ill-usage of Jews' while stressing that it 'foreclosed' evangelising opportunities, and Budapest delegates repudiated Jewish prejudice while emphasising that the 'unchristian treatment of the Jew' was a stumbling block to accepting the Christian message.[18]

But it was also the case that repentance for deplorable historical treatment of Jews was equivocated by claims such as 'the Jew began the sorry business'. Jews were distinguished for ongoing hatred of Christ, for 'turning gentle-minded people into angry fanatics', for inciting non-Jews with provoking traits and behaviours. While granting that some 'Jewish' traits may have resulted from harsh Christian treatment, it was simultaneously held that there had 'always been something in the character or conduct' of Jews that provoked their non-Jewish neighbours.[19] Among other such traits appearing in the conference volume were 'pride', 'superiority', 'uncanny power of exploiting', 'repelling arrogance', 'acquisitiveness' and 'shrewd if not cunning, thrifty if not niggardly, self-assertive if not unscrupulous, tenacious if not obstinate, gain-seeking if not grasping' tendencies.[20]

Such 'Jewish' traits were explained in the closing chapter on antisemitism by way of distinctions between anti-Judaic and antisemitic *reactions* to Jews. Anti-Judaism was designated as oppositional reaction 'to the religion of the Jew', as well as reaction to a whole category of provoking Jewish traits which Judaism was said to engender. In a corresponding distinction, non-Jewish reactions to Jewish racial pride, refusal to assimilate and establishment of an '*imperium in imperio*' in every nation inhabited' were said to be more properly designated as antisemitic 'opposition to the Jewish race'.[21] The overall effect, whether intended or not, was that the carefully differentiated terms constituted one long inscription of Jewish blame for provoking both anti-Judaic and antisemitic reactions in non-Jews, a blame that was not undone by conference repentance for past Christian injustices to Jews.

As part of the assessment on current responses to Jews, widespread antisemitism, though 'not so violent' as in the past, was said to be 'rapidly on the rise in Central and Eastern Europe', with 'strong tendencies at work' in England, South Africa, Egypt, Palestine, Japan and the United States. That the Church was 'in no way directly connected', and that Protestant churches in particular gave it 'no countenance', was part of this understanding. Giving antisemitism no countenance, however, did not mean being unsympathetic to its social, political and economic claims. But convergence on some points did not mean being in concert with its racial or persecutory aspects. Beyond violating the universality of the Church and hindering Jewish missions, neither antisemitism nor anti-Judaism were said to have worked. Systematised bias and persecution, whether along religious or racial lines, had not solved the Jewish problem, nor had 'learning and civilisation', 'democracy', 'assimilation', 'segregation', 'opportunity' or 'equality'.[22]

If the Jewish problem was to be solved, the only viable solution lay within the purview of the Church, one that had the tri-advantage of insight about conversionary failure, changed Christian attitudes and a unified ability to withstand the underlying unity of world Jewry. Concern that the work of the Church would be harmed or hindered was part of this, but it was not to be seen in terms of threat only, for it was recognised that a 'race numbering over 15 million' offered 'unparalleled opportunity' for spreading the gospel. There was also avid belief that the Church was being called to repentance, greater tolerance, and love for Jews. Shouldering the burden of repentance and taking a stand against current 'forces of prejudice' were understood as requisite steps on the path of reparation. But these alone were not enough to meet the challenge of the world situation. The Church also had to openly declare that conversion to Christianity was the only way to help Jews, the only way to solve society's Jewish problem, the only way to solve society's enmity against the Jews.[23]

In search of solution, structure and science

With all of this encased in conference statements of urgency, ecumenical Protestant response was swift and broad. Some 6700 copies of the conference volume, *The Christian Approach to the Jew*, were distributed to international leaders by the interim committee shortly after the April 1927 conferences. By February 1928 a non-denominational conference had been held in London on 'the urgency of the Jewish problem', small mini conferences had convened on both the Continent and in the United States, and a Church of England commission had been designated to study 'the problem'. As summarised in an interim committee memorandum to the IMC that month, failure to respond to the 'urgency' of the developing situation would affect the Church, hindering it in all lands 'by the aggressive presence of a people who deliberately rejected Christ'.[24]

Equally crucial was the quickening of corporate approval. Two months later the Budapest–Warsaw mandate for a centralised body dedicated to evangelisation of Jews was approved by the IMC world conference in Jerusalem, along with a resolution calling on 'all churches in Christendom' to study the Budapest–Warsaw volume. The mandate was ratified in July 1929 by the IMC Administrative Committee, and ICCAJ was brought into existence as a subsidiary body.[25] By fall 1930, with offices in both London and New York, an executive director had been appointed to spend six months of each year on either side of the Atlantic, criss-crossing the European and North American continents with the messages of the Budapest–Warsaw conferences.[26]

What this meant in terms of immediate effect, as recounted by IMC chairman John Mott, was that the series of orchestrated administrative actions placed the 'official representatives of the missionary movement of over fifty countries' in support of a 'comprehensive progressive program to further a truly Christian approach to the Jews'.[27] What it meant in terms of structure was that the conversionary initiative would remain small but far from peripheral. The framework was divided into North American, British and European Continental sectors, with IMC appointees from each region comprising one-third of the international governing body, initially fixed at 15 and then expanded to 25 and 36 in 1932 and 1947, respectively.

Each sector, however, was empowered from the beginning to co-opt members sufficient to meet regional needs. By 1931 the North American sector (NAICCAJ) included twenty-five appointees from what were said to be 'all of the more important Christian churches and auxiliary agencies of America'. By early 1932 a three-way pro tem alliance had been forged between the regional sector, the

Federal Council of Churches, and the Home Missions Council to act as 'the central body for the promotion of the Christian approach to the Jews in North America', one that represented the mission boards of twenty-seven Protestant denominations in Canada and the United States.[28]

Two other collaborations formed the basis of the British regional sector (BICCAJ). The Conference of Missionary Societies in Great Britain and Ireland, which was founded in 1912 and comprised forty Protestant church and church-supported agencies, made its Jewish mission committee a primary constituency. A second major constituency was formed in Scotland when the Jewish mission committees of the Church of Scotland and the United Free Church, both of which had histories dating back to the 1840s, merged into a single entity in 1929. Each was integral to ICCAJ, and each held continuous positions of power within its regional and international structures.[29]

The European Continental sector (EUICCAJ) was also based on collaboration. The West German Association for Israel (Westdeutscher Verein für Israel, 1843), Berlin Society for Promoting Christianity Among the Jews (Gesellschaft zur Beförderung des Christentums unter den Juden zu Berlin, 1822), Central Association of the Evangelical Lutheran Church for Missions to Israel (Evangelisch-Lutherischer Zentralverein für Mission unter Israel, 1871) and Institutum Judaicum Delitzschianum (1871) entered into cooperation in support of the international initiative. Following in tandem, the mission societies of Scandinavia, Switzerland, Germany and Holland consolidated support for the Delitzschianum in Leipzig, which was to be promoted as an associated training centre for English-speaking missionaries to Jews. The Continental sector also had IMC appointees from Czechoslovakia, Austria, Finland, Hungary, Poland and Romania, but only Germany, Switzerland, Sweden, Holland and Hungary held continuous seats on the international executive committee.[30]

The aim of these nationally and denominationally diverse allies was to move ICCAJ front and centre of world Protestant efforts to evangelise Jews. What was being advanced, however, must not be confused with a mission agency. ICCAJ was brought into existence as a consulting, planning and lobbying initiative for transnational adoption of Church attitudes on Jews and Jewish missions, one charged with the study of world Jewish populations for the purpose of laying down future policy and planning for the global mission field.[31] The main objectives were to revitalise mainstream Jewish missions and unify Protestant 'forces' by rallying a collective sense of oneness, solidarity and duty in Christianising the Jews. The unifying effort was to spread both horizontally and vertically from regional cores in Britain, North America and Continental Europe by way of printed materials, conferences, workshops and lectures to theological colleges, seminaries, denominational synods, ministerial bodies, mission boards, university, women's and youth group organisations, all of which were to be approached at the local, national and world levels.

The language of planning reflected the 'enter and occupy' aims of the Protestant Great Awakening, but it also signalled the inadequacies of that legacy as it came to rest on the 1927 Budapest–Warsaw conferences. As noted by church historian Timothy Yates, the Edinburgh world mission conference chaired by John Mott in 1910 had been preached and understood in terms of battle lines and world conquest. The metaphors of 'occupation' seventeen years later at Budapest and Warsaw, however, had different connotations.[32] Jewish mission geography was still based on a metaphysical map of borders between the 'saved' and 'unsaved', but the approach to the Jewish 'unsaved' had to be reassessed if the historical failure of the Church was to be reversed. The postwar dispersions of both Jews and the Jewish problem required 'more definite and methodical' thinking from a global perspective that had real-time correspondence to changing reality. It was no longer just a matter of sending Christians into foreign areas populated by Jews, for millions of Jews were now 'living in the midst of Christian communities and under the shadow of Christian churches'. The whole field of world Jewry, in other words, the Jews next door and the Jews abroad, was to be re-examined, re-thought and restated in the light of 'scientific' demographic studies and strategies.[33]

While all Jews were to be regarded as valued prospects, women and youth of all ages were seen as vital subgroups of incalculable worth. Arguments for the evangelising value of Jewish women and girls, estimated to be 7.5 million, rested on two suppositions, both of which stressed the influential power of Jewish women and the need to harness it for Christian purpose. The first was grounded in the belief that Jewish women were 'particularly influenced' by the social revolution over women's status, and that 'wider social freedom' made liberated Jewish women 'a centre of the new power, either for good or ill'. The second rested on the belief that the Orthodox Jewish wife and mother could be 'a source of ignorant and fanatical opposition to the Christian message', or 'a channel in the home for the free flow of Christian influence'. In either case, whether liberated or Orthodox, Jewish women were to be looked upon as prospective routes of entry into the Jewish community.[34]

Central to this reasoning was the belief that Christian schools had long-term effects even when baptism was not possible, and that Jewish students saturated with influence from an early age had the potential to become 'secret followers of Christ'.[35] Such reasoning was fortified by the methodology practised by Macdonald Webster at the Church of Scotland Jewish Mission School in Budapest in the decade before World War I. Faced with Hungarian laws prohibiting baptism under the age of 18, he discontinued the enrolment of boys in order to increase the number of girls who might become secret channels of Christian influence in Jewish homes.[36] Such indirect evangelisation of 'the future mothers of Israel' was understood to be crucial to the overall aim of leavening 'the whole people', even though the results would be 'far reaching' rather than immediate.[37]

Whether girl or boy, however, every Jewish student was to be seen as a door to a Jewish family. Winning the 'hearts of the youth of Israel' was to be presented as the 'duty' of the Church. The guidelines to be conveyed to churches and missions included that 'schools and hostels should be maintained or started' wherever possible; that pupils should be kept 'under Christian influence' as long as possible; that provision should be made for teachers to stay 'in touch' with students through 'clubs, classes, and correspondence'. The same principles were to apply to youth outside the milieu of education, for the 'duty' to 'attract and influence' Jewish youth was to be extended to neighbourhood play centres, summer camps, vacation Bible school, YMCA, YWCA, Boy Scouts and Girl Guides.[38]

Emphasis on Jewish youth extended to the university level. Students who were often 'separated from their homes and synagogues ... in great loneliness' were to be heralded as a field of unlimited possibility. The 'duty' to mine that field was to be placed in the hearts and minds of all Christian student leaders in university centres across Europe and North America. Arguments for the need and validity of evangelising Jewish students were to be driven home to 'theological and other Christian students in every possible way', particularly through the venues of the WSCF and its affiliated national Student Christian Movements. The 'more educated' Jews at the university level were to be presented to Christian student leaders as 'a special need and opportunity' that could be influenced by Christian apologetics, 'but even more so by sympathy and Christian help of every kind'.[39]

These transnational ambitions for penetrating the untapped fields of Jewish youth were in many ways reflected in the 1930 appointment of the first ICCAJ director. As a seasoned ecumenist of eighteen years, sixteen of which had been carried out in Europe, Dr Conrad Hoffmann Jr had to his credit two impressive firsts for achieving success under the most daunting conditions. Appointed in 1915 by John Mott, who administered the International Committee of YMCAs, Hoffmann pioneered the *first* organisational relief mission to Allied prisoners of World War I in Germany. It was, significantly, the only international humanitarian body allowed inside Germany's system of POW camps. Moving in and out of German camps and hospitals to supply aid to prisoners, whose number by the war's end approached 2.8 million, his work was held in such high regard that he was the only American allowed to remain on German soil after America entered the war.[40]

After serving in Germany until 1919, Hoffmann was tapped again by Mott, who was also chair of the World Student Christian Federation. This time it was to head a humanitarian programme for the struggling students of war-torn European universities. As director of European Student Relief, his operations by 1923 included administration of some 120 field workers serving 25 million meals in 20 European countries. Travelling widely to university campuses in 36 countries, he had also raised by 1926 some 2.2 million dollars, while earning the reputation of a humanitarian of the utmost impartiality, one said to know 'more of student life than anyone else in the world'.[41]

While all of this factored in when Hoffmann was tapped by Mott again as director of ICCAJ, it was but part of the reasoning. The final determinants rested on a far more reaching assessment of his value and assignment. With a PhD in agricultural biology, he had no theological training, no experience in organised Christian missions, no history in Christian–Jewish relations. What he had that was deemed vital was unmitigated focus on whatever ecumenical issue was at hand, along with the organisational skills and fortitude to pioneer an international groundbreaking venture. It was also imperative that he was imbued, in Mott's words, with 'strong evangelistic conviction' while believing that the cure of world problems lay in the application of Christian principles.[42]

Hoffmann's humanitarian reputation was also crucial, for this first attempt to globalise Jewish evangelisation was understood as

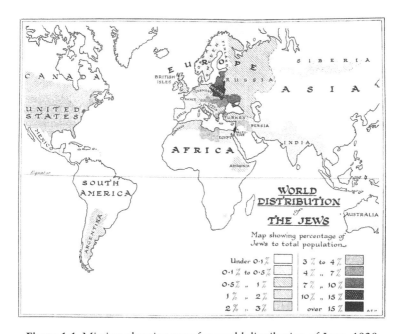

Figure 1.1 Mission planning map for world distribution of Jews, 1928

Sourced from *The Call to West and East: The Sixth and Final Report of the World Call Series* (Westminster: Press and Publications Board of the Church Assembly, 1928).

a matter of world concern that had to be implemented with the utmost sensitivity. In Mott's assessment, there was 'probably no man living' who fitted the bill better: none who had 'ministered to wider areas and greater depths of human need', none who could lead with such 'statesmanlike measures, cooperative spirit, unselfish abandon'. Under his hands, Mott assured, the planning and expansion of world Jewish evangelisation would be 'positive, constructive, irenic, and sympathetic'.[43] The question before Hoffmann as he embarked from New York for his first directorial tour of Europe in late 1930 – England, Scotland, Germany, Austria, Czechoslovakia, Hungary, Romania, Poland – was how to deliver that beneficent vision within the social, political and geographical boundaries of time and events.

Oppositions and hindrances

Opposition to this unprecedented surge of conversionary planning was mounted even before the Budapest–Warsaw conferences convened. To understand the context of the controversy it is important to understand that a different form of Christian benevolence was also emanating from postwar Protestantism. While both found root in a social gospel of Christian service, there were critical differences in how benevolence towards Jews was understood. In contrast to those who believed that evangelisation was the highest form of Christian benevolence, there were those who believed that evangelisation could be held in abeyance in order to advance goodwill relations between Christians and Jews.

The Central Conference of American Rabbis (CCAR) had entered into such relations with the Federal Council of Churches (FCC) in 1924 on the grounds of mutual goodwill, 'mutual respect for the integrity of each religion', and absence of 'proselytizing purpose'. The five-year history leading to the agreement, as historian Benny Kraut has shown, was burdened with conversionary slips (by Christians) and suspicion of motives (by Jews). Yet each side persevered the missteps to form the Joint Commission on Goodwill, which functioned without incident until CCAR learned in December 1926 that FCC would be part of the 1927 Budapest–Warsaw conferences.[44]

The headline 'Rabbis Appeal Against Missionary Plans of Christian Conference in Budapest' on 20 January in the *Jewish Telegraphic Agency* made clear that Jewish leaders would not stand silently by as the proposed train of conversionary planning passed through.[45] After learning of the scheduled conferences, leaders of CCAR cabled the chairman of the FCC Goodwill Committee with a diplomatic reminder of their 'no proselytizing' agreement. Rev. Dr A.W. Anthony, who was instrumental in founding the FCC Goodwill Committee in 1923 and current chair of the Joint Commission on Goodwill, responded by bringing John Mott and CCAR rabbis together on 28 February.

While neither the meeting nor a subsequent letter from CCAR to Mott had an effect on the opening of the conferences on 7 April, it did set into motion a manoeuvre that shifted the negative news coverage of the conferences. In a New York interview on 11 April with the *Jewish Daily Bulletin* (*JDB*) Anthony announced that he had cabled Mott in Budapest to recommend that the conferences condemn antisemitism. The next day the *Jewish Telegraphic Agency* carried the far more positive headline, 'Federal Council's Goodwill Commission Urges Protestant Congress in Budapest to Raise Voice Against Anti-semitism'.[46]

The change in focus was both strategic and misleading. Beyond the improbability that Anthony would publicise a cable to the most powerful ecumenist in America without advance consent, the so-called 'recommendations' to Mott were points already made in the pre-conference package. It was known to all in advance, as part of the new platform, that Christians were being called to a greater love for Jews, one that was to be manifest in repudiation of persecution and prejudice, as well as an overhaul of evangelising methods. None of this was known to CCAR, of course, so the timing of the cable and interview gave the appearance that FCC had risen spontaneously to influence Mott and the Budapest–Warsaw conferences. Anthony carefully distinguished that, although members were present, neither FCC nor its committees were officially represented. He also reasoned that even though FCC and CCAR had goodwill committees with 'no proselytizing purpose', they had 'no power ... to bind either all Jews or all Christians' to that purpose.[47] The overall effect on the rabbis, according to Kraut's analysis, was that CCAR accepted at face value the good intentions of the FCC Goodwill Committee, as well as its perceived commitment to dissuade Protestants from the use of goodwill as 'a smokescreen for conversion'.[48]

Whatever placating effect this had on the belief that Anthony himself was committed to 'no proselytizing' was dissipated in June 1929 when constitutional lawyer Louis Marshall released letters in which Anthony insisted that Christians would not be 'muzzled' by Jewish opposition to evangelisation. The correspondence between the two was initiated by Anthony after complaints by both Protestants and Jews against the Goodwill Committee. The United Presbyterian General Assembly had cut its financial pledge to FCC on the grounds that its Goodwill Committee was too liberal in Jewish policies, and Jews had complained again that it was a smokescreen for conversionist motives. Anthony associated the Jewish claim with Marshall and, on 8 June, penned a letter averring, 'you have been quoted' with characterising the Goodwill Committee as duplicitous.[49]

Marshall's response two days later was that he 'never questioned the good faith' of the FCC Committee, but did object to Anthony's approval of the 'propriety of efforts' to evangelise Jews even when directed at Jewish youth. Anthony ignored the sensitive issue of youth on 17 June, arguing instead that it would be lacking in goodwill as well as discrimination if the Church abandoned Jews from its mission commission. Marshall, who was also president of the American Jewish Committee, rebutted that it was not 'offensive discrimination' to be deprived of 'the suffering humiliation of becoming the victim of conversionist zeal', emphasising that Jews did not view the attention of missionaries as 'evidence of goodwill'. What received most of Marshall's eloquent ire in the long exchange, however, was a refutation of Anthony's claim that Jewish opposition was a masked attempt to muzzle Christian witness and thereby breach the constitutional right to free speech.[50]

The full correspondence was widely disseminated after Marshall handed it to *Jewish Telegraphic Agency* for publication on 24 June 1929. In the New York *Jewish Daily Bulletin* it appeared beneath the headline 'Christian Missionary Work Among the Jews Menaces Goodwill Activity'. The next day, the New York based FCC officially entered the fray by way of the disclamatory headline, 'Dr. Anthony's Views On Conversion Not Those of Goodwill Committee'. The statement of disassociation by Everett Clinchy, secretary of the FCC Goodwill Committee and newly formed National Conference of Jews and Christians, stressed that Anthony 'was not speaking for the Committee', that his views were 'purely personal', and that the FCC Goodwill Committee was 'not interested in converting Jews'.[51]

Yet that was not the end of proselytising revelations to North American Jews. Later that summer the North American Home Missions Council – with which Anthony, Mott, FCC, IMC and the emerging ICCAJ were all connected – issued its own statement in support of Jewish missions. It was drafted in response to the New York Board of Rabbis request that proselytising of Jews cease, and it made clear that its thirty-eight mission boards in the United States and Canada reserved 'not only the right but the duty to present the gospel of Christ ... to every man and woman within the bounds of this Continent'.[52] The head of the committee issuing the statement was Dr John Conning, newly named chair of NAICCAJ and soon to be vice-chair of the international ICCAJ.[53]

Revelations continued to unfold when John Mott argued before the Foreign Missions Conference of North America in December 1930 that 'Christian missions among Jews is a duty of the Christian Church in spite of protests raised against it'. Under that headline the *Jewish Telegraphic Agency* reiterated the history and deepening frustration of Jewish leaders. Roger Strauss, Jewish co-chairman of the National Conference of Jews and Christians (NCJC), pointed to the incongruity of Mott claiming that the evangelising programme would result in 'better understanding between Jews and Christians'. Dr Herbert Goldstein, president of the Association of Jewish Orthodox Communities, went further by urging that such claims should 'open the eyes of Jewish leaders who have been caught in the loving goodwill propaganda'. Strauss, however, pointing to his NCJC colleagues, had hope that not all Christian goodwill was stained by conversionary intentions. As for 'Dr Mott and his associates', he had little concern that ICCAJ 'would actually succeed' in converting Jews, but he was greatly concerned that it was doing America 'an evil service' by fanning 'the flame of religious prejudice'.[54]

ICCAJ reaction to this three-year stream of publicised Jewish opposition, which was coming from Jewish leaders in Britain as well,[55] was a mix of anticipation, resolve and calculated attempts to avoid or temper public Jewish protests. The Budapest–Warsaw conferences had warned that 'official Judaism ... does its utmost to create hindrances', but there was also increasing awareness that methods which 'needlessly awaken[ed] the opposition of the Jews' should be avoided. At the same time the protesting claims of Jews were recognised as fodder for developing 'more effective means of meeting Jewish defensive measures and propaganda'. It was also the case that empirical lessons were being learned about the circumstances and negative publicity value of Jewish protests. As oppositions became more vocal a decision was made in the fall of 1930 to *not* put at risk an upcoming conference in the New York area by publicising it in advance. Mott and the newly appointed leaders of NAICCAJ chose instead to outmanoeuvre Jewish opposition by holding a 'confidential' conference that would not be discussed publicly until after it had ended.[56]

What had not been expected was that formidable opposition would come from within. The presumed hindrances within the Church had been those of apathy and misunderstanding, indifference, or anti-Judaic enmity, each of which was thought to be correctable by Christian education and rallying. As recorded by Mott on the first day of the Budapest conference, his life had been spent 'in drawing together Christian forces', and nowhere in his notes on the developing 'grand strategy' of 'vision, vitality and victory' were dissenting Christians mentioned.[57] The FCC Goodwill Committee had not been a major concern, for even though Anthony was not part of ICCAJ he was sympathetic to its conversionary agenda. Moreover, FCC general secretary Samuel Cavert was a Mott protégé who was part of the 1928 Jerusalem meeting that set in motion the creation of ICCAJ, and by 1930 he was on the executive committee of NAICCAJ. The other goodwill body, the National Conference of Jews and Christians, was viewed with more caution since it had risen in the wake of Jewish protests to the Budapest–Warsaw conferences, but there was no indication by fall 1930 that Christian members would formally and publicly oppose the emerging ICCAJ programme. Neither group had given any hint of the oppositional tenacity that arose from Britain in the fall of 1930.

When British Anglican James Parkes began working within the ecumenical movement, ICCAJ did not exist, but relations established there placed him in the path of those who would be its leaders. After graduating from Oxford in theology in 1923 he was named International Study Secretary for the British Student Christian Movement (SCM), a constituent of WSCF in Geneva. In that capacity he served on the international committee of European Student Relief, the humanitarian programme under Conrad Hoffmann's direction. As the postwar student crisis subsided, the organisation was restructured in 1926 under the name International Student Service (ISS), and the focus was changed to relief of student social problems through education, mutual understanding and self-help.[58] Hoffmann remained head until moved to a WSCF secretariat in December 1927, at which time ISS leadership was handed to Walter Kotschnig, a 26-year-old political scientist from Austria. Parkes, who was by then 32 and ordained in the Church of England, was brought on board to create a programme of international cultural cooperation in European universities, one to be carried out within the boundaries of ISS neutrality 'to students of all countries, whatever their race, nationality or convictions'.[59]

By all ISS accounts, the greatest challenge to international cultural cooperation in European universities in 1928 was the mounting aggressions of east European nationalists toward Jewish minorities. Although the redrawing of national borders at the end of World War I was supported by mandatory Minorities Treaties that guaranteed civil and religious rights of peoples within newly created or expanded eastern European states, avid discontent over who was and was not 'national' erupted in Hungary, Poland and Romania. Just three months after the June 1920 Treaty of Trianon guaranteed political and civic rights in Hungary without distinction of birth, race, religion or language, a *numerus clausus* was issued that restricted university education to those 'known to be of absolutely unimpeachable national loyalty and morality', and only in proportion to each minority in the overall population. For Jewish students, to whom the law most radically applied, that meant a crippling decrease in university enrolments, even though the treaty made clear that Jews 'were in fact and by law Hungarian nationals'. Similar de facto exclusions were soon manifest in Poland and Romania even though the enforcing body of the Minorities Treaties warned against the use of *numerus clausus*.[60]

By 1923 nationalist agitation against Jewish students in all three countries had spread even to European Student Relief, turning to bitter controversy an international conference in Parad (Hungary), and then erupting again in 1925 in a 'venomous speech' by a European student Christian leader at a WSCF conference in Switzerland, which Parkes was chairing. By the time he assumed the post in cultural cooperation with ISS in March 1928, the National Socialist Student League in Germany had been created for the purpose of integrating Nazi ideology in universities; the leader of the Romanian antisemitic party was a university professor; and the combined effects of *numerus clausus* in Hungary, Poland and Romania, both by law and de facto, had driven as many as ten thousand eastern European Jewish students to expatriation in search of university enrolment.[61]

With no blueprint, no Polish, Romanian or Hungarian language skills and bound on all sides by ISS parameters of conciliatory neutrality, Parkes looked for a way to mitigate the agitation and violence. His approach was both innovative and daring. He brought Jewish and non-Jewish nationalist students together at mediated discussions, on the one hand, while launching a major research initiative into the historical causes of the problem, on the other. With respect to the former he developed a series of international conferences and study groups, the first of which was held outside Paris in December 1928 with students from Czechoslovakia, Germany, Austria, Hungary, Poland, Romania, France, the United States and Great Britain. In the wake of its success, Jewish and non-Jewish students were organised into informal local and regional groups to document and study the cultural, political and economic aspects of 'the Jewish question in universities'. Such hands-on work allowed Parkes to witness the issues of accelerating nationalist antisemitism at first hand, not only when bringing Jewish and non-Jewish students together in study groups and conferences, but also by travelling to the European countries affected by anti-Jewish nationalist aggressions.

Conversion and the Jewish problem: 1925–1932 45

Parkes's concomitant engagement in the collection and analyses of historical documents also led to the first of two groundbreaking books on antisemitism.[62] Recognising that the issues in European universities could not be reduced to either the 'malevolence' of Jews (as nationalist opponents claimed) or the anti-Jewish oppression of *numerus clausus* laws (as Jewish students claimed), he framed his research in the broader context of a European society that could not be shorn of its historical Christian past.[63] As his one presupposition, 'more firmly established' by each piece of historical data acquired, he argued that the roots of antisemitism lay in human history and not in any supernatural event. He thus dismissed any claim that attributed antisemitic cause to either the 'direct action of God' in 'the condemnation of the [alleged] deicide race', or to Jews as a people 'hostile to the rest of humanity'. Both, he stressed, resulted in explanations that focused on Jewish actions and behaviours, either 'self-causing' backlash from non-Jews or 'self-causing' an alleged divine punishment. In addition to antisemitism having no roots in the supernatural, he argued that *no* solution was to be found there either. As a human phenomenon it would have to be 'unravelled by human intelligence and resolved by human action'.[64]

The findings of Parkes's research were unfavourable to Christianity. He argued evidentially that anti-Jewish decrees of early Church councils served as the basis for an official Church attitude toward Jews, one sustaining in hostility after the Church came to power under Constantine. Recognising that the eleventh century marked a violent turning point, he argued that the justifying cause for the crusader violence rested in the foundational 'hostility of the Church', as did 'the sustained hatred which mark[ed] relations between Christians and Jews from the eleventh century onward'. Moreover, the centuries following the crusade 'sowed the seeds' of modern antisemitism in two crucial ways: by 'instilling hate into Christians' and forcing Jews into a state of degradation that provoked and nurtured the development of atypical traits.[65] While Parkes was refuting the Nazi claim that Jewish characteristics were inherent and unalterable, he was at the same time levelling a powerful indictment against the Church in its ancient, medieval and modern aspects. Christianity was being implicated in not just one but two dimensions, for not only did the hatred that sowed the seeds of modern antisemitism have its origin in Christian religious motive, so did the alleged 'Jewish' traits associated with the exclusivity that antisemites and others (including ICCAJ) claimed as provoking causes of antisemitic backlash.

When Parkes's book was published in the fall of 1930, John Mott instructed H. L. Henriod, general secretary of WSCF, to 'procure' a copy.[66] A month later the judgment of Mott and ICCAJ protégés in New York was delivered to Parkes in a letter from Conrad Hoffmann. To understand why Hoffmann would be the bearer of judgment, it is necessary to look back to Geneva a few months earlier. Hoffmann was twelve years older than Parkes, as well as fifteen years senior in ecumenical status, but Parkes was two years senior in terms of work related to Jews. As such, Hoffmann approached him as he was leaving Geneva for his New York introduction to ICCAJ, with the professed hope of working cooperatively. Parkes's understanding at the time was that he wanted to make changes in mission policies and guide ICCAJ along the same goodwill lines as the National Conference of Jews and Christians.

Sixty days after Hoffmann's introduction to ICCAJ he relayed a 'much better understanding' of his new role. The early November letter was dated three days after his last meeting with Mott and NAICCAJ members, immediately before embarking from New York for his first directorial tour of Europe, and it included the verdict on Parkes's book, offered in his own best interest. *The Jew and His Neighbour: A Study of the Causes of Anti-Semitism* was judged to be an uninformed and 'hurried piece of work', 'written without adequate background', 'premature', 'shooting off half cocked', and damaging to his future ecumenical career.[67]

Although decades later Parkes would refer to Mott as a 'Christian imperialist', his response in December 1930 was to discount the warnings and focus instead on the abyss between his work and theirs.[68] Referring to an outline of ICCAJ plans in Hoffmann's two letters, he pointed out that the chasm between them was not merely a difference in emphasis but 'of kind'. In looking at his own work, which had no ulterior conversionary motive, it seemed to him that the motives of ICCAJ were more along the lines of 'how to take advantage of the present difficulties of Jews [in order] to convert them'. Parkes went on to challenge the contradictory duality of ICCAJ intentions, positing as improvident the claim that ICCAJ could improve Christian–Jewish relations while launching a programme of global evangelisation. He roundly rejected the organisational concept of 'right' Christian thinking about Jews, namely, that one 'believes in converting the individual Jew ... or one does not accept responsibility for the Jews'; and he did so on the grounds that such narrowness in thinking ignored the Christian responsibility 'to give the Jew a square deal to be a Jew'.[69]

To say that Parkes's critique was unexpected and that it breached ICCAJ consciousness with the reality of Christian opposition would not be an overstatement. Indeed, it was at this point in December 1930 that Mott argued before the North American Foreign Missions conference that 'Christian missions among Jews is a duty of the Christian Church in spite of protests raised against it'. By spring, Hoffmann too was alerting ICCAJ associates that protests from 'good-will' Christians, a category into which Parkes was now placed, would have to be 'reckoned with'.[70] Yet even as Parkes opposed the claims and goals of ICCAJ, he initially saw Hoffmann as one who had been thrown unknowingly into the midst of a *déformation professionnelle*, and he did so in deference to his sixteen-year reputation for humanitarian impartiality in the European fields of wartime and postwar suffering. The idea that Hoffmann would use his trusted reputation to carve a path of partiality in Jewish evangelisation was inconceivable to him, until he learned of Hoffmann's directorial tour to assess the Jewish mission fields of central and eastern Europe, the same fields in which he was labouring to mitigate anti-Jewish and antisemitic aggressions.[71]

The thin line of distinctions

Opposition was not the only problem shaping the developing grand strategy of the conversionary initiative. According to Mott, discerning ecumenists would always associate the 1928 IMC world conference in Jerusalem with identification of secularism as 'the chief antagonist' to religious faith.[72] The 'mountain range of problems' resting under the secular threat, as catalogued by Mott's conference interpreter, included atheism, Bolshevism, fascism, 'racial

Figure 1.2 European mission agencies associated with ICCAJ by 1932

Of 210 agencies and branches in 36 countries, the 12 non-European nations included Abyssinia (1), Australia (1), Egypt (2), India (2), Morocco (1), Palestine (15), Persia (2), Syria (1), Tunisia (1), Union of South Africa (4), Canada (17), United States (82). *Directory of Agencies Promoting the Christian Approach to the Jews* (NY and London: ICCAJ, 1932), IMC.261202.

and national demands for self-determination', materialism, relativism, demise of moral authority and all such irreligious elements that derogated the status of Christianity in western civilisation.[73] Everything under the umbrella of secularism, in other words, was seen as a gathering collective force eating away at the pillars of Christendom's authority, a 'single great enemy' which the Church had the 'single supreme duty' to surmount. The need for a unified stand against the 'secular civilisation' flourishing in the midst of western Christendom was recognised as urgent. United Christian 'forces' would have to be rallied and educated to the fact that battles would have to be fought on a landscape of competing worldviews, and that gaining access to 'unoccupied areas of thought' would be as vital as gaining unoccupied geographical ground.[74]

One of the ways in which this played out in ICCAJ was increasing focus on Jewish mentalities. The Budapest–Warsaw conferences had realised that understanding the Jewish mind was key to mission success, but it was also held that Jewish mentalities varied according to national, regional and local cultures. The alleged universal aspects of Jewish mentalities, however, began to move front and centre after Hoffmann consulted German universities that paid 'special attention ... to the Jewish question', meeting with Gerhard Kittel and his habilitated student Karl Heinrich Rengstorf on his first directorial tour of Europe in late 1930 and early 1931. Shortly after his return, Kittel's University of Tübingen was recommended as an academic centre with 'excellent research opportunities' in the field of Jewish missions, and Rengstorf was appointed to the ICCAJ international committee.[75]

Professor Julius Richter, a seasoned ecumenist at the University of Berlin, who was Mott's consultant for Continental appointees to ICCAJ, was also brought in as a keynote speaker for a conference in Atlantic City in May 1931 under Mott's chairmanship.[76] With Germany as a model, Richter taught from a place of revered percipience that Jewish mentalities had to be understood in order to recognise the mechanisms of anti-Jewish reactions in society. He outlined four categories of Jews encountered in missionary operations: Zionists, impassioned with nationalism; reactionary ghetto Jews who clung to old traditions; reform Jews, predominately assimilators; and renaissance Jews, whose primary concern was Jewish culture and heritage. His guiding point was that even though the general categories were highly divergent with 'endless variations and crosses', the 'tendencies' in each remained more or less convergent in terms of the ways in which non-Jewish reactions to Jews were provoked. Jewish tendencies toward 'secularism', 'agnosticism, 'anti-moralistic sensualism' and 'engrossing materialism' caused Jews to be 'regarded as a dangerous poison' in guest nations, on the one hand, while 'intellectual superiority, unparalleled business activity and ingrained will to power' caused Jews to be judged as feeling predestined 'to become the leaders of their host peoples', on the other. The end result, which Richter said should not be surprising, was that the 'imperious intrusion of Jewry' generally evoked non-Jewish reactions in the form of antisemitism. As example of *why* antisemitic reaction was 'cropping up in accentuated force' in Germany, he explained that even though Germany was 'suffering under the postwar burden of poverty and distress', Jews were 'parading in luxury and licentiousness, filling the most expensive theatres and hotels, riding in fine autos, and seeming to riot like vampires in the blood of their host peoples' – without any discernment of their provocative behaviours.[77]

Relations between Jewish mentalities and provocations of non-Jews was a theme brought out by other conference speakers as well. Dr John Conning, chairman of NAICCAJ and vice-chair of ICCAJ, had argued regularly since 1927 that Jewish exclusivity made Jewish patriotism suspect and that Christians were 'disturbed by the persistent efforts of Jewish leaders to secularize America'. Here, in May 1931, he stressed the impact of 'the largest and most influential Jewry in the world' on the 'great Christian nations' of the United States and Canada.

> Across [the] pathway [of North America] lie 4,500,000 of the most virile and resourceful people in all the world who are not in accord with the Christian program, and who deny that these countries are or ever can be Christian ... We have now in this country not only the largest Jewry in the world, but the most influential. Jews are now at the peak of Jewish experience with respect to freedom of opportunity and achievement. Already their influence is widely felt in journalism, art, science, law, medicine, and many other spheres. They are largely

under the sway of secular civilization and furnish leadership in communistic and other movements [that are] definitely irreligious in their outlook and intent.[78]

Conning was not alone in his concern about the increasing sway of secular views from world Jewry, nor was he the first to warn about the threat of Jewish secularism. It had been basic to the discourse since Macdonald Webster's *IRM* arguments in 1918 and 1925 about relations between eastern European Jewry and the spread of the Jewish problem to the west. C.H. Gill, general secretary of Anglican Church Missions to Jews and future chairman of ICCAJ, was in fact the bearer of the same message from Webster and other British colleagues to the Atlantic City conference. While positing that the universality of the Jewish problem was a reflection of Christianity's failure 'to evangelize Europe's Jewry in the past', Gill urged that no solution to the problem in America would be found without 'touching the source' of secular freethinkers flowing from eastern Europe to the west.[79] Basil Mathews, Mott's interpreter of the Jerusalem conference who had just published *The Clash of World Forces: A Study in Nationalism, Bolshevism and Christianity* in English, Danish and Swedish, added to the discussion that 'the Jew of genius, Karl Marx', would never have produced 'the greatest rival to Christianity since the birth of Islam' if the Church had dealt historically in 'Christian ways with the Jews'. He also reminded that other disintegrating secular ideas 'battling for ascendancy' had emerged from 'two other great Jews, Freud and Einstein'.[80]

The conference understanding was that the Church could no longer afford to ignore Jews, not only in the divine imperative to bring them to spiritual destiny but also, in Conning's words, 'as a people able, virile, persistent, but non-Christian, menacing many of our cherished ideals'.[81] How Jews thought, how Jews behaved, how Jews influenced society were matters of concern in both missions and in meeting the subtle menace of a secular civilisation. Unlike an identifiable enemy that cast single deadly blows, the secular complex was understood as an eroding enemy of many faces, some of the more dangerous elements of which resulted from disintegrating Judaism and the flow of Jews toward atheistic, nationalistic and other non-religious elements. That world Jewry was becoming more irreligious, with Jewish predilection toward a cohort of secular forces, was in fact one of the takeaways of the conference. Another, in the conclusions of Hoffmann's 37-page directorial report, was framed as a valid argument for preoccupation with the mentalities of postwar Jewry:

> In many lands the Jews occupy a predominant position and exercise a directing influence in the life of society out of all proportion to their number. This being true, it matters a great deal for the cause of a Christian world community what the religious outlook ... of this dominant element in society is.[82]

That all of this fell under the banner of perceived Christian benevolence, and that none of it was seen as anti-Jewish, harmful or related to antisemitic attitudes, was made clear by Hoffmann's post-conference assessment. In an attempt to pry James Parkes from his negative critique of ICCAJ, he had written prior to the conference to say that it would conduct an 'intensive study' of Christian attitudes that might contribute to antisemitism. A few days after the conference he wrote again to report that seventy-five 'outstanding Christian leaders' had lifted 'the whole enterprise ... to a much higher plane'. While failing to mention that papers emphasised Jewish provocations rather than Christian causes of anti-Jewish attitudes, he reported accurately that the conference confessed 'with shame' the past negative attitudes of Christianity, and urged 'repentance for prejudice and unjust discriminations' against Jews. Yet neither Hoffmann's letter nor the enclosed conference findings had the intended effect.[83]

Parkes rebuked the 'clear and compelling evangelistic purpose' of the ICCAJ initiative and rejected as unacceptable any 'official conversionist policy', regardless of how beneficently it was framed. While granting the importance of confessing 'with shame' the attitude and conduct of Christians in the past, he was roundly critical that no responsibility had been claimed for the 'ultimate' cause of historic Christian attitudes toward Jews, and that no repudiation had been made for some two thousand years of 'ignored facts'. For Parkes, it was one thing to encourage Christians to repent for 'prejudice and unjust discrimination', as one finding did, but altogether another to

Conversion and the Jewish problem: 1925–1932

acknowledge and accept responsibility for the anti-Jewish Christian attitudes that permeated western history and culture. Even those findings that touched on discrimination and repentance, he urged, were 'inadequate to express the historic facts'.[84]

What was not revealed in the correspondence that so lucidly draws a hard line between Parkes and ICCAJ was that none of the conference findings explicitly repudiated antisemitism. In keeping with the Budapest–Warsaw findings the terms 'prejudice' and 'discrimination' had been used instead. 'Prejudice', 'un-Christian treatment', 'ill-usage', 'injustice', 'persecution' and 'sins of Christendom against the Jews' had all found place there, but the term 'antisemitism' was missing from the list of Christian admissions, just as in 1931. 'Race prejudice' and 'race discrimination' did appear in one of the 1931 resolutions but it was in the evangelising context of declaring that racial discrimination had no place in Christian missions. When calling Christians to repent for past and current anti-Jewish attitudes, however, only 'unjust discrimination', 'prejudice' and 'ostracism' were used. That this was neither oversight nor coincidence will become clear when viewed in the context of a third conference in June 1932.

The year and setting are important, for it was the first joint meeting since the British, North American and Continental European regional sectors were formed. As such, the conference was poised to address three international matters: adoption of an organisational constitution; the drafting of a positional statement on antisemitism; and the unveiling of a directory of agencies promoting ICCAJ in thirty-six countries, twenty-four of which were in Europe. At its convening Hoffmann called for a statement that disavowed antisemitism as an 'un-Christian racial manifestation', on the grounds that official repudiation could influence European churches to 'protest against the violence and outrages' of antisemitism.[85] It was to be drafted by an appointed committee after discussion of papers by three ICCAJ executives who had been centrally involved since the Budapest–Warsaw conferences: Rev. J. van Nes, Reformed Church of the Netherlands, Dr Otto von Harling, director of the Delitzschianum in Leipzig, and Dr John Conning.

Addressing antisemitism in Europe, Germany and North America respectively, three common points were brought forward.

Antisemitism was understood as having political, economic, social, racial and religious aspects; the religious aspect was understood as the most inconsequential; and each included an aspect of Jewish guilt in explanation. For Rev. J. van Nes, the deicidal guilt of the Jews was a measuring stick for the guilt to be borne by Christians who became involved. In his analysis, antisemitism was an anti-Christian manifestation divinely used as 'a scourge ... to punish Jews for their sins', and its anti-Christian nature meant that 'good' Christians could not be involved, and that nominal Christians who became involved would be punished just as God punished the Jews.[86]

Dr Otto von Harling, echoing many of Julius Richter's points from 1931, argued that every country had its 'point of limit' in absorbing Jews, and that a 'too many of the Jews' attitude would be stronger in countries like Germany where Jews penetrated the 'spiritual organism' as well as its economic and political realms. 'Factual' conditions said to be contributing to Germany's current 'struggle' were set out in three ways. First, in keeping with ongoing concerns about the eastern 'fountain' of secularism and atheism flowing to the west, he emphasised the movement of 'unscrupulous' eastern European Jews into German society to profit from 'Germany's helplessness'. Second, he pointed to the left-wing interests and international loyalties of Jews, and, third, he invoked increasing Jewish influence on German culture and intellectual life. Urging for the sake of 'justice' that ICCAJ members try to understand why such a 'passionate struggle' had risen in a people who were 'otherwise rather peaceful', Harling went on to ask for confidence that Germany would deal with its problem as 'conditions demand'. The struggle had become 'very ugly and rough', but 'it had to come', he urged, and it would be 'unjust to blame [solely] either the Jews or the Germans ... for guilt is found in both, and guilt and fate are not easy to separate in the Jewish question'.[87]

John Conning, in the same vein as Harling's 'point of limit' theory, pointed to the provocative nature of Jewish behaviours and ingresses, stressing as he had since 1927 that antisemitism did not appear in America until Jews 'increased to millions' and the 'Jewish ferment' began to break through with 'racial peculiarities' and 'disproportionately large numbers of Jews' in the professions. As a way

Conversion and the Jewish problem: 1925–1932 55

of moving into discussion, Conning closed with a series of leading questions intended to elicit a summation of claims implicit in ICCAJ arguments about antisemitism, namely, that Christianity alone possessed the solution; that Christians had 'a right' to expect Jews to remove self-causes; that the Church was duty-bound to cultivate the 'correct' Christian attitude toward Jews.[88]

Two points stand in bold relief in the statement forged in the wake of these papers and discussion. The first is that even though the statement was titled 'Finding on Anti-Semitism', the term 'antisemitism' was nowhere to be found. The second is the inclusion of a mutual blame clause that had not appeared in earlier findings, even though Jewish blame for provocation of non-Jewish attitudes was widely discussed in papers, reports, meetings and conferences.

To cast light on *why*, it is necessary to look first at the internationalism around which ICCAJ was structured. As subsidiary of the IMC, ICCAJ was bound to the supranational idea that 'spiritual unity ... demands manifestation in international missionary cooperation'.[89] But ICCAJ was more than just a subsidiary of a supranational collaborative: it was itself an international body comprising multinational interests channelled into supranational goals and, like IMC, it operated along the lines of organisational neutrality grounded in the supranational purpose of evangelising Jews.

What this meant in terms of speaking officially is that organisational statements consciously reflected ICCAJ's international structure, as well as the cautionary implications of IMC's troubled history. As noted, Mott was harshly censured by German mission constituents during World War I for a presumed negative bias against Germany, one framed by Julius Richter as 'offence' against the supranational nature of Christian missions. The postwar need for measured neutrality in regard to Germany was thus understood. It was also the case that the 1931 and 1932 statements were formulated in the wake of German constituent papers that characterised German antisemitism as justified backlash to Jewish ingressions. Moreover, both authors, Richter and Harling, were part of the discussions that preceded the statements, and Harling himself was part of the 1932 drafting committee. Indeed, it was only after Harling's appeal for the understanding of Germany's Jewish problem that a mutual blame clause appeared for the first time in an official organisational statement. It is also clear that all who were involved were self-consciously aware that the 1932 statement would be presented at a twelve-day conference of the IMC executive committee in Germany a fortnight later, with Julius Richter in attendance.[90]

To probe further why the term 'antisemitism' was not used in ICCAJ official statements, it is important to point out that ICCAJ leaders were involved in drafting two other statements that *did* use the term 'antisemitism'. The first was issued in the name of the North American Home Missions Council in December 1930,[91] the second as a joint North American statement of twenty-five Protestant organisations in December 1931.[92] The relevant point is that statements using the term (December 1930 and 1931) as well as those omitting it (May 1931, June 1932) were drafted by the very same circle of ICCAJ executives in the same precise period. The crucial difference is that the two statements of North American scope repudiated 'antisemitism' per se while the ICCAJ organisational statements did not. In fact it would not be until July 1937 that an official ICCAJ statement actually used the term 'antisemitism' when condemning racial prejudice against Jews.

Yet it should not be presumed that international protectionism was the only factor in organisational attempts to disavow antisemitism as 'an un-Christian racial manifestation' while avoiding use of the specific term. Reluctance to use 'antisemitism' in official statements also reflected a theoretical concern about undistinguished conflation of all negative attitudes toward Jews as 'antisemitic'. This held true in regard to German constituents who had argued since 1927 that 'the warding off of Jewish anti-Christian encroachments' was not antisemitic.[93] But it was also true of constituents who were not German. As shown throughout this chapter it was widely accepted among international conferees that defence of Christendom against so called anti-Christian advances of Jews was neither antisemitic nor unjustly prejudicial.

The conscious choice to use words other than 'antisemitism' in official statements was also informed by distinctions between racially motivated and non-racially motivated 'prejudice', a term prominent in all statements between 1927 and 1932, including the Budapest–Warsaw findings. While it could be presumed that 'prejudice' was used substitutively, a comparative analysis belies that synonymatic exchange was being made. The pattern in all instances was that of naming unjust 'prejudice', 'discrimination', 'ill-usage' and 'ostracism' as forms of anti-Judaism that were being renounced as past and present sins of the Church and Christendom. 'Race prejudice', 'race discrimination' and 'antisemitism', in contrast, were used to acknowledge and refute violations of the universality of Christianity.[94] Such distinctions appeared in contrasting pairs whether the term antisemitism was used or not: unjust Christian treatment of Jews *and* racial prejudice (B-W Apr. 1927); unjust Christian discrimination *and* antisemitism (HMC Dec. 1930); unjust Christian prejudice *and* racial prejudice (NAICCAJ May 1931); Christian anti-Jewish prejudice *and* antisemitism (NA Protestants Dec. 1931); Christian prejudice *and* racial discrimination (ICCAJ June 1932).

Recognition of these subtleties is critical, particularly by 1932, for it was at that conference that ICCAJ proclaimed itself the 'responsible' body for making known the causes of 'race hatred', discrimination and prejudice against Jews. The point heralded in the self-christening was that ICCAJ was being called to educate world Protestant populations on 'the realities of the situation', an elaboration of which appeared in an article on the 'missionary significance of the Jews' in *IRM* the following month.[95]

What is most striking is how little had changed in the seven-year interim since the call for Christian experts appeared in the same journal in 1925. The 1932 article was not only structured around the same points, it made generous use of the same text and listed the same postwar developments that signalled societal need for international expansion of Jewish missions: world emancipation of Jews, universal Jewish problem, increasing Jewish influence, increasing antisemitism, disintegration of Judaism, movement of Jews toward atheism and/or racial-national consciousness. What was new relative to the seven-year argument was that racial consciousness among world Jewry was now said to be fanning 'the flame of anti-Semitism'. Such linking of Jewish racial consciousness to antisemitism was not itself new – Conning had argued since 1927 that Jewish racial pride provoked antisemitic response and that Jewish leaders groomed 'racial consciousness and emphasized racial claims' – but the claim by 1932 was that 'Judaism to multitudes of Jews was more a matter of race than religion'.[96]

That this was finding place as a fixed category of thought was made clear a few months later when ICCAJ executives met with a group of American rabbis for the purpose of quelling their protests against organised Jewish missions. The November Chicago meeting – which included among others Rabbi Professor Samuel Cohon, Chair of Theology at Hebrew Union College (Cincinnati), Rabbi Solomon Freehof, Reform Congregation (Chicago), Rabbi Professor Meyer Waxman, Hebrew Theological College (Chicago) – was unsurprisingly a stalemate. The group of nine rabbis were 'irreconcilably opposed to any attempt on the part of Christians to evangelize the Jews', while ICCAJ remained 'irrevocably convinced' that Jews had to be included in all missionary programmes. Yet rather than just granting that differences persisted between Jewish and Christian leaders, ICCAJ leaders concluded that 'the real problem' centred around the question of whether Judaism was 'a Race or a Religion'. Among claims passed along in the wake of the meeting was that 'the whole problem [was] essentially one of racial pride and not of religion', that 'the aim of Jews was to preserve the integrity of the Jews as a race', that the 'real problem' was 'fundamentally a racial problem which pretends to be a religious problem'.[97]

Although the mounting argument about Jewish racial identity would not reach fullness until after Hitler's ascent to power in 1933, all of the fundamental elements were present in 1925. In that critical respect, the emerging racial-identity theory cannot be separated from the call for Christian experts to study the Jewish problem, *or* the unanimous mandate of the Budapest–Warsaw conferences to create a planning body for global expansion of Jewish missions. That the conversionary initiative was brought into existence as a problem-solving body was not only understood but mandated. As solemnly appraised by John Mott in his closing address of the June 1932 conference, ICCAJ 'had been called to deal with the most difficult set of problems that any group of Christians have had committed to them'.[98] The overarching belief was that antisemitism was an unchristian racial response to the advancing reality of an international Jewish problem, and ICCAJ viewed itself as the benevolent bearer of a divinely mandated non-racial Christian solution. Its imprecise condemnation of antisemitism as 'racial prejudice' fitted well with the IMC aim of uniting world Protestant forces to seek 'justice in international and interracial relations', and ICCAJ took most seriously its duty to learn 'the mind of Christ' and 'press forward boldly in spreading worldwide understanding'.[99]

Yet it is also the case that ICCAJ propagation of Judaism as a breeder of racial traits that provoked non-Jews to antisemitic backlash was itself a troubling theory of troubled international and interracial relations. By the eve of Hitler's rise, while claiming (and believing) itself diametrically opposed to all doctrines and solutions of antisemitic racism, ICCAJ was categorising Jews as a race with society-troubling attributes, and, in its pronouncements of Judaism as a conveyor of racial advancement, it was thoughtlessly and dangerously in agreement with mainline tenets of Nazi antisemitic theory.

Notes

1 Macdonald Webster, 'The Jewish Problem: Some Newer Aspects', *IRM*, 14:4 (1925), 598–607, quot., 598–601, 603.
2 Ibid., 603.
3 Clark, *The Politics of Conversion*, 252, 270–1, 278, 283; for incisive analysis of Johannes de Le Roi, to whom Clark attributes the first outlining of mission theory, 242–81; also 'Missionary Politics: Protestant Missions to the Jews in Nineteenth-Century Prussia', 33–50. For de Le Roi, *Die evangelische Christenheit und die Juden unter dem Gesichtspunkte der Mission geschichtlich betrachtet* (1884–1892).
4 Quot., John Wilkinson, *Israel My Glory: Israel's Mission and Missions to Israel* (1894), 117–20. For Danish use of de Le Roi in late nineteenth century, Martin S. Lausten, *Jews and Christians in Denmark: From the Middle Ages to Recent Times, 1100–1948* (Leiden: Brill, 2015).
5 Webster, 'The Need of a New Policy in Jewish Missions', *IRM*, 17:2 (1918), 206–18, quot., 214, 207, 210.
6 IMC Minutes, Oxford, 9–16 July 1923, IMC.261231.
7 Webster, 'The Jewish Problem' (1925), 606, 603.
8 Webster to Mott, 3 June 1927, IMC.261230.

9 Delegate nations included Austria, Belgium, Bulgaria, Canada, Czechoslovakia, Danzig, Denmark, England, Egypt, Finland, France, Germany, Greece, Holland, Hungary, India, Ireland, Norway, Palestine, Poland, Romania, Scotland, Sweden, Switzerland, United States, Yugoslavia.
10 *The Christian Approach to the Jew*, ed. James Black (London: Edinburgh House Press, 1927), hereafter CATJ, 11–17, 18–45, 46–77.
11 CATJ, 18–20.
12 CATJ, 100–2.
13 CATJ, 18–19, 36–7.
14 Min. Interim Comm., 1 Feb. 1928, IMC.261230.
15 CATJ, 27, 42–3.
16 CATJ, 7–11, 27–8, 36–7, 42–3, 91–9, 166–71.
17 CATJ, 5–7.
18 CATJ, 18–19, 28, 36–7, 44.
19 CATJ, 3–5.
20 CATJ, 190–1; 99–100 for traits of lying, boastfulness, selfishness, love of money, dishonest dealings, absence of a sense of sin.
21 CATJ, 190–1.
22 CATJ, 195–7.
23 CATJ, 18–19, 27, 37, 42, 44.
24 Memorandum on B-W Conferences, 9 Feb. 1928, IMC.261230.
25 Conference summary, Feb. 1928; IMC Jerusalem report, 24 Mar.–8 Apr. 1928, 73; min., Informal Group, 26 Sept. 1928; NAICCAJ min., 28 June 1929; IMC min., 11–21 Jul. 1929; IMC.261230, 261202, 261207.
26 ICCAJ offices were located in IMC headquarters in New York, 419 4th Avenue until winter 1934–1935 then 156 5th Avenue. London offices at Edinburgh House, 2 Eaton Gate, also housed the British Conference of Missionary Societies, *IRM*, Missionary Press Bureau and, by 1938, the London office of WCCIF.
27 John Mott, 'Purpose of the Conference', 4, *Christians and Jews* (New York and London: IMC, 1931), 3–5, quot. 4.
28 NAICCAJ included rep. from FCC, Home Missions Council, Church of England in Canada, Protestant Episcopal Church, United Lutheran Church in America, Methodist Episcopal Church, Presbyterian (USA), American Baptist Home Mission Society, Missionary Education Movement, Council of Women for Home Missions, Hartford Theological Seminary, International Committee of the YMCA, Student Division of the North American YMCA, and Student Volunteer Movement.

29 Conference of Missionary Societies in Great Britain and Ireland included the Baptist Missionary Society, British Jews Society, British Syrian Mission, Churches of Christ Foreign Missions, Church Missionary Society, Church of Scotland Foreign Missions, Church of Scotland Women's Missionary Committee, Dublin United Missionary Council, Edinburgh Medical Mission Society, Episcopal Church of Scotland Foreign Missionary Society, Friends Service Council, Jerusalem & East Mission Society, London Missionary Society, Methodist Missionary Society, Mission Council Church Assembly, Moravian Missions, National Bible Society of Scotland, National Laymen's Missionary Movement, Presbyterian Church of Ireland Foreign Mission Committee, Presbyterian Church of Ireland Jewish Missions, Presbyterian Church of Wales Foreign Missions, Presbyterian Women Missionary Association, Scottish Missionary Movement, Society for Promotion of Christian Knowledge, Society for Propagation of Gospel, South American Mission Society, Student Christian Movement, United Society of Christian Literature, University Mission of Central Africa, World Dominion Movement, World Sunday School Association, YMCA, YWCA, Zenana Bible Mission.
30 Interim Comm., 28 June 1927, 1 Feb. 1928; Informal Group, 26 Sept. 1928; Conf. of Officers, 28 June 1929; Otto von Harling to Webster, 18 Oct.; Webster to Paton, 21 Oct. 1929; NAICCAJ Min., 12 June, 28 June, 29 Sept., 10 Dec. 1931, 19 May 1932; DRs, Mar. 1931, June 1932, IMC.261207, 261230, 261202; Survey 1930, *IRM*, Vol. 20 (1931), 67–70.
31 *CATJ*, 26–7, 39–40, 43.
32 Timothy Yates, *Christian Mission in the Twentieth Century* (Cambridge: Cambridge University Press, 1996), esp. 3–33. For militarised language, *CATJ*, 103, 117, 119, 123; 27, 42–3.
33 'Jewish Conference at Budapest', 7 Apr. 1927, Mott Papers, YDL: G45 SIV, Notebooks, B124 F204.2, 'Jews'. *CATJ*, 18, 26–7, 43–5; 102–3; Memorandum, 9 Feb. 1928, IMC.261230.
34 *CATJ*, 34–5, 38.
35 *CATJ*, 21.
36 For laws on mission schools and proselytising in Europe and Asia, *CATJ*, 106.
37 For more on Webster's evangelising theory, David McDougall, *In Search of Israel* (Edinburgh: Thomas Nelson and Sons, 1941), 122–4.
38 *CATJ*, 20–2; 104, 110–14.
39 *CATJ*, 28, 31, 33, 38.
40 Conrad Hoffmann, *In the Prison Camps of Germany* (New York: Association Press, 1920).

41 *International Student Service* (Geneva: ISS, 1928); *Harvard Crimson*, 17 May 1922; *Carolinian*, Vol. 5, Oct. 1923; *Wisconsin Alumni Magazine*, Vol. 25 (May 1924), 256–7.
42 John Mott, Memorandum on appointment of ICCAJ director, summer 1930, IMC.261230.
43 John R. Mott, 'The Purpose of the Conference', *Christians and Jews* (New York and London: IMC, 1931), 4–5.
44 Kraut, 'Towards the Establishment of the National Conference of Christians and Jews: The Tenuous Road to Religious Goodwill in the 1920s', *American Jewish History*, 77:3 (Mar. 1988), 388–412; quot., 401. The FCC Committee of Goodwill Between Christians and Jews was formed in February 1923, CCAR Committee of Goodwill (Oct. 1924), Joint Commission (Dec. 1924). While unaware of the ICCAJ archives, Kraut argues that its evangelising initiative and Jewish opposition to it was the 'spark' and 'immediate cause' of the emergent National Conference of Jews and Christians in spring 1927. See also *Yearbook of Central Conference of American Rabbis*, Vol. 35 (1925), 90–1; Vol. 37 (1927), 98–105.
45 *JTA*, 20 Jan. 1927.
46 Ibid., 11, 12 Apr.
47 *JTA*, 12 Apr., for extended coverage, 11 and 12 Aug. 1927
48 Kraut, 408; he argues that the initial formation meeting for NCJC on 20 April was called by Anthony and John Herring on 12 April, which was the same day the interview was published in *JTA*. For more on NCJC's founding and the demise of FCC's Goodwill Committee in 1932, 388–99, 403–12; also 'National Conference of Jews and Christians', *NYT*, 11 Dec. 1927. For NCJC's later work and name change to NCCJ, Victoria Barnett, 'Fault Lines: An Analysis of the National Conference of Christians and Jews, 1933–1948', PhD, George Mason University (2012).
49 *JDB*, 10 June 1929.
50 *JTA*, 24 June 1929.
51 *JDB*, 25 June; 28th, *Detroit Jewish Chronicle* and *The Jewish Times*; Kraut, 396 n.18, 411.
52 Robert Handy, *We Witness Together: A History of Cooperative Home Missions* (New York: Friendship Press, 1956), 141–3.
53 NAICCAJ min., 28 June 1929, IMC.261230.21.
54 *JTA*, 1 Jan. 1931; also *Neue Welt* (Vienna), 13 Feb. 1931, PP MS60/17/8/1.
55 For early Jewish opposition in Britain, Claude Montefiore, 'The Attempted Conversion of the Jews', *Hibbert Journal* (Jan. 1930),

250–1, where, in referring to the Budapest–Warsaw volume, he argued that 'over and above anti-Semitism there is nothing that militates against good ... relations between Jews and Christians as the efforts of conversionists'.
56 *CATJ*, 19, 97, 100–2; NAICCAJ Min., 28 June 1929, 6 Nov. 1930; DR, Mar. 1930–Mar. 1931, IMC.261202, 261230, 261207.
57 Mott Papers, YDV: G45 Series IV, Notebooks, B124 F204.2, 'Jews', 7 April 1927.
58 The restructure was complete by Aug. 1926, after which ISS operated as an independent body under auspices of WSCF but governed by a self-electing board, two-thirds of which from WSCF. By 1928 the remaining third of the board included both Catholics and Jews.
59 Walter Kotschnig, *International Student Service* (1928), 4–6; ISS exec. min., Paris, 26–27 Apr. 1928, ISS.213.09.39.
60 The Paris Peace Conference created the charter for the League of Nations and set new European national boundaries, requiring each new or expanded state to guarantee equal civil rights and preserve religious rights. Minorities Treaties were signed between 1919 and 1920. The Trianon Treaty was signed in June 1920, and the Hungarian Numerus Clausus (Law XXV) was passed by 26 September. But even with warnings from the League of Nations the Polish government imposed 'in practice' use of *numerus clausus* in universities by 1923. For postwar pogroms in Poland both before and after the Minorities Treaty, British and American Commission reports: *Morgenthau Report* (1919), *Jadwin and Johnson Report* (1919), *Samuel Report* (1920). See also Andrzej Kapiszewski, 'Controversial Reports on the Situation of Jews in Poland in the Aftermath of World War One', *Studia Judaica*, 7:2 (2004), 257–304.
61 Jules Stone, *Numerus Clausus in the Universities of Eastern Europe* (Birmingham: Interuniversity Federation of Great Britain and Ireland, 1927), 3–19; 'Issues to be Discussed on Race, Minorities, and Anti-Semitism at WSCF Conference', 17 Feb. 1925; minutes and reports on WSCF conference at Oberaegeri, Switzerland, 29 Aug. 1925, WSCF 213.07.
62 Min., ISS Assembly, 25–7 Apr., 12 Aug. 1928; ISS news report, Dec. 1928; Conference on the Jewish Question in the Universities, 29 Dec.–2 Jan.; Memoranda to ISS Assembly, 2 and 5 Jan. 1929; ISS min., Paris, 22–5 Apr.; Commission II, ISS conference, Krems, Austria, 30 July–7 Aug. 1929; ISS.213.09. 39.
63 Parkes first argued this in 'Some Aspects of the Jewish Situation in Europe' in a Geneva address to the National Student Union, May 1929, PP60/9/1/1.

64 James Parkes, *The Jew and His Neighbour: A Study in the Causes of Anti-Semitism* (London: SCM Press, 1930); quot. from 1931 edn (New York: Robert R. Smith), 11, 39–40.
65 Ibid., 16–17, 35–51, 76–7, 101.
66 B.R. Barber on behalf of John Mott to H.L. Henriod, 22 Oct. 1930, PP60/7/1/2.
67 Hoffmann to Parkes, 9, 11 Nov. 1930, PP60/17/8/2.
68 Parkes, *Voyage of Discoveries*, 116.
69 Parkes to Hoffmann w/copy to Kotschnig, 9 Dec. 1930, PP60/7/1/2, 60/17/8/2.
70 For Mott quot., 'Christian "duty" to Conduct Missionary Activity Among Jews', *JTA*, 1 Jan. 1931. Hoffmann, 'Notes on Goodwill'; DR, Mar. 1931; also NAICCAJ Min., 29 Sept. 1931; IMC.261202, 261207.
71 Parkes to Kotschnig, 9 Dec. 1930, PP60/17/8/2.
72 Mott, 'At Edinburgh, Jerusalem and Madras', *IRM* 27:3 (1938), 297–320; 306.
73 Basil Mathews, *Roads to the City of God: A World Outlook from Jerusalem* (London: Edinburgh House Press, 1928), foreword by Mott, 13–14, 26–7, 34–5.
74 *The Call to West and East* (London: Church of England Missionary Council, Oct. 1928), v, 149, 153, 158.
75 DR, March 1931, 18; IMC.261202. For the standard work on Kittel's anti-Jewish views, Robert Ericksen, *Theologians Under Hitler* (New Haven: Yale University Press, 1985) and *Complicity in the Holocaust: Churches and Universities in Nazi Germany* (Cambridge: Cambridge University Press, 2012). For anti-Jewish views of Rengstorf, Horst Junginger, *The Scientification of the "Jewish Question" in Nazi Germany* (Leiden: Brill, 2017), 124, 127–8, 130, 155, 376. Rengstorf was Kittel's research assistant during habilitation, after which he taught at Tübingen until 1936; he was co-editor with Kittel of *Rabbinische Texte* and wrote multiple entries to Kittel's *Theologisches Wörterbuch zum Neuen Testament*, the first volumes of which were published in 1933 and 1935. He was appointed to ICCAJ from 1932 to 1935, with further association before outbreak of war, then again in 1945.
76 *Christians and Jews* (New York and London: IMC, 1931), hereafter *CAJ*.
77 Julius Richter, 'The Gospel for the Modern Jew from the Standpoint of the German Churches and Missions', *CAJ*, 70–8.
78 John Conning, 'Major Problems and Issues in a Christian Approach to the Jews', *CAJ*, 13–33, quot. 28–9; *Our Jewish Neighbors: An*

Essay in Understanding (1927); 'The Jewish Situation in America', *IRM* 16:1 (1927), 64–75; 'Religion and Irreligion in Israel', *IRM* 19:4 (Oct. 1930), 538–49.

79 C.H. Gill, 'Present Day Emphases in Work for Jews in Europe and the Near East', *CAJ*, 34–44.
80 Basil Mathews, 'What is the Central Objective of the Christian Approach to the Jew?', *CAJ*, 61–9.
81 Conning, 'Major Problems and Issues in a Christian Approach to Jews', *CAJ*, 17.
82 Hoffmann, 'The First Six Months as Director' (March 1931), 36, IMC. 261202.
83 Hoffmann to Parkes, 26 May 1931, PP 60/17/8/2.
84 Parkes to Hoffmann, 11 June 1931, PP 60/17/8/2.
85 ICCAJ min., Digswell Park, England, 12–14 June 1932, IMC.261202.
86 J. van Nes, 'Anti-Semitism on the Continent of Europe', IMC.261202.
87 Otto von Harling, 'Antisemitism in Germany', IMC.261202.
88 John S. Conning, 'Anti-Semitism in America,' IMC.261202.
89 International Missionary Council, *The World Mission of Christianity: Messages and Recommendations* (London and New York: IMC, 1928), 80.
90 IMC exec. comm. min., Herrnhut (Saxony), 23 June–4 July, IMC.261202; Paton, 'Herrnhut', *IRM* 21:4 (Oct. 1932), 488–97.
91 The HMC statement in December 1930 was drafted by John Conning, chair of NAICCAJ and vice-chair ICCAJ, and Dr Josh McDowell, NAICCAJ executive.
92 The NA Protestant statement in December 1931 was drafted by Conning, Hoffmann and Samuel Cavert, general secretary of FCC and member of NAICCAJ executive. It was issued under the signatures of representatives from the General Assembly of the Presbyterian Church in Canada, General Conference of the Methodist Protestant Church, General Convention of the Christian Church for US and Canada, National Council of Canadian YMCA, United Church of Canada, Church of England in Canada, General Conference of the Methodist Episcopal Church South, African Methodist Episcopal Zion Church, United American Lutheran Church, Missionary Education Movement, Moravian Church North, Lutheran Church in America, Home Missions Council, Evangelical Synod of North America, Federal Council of Churches, General Conference of the Methodist Episcopal Church, Meeting of Friends in America, Southern Baptist Convention, Presbyterian Church USA, International Convention of the Disciples of Christ, National Council of Congregational Churches, National

Council of the Protestant Episcopal Church, General Synod of the Reformed Church in the US, Reformed Episcopal Church, General Synod of the Reformed Church in America. NAICCAJ was listed only as affiliation; IMC.261230.
93 *CATJ* (1927), 124.
94 The statement adopted by IMC at Herrnhut, 23 June–4 July 1932, followed the same pattern, see min., IMC. 261230.
95 Resolution on Anti-Semitism, ICCAJ min., 13–24 June 1932, 7–8, IMC.261202.
96 'The Jews: The Missionary Significance', *IRM*, 21:3 (Jul. 1932), 337–48; Conning, 'The Jewish Situation in America', *IRM*, 16:1 (1927), 73.
97 Confidential report on meeting in Chicago, 13 Nov. 1932; Meeting of Jewish and Christian leaders in Chicago; NAICCAJ Min., 23 Nov. 1932, IMC.261207.
98 ICCAJ Min., Digswell Park, England, 12–14 June 1932, 7, IMC.261202.
99 IMC, *World Mission of Christianity, Messages and Recommendations* (1928), 82.

2

In the shadows of response: 1933–1936

The peril of protest

Inflaming words, as well as silences and protests, can have unsuspecting effects in unexpected places. Four days after the German election of 5 March 1933, which fortified Adolf Hitler's appointment as German Chancellor in January, emboldened pockets of Nazis carried out widespread intimidation of Jews in varying parts of the country. On the other side of the Atlantic, major news outlets reported eyewitness accounts of German Jews being slapped, 'hit over the head with blackjacks, dragged out of their homes in night clothes and otherwise molested'.[1] As news reports of the atrocities multiplied, three Federal Council of Churches (FCC) executives seasoned in ecumenical diplomacy published a statement in *The New York Times* on 25 March, calling the reports a matter of concern to 'all men of brotherly ideals'. The statement was a protest against 'racial and religious intolerance' as well as a vote of confidence that German church leaders would repudiate the antisemitism 'within their borders'.[2] Yet rather than disavowing antisemitism, the riposte from German church leaders was a barrage of cables refuting 'exaggerated', 'deceitful', 'untruthful and disastrous' reports about Germany. Under pledge of 'honour and conscience', German Protestant leaders insisted there had been 'no pogroms against Jews', while urging FCC officials to exercise 'Christian righteousness and veracity' and counter the 'erroneous propaganda of horrors against Germany'. Hermann Kapler, president of the German Federation of Evangelical Churches who had warned at the 1925 Stockholm conference that ecumenical relations would cease if claims of German war guilt persisted, now implored the FCC officials to use their 'influence' to quell protests against Germany's 'alleged persecution of Jews'. As head of UCCLW's Continental European division, he also warned that further protests 'will do harm to ecclesiastical cooperation'.[3] Similar cables were sent to UCCLW chairman Bishop George Bell in London, general secretary H. L. Henriod, and Adolf Keller, director of the European Central Bureau for Inter-Church Aid, both of whom were headquartered in Geneva.[4]

The FCC officials who were also executives of the American sector of UCCLW – Samuel Cavert, Parkes Cadman and Henry Leiper – responded from New York on 30 March in three cables, assuring Kapler and others that the 'message of warning' was gratefully acknowledged, that they 'sympathize[d] deeply with German claims for equality in international affairs', and that concern over reported antisemitism did not imply 'loss of esteem for German people or lessened affection for our Christian brethren'.[5] Over the next two days follow-up letters were written on UCCLW letterhead to colleagues in Europe, requesting intervention in what was seen as a brewing ecumenical crisis. They were a first attempt to try and explain what had happened. Penned by Leiper, the best that could be surmised was that joint protests by American Christians and Jews against reported Jewish persecution had been interpreted in Germany as 'unmistakable confirmation ... that Jews had the power to swing whole nations into line'. The FCC statement, coming as it did between a rally on 12 March and a publicised protest in Madison Square Garden two weeks later, had likely fuelled the myth that 'there really was a world-wide organization of Jewry, capable of mobilizing public sentiment on a wide scale'. The immediate concern was Kapler's warning that further 'participation ... in protests' would endanger ecumenical relations. What was 'needed', and what was being requested, was for William Adams Brown, American chair of the UCCLW Administrative Committee who was liaising in Europe, to 'go at once' to Berlin and 'reassure Dr Kapler and others of the basic and unaltered friendliness of the American people'.[6]

As Leiper was writing from New York to Geneva, Henriod was writing from Geneva to Berlin to assure Kapler that the UCCLW office would do everything it could to 'prevent demonstrations being taken against Germany on false reports'. Henriod agreed with Kapler that the protests could 'do serious harm to cooperation between the churches', and that actions 'based on unconfirmed reports' could 'endanger the situation in an irreparable manner'. But he also made clear that news reports about Germany were causing concerns and that UCCLW was faced with the problem of constructing 'a satisfying answer' to church circles calling for action. In that context he asked Kapler to advise 'as quickly as possible' on the German church attitude to the state boycott, which was being levied against Jews as he wrote.[7]

Henriod's concern was heightened when, without word or protest from German church leaders, the German Law for Reconstruction of the Civil Service was issued on 7 April and its first ordnance defining 'non-Aryan' according to Jewish lineage of one parent or grandparent appeared four days later. Writing that day to Bishop Ammundsen of Denmark, who was vice-chair of UCCLW and chair of the World Alliance, he described the situation as 'becoming too serious' to do nothing but that isolated church protests would be as 'dangerous' as 'no action at all'. His fear, as he prepared for meetings with church leaders in Berlin while advising other church constituencies 'to wait if possible for public action', was that 'we are coming to a divisive turning point for the whole of the ecumenical movement'.[8]

As part of Henriod's preparations, he met with other ecumenical leaders in Geneva the same day, 11 April, to coordinate information for churches abroad. Two positional papers prepared by colleagues appear with the preparatory correspondence. Both were dated 13 April, both warned about the dangers of 'being lured into the poisoned atmosphere of a propaganda of lies and hatred', and both invoked the history of the war-guilt debacle that nearly severed burgeoning ecumenism during and after World War I.

The first was weighted by the reputation of its author, one of the most respected ecumenists in Europe and North America. In Dr Adolf Keller's 'Facts and Meaning of the German Revolution', the Nazi state attitude toward Jews was but one aspect of the National Socialist revolution, an 'incidental outburst of race antagonism' as compared to the 'more permanent' state–church issue over spiritual liberty. He accepted as fact reports from German churchmen who claimed that atrocities against Jews had been 'distorted', and he urged as 'duty' that Christians abroad look at the 'entangled situation in the cold light of real facts before forming hasty judgments'. In reviewing those 'facts', he argued that 'hatred against Jews' involved more than blind racial prejudice, for the 'Jewish element played an important role in Russian Bolshevism as well as ... German communism and atheism'.[9] Indeed, as framed in a confidential paper a week earlier, what was happening to Jews could not be adequately explained outside the German struggle 'against the spirit of Marxism and Bolshevism whose strongest exponents may be the Jews'.[10] German antisemitism was thus a response to 'the destructive ... influence of the revolutionary Jewish mind', as well as a charge against 'the Jewish element ... responsible for the lowering of moral standards in public life'. Such 'facts and meaning' had to be taken into account when assessing German state policy on Jews, even while deploring the harsh and unjust forms it had taken. Instead of forming hasty opinions 'based on insufficient information or a propaganda of hatred', Keller advised, churches abroad needed to 'listen attentively' to what the German churches were going to say and do in order to save their 'liberty of speech and spiritual life'.[11]

Many of the same points were made in the second paper, which was published a few weeks later in *Christian Century*. Like Keller, W. A. Visser 't Hooft, general secretary of WSCF, warned against the 'mob psychology' causing a rush to judgment on Germany without looking into 'the deeper reasons' for its action. While not denying that Jews were having 'a difficult time in Germany', distinctions had to be made between German actions based on 'prejudice and ignorance' and actions that were 'explicable and to some extent justifiable'. With respect to the latter, he held that two points had to be kept in mind. The first was that 'certain types of Jews insisted on constituting a nation within a nation', which would understandably create problems for a nation threatened by 'disunity and internal division'. The second was that Germany's new civil service laws did not exclude Jews employed before August 1914, which gave him reason to think that National Socialism was progressing from blind antisemitism to a 'somewhat less crude policy of distinguishing between anti-national and pro-national Jews'. But the 'great issue' for Visser 't Hooft, like Keller, was the freedom of the German Protestant churches and, as such, churches abroad needed to stand in unity with sister German churches 'instead of judging prematurely'.[12]

Four days after the Geneva papers were written a critical round of meetings took place. On 17 April Henriod left Geneva for consultations with church leaders in Berlin, accompanied by research director Hans Schönfeld (whose half salary was paid by the German Evangelical Church). Following two days of meetings in Berlin, Henriod travelled to France and Schönfeld returned to Geneva. On 22 April Samuel Cavert arrived in Berlin from New York for six days of meetings, leaving on the 27th for London to meet with J. H. Oldham and William Paton, general secretaries of IMC and *ex officios* of ICCAJ. On the same day, W.A. Brown, UCCLW administrative chair, who was in Rome when he learned of the pending crisis, arrived in Geneva to meet with Henriod, Keller, Schönfeld and Visser 't Hooft.[13]

From the meetings in Berlin, London and Geneva came three reports which, along with those of Keller and Visser 't Hooft, had critical bearing on UCCLW interpretation of the situation in Germany. The first, dated 25 April, marked 'Strictly Confidential' and unsigned, has been attributed to Schönfeld, but new evidence suggests it was an early version by Brown.[14] The second, dated 28 April and marked 'Private and Confidential', was signed by Henriod and written officially for the UCCLW Administrative Committee.[15] The third, unsigned but identified as Brown, was written in Geneva after meeting with Henriod, Schönfeld and Visser 't Hooft between 27 and 30 April.[16]

Emerging from all three reports was a sympathy for the German churches that had been well plied by German appeals for brotherly understanding. This is not to say that the plight of German Jews was ignored, but that it was not at the forefront of consideration. Emphases instead were placed on the 'drastic changes imposed on the Church by the National Socialist revolution', and, this, in such a way that what was happening to Jews, and German church silence about it, were relegated to a subcategory of concern.

Each of the reports, like Keller and Visser 't Hooft, placed current antisemitic acts within the context of a National Socialist revolution. While none of the reports justified Nazi persecution of Jews in any way, all depicted the German state attitude as in some way explicable, each reciting claims about Jewish influence, disproportionate representation in universities and professions, lowering of moral standards, or involvement in socialist and communist parties. In both of Brown's reports the Nazi state attitude to Jews was explained but not justified as a 'response to real grievances and dangers', with a reminder in the second that 'it is not in Germany only ... that Jews have abused privileges that were granted to them'.[17] The most pressing issue in all the reports was the struggle of the German Protestant church against incursions by the Nazi state, a matter said to be so complex that 'public statements' by German church leaders 'against actions such as the Jewish boycott is out of the question'.[18] As to who should attend to what, the responsibility of German church leaders was to 'safeguard the independence of the church against the state', while the 'most important thing' for churches abroad was 'to leave the Germans alone to work through their national crisis'. In so advising, each report called for Christian humility and patience, with Henriod stressing the 'imminent' Christian duty to learn the facts and not judge hastily what was happening, including 'the current silence of the German churches'.[19]

On 1 May, with reports in hand, a second and wider round of meetings ensued. Brown and Henriod left Geneva: Brown to London for meetings with Cavert, and Henriod to Paris to speak on the German church situation to the executive committee of the French Federation of Protestant Churches. On 3 May Henriod rejoined Cavert and Brown, and the three travelled from London to join with Visser 't Hooft, Oldham, Paton and others at the home of William Temple, Archbishop of York, for a prearranged meeting on how to draw the various ecumenical bodies together.[20] After two days of discussions Henriod, Cavert and Brown returned to London for a UCCLW Administrative Committee meeting on 6 May, chaired by Bishop George Bell.

At this juncture the Henriod report that had already been widely shared and discussed was presented officially in the context of whether UCCLW action should be taken on the situation in Germany. The 7 May letter resulting from that decision has been

In the shadows of response: 1933–1936 73

cited consistently in scholarly literature as example of UCCLW official protest on behalf of German Jews.[21] Like the events preceding it, however, newly found documents reveal a far more complex story. While it was indeed the case that UCCLW agreed to send a letter of concern to the German church president, it was also the case that the incumbent German church president, Dr Hermann Kapler, was chairman of the Continental division of UCCLW, and that the letter was sent to him for pre-approval and revision at his discretion. The 'Private Draft' from UCCLW chairman George Bell to Kapler, marked in bold red by the words 'Private and Confidential', included this request:

> The Bishop of Chichester sends the accompanying draft of the proposed letter to Dr. Kapler, with the particular request that it may be carefully scrutinized all through and especially in the sentences about the Jews and about the Church. Is enough said? or too much?
>
> With regard to the Jews, would it be wise or unwise to go a little further, implying that we realize there were special difficulties? E.g., put 'undiscriminating action taken' instead of 'action taken'; or add after 'Jews' 'whether worthy or unworthy'; or add at end of paragraph 'lest a whole race should be forced to suffer for the faults of some of its members'? Or leave simply as in Draft?
>
> ... Again does the letter say enough or too much about the Nazi movement itself?[22]

When the revised version appeared ten days later there was subtle but marked editing that changed the tone of the letter. The introductory context associating the letter with the general 'substance' of Henriod's letter to Kapler on 1 April was unchanged. All revisions were made in the next paragraph. The original draft expressed four sentiments of the Council: *realisation* of the importance of Germany's national movement; the *wish* to not enter into political questions; the *hope* for peace and brotherly love in Germany and Germany's relations with others; and *concern* about German national actions against Jews. The only one restyled was the first, and in so doing 'realisation' was restated as 'we appreciate the immense importance of the national movement now proceeding amongst the German people'. The other changes were either inclusions (noted by italics in square brackets) or, in one place, a deletion of text (indicated by crossing-out). The two most critical revisions were the removal of 'other races' in sentence two and an insertion in sentence four which changed the document from a statement of concern about Jews to one of concern about Jews *and* the German church:

> We do not wish to enter into [*special*] political questions [*in which you and your fellow citizens are engaged*], nor indeed is it our business to do so.
>
> But we believe that you will welcome an expression of the deep interest with which we and ... our colleagues in many different Churches in Europe and America follow the developments of the movement, and of our earnest hope that the forces which make for good and for peace and brotherly love, alike within the German Reich and in relation to ~~other races and~~ nations, may be in every way helped and strengthened.
>
> [*We are not yet perhaps fully informed of all the circumstances of the case and we should be thankful for further information.*]
>
> But at the same time it would not be fair to disguise from our friends in Germany that certain recent events, especially the action taken against the Jews [*and the serious restrictions placed upon freedom of thought and expression*], have caused and continue to cause us anxiety and distress; and we feel that we ought to share our concern with you here.[23]

All racial implications were removed with deletion of 'other races', which, along with insertion of 'special' before 'political questions' in the first sentence, suggested that 'the action taken against the Jews' was politically rather than racially motivated. But that, of course, was what Bell was getting at when asking Kapler whether the statement should distinguish 'undiscriminating actions against Jews', imply that there were 'special difficulties', or suggest by adding 'whether worthy or unworthy' that at least some state actions against Jews were valid. Moreover, by adding that 'you and your fellow citizens' are engaged in those 'special political questions', the impression was given that there was at least some agreement between state and church as to what constituted those 'special' political concerns. Further, by inserting in the last sentence 'and the serious restrictions placed upon freedom of thought and expression', the issue of the spiritual liberty of the

In the shadows of response: 1933–1936 75

German church was written into the letter, and the document was no longer a matter of sole concern about the plight of German Jews.

While it is by no means certain which changes Kapler initiated, it is unmistakably clear that after being invited to do so he was involved not only in the revision of the 7 May letter, but its disposition as well. The revised version of 17 May, which cancelled the original letter, was circulated to UCCLW leaders only, with a labelled note that it was 'not to be published in any way at present, by request of Dr. Kapler'.[24] Yet significantly more crucial than who initiated which change is that the revised and shelved letter of 17 May reflected UCCLW acquiescence to the interpretative line emanating from Kapler and other German church officials. It was also the case that this was allowed even after Henriod, Cavert and Brown learned from German church leaders that on 11 April – the day non-Aryans were defined according to Jewish lineage – a commissioned paper on 'The Church and the Jewish Question in Germany' was debated under Kapler's gavel, with church consensus that the Aryan paragraph 'was an act of harsh but necessary justice' to 'safeguard the German people'.[25]

When FCC executive Samuel Cavert, who was also a member of the North American sector of ICCAJ, returned to New York after the UCCLW meeting on 6 May, he wrote to ecumenical colleagues in Switzerland and Germany that his intention was to 'interpret the situation in German Protestantism as sympathetically as possible'.[26] Cavert began with an essay in *Christian Century*, which appeared exactly sixty days after he, Cadman and Leiper published the *New York Times* statement that reignited the threat of German withdrawal from the ecumenical movement. Although the two pieces were distinctly different in type, each addressed relations between Nazi persecution of Jews, German church responses and the attitudes of the rest of the Christian world. In the *New York Times* statement on 25 March, all forms of racial and religious intolerance were protested, German churches were expected to repudiate antisemitic violence in Germany, and Christians were urged to 're-examine their own racial attitudes and relationships'.[27] In the article of 24 May for *Christian Century*, 'cruel discriminations against the Jews' were pointed to but not protested, explanation was given on *why* German churches had *not* protested 'the injustice done to the

Jews', and appeal was made for non-German Christians 'to avoid rash judgment' and strive for 'unbroken fellowship' in the spirit of ecumenical unity. Cavert's essay was aptly titled 'Hitler and the Churches', for the predominant emphasis was no longer violence against German Jews, but survival of the German churches under the National Socialist advances of Hitler.[28]

The threat of Jewishness

On a parallel plane of responses, John Mott made known his own view of Christian protests against Germany's suppression of Jews as 'unavailing and provocative'. He was one of many ecumenical Protestant leaders moving in and out of Germany who carried opinions and reports to the Archbishop of Canterbury in London. According to Archbishop Lang's notes of their meeting on 31 May, Mott confided that 'even the most spiritually-minded' of Protestant churches in Germany were not 'disposed to make any kind of public protest'. He added that he could not but have 'at least some understanding of the reasons that had made the Jews so unpopular ... in Germany'.[29] While Mott was just one in a train of ecumenical opinions moving through Lambeth Palace, there was enough similarity in views by 7 June for Lang to doubt that he could speak as 'Jews might expect' at an upcoming event in London. Archbishop Lang penned that concern to Tissington Tatlow, chairman of the ISS assembly, after reading a report by Walter Kotschnig that also dissuaded criticism of Germany.[30]

James Parkes, who worked closely with Kotschnig and was versed in the report, was with Tatlow when the letter arrived. After hearing Parkes's different perspective, Tatlow arranged for him to meet with Lang's secretary and then followed with a letter to Lang, recommending Parkes as 'one of the most reliable sources ... about Jewish affairs on the Continent'.[31] Parkes followed his meeting with Dr A.C. Don with a four-page letter, along with three pages of notes on issues that Don had raised, urging that Archbishop Lang use his weight and authority as Primate to make 'a deep and serious appeal to German Christianity' to dissociate from the lies of racial superiority. He also urged, in opposition to the prevailing apologetic, that the National Socialist threat in no way justified the pervasive silence of the German church.[32]

Parkes's intervention with the Archbishop of Canterbury is all the more significant, having just been publicly silenced in Germany. After his initial success in bringing Jewish and nationalist students together in conferences, German National Socialist students insisted on the grounds of ISS impartiality that their leaders be granted equal hearing. By 1931 he was thus sharing the same podium with Nazi defenders of antisemitism, such as Dr Wilhelm Stapel, the Protestant editor of an antisemitic journal who would become advisor to Hitler's Reich Minister of Church Affairs in 1935. Parkes's outspokenness on antisemitism, along with coverage in European newspapers as a defender of Jewish students, led to increasing irritation in Germany. In December 1932, as university violence persisted in eastern Europe and Germany, he published a scathing editorial in the tri-language *Vox Studentium*, calling out adult leaders of National Socialists in Germany, National Democrats in Poland and the Iron Guard in Romania for using and abusing nationalist students to advance antisemitic goals. Immediately after Hitler came to power in January, German nationalist students retaliated in the German *Student Rundschau* charging Parkes with misrepresentation, falsity and prejudice. The publicised uproar was so laden with tension by March that ISS director Walter Kotschnig was forced to publish an apology for the editorial, promising to avoid future actions that might 'injure' the impartial work of ISS.[33]

Yet Parkes's resolve to not keep silent about what was happening in Germany was unabated. After intervening with Lang in June he penned an essay in July for a Christian mission journal, castigating Germany again as 'the disgrace of a supposedly Christian country'. He repudiated its 'nonsensical and unscientific' Aryan laws, as well as those who supported them 'from the pulpit and in the press'. Moreover, Parkes turned the table by arguing that 'the problem of the Jews' was due neither to race nor religion but to their history of suppression in 'Christian Europe', stressing that the only way they survived as a people was through their refusal to convert. For him, the 'first step' in dealing with 'the catastrophe of Germany' was thus to start making the world safe 'for a Jew to be a Jew'.[34] By arguing this way in a mission journal he was countering more than one argument and addressing more than one audience. Parkes was also taking aim at the recent ICCAJ surge of conversionary lobbying across Europe.

Beginning with three addresses on the 'Jewish Problem and Jewish Missions' to two thousand students at an SCM quadrennial conference in Edinburgh earlier in January, Conrad Hoffmann had been criss-crossing Europe on a five-month lecture tour of England, Ireland, Scotland, Denmark, Sweden, Norway, Finland, Estonia, Latvia, Poland, Germany, Belgium and the Netherlands. By May the themes of his lectures had been packaged into a 21-page pamphlet that was being distributed in the wake of this fourth European tour as ICCAJ director. It was the first of three published pieces over eleven months to reflect the conversionary discourse being delivered to Protestant audiences immediately after Adolf Hitler came to power.

Assayed together they represent an elaborate argument of *increases*: increasing disintegration of Judaism, increasing Jewish influence and increasing antisemitism, all of which increased the urgency of Christianity's mission call. Each bore the title or subtitle of 'Modern Jewry', each was argued relative to the Jewish problem and Jewish missions, and each held a complexly winding argument about postwar modern Jewry and the consequential societal dilemmas that it and the Christian world had to recognise and face. Each of the pieces also urged Christians to embrace and promote a Christian attitude toward Jews, to disavow and combat antisemitism and strive for Christian justice.

The May pamphlet, 'A New Approach to an Old Problem', was a play on the title and content of Macdonald Webster's 1925 call for Christian experts on the Jewish problem. Like the rest of the series, it advanced themes that had been developing since that call was made. The somewhat sympathetic picture in the opening pages portrayed a confused postwar Jewry, adrift and 'buffeted about on the sea of modernism', trending 'away from organized religion', falling 'prey' to idealism, cults, atheism and communism in a world of rising antisemitism.[35] By page 6, the Church was being urged to increase its awareness of 'the increasing influence of Jews in all fields of human endeavour' and recognise that 'every world movement' had to 'reckon with the Jew who is such a dominant element and force in human society today'. Layered in between sympathies and warnings, the pamphlet sketched a 'baffling phenomenon' of rising antisemitism and a 'vicious circle' in which modern postwar Jewry was said to be caught. Disintegrating Judaism was 'losing the Jew religiously', Zionism was 'striving to hold the Jew racially', and the more racially conscious the Jew became the more bitter the antisemitic backlash. 'The Jew', Hoffmann explained, worsened the situation by demanding 'full equality and recognition' while simultaneously insisting on 'retention of Jewish characteristics and loyalties'.[36]

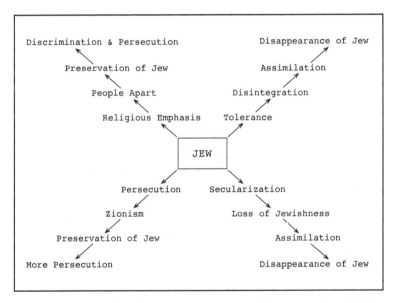

Figure 2.1 Facsimile of 'Disappearance of Jew' illustration chart, 1933

The 'vicious circle' and its implications were painted more fully in September 1933 in a report on 'Modern Jewry and Christian Responsibility', which included a lecture chart on the 'Disappearance of Jew' (Figure 2.1). Here it was argued that religiously based Jewish consciousness had been disintegrating along with Judaism until Hitler's antisemitism provoked a 'renaissance' of Jewishness. The contention was that Nazi antisemitism provoked racial and national consciousness of Jewishness which, in turn, provoked antisemitic backlash which, in turn, provoked Jewishness, and vice versa in a deadlock 'vicious circle'.

The theoretical presumption argued in winding detail was that antisemitism would disappear when did Jewishness, but that antisemitism and persecution would sustain and increase so long as Jewishness was preserved. In contrast, if Jews assented to assimilation and conversion, toleration would follow as Jewishness and 'Jew' disappeared. That Jews had to choose between preservation and persecution *or* assimilation and disappearance was posited as a critical dilemma bearing heavily on modern Jewry as well as the world. Christians were urged to recognise the seriousness of the situation and develop 'convictions' on the issue, for 'unless Christianity can Christianize Jewry, Jewry will Judaize the world, and in modern Jewry today the antireligious, atheistic and unscrupulous Jew is gaining the ascendancy'.[37]

Layered between descriptions of the 'vicious circle' and warnings about Jewishness and Judaisation was repudiation of Nazi racial antisemitism. Yet while condemning Nazi persecution and praising international protests of Christians and Jews, Hoffmann stressed that 'in all of the protests and denunciation by world Jewry' there had been 'little or no admission by Jews of any possible blame'. The point was argued in the context of the leading question, 'are gentiles alone responsible or guilty, or are the Jews themselves also to blame for much of the persecution and discrimination ...?' In answering in part, he invoked again the racially conscious surge of Jewishness that allegedly provoked antisemitic backlash, going so far as to claim that 'the racial emphasis of Hitler and his followers' was 'more or less identical with the racial emphasis on Jewishness'. The widely distributed report also drew attention away from Nazi antisemitism by arguing that there were 'larger issues' and 'greater menace in Hitlerism than its repercussions on Jewry'. Citing danger of war, as well as political, religious and economic freedoms, Hoffmann went on to criticise that 'our Jewish friends seem to overlook these entirely in the frenzy and preoccupation of protests against the anti-Semitic manifestation of Hitlerism'.[38]

Most of the same argumentative elements appeared in 'Modern Jewry and the Christian Church' in *International Review of Missions* in April 1934, with 2,400 reprints distributed internationally.[39] The lines of argument were ambiguously layered with statements of benevolent concern, including the need for a united Christian front to disavow and combat antisemitism, 'strive for Christian justice', and 'educate the Christian world to an intelligent and sympathetic understanding of the Jews'.[40] Other formulaic elements repeated from earlier pieces that 'no better publicity agency could have been found than Hitler's anti-Semitism' and that opportunity had never been 'so ripe ... for an aggressive constructive program involving a Christian approach to the Jews'.[41]

Holding centre stage, however, was the deadlocked problem of antisemitism and the 'vicious circle'. In the opening lines of the article antisemitism was presented as one of the 'profound influences' transforming modern Jewry and, over the next five pages, repeatedly imaged as the *provoker* of 'a rebirth' and 'revival' of Jewishness, 'a veritable renaissance of Jewishness', a 'new sense of racial and national solidarity'. The conscious repetition brought home with intended force that the emphasis of postwar modern Jewry was increasingly atheistic and that Jewish racial loyalties increased as secular 'atheistic Jewry' evolved.[42] The September memorandum had already argued that Jewish racial loyalties could lead to the 'grave danger ... of a Jewish state within the body politic',[43] but here the 'racial and national emphasis' of Jewry was presented as a two-edged sword that hastened Jewish solidarity while creating 'a serious conflict of loyalties'.[44] The Jew was 'torn between loyalty to Jewry as a national and racial entity, and loyalty to the land of which he is a citizen or which he resides'. The issue once more was that the Jew had to choose between preservation of racial and national identity (which would involve persecution) or assimilation (which implied 'his possible disappearance as a Jew'). For Hoffmann and those he represented, the question for world Jewry as well as for all 'engaged in the Christian approach to the Jew', was once again in the form of the Judaising threat:

> Shall Jewry become a nation with a national home somewhere, or shall Jewry disappear in humanity, like salt in a solution, no longer existent as Jewry, but permeating all mankind with Jewish spirit and influence?

That such questions were subtly framed as a 'matter' brought 'prominently into the limelight by Germany' is revealing on several levels.⁴⁵ First, it strongly implies that the alleged sociopolitical problems that modern Jewry presented to the Church were similar to the 'matter' with which Hitler was dealing in Germany. Second, conspicuously obvious are the ways in which concepts that were rampant in Nazi antisemitic theory were being used in Hoffmann's explanations of the same alleged universal Jewish problem, Jewishness and Judaisation. Third, that the use of such language and concepts could appear *unchallenged* in a highly respectable Protestant journal suggests, or implies, a widely accepted or tolerated understanding that such issues existed. But *why* would it be so unabashedly embodied in the discourse of a Protestant initiative that denounced Nazi racial antisemitism, and why would it be so tolerated?

As director of ICCAJ, Hoffmann was robustly engaged in rallying Protestant forces to the cause of Jewish missions. His religio-socio-political argumentation was organisationally accepted as justification for world expansion of Jewish evangelisation, as well as 'intelligent' education on the attitudes Christians should take about current trends and tendencies in world Jewry. The broad base of international consensus informing his role as spokesman provided legitimacy and moral authority to his arguments. This did not mean of course that each aspect of each claim was held by all in support of the initiative, or that there were no variations within sets of given theological and theoretical premises, but it did mean broad agreement about a universal Jewish problem and the societal need for conversion as the only viable solution. Hoffmann's arguments on causal relations between Jewish racial–national consciousness and antisemitism, as well as the threats of Jewish influence and Judaisation, were accepted as an appropriate *entrée* to the web of societal issues said to be linked to the Jewish problem and the need for Jewish conversion. Under his hands, antisemitism had become an expedient way to talk about the conversionary 'opportunities' afforded by the notoriety of Nazi persecution of German Jews.

Indeed, a few months before Hoffmann's essay appeared in the April 1934 issue of *IRM*, Rabbi Israel Newman, whose critical study on *Jewish Influence on Christian Reform Movements* revealed in 1925 that 'Judaising' had entered the language of 'every Christian people', published a warning about the unethical way in which antisemitism was being used by ICCAJ. His editorial in the Chicago *Sentinel*, naming Hoffmann as leading spokesman, accused ICCAJ of using benevolent concern about Nazi antisemitism as a lure to events that ended in missionary appeals to Jews.[46] Rabbi Samuel S. Cohon, one of the nine who met with ICCAJ leaders in Chicago in 1932, had also warned a few months earlier that its claimed benevolence was intended 'to disarm Jewish opposition to … proselytizing endeavours' while, in actuality, 'the people whose souls they seek to save' are painted 'in the blackest colours' in order 'to demonstrate the urgency of their redemptive work'.[47]

Yet without halt or reflection, the charges of the rabbis were denied with aplomb, and explained away as ongoing Jewish opposition to Jewish missions.[48] What Newman, Cohon and other Jewish leaders did not realise was that the overwhelming majority of Hoffmann's lectures on both sides of the Atlantic, like the three published pieces discussed here, were directed to Protestant audiences rather than Jews, with the aim of educating and spiritually conscripting evangelising forces.[49] By the time Hoffmann's questions about the 'disappearance of Jew' appeared in April 1934, they had already been asked in one form or another in sixty-five British lectures between January and March, before he set off on an eight-week tour of uncounted lectures in central and eastern Europe, the Balkans and Middle East. Another 250 lectures were delivered in Britain, Continental Europe and North America between summers of 1934 and 1935, after which numbers increased so much that counting was no longer a priority (Figure 2.2).

Although it is impossible to know in more than general outline the make-up of Protestant audiences hearing and reading the discourse as Hoffmann criss-crossed the European and North American continents, what can be known with certainty are the tenets of conversionary arguments that were being transmitted in the early years after Hitler came to power. The robust calls to strive for Christian justice and unite in a world alliance against Nazi racial antisemitism did not cancel out the forceful warnings about the threats of Jewishness, Judaisation and causal relations to antisemitism, *nor* were they intended to do so. The claims were as central

Tracking the Jews

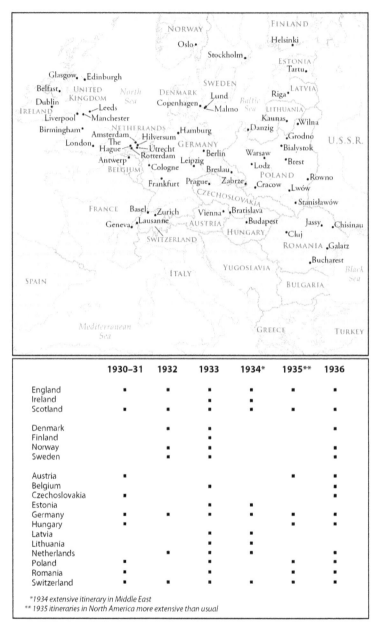

Figure 2.2 ICCAJ Director European itineraries by nation, 1931–1936

to the discourse as the juxtaposed claims of love and benevolence in which they were wrapped.

Conscience and apologia

As Conrad Hoffmann's second report on 'Modern Jewry and Christian Responsibility' was being disseminated in early September 1933, UCCLW was immersed in the rekindled issue of the German church at its Novi Sad meeting in Yugoslavia. On 5 September, just four days before the Council meeting, the faction of *Deutsche Christen* who sought to align German Protestantism with Nazi ideology had prevailed at the Prussian Synod and the Aryan paragraph had been voluntarily adopted. All of the delegates at Novi Sad – England, Denmark, Sweden, France, Switzerland, Greece, Yugoslavia, Hungary, United States, Germany – understood the fragility and dangers of the moment.[50] Yet of eleven documents drawn up during three days of deliberations, none were believed satisfactory and any that 'implied a joint action amounting to censure' of the German church were deemed as 'unfit instruments for what the Council wanted to accomplish'. What that entailed, as framed in the report by Henry Leiper that became the basis for future ecumenical reports, was avoidance of UCCLW division while making peace with the demands of conscience.[51]

The diplomatic solution, in lieu of harsh censure, proposed by chairman George Bell and adopted by the executive council, was an official Minute which recorded that differing opinions existed while emphasising the need to maintain Council unity. Within that context the official Minute of 12 September stated two 'grave anxieties': 'the severe action taken against persons of Jewish origin', and 'the serious restrictions placed upon freedom of thought and expression in Germany'. The Minute was to be followed by an official letter, not to President Hermann Kapler who had resigned in July, but to Reich Bishop Ludwig Müller, who was put into place by Hitler and then elected by a national synod on 27 September.

As this intention played out on paper on 23 October, the equivocal phrase 'persons of Jewish origin' was clarified to mean those within the boundaries of Christianity, a subtle but critical point made explicit in the official letter to Müller.[52] The two grave anxieties of the Council were clarified in three different ways, leaving no doubt that 'persons of Jewish origin' referred to Christians of Jewish descent. The letter stated 'distress and anxiety' about the Prussian church adoption of the Aryan clause *and* the 'suppression or forcible silencing' of Christians who opposed the *Deutsche Christen* majority that sought alignment with the Nazi state. It expressed 'shock' that race was allowed to be 'a determining factor in the status of the Christian', and that the Aryan clause was used to move Christians from their posts 'simply because they are Jews by birth or Jewish descent'. Third, the letter repeated that the 'two matters gravely disturbing to the Christian conscience' were 'suppression and silencing of opponents' *and* 'discrimination against Church members of Jewish descent'.[53] The same two 'disturbing' matters were delineated a fourth time in a second letter to Müller on 18 January as 'the application of the Aryan Paragraph to Church officers' *and* 'the suppression and silencing of opponents'.[54]

It is important to recognise, however, that the relegation of Jews per se to a category of lesser concern was not unique to UCCLW. At the same time suppression of non-Aryan Christians was being stressed in the January 1934 letter to Reich Bishop Müller, the Aryan law that 'cut at the heart of Christianity' was being stressed by an 'influential conference' of British missionary executives in London.[55] The keynote speaker was Ruth Rouse, a member of the British ICCAJ who was secretary to the Council on Foreign Relations and Missionary Council of the Church of England. In the latter two capacities she conducted onsite evaluation of the situation in Germany in late October, holding some forty-five meetings with German state and church leaders, missionary societies, student bodies, many of whom were in SA uniforms, members of the Nazi Party, Disarmament Conference delegates, secretaries of Home and Foreign Offices, and Reich Bishop Müller.

Yet in Rouse's three confidential reports there was nothing on the general plight of German Jews or the general implementation of the Aryan clause.[56] The report to the Council on Foreign Relations did not even use the word 'Jew', even though like the other two it addressed the Aryan clause as it applied to Christians of Jewish origin. Her conference address, however, included the 'intolerable'

Jewish elements that German statesmen, churchmen and youth groups said they were 'determined at all costs to do away with'. After listing a few – 'domination of Jews in certain professions', 'Jewish influence and control of cinema and theatre', 'spread of Communism', 'bad influence exercised by Jews from Poland and Russia' – she cautiously pointed out that, although 'tremendous suffering' had been inflicted on German Jews, 'the Hitler regime had done much to improve the moral situation'.[57]

Rouse's point – that there were both negative and positive effects to be weighed when forming a Christian opinion about Germany – agreed in principle with Leiper's report on Novi Sad, which appeared roughly at the same time. For both ecumenical leaders, the Christian duty was 'to try and understand' rather than alienate 'by hasty criticism and self-righteous condemnation'. In that vein, Leiper's time in Germany before the Novi Sad meeting, as well as his first-hand view of its so called 'anti-Jewish crusade', were included in the Novi Sad report. His intention was not to 'minimize the terrible injustice and inhumanity' of what was happening to Jews, but after visiting with numbers of church leaders he found 'little evidence to support' the view that the lives of all 'pure Jews and … part Jews' were 'in danger'. This, along with his take-away belief that most German people had 'never seen anything happen to any Jew', led him to advise that 'attitudes toward the State and toward the Jews' were 'not the only attitudes that matter' in the new German church: there were also 'points of strength', and they had to be taken into account so as to 'judge not that ye be not judged'.[58]

In advising this way, both Leiper and Rouse were in line with the earlier advice of Keller, Visser 't Hooft, Henriod, Brown and Cavert; and Henriod was still hoping in October that churches abroad would comply by not forming attitudes before consulting ecumenical leaders. To do otherwise, he urged, would run counter to the 'crucial importance of the ecumenical movement'.[59] That the same advice was still being issued after the Novi Sad decision was testimony to its diplomatic success. The diplomacy had smoothed the way for Rouse's access to German state officials and, according to her reports, German church leaders were praising the moderate action in lieu of the public condemnation that some demanded.[60] It also smoothed the way for Dr Charles Macfarland, emeritus general secretary of FCC, to receive an invitation from Germany. Just three weeks later, while consulting in Geneva, a state approved proposal for him to conduct an onsite study of the German church situation was issued by UCCLW German delegate A. W. Schreiber. The invitation provided access to some sixty German state and church officials, including Reich Bishop Müller, Alfred Rosenberg and Adolf Hitler.[61]

Macfarland's published study in January 1934 was the most comprehensive ecumenical report to date. *The New Church and the New Germany* was also a critically important apologetic for the UCCLW decision at Novi Sad. At 209 pages and dedicated to German ecumenists who led 'the Evangelical Church of Germany into enduring relations with Ecumenical Christianity', it painted an enduring portrait of a German Protestant church steeped in revolutionary struggle of world importance, with UCCLW standing as 'providential' mediator and interpreter to the rest of the Protestant world.[62]

Once fitted into this context, Macfarland's analysis followed familiar lines of explanation: there were grounds for German concern about its Jewish problem; the problem had been addressed with legislative action; the law had made its way into the German Protestant church by way of the majority *Deutsche Christen* sector that sought alignment with the Nazi state. In examining the state corrective, he pointed to 'extenuating circumstances' that had to be taken into account: (i) There was 'altogether too much truth in identification of certain members of the Jewish race with wrongdoing'; (ii) 'The presence of the Jews ... cause a real economic, cultural, social and institutional problem in Germany, as it has to a lesser degree in other nations'; (iii) Hitler's 'hatred and horror of atheistic Marxism and communism' was directed at Jews specifically because 'many of that race identified with those economic and social theories'.[63]

Consequently, so Macfarland assessed, 'Adolf Hitler faced a problem of the State that had to be met.' But he was also clear that Hitler's corrective was wrong in 'spirit, method and practices', abounding in 'discriminating ruthless process' and lacking everything 'essential to any reasonable regulation of the problem'.[64] The hard to reconcile issue was that there was enough Protestant agreement with the state on the gravity of the Jewish problem for the Prussian Synod to apply the Aryan clause on 5 September 1933.[65] That roughly half of German Protestantism had agreed that Christian brotherhood could be determined by race and nation was something that could not be overlooked by UCCLW at Novi Sad a few days later.[66]

Here Macfarland spoke in the voice of Henry Leiper, quoting long passages from one who had 'a large share' in solving the two-horned dilemma with which the Novi Sad Council was faced. On the one hand, the German church abandoned the supraracial attributes of the universal Church when it adopted the Aryan clause, but if the German church was denounced and abandoned, Germany would be left without the 'spiritual and moral force' of world Christianity. On the other hand, German church endorsement of racial discrimination could not be overlooked, but neither could the long Christian history of splitting the Church every time there was 'disagreement'. That UCCLW chose the latter and remained in fellowship with the German church was explained by both Macfarland and Leiper as an official ecumenical attempt at changing the centuries-long habit of Christian division, even 'at the risk of being thought willing to acquiesce to immoral and un-Christian actions'.[67]

The ecumenical diplomacy of Novi Sad was hailed as a feat that could only have happened within the supranational Council. 'Only men who knew and trusted one another and were surrounded with the evidences of Christian life as a bond across all race and national lines could have gone through that discussion without the lifting of a voice in anger or the speaking of a harsh word'.[68] While the decision of Novi Sad was 'a black hour for the Church', both Macfarland and Leiper admitted, it would have been 'even blacker' if the attempt to maintain unity among the churches had broken down.[69]

To bring that diplomatic decision into sharper focus, the World Alliance for Promoting International Friendship through the Churches (WA), whose general secretary Henriod was the same as UCCLW, *did* in fact unequivocally protest against persecution of the 'Jews', 'the Jewish race' and German church adoption of the Aryan clause at its own meeting in Sofia the following week.[70] Chairman Bishop Valdemar Ammundsen made clear as early as

9 April that the WA could not issue a peace statement without addressing Jewish suppression in Germany. Yet as vice-chairman of UCCLW, Ammundsen was also in accord with the measured diplomatic solution at Novi Sad.[71]

To ask why the WA did and UCCLW did not explicitly protest on behalf of German Jews as Jews is to spotlight the tightrope that the Council was walking in order to maintain relations with the official church government of the Nazi state. As distinguished by Leiper, the WA was a peace consortium made up of individuals rather than churches, and its German branch had little dependence on the Nazi church government. UCCLW, in contrast, was a body of churches bonded together by supranational principles of unity, one in which the German church had played a major role since inception of the Council. It was, in fact, the only ecumenical body that 'even pretended to be representative' of churches united in the aim of applying Christian principles to national and international social issues.[72] Such bonding, as publicly stated by chairman George Bell immediately after the Novi Sad decision, was based on an undivided unity in the belief that 'a Christian world order, *the* Christian world order, is ultimately the only one which, from any point of view, will work'.[73]

That the 'black hour' of Novi Sad had to do with the issue of ecumenical unity, rather than with UCCLW failure to condemn Nazi state suppression of German Jews as Jews, was underscored by the fact that, after Bell's letters to Reich Bishop Müller on 23 October 1933 and 18 January 1934, in which Jews per se were not listed among UCCLW 'grave concerns', numerous reports on the situation in Germany were circulated over the following six months without even the word 'Jew'.[74] Moreover, as this graduated slide continued, neither Jews, Christians of Jewish origin nor the catalysing Aryan paragraph found mention in the next UCCLW conference statement.

Where Novi Sad has been recorded as settling 'the most outstanding problem before the Western Churches', the conference in Fanø (Denmark) in August 1934 has been memorialised in the official history as 'the most critical and decisive meeting in its history'.[75] Nils Ehrenström, who with Hans Schönfeld manned the UCCLW research department, was instrumental in planting that memory as the moment when UCCLW 'resolved to throw its weight on the side of the Confessing church in Germany against the so-called "German Christians", and by implication against the Nazi regime'.[76]

This has been cited and interpreted to mean that UCCLW aligned itself with the Confessing church as 'the sole legitimate representative of Protestant Christianity in Germany', but a closer look at the archives brings a far more complex picture into focus.[77] Leiper's first-hand report stated clearly that it was not the intention of UCCLW 'to put the mark of approval upon any system of theology' at Fanø, going so far as to say 'when it comes to theology the Council probably represents in the main churches which are more in sympathy with the pragmatism and creationism of the Reich Church than the Barthian tendencies of the Confessional Synod'.[78] This distinction by one involved in every stage of deliberation at both Novi Sad and Fanø becomes all the more significant when the official conference minutes are juxtaposed with recently unearthed private session minutes marked 'for record only, not for minutes'. The twenty-one pages of privately recorded deliberations leading to the Fanø statement fill a critical gap between Leiper's report, the official minutes and the resolutions adopted at the conference.[79]

While UCCLW indeed censured the Reich church on the grounds of autocratic church rule and endangered church liberty, it did not weight itself against the Reich church or in favour of the Confessing church, nor did UCCLW cease to seek relations with the Nazi church government. The week before Fanø, Bishop Ammundsen reported to Council principals that, unlike Confessing church 'friends' who wanted UCCLW to 'declare the official church in Germany to be no longer a Christian church', he was not in favour of that step at Fanø, even though he was being urged that 'excommunication of even a single church would help them greatly'. As revealed in his report of private meetings with Confessing church leaders the day after the Reich Synod adopted the Hitler oath and consolidated the powers of the Reich Bishop on 9 August, Ammundsen was in 'warm sympathy' with the Confessing church stand on Christian principles, but he saw as a 'serious' fault that its leaders 'emulated with "German Christians" in proclaiming their loyalty to Hitler'.[80]

Distinctions between personal sympathies and what he was prepared to say officially as vice-chairman of UCCLW were clearly being made. Moreover, Ammundsen was not alone in his refusal to officially judge, declaim and abandon the Reich church at Fanø. To his concern that 'in every church there is something unchristian and who can say how much can be tolerated?',[81] Leiper and others pointed to their own shortcomings in the private sessions, to which Jezéquél from France added 'Who art thou to judge thy brother?[82]

What had happened in the eleven months between Novi Sad and Fanø had sharpened Council concerns to the point where they now realised that the 'black hour' could not be repeated, but it had not diminished commitment to the ecumenical ideal embodied in the supranational structure of the Council. Those involved in drafting the Fanø resolution were clear in the private sessions that it was 'essential to abstain from any semblance of constituting a court' and that only the 'religious basis and motive' would be stressed.[83] Indeed, as requested by Joseph Oldham after review of the initial draft, the first paragraph was also to show that UCCLW was *not* 'solely concerned with aspects of the problem in Germany', but rather with the greater problem of state interference with the Church wherever it occurred.[84]

Further, as stated in the resolution and substantiated by the private sessions minutes, UCCLW intended 'to remain in friendly contact with *all* groups in the German Evangelical Church'.[85] 'Feelings of cordial goodwill' were extended to the German people and sympathy was conveyed to all 'fellow Christians in the difficulties of the present time'.[86] In addition, as highlighted by Ammundsen in the last private session, because the Confessing church had not been involved in the deliberations, the Council had an 'imperative duty to say or do something in an unmistakable manner', showing 'them and the world that we had a spiritual fellowship with them' as well.[87] The penultimate paragraph in the final resolution was therefore intended to assure 'brethren in the Confessional Synod … of its prayers and heartfelt sympathy in their witness to the principles of the Gospel', as well as UCCLW 'resolve to maintain close fellowship with them'.[88]

UCCLW leaders recognised in advance that it risked a break in relations with the Reich church by censoring its autocratic rule or striving for fellowship with all German church groups, but there was no intention whatsoever to sever relations. Indeed,

Bishop Theodor Heckel, head of the newly formed Reich Church Foreign Office, was praised both privately and publicly for the way in which he conducted himself, and Heckel responded in kind with praise for the way the Council 'bound' him to it 'by so much brotherly feeling'.[89] On the last day of the conference Heckel formally opposed and denied the grounds of the resolution, protesting against the penultimate paragraph as a 'one-sided stress on a particular group in the German church' – which Leiper framed as a clever strategy – but he did so while pledging 'to consolidate the bonds between the German church and Oecumenical Movement', which was a clear product of the 'brotherly' sessions.[90]

Both parts of Heckel's formal response have to be weighed equally when considering the outcomes of Fanø. Moreover, all of UCCLW's responses have to be given equal light in order to grasp the complexities of what was happening. Much has been made of the co-opted appointments of Confessing church members Karl Koch and Dietrich Bonhoeffer, but nothing is said about the concurrent nomination and election of Bishop Heckel and Dr Friedrich Krummacher of the Church Foreign Office to the UCCLW administrative and executive committees.[91] Whether or not Krummacher's membership in the National Socialist German Workers' Party (NSDAP) was known to UCCLW, his appointment, and that of Bishop Heckel, to the highest administrative committees is itself compelling witness that something far more complex and layered than has been memorialised was in play at Fanø.[92]

What was *not* risked in the official Fanø statement was any further mention of Jews, Jewish Christians, antisemitism or the Aryan paragraph. Indeed, Leiper met with Heckel the week before Fanø and in the nine points of UCCLW concern delivered in a memorandum for his consideration, there was not a single mention of Jews, race, or the Aryan paragraph.[93] Moreover, Leiper, who was part of the drafting committee, made clear in the last private session before the resolution was presented that it 'had not the right to produce a document in any sense purporting to express our views ... about the Aryan paragraph', even though the Council 'had said things about it before'.[94] In bold contrast, the WA, which was meeting simultaneously in the same hotel with some joint sessions, called 'attention to the growing menace of anti-Semitic propaganda'. The WA resolution stated clearly that deprivation of civic rights to 'people of Jewish race' was 'a deep injury to the Jews themselves', 'a moral poison in the social life of any community', and was 'contrary to the teaching and spirit of Jesus Christ'.[95] Yet for UCCLW – if Fanø was indeed 'the most critical and decisive meeting in its history' – it was also the third time in the first twenty months of Hitler's rule that statements on what was happening to Jews *as Jews* were sidestepped in order to not ruffle the issues of Council unity.

Antisemitism and refugees

In April 1934, four months before Fanø and concurrent with Hoffmann's *IRM* article on 'Modern Jewry and the Christian Church', the secretary of the British Student Christian Movement called on James Parkes to 'balance' out the barrage of conversionary lectures on Jews being delivered across Britain. The SCM concern was that it had compromised itself when allowing Hoffmann to address the Jewish question and Jewish missions at the 1933 Quadrennial, thereby creating an atmosphere in which 'pressure' was being exerted to adopt official evangelising policy. Parkes was eager to help but immersed in Jewish refugee issues and could not give the lectures until early 1935.[96] He had been at the head of an autonomous ISS committee charged with creation of a student refugee programme since May 1933.[97] While raising funds in Canada that fall he was called to New York as a consultant to James McDonald, a newly appointed League of Nations High Commissioner for Refugees from Germany. Parkes sailed from New York in early November as part of his initial entourage, meeting regularly during the passage and then attending the first informal High Commission meetings at the Hotel du Rhin in Paris. Although the association did not result in Parkes's acceptance of a permanent position,[98] the ISS committee he headed became the official student arm of the High Commission for Refugees, and by April 1934 some 1,325 Jewish students had been assisted with emigration from Germany by the committee he created.

But Parkes's efforts had not been without hazards. After the 1933 uproar in Germany over his *Vox Studentium* editorial, an ISS conference in Bavaria that summer (which he and Jewish students refused to attend) was unexpectedly attended by Heinrich Himmler and Ernst Röhm. Eleven months later on 30 June 1934, the German assemblyman in charge of the ISS conference arrangements was taken from his Munich flat and brutally murdered in what became known as the Röhm Purge. Within weeks ISS ties with all student groups directly or indirectly linked to the Nazi state had been severed and ISS had withdrawn from Germany. As it turned out, the withdrawal coincided with the fall publication of Parkes's Oxford doctoral study and his subsequent move into the field of independent scholarship, but the Nazi threat did not end there.[99]

While delivering the SCM lectures in Britain and making plans to relocate there the following spring of 1935, his Geneva flat was placed under police protection after learning that it was targeted by Swiss Nazis. When returning two weeks later, a male employee helping with the move was mistaken for Parkes and critically injured in an attempted murder plot resulting in long-term impairment. The 'Nazi plot' on Parkes's life was widely reported, with headlines reaching as far as the front page of the English newspaper in Buenos Aires. As explained by the general secretary of SCM to the British press, Parkes had just finished lecturing on the 'Jewish question' in British theological colleges when it happened, and there 'was no doubt' that his scholarship and activism on Jewish issues was 'the reason' for the attempted murder.[100]

During those eight weeks of lectures in early 1935, Parkes drew on his published Oxford thesis, *The Conflict of the Church and the Synagogue: A Study in the Origins of Antisemitism*. His use of the non-hyphened term, which began in 1932, was grounded in his refusal to legitimise neither the artificial construct 'Semitism', which antisemites claimed was a real and existent threat to national and world societies, nor a universal Jewish problem, which antisemites insisted was the target of 'anti-Semitism'. His lectures, as well as the chapter analyses that lay behind the non-hyphened title, argued incisively that the provenance of modern antisemitism and its accessory Jewish problem were firmly rooted in Christian history.

Analysing from a broad range of ancient sources preserved by the Church as theological and historical legacy, Parkes argued that the conceptual portrait of Jews and Judaism drawn by church fathers in the first centuries of Christian history was one of theological necessity rather than historical reality. He demonstrated evidentially that the 'Old Testament' was used as 'a mine' from which 'proof texts' were extracted to prove the predominance and truth of Christianity. Claims derived from such 'proofs' were used interpretatively out of context to define 'a theological position of Jews' as God-betraying and God-abandoned enemies of the Church and Christianity. Further, universalisation of 'the Jews' – 'the Jews' killed Christ, 'the Jews' were rejected by God, 'the Jews' were the enemy of God – was central to the development of an anti-Jewish theological position. By the time the fourth gospel was written in the early second century, 'the Jews' was an all-inclusive reference to those 'considered equally the enemies' of Christianity, with the result that 'a Jew' and 'some Jews' were almost unknown to later patristic writings, having been replaced by a stream of universalisations used to portray 'Jews' as always and everywhere 'a perpetual and present danger'.[101] The sobering result, on Parkes's analysis, was a perdurable foundation of Christian anti-Jewish beliefs and teachings that held through the centuries, one on which modern antisemitism 'reared a structure of racial and economic propaganda'. While stressing that antisemites were and would continue to be culpable, he yet argued that the ultimate responsibility rested 'with those who prepared the soil, created the deformation of the people, and so made these ineptitudes credible'.[102]

The inroads made by this scholarship into the milieu of ICCAJ thought and theory were apparent in one immediate way. Parkes's mountain of primary source evidence on the development of foundational anti-Jewish teachings in the Church could not be ignored, but his emphasis on causal relations between Church teachings and antisemitism conflicted with Hoffmann's claims on the causal role of modern Jewry. Awareness of the degree to which anti-Jewishness permeated Church teachings was heightened among ICCAJ leaders, but Hoffmann's insistence about Jewish causes was not affected. The obdurate belief, as illustrated by a lecture in London in May 1935, was hardening into a formulaic pattern.

Antisemitism, as had become common, was introduced as a problem that 'compelled' Christianity to 'face its responsibility and attitude to the Jewish people', but on the other side of that seemingly unshadowed benevolence was the claim 'whether we like it or not, the Jew is still a problem'.[103] Following in tandem was the line-up of racial-identity elements that had been developing since the 1925 call for Christian experts on the Jewish problem. Zionism and Palestine were presented as provokers of 'racial pride and national ambitions', which provoked antisemitic backlash that, in turn, provoked the 'renaissance' of Jewishness that was fuelling racial antisemitism. The 'whole secularist drift', as Hoffmann termed it, was creating 'a danger, not only to Judaism but to the Christian faith as well'. His plea for action, in this case to a group of Protestant missionary societies, was stated in plain language that could not be misunderstood:

> You and I somehow have got to win the Jew to Christ to save the Jew from becoming a problem and even a menace to the Christian faith. The more he becomes a menace, the more likely are we to have anti-Semitism: it is a vicious circle. The only way out is Christ. And we must save the Jews for Christ and by Christ and through Christ. The need was never greater than today in view of the geographical dispersion of the Jews to the ends of the earth, his racial pride, his aggressiveness.[104]

The same arguments in different form appeared in Hoffmann's five-year report two months later at an ICCAJ conference in London, with delegates from Ireland, Scotland, England, Sweden, Hungary, Switzerland, Germany, Canada, the United States and the Netherlands.[105] While efforts were made to degeneralise claims, undoubtedly in response to Parkes's book, the greater part of his causal discourse still curved around Jews. In each case in which 'manifold' causes of antisemitism were discussed – economic hardship, intense nationalism, rising secularism – explanations invoked 'certain Jews' or 'some Jews', often with harshly provocative depictions.[106] Familiar claims about modern Jewry's threats to Christianity were also in play: Jewish involvement in anti-religious movements, a 'renaissance' of Jewishness stressing racial and national aspects, disintegration of Judaism which increased numbers of atheistic Jews, all of which gathered toward the conclusion that each was part of an 'undeniable entrenchment of Jewry in opposition to Christianity'. 'How are we leavening this type of modern Jewry?' was the question being put forth here.[107]

The answer, after nearly seven pages on limitations and failures, was that the objectives of the Budapest–Warsaw conferences were far from realised. Chief among stated factors was the 'rising tide of anti-Jewish feeling' but, at the same time, increasing anti-Jewishness was argued as warrant for expansion of Jewish missions, for Hitler was making the world more 'Jew conscious than ever before'. IMC chairman John Mott was in accord with both thoughts, but he also held that 'much more thinking on the Jewish problem' and conversion was needed. It had become more apparent with each passing year that there was 'no hope of evangelizing the Jews without Christianizing the Christians'. The often repeated motto had initially referred to educating Protestant forces on the need and duty of Jewish missions, but growing awareness of anti-Jewishness and antisemitism among church populations in Germany, eastern Europe, Balkans, Palestine, Egypt, Britain and America had deepened the meaning. While such awareness did not extend to organisational reflection on the claims and language of its own discourse, the degree to which members now recognised antisemitism in the churches was enough to move 'combating' it to a higher priority on Hoffmann's agenda. Teaching on the 'right' Christian attitude toward Jews was thus to be expanded in conjunction with work against unjust anti-Jewishness and racial antisemitism. With this focus, and a recognised need 'for much more thinking on the Jewish problem', the July 1935 delegates mandated as 'urgent' new research into both the causes of antisemitism and the refugee problem emanating from Germany's Aryan laws.[108]

ICCAJ had three major concerns about the Aryan laws creating the refugee crisis. Like UCCLW, the racial system underlying the Aryan laws was seen as a direct violation of Christian universalism and the sanctity of baptism, but, along with protecting the irrevocable nature of baptism for Christians of Jewish descent, ICCAJ had charged itself with protection of the baptismal sacrament before it was implemented. The Budapest–Warsaw conferences had mandated planning for evangelisation of 'the whole Jewish people, fifteen and a half million Jews of the present day dispersion', which meant that individual Jews and 'the whole people' were conceptually linked in a specialised meaning that carried with it the 'duty' of not risking the overall goal by baptising unfit individuals who could be stumbling blocks to other Jews.[109]

Obstacles standing in the way of meeting that goal, as understood, were that no standardised policy for baptism existed among Protestant churches, and that emancipation had brought with it ulterior Jewish motives to convert for political, social and economic gain. Among actions advised to dissuade such motives were to make baptism more difficult for Jews by instituting longer periods of instruction, set periods of observation, and 'testing' of Jewish faith by 'proof' of changed lives. Those emphases increased after Hoffmann criticised in 1931 the tendency in eastern Europe to baptise Jews even when recognised as 'purely for economic or political prestige purposes', and they increased again after Germany's Aryan clause was introduced in 1933. By July 1935, when research on non-Aryan refugees was mandated, ICCAJ was urging Protestant churches to adopt as a 'uniform modus operandi' a six-month probationary period that had just been unanimously mandated by the Reformed Church of Hungary. It would not solve the problem of 'what to do with converted Jews' already in churches 'to hide themselves', as ICCAJ Hungarian member Gyula Forgács explained, but the stricter policy provided stronger assurance that Jewish baptism would be 'evidence of a sincere religious experience and conversion', and not merely, as Hoffmann had warned, 'a means to social or commercial prestige or an attempt to escape from the stigma of being a Jew'.[110]

Second, according to data from the Office of the High Commissioner in July 1935, which ICCAJ closely monitored, Palestine was the main country of refuge for Jews fleeing Germany.[111] Concerns about a build-up of 'anti-Christian' elements in Palestine had been a platform issue since the 1925 call for Christian experts on the Jewish problem.[112] By 1929 the belief that 'Jewish Palestine' was becoming the new 'spiritual centre' of Jewry was well established, and by 1933 the 'reality' of relations between Palestine, Zionism and the dangers of Jewish racial-national consciousness was one of Hoffmann's inflexible mantras.[113] Indeed, warnings about the a-religious and anti-religious aspects of Zionism increased with the rate of Jewish immigration to Palestine. By mid-1935 when the High Commission reported that Palestine had absorbed more refugees from Germany 'than all of the other countries of the world together', Hoffmann's warning was that the Jewish population, growing 'at the rate of thirty to fifty thousand per year', could reach 'one million by 1945'.[114] That 'a land largely controlled by Jews' would negatively impact mission efforts was part of the argument, but even more so was the 'intensely ambitious' Zionism that was said to be gaining ground. That Jews might control Palestine 'economically, politically, numerically and culturally' had far-reaching implications for ICCAJ's director, for as Zionism grew so did 'the racial pride and national ambitions of Jewry'[115]

The third area of marked concern about the Aryan laws was highlighted at the conference of July 1935 in an appended paper by Parkes Cadman, chairman of both the American sector of UCCLW and the American Christian Committee for German Refugees. The opening words of his report on 'German Christian non-Aryans' summarised the relevance for Christendom by framing the date of the first Aryan law, 7 April 1933, as 'a famous date in the history of Christianity'. The stated significance of the legislation, in other words, was not the suppression of the Jewish people, but 'the first time a government ... challenged the validity of baptism'. The Aryan laws were said to have precipitated 'a serious crisis in Church history', creating a 'desperate' plight for Christians of Jewish descent, one that was markedly different from that of Jews. Citing the German Protestant paper *Auf der Warte*, Cadman went on to argue that Jewish conditions in Germany were 'essentially more favourable than those of non-Aryan Christians', that the number of non-Aryan Christians was far greater than Jews, that the aid provided them was pitiful compared to that given by world Jewry to Jews. He also posited, as 'a living refutation of the preposterous nonsense about race, religion, and Germanism', that non-Aryan Christians posed a greater 'threat' to Nazism than Jews.[116]

When Hoffmann's confidential report on the condition of non-Aryans followed on 1 September, twice the length and more broadly focused, it agreed with all aspects of Cadman's paper. It heralded as an 'ominous' warning that the Aryan laws were evidence that Nazism could 'not tolerate the Christian religion', it lamented the suffering of all who were classified as non-Aryan, and followed Cadman's focus on numbers and aid. While inconsistent in his usage of the non-Aryan terminology – 'Jew and partial Jew', 'Christian and partial Jew', 'Jews and non-Aryans', 'non-Aryan and Hebrew Christian' – Hoffmann like Cadman was clear that Christian non-Aryans were reacted to more harshly, their economic position was worse than Jews, and their numbers were as much as six times greater.[117]

The goal in both reports was to raise awareness and stir Christian indifference toward non-Aryan Christians, which by all accounts had to be stirred, but it must not be overlooked that the reports depicted suffering as if it could be measured. It was not just a matter of making needed appeals for non-Aryan Christians, which had to be made, but that the plight of Jews was being diminished to rally support for Christians of Jewish descent. That the 'needs' of non-Aryan Christians were 'greater than even those of the Jews' was a point circulated by Hoffmann even before Cadman's report appeared, but it is important to recognise that it was not just an ICCAJ idea. As stated in a report by UCCLW general secretary Henriod the following summer, 'the fate' of non-Aryan Christians was being broadcast as 'more tragic than that of the Jews' from Geneva as well.[118]

The weight of these perceptions increased dramatically when the Nazi state introduced the Nuremberg Laws two weeks after Hoffmann's report on non-Aryans. In the words of High Commissioner James McDonald, the new legislation 'altered the entire complexion of the refugee problem'.[119] The Reich Citizenship Law and the Law for the Protection of German Blood and Honour on 15 September 1935, along with supplementary decrees two months later, deprived German Jews of citizenship, forbade marriages or extramarital relations with German nationals, and laid the framework for a complexly constructed legal definition and conception of who was and was not a Jew.

Jew, Anyone with 3 or 4 Jewish grandparents
Jew, 2 Jewish grandparents belonging to Jewish congregation on 15 September

Jew, 2 Jewish grandparents + married to a Jew on 15 September or later
Jew, 1st degree *Mischling* + married to a Jew
Jew, 1st degree *Mischling* + spousal member of Jewish congregation
Jew, Aryan converted to Judaism
1st degree *Mischling*, 2 Jewish grandparents with no connection to Jewish religion
2nd degree *Mischling*, 1 Jewish grandparent with no connection to Jewish religion

The Nuremberg disenfranchising laws expanded non-Aryan terminology and formulated definitions of 'Jew' according to degrees of alleged hereditary 'Jewishness' rooted in the religious background of one's forebears.[120] Secular Jews who had never been involved with Judaism, generational Christians of Jewish descent who had never associated with Jews, and Jews who had converted on their own initiative were thrown into the net of marginalisation based solely on the religious association of their grandparents, by which was deduced their degree of 'Jewishness'. Although the exact number caught in the expanding classification was not known, all 'Jews' in Germany were being disenfranchised, deprived of citizenship, freedoms and rights, while German churches, some willingly and some not, were being pulled into the system by virtue of their religious roles as keepers of baptismal records, conveyors of baptismal sacraments and dispensers of baptismal certificates.[121] By the end of 1935 more than 80,000 non-Aryans had fled Germany during the three years of Nazi rule, and for those remaining possession or non-possession of the documents was the basis on which the status of 'Jew' was being officially assigned.

All of this was to be taken into account in the newly mandated study on antisemitism. The 'ecumenical' significance of the study is that it was to be a first collaborative effort with UCCLW, who had just launched an international research programme on 'Church, Community and State' in preparation for a 1937 world conference at Oxford. In accord with the mandate, Hoffmann invited the participation of IMC general secretary Joseph Oldham, who had been tapped at Fanø as organiser of research for the Oxford conference. Oldham responded favourably, and in both February and April Hoffmann reported that a study on the causes, consequences and cures of present-day antisemitism would likely be forthcoming. At the same time an ICCAJ study commission was formed under Hoffmann and William Paton, who was Oldham's co-general secretary of IMC. The working arrangement was for ICCAJ to present a study on antisemitism at a conference in Vienna immediately before Oxford, where a parallel UCCLW study would be brought to the fore.[122]

The two-study plan was unexpectedly altered, however, after a meeting of UCCLW in Chamby (Switzerland) in August 1936, where yet another issue on antisemitism arose. The setting and details are important, beginning with UCCLW's reconfirmation of Heckel and NSDAP member Krummacher to its executive and administrative committees.[123] In this milieu of cooperation with the Reich church, delegations from both the Confessing and Reich churches had been brought together around the common goal of planning for the 1937 UCCLW Oxford conference.[124] Bishop Bell had spent the week working behind scenes to broker enough peace between the opposing German groups for them to meet and discuss choices for a united Oxford delegation, which their leaders did amicably on the last morning of the meeting.[125] That afternoon, as the last item on the agenda, Bell reported that, after extensive discussion on 'Christians who were suffering on account of faith, nation or race in different parts of the world', the Administrative Committee concluded that 'it was not possible to adopt a resolution adequate to the situation' while giving 'due justice' to both 'the necessities of the case and the rights of members of the Council specially concerned'.[126]

Not everyone, however, agreed that the *rights* of UCCLW members should be weighed against a statement on antisemitism. Five of those present held that antisemitism was 'penetrating like a contagious disease into all parts of the world', and each of the five – Henry Leiper, Joseph Oldham, Marc Boegner, Canon Lewis-Crosby and Mrs. Söderblom, the Archbishop's widow – argued in some way that 'a clear and definite statement ... was urgently awaited from the Christian churches'. Arguing otherwise, and in agreement with Bell, was Reich Church Commissioner Wilhelm Zoellner and General Superintendent Otto Dibelius, who urged 'that no notice had been given of the subject' and that the Council should consider whether 'a statement was ... the best form of expression that its sympathy could take'. Their argument was that 'the Council would be acting in the fullest interest of the Una Sancta' *if* it refrained 'from issuing a statement at this juncture'. They also assured that in Germany 'the matter of Christians who were suffering on account of faith, nationality or race was receiving far more serious consideration than could be provided in any rapidly drafted resolution'.[127]

At this point Bell adjourned for 'further reflection', at which time he consulted the heads of the German delegations. When the session reconvened two hours later, Bell reminded the Council that they 'had to consider the interests' of all concerned. The 'expressions of anxiety' brought out in the earlier session had given him hope that 'a more personal sense of responsibility in the matter might be brought home individually', but little had changed in terms of a collective statement. What was 'necessary', he concluded, was to show that 'the Church had been keenly exercised' by the issue and that the Council realised 'the trouble was by no means confined to a single country'. Bell's resolution, seconded by Ammundsen and unanimously adopted by the rest of the Council, said as little as possible without using the term antisemitism or identifying its sufferers. It simply stated that UCCLW was aware 'that the mind of the churches in different parts of the world is greatly exercised by the distress of those who suffer in consequence of faith, nationality or race', and that 'in profound sympathy' the matter was referred to the administrative committee for 'earnest consideration' of how to 'alleviate and remedy the present distress'.[128]

Not a word of the decision to sidestep another statement on antisemitism was mentioned when Joseph Oldham informed Hoffmann two weeks later that UCCLW could not be involved in the study on antisemitism. It had become 'increasingly clear', he said, that the research on Church, Community and State would exhaust all 'available energy', with 'little hope' of an 'effective contribution to the problem of anti-Semitism before the Oxford Conference'. What was most startling to Hoffmann was not that preparations for Oxford had interfered with the parallel study on antisemitism, but that Oldham had commissioned the initial research from James Parkes, whose paper he had adjudged as 'too historical'.[129]

Hoffmann assured Oldham that the ICCAJ study would proceed while asking to be informed if Parkes undertook 'something new' so he could coordinate the effort. At the same time he began a course of action that made no room for Parkes's historical views. Over the next nine months every stage of planning was set on current and not historical causes of antisemitism, with one precise exception. While it was traditionally held that Jewish hatred of the Church was universal and constant, Parkes argued that the alleged hatred was based on theological exegesis that *required* Jewish hostility rather than any historical reality, so Hoffmann went in search of substantiation for the traditional view. What he had in mind, as framed to expositors, was 'Jewish opposition to the growth of the early Church', for it was there that at least some roots of current antisemitism were 'lodged'. With that exception, which so clearly sought Jewish causation, the mandated study was to focus on immediate causes and not historical anti-Jewishness, for 'the more important question' was what could be done in the face of the 'current persecution'.[130]

To think briefly about what that 'current persecution' entailed, one week after FCC protested against Germany's persecution of Jews in the *New York Times* on 25 March 1933, the new Nazi state called for a boycott of all Jewish businesses. The first Aryan laws that defined Jews as non-Aryan and began their elimination from influential spheres of German society were enacted on 7, 11, 22 and 25 April, followed by decrees in July, September and October. As part of the summer and fall laws, Nazi cultural ministries were created in broadcasting, press, film, literature, theatre, fine arts and music under the Propaganda Ministry of Joseph Goebbels, who pledged the removal of every vestige of Jewishness from German life. Definitions of 'Jew' according to stipulated degrees of hereditary Jewishness followed with the enactment of the Nuremberg Laws in September 1935.[131] One immediate result was the marked increase in 'scientific research' on Jews in all spheres of German society. Research on the Jewish problem and Jewish influence became the publicly stated goals of major Nazi institutions, three of which – the Institute for the Study of the Jewish Problem (Berlin 1935), Reich Institute for History of the New German (Berlin 1935), Research Department for the Jewish Problem (Munich 1936) – were up and running by 1936, with publicised findings in the language of 'Jewish influence', 'Judaisation' and the societal need for 'de-Judaisation'.[132]

The relevance of these ideological elements cannot be overstated, for it was around the same issues of 'Jewishness', 'Jewish influence' and 'Judaisation' that ICCAJ director Hoffmann was educating international Protestant audiences on the 'realities' surrounding the 'Jewish problem'. The language and concepts were central to the racial-identity theory that stressed causal relations between racially conscious Jewishness and rising antisemitism. Causality – and not just correlation between modern Jewry, Jewishness, and antisemitism – was a hallmark feature of the conversionary discourse throughout the first four years of Nazi rule. It went hand in hand with assertions on the dangers of Jewish influence, including that Jewry would Judaise the world unless Christianity could Christianise Jewry, with no hint of awareness that concepts and language were dangerously shared with the antisemitism it claimed (and believed) it was called to combat. That some *or* all of this would carry over to the new study on antisemitism was clear by the turn of the year when Hoffmann advised those drafting it to keep in mind that:

> owing to the constant insistence of the Jew regarding his *racial and national identity*, he becomes a suspicious minority against whom anti-Semitism is inflicted whenever an economic crisis or other national crisis arises.[133]

Notes

1 Deborah Lipstadt, *Beyond Belief* (New York: Touchstone, 1985), 14.
2 FCC Statement, WCC.301.4317; *New York Times (NYT)*, dated 24 Mar., pub. 25 Mar. 1933, p. 10.
3 Cables to FCC, 25–31 Mar., incl. G. Burghart (German World Alliance); Gerhard Ohlemüller, Fahrenhorst, Luther (Int. Protestant League), Kapler (UCCLW), FCC. B9.F15.
4 Kapler to Bell, Henriod and recipient list, 30 Mar.; Professor Heimann to Christian Social Institute, 30 Mar; Kapler to Henriod, 31 Mar., 3 Apr. WCC.301.4318, 42.0041.
5 FCC to Kapler (2), to Ohlemüller in Berlin, 30 Mar., WCC.301.4317, 4318.

In the shadows of response: 1933–1936   107

6 Leiper to Brown, 31 Mar; to Visser 't Hooft, 1 Apr.; Cavert, Leiper to Brown, 1 Apr., WCC.301.4317, FCC.B9F15.
7 Henriod to Kapler, 1 Apr., w/c to Cadman, Cavert, Leiper, Bell, WCC.420041.
8 Henriod to Ammundsen, 7, 11, 14 Apr. 1933, WCC.301.4317.
9 Adolf Keller, 'Facts and Meaning of the German Revolution as Seen from a Neutral Point of View', 13 Apr. 1933, WCC.301.4317.
10 Keller, 'European Survey', Confidential, 6 Apr., FCC.B9F15. Keller accepted the explanation of church superintendent Otto Dibelius in a radio broadcast to American churches on 6 Apr. For text of broadcast, John Conway, *The Nazi Persecution of the Churches, 1933–45* (Toronto: Ryerson Press, 1968), 342–4.
11 Keller, 'Facts and Meaning', WCC.301.43.17.
12 W.A. Visser 't Hooft, untitled, 13 Apr., WCC.301.4317, published in *Christian Century (CC)* as 'Christ or Caesar in Germany', 3 May 1933.
13 Cavert to Henriod, 15 Mar.; Henriod to Cavert, 22 Mar.; Henriod to Ammundsen, 11 Apr.; Cavert to Henriod, 4, 15 Apr., WCC.301.4317, FCC B9 F15.
14 Report 1, 'The Situation in Germany', 25 Apr. 1933, WCC.301.4317, FCC B9F15. The author has been difficult to pin down due to conflicting copies in WCC and FCC archives. While neither bears a signature, the FCC copy has pencilling ('by H. Schönfeld') on the first page, which has led researchers from FCC archives to assume his authorship. In the WCC archives the document appears without such marking in two places related to Leiper's request for Brown's intervention and Brown's second report. Brown's authorship is based on similarity of voice, style, content, points of discussion, unusual names mentioned, use of a curious mix of roman and decimal numerals, and the fact that UCCLW did not typically assign duplicate reports on the same meetings. Pencil marking in the FCC archives, as suggested by other archival notations in the same handwriting on other documents, may have been added when archivists sorted and catalogued the World War II era documents.
15 Report 2, 'On the Visit to Berlin', 28 Apr. 1933, in French and English, WCC.301. 4307; French is also in Armin Boyens, *Kirchenkampf und Ökumene, 1933–1939: Darstellung und Dokumentation* (Munich: Kaiser, 1969), 291–5.
16 Report 3, 'Impressions of the Situation in Contemporary Germany with Special Reference to its Bearing on the Future of International Cooperation', WCC.301.4317.
17 Quot. resp., Brown report 3, 5; Brown report 1, 4; Henriod report 2, 2.

18 Quot., Brown report 1, 4; Henriod report 2, 4.
19 Quot. resp., Brown report 3, 6–7; Henriod report 2, 3.
20 This was the first in a series of meetings that led to the founding of WCC; it had been in planning since January. See Henriod to Paton, 9 Jan., to Cavert, 21 Feb., 27 Apr. 1933; IMC.261142, FCC.B9F15.
21 As example, R.C.D. Jasper, *George Bell, Bishop of Chichester* (Oxford: Oxford University Press, 1967), 101; Boyens, *Kirchenkampf und Ökumene* (1969), 52–3, 308–9; Johan Snoek, *The Grey Book* (New York: Humanities Press, 1970), 94; Victoria Barnett, 'Christian and Jewish Interfaith Efforts During the Holocaust', *Gray Zones: Ambiguity and Compromise in the Holocaust and Its Aftermath* (Oxford and New York: Berghahn Books, 2005), 20.
22 Bell to Kapler, 'Private and Confidential Draft', 7 May 1933, WCC.42.0041.
23 'Private and Confidential' Draft, 7 May; the 17 May changes are in italics; WCC.42.0041.
24 Bell to Kapler, 17 May 1933, with no publishing noted, WCC.42.0041.
25 Klaus Scholder, *The Churches and the Third Reich*, Vol. 1 (Philadelphia: Fortress Press, 1988), 274–9.
26 Cavert to Keller, 22 May; to Kurt Böhme, 31 May; to Visser 't Hooft, 13 July 1933; for praise of Cavert's essay, Keller to Cavert, 9 June; FCC.B9F15, F16.
27 FCC statement, *NYT*, 25 March 1933, WCC 301.4317.
28 Cavert, 'Hitler and the German Churches', *CC*, 24 May 1933, 683–5.
29 Memo by Lang on meeting with Mott, 31 May 1933, in Andrew Chandler, *Brethren in Adversity* (Woodbridge: Boydell Press, 1997), 47.
30 Lang to Tatlow, LPL Lang Papers, Vol. 38, fol. 31. Kotschnig, 'Reflections on a Visit to Germany', 15 May 1933, w/copies to Tatlow, Mott, Cavert, Keller, Henriod, Temple and 20 other ecumenical leaders. He did not discuss German churches; his concern was that 'wholesale condemnation' of Germany would aggravate German sensitivities over war guilt in the Versailles Treaty, and 'bring the spectre of war dangerously near' again, WCC.301. 4317.
31 Tatlow to Lang, 9 June 1933, LPL Lang Papers, Vol. 38, fol. 39.
32 Parkes to Don, 9 June 1933, LPL Lang, Vol. 38, fols 32–38; Don to Parkes, 10 June, fol. 40. See also Andrew Chandler, *British Christians and the Third Reich* (Cambridge: Cambridge University Press, 2022), 74–7; 'A Question of Fundamental Principles: The Church of England and the Jews of Germany, 1933–1937', *Leo Baeck Institute Yearbook* (1993), 231–3; Parkes, *Voyage of Discoveries*, 106.

33 *Vox Studentium* was the ISS tri-language journal distributed to all national student unions; for *JTA* coverage, 20, 22 Dec. 1932; 1, 3 March; 13, 24, 31 May 1933.
34 Parkes, 'The Nature of Antisemitism', July draft for *The Church Overseas, An Anglican Review of Missionary Thought and Work*, 6:24 (Oct. 1933), 302–10; PP60/9/1/9.
35 Conrad Hoffmann, *A New Approach to an Old Problem: Modern Jewry and the International Committee on the Christian Approach to the Jews* (New York and London: ICCAJ, May 1933), 1–5.
36 Ibid., 6.
37 'Modern Jewry and Christian Responsibility', Sept. 1933, circulated as a confidential report and then publicised 'available on request', 2–5, 20, IMC.261207.
38 Ibid., 6–8, quot. 7.
39 Conrad Hoffmann, 'Modern Jewry and the Christian Church', *IRM*, 23:2 (Apr. 1934), 189–204.
40 Ibid., 198–9.
41 Ibid., 193, 195–8, 200.
42 Ibid., 190–4.
43 Hoffmann, 'Modern Jewry and Christian Responsibility', 4.
44 Hoffmann, 'Modern Jewry and the Christian Church', 190–4.
45 Ibid., 195.
46 Louis Israel Newman, *Jewish Influence on Christian Reform Movements* (New York: Columbia University Press, 1925), quot. 2; 'Telling it in Gath', *The Sentinel*, 93:4 (25 Jan. 1934).
47 Cohon, 'The Jew and Christian Evangelization', 470–80.
48 For commissioned rebuttal to Cohon, see 'Considerations on a Complaint Regarding Christian Propaganda Among Jews', *IRM*, 22:4 (Oct. 1933), 481–99, by Edwyn Bevan, who delivered the 1933–1934 Gifford Lectures and often defended ICCAJ's conversionary agenda. For Hoffmann's denial, *News Sheet* (Mar.–Apr. 1934), 1.
49 The mandate for ICCAJ was for policy, planning, coordination and enlistment for evangelising Jews rather than direct evangelisation, but it is clear that intent to evangelise was always present and opportunity always looked for. Even the November 1932 meeting to dissuade rabbis from opposing ICCAJ had at root the message that Christianity was Judaism's fulfilment. Jews were also occasionally addressed in mixed lectures on Christian relief, antisemitism, or the situation in Germany, and small groups of Jewish students were engaged wherever possible, as in Romania 1931, Warsaw and Oxford 1933, Canada 1933 and 1935; see DRs 1931–35, IMC.261202, 261207.

50 The German delegation included Drs Heckel, Schreiber, Wahl, Hinderer, Böhme, Menn, M. Dibelius.
51 Henry Leiper, *Personal View of the German Churches Under the Revolution: A Confidential Report Based on Intimate Personal Contact with Leaders on Both Sides of the Church and State Controversy in the Third Reich* (New York: UCCLW, 1934), 18–20.
52 UCCLW Min., Novi Sad, 9–12 Sept. 1933, 10, 15–16, 20, 37–42, HSL.971027.B2.
53 Bell to Müller, 23 Oct. 1933, in Novi Sad Min., 39–41. Also Henriod to Bell, 25 Oct.; Henriod to Fezer, 7 Nov.; UCCLW press release, 29 Nov.; WCC.301.4317, FCC.B9F17.
54 Bell to Müller, 18 Jan. 1934, WCC.301.4306.
55 Paton to Henriod, 6 Feb. 1934, IMC.261142. Delegates included Conference of British Missionary Societies, East London Fund for the Jews, Church Missions to the Jews, British Jews Society, Church of Scotland Jewish Mission Committee, Jerusalem and the East Mission, International Hebrew Christian Alliance, Barbican Mission, British & Foreign Bible Society, Missionary Council of the Church Assembly, Presbyterian Church of England, Baptist Union, Congregational Union, Methodist Missionary Society, Student Christian Movement, ICCAJ, IMC.
56 The 1933 Rouse reports are in three confidential versions: Church of England Council on Foreign Relations, 31 Oct.; Conference of Missionary Societies in Great Britain and Ireland, 24 Oct.; Report on Missionary Situation in Germany, 24 Oct., WCC.301.4317, 301.4318.
57 Confidential conference on the Christian Approach to the Jews, min., 11 Jan. 1934, 2–3, IMC.261201.
58 Leiper, *Personal View of the German Churches*, 4, 6–7, 22: compare to his 'Anti-Semitism in Germany', *American Hebrew* (23 Dec. 1932), 113–19; also Confidential to Cavert, 2 Sept. 1933, FCC.F17B2.
59 Henriod to Bell, 19 Oct. 1933, 4, WCC.301.4317.
60 Rouse, Report to Council of Foreign Relations, 31 Oct., 9.
61 After Schreiber's invitation was accepted, ecumenists in and out of Germany contributed materials for Macfarland's study, including Bonhoeffer; see Winterhager to Henriod, 17 Oct. 1933, WCC.301.4317.
62 Charles Macfarland, *The New Church and the New Germany: A Study of Church and State* (New York: Macmillan, 1934), v, 7, pointing to the 'providential' existence of UCCLW in relation to the struggle of the 'new' German church.

63 Ibid, 63–7.
64 Ibid., 65–8.
65 Ibid., 69–72, 78–89.
66 Ibid., 169–70.
67 Ibid., 170–4.
68 Ibid., 174–6; Leiper, *Personal View of the German Churches*, 20–1.
69 Ibid., 175, quoting Leiper directly.
70 WA Statement on Racial Minorities, Sofia, 14–21 Sept. 1933, WCC.301. 4318.
71 Ammundsen to Henriod, 9 Apr. 1933, WCC.301.4318.
72 Henry Leiper, *The Church–State Struggle in Germany* (London: Friends of Europe, 1935), 19; also 'The Churches' Answer to a Divided World', *Community Churchman* (May 1931), 7.
73 Bell, Letter to Editor, *The Times*, 4 Oct. 1933, orig. ital., WCC.301.4317.
74 Bell to Heckel, 10, 13 Feb. 1934; Visser't Hooft, Confidential report on latest developments in the German Church, 19 Feb.; Bell, letter to editor, *The Times*, 19 Mar.; Bell to Karlström, confidential, 23 Mar.; Henriod, Confidential report of journey to Haderslev, Lund, Berlin and Kassell, 28 Apr.–8 May, WCC.301. 4306, 4317, 4319; Leiper, 'The Church Situation in Germany', Aug. 1934, FCC.B12F4.
75 Leiper re Novi Sad, *Personal View of the German Churches*, 20; Ehrenström re Fanø. 'Movements', *HEM*, 583.
76 Ibid., Ehrenström.
77 As example, Eberhard Bethge, *Dietrich Bonhoeffer* (London: Collins, 1970), 381; Wolfgang Gerlach, *And the Witnesses Were Silent: The Confessing Church and the Persecution of the Jew* (Lincoln: University of Nebraska Press, 2000), 130, quotes Bethge; Burton Nelson, '1934: Pivotal Year of the Church Struggle', *HGS*, 4:3 (1989), 291; Keith Clements, *Faith on the Frontier* (Edinburgh and Geneva: T&T Clark and WCC, 1999), 282. For interpretation: Michael Kinnamon, *Unity as Prophetic Witness* (Minneapolis: Fortress Press, 2018), 30; Keith Clements, *Dietrich Bonhoeffer's Ecumenical Quest* (Geneva: WCC, 2015), 176.
78 Leiper, *The Church–State Struggle*, 26.
79 The detailed minutes of Fanø private sessions for Council members are at WCC.24.248, hereafter cited as PS.
80 Ammundsen, 'Report on my interview with Dr Koch and Friends in Hamburg, 10 August', dated 13 Aug. 1934. Koch, Asmussen, Fiedler, Hildebrand, and later Mathiesen and Tonnesen were in attendance. 'Friends' apparently referred to earlier letters from Bonhoeffer, while

the direct reference to 'leaders' was to Koch and Asmussen; quot. resp. 2, 1, 2, 4, WCC.24.248.
81 Ibid., 4.
82 Leiper, PS 25 Aug, 9; Jezéquél, PS 29 Aug., 1.
83 Boegner, Leiper, PS 29 Aug., 1, 3. The drafting team was made up of Boegner (France), Leiper, Ammundsen, Bell, Henriod, Keller, Brun (Norway), Bishop of Novi Sad.
84 Oldham, PS 29 Aug., 1; Brun, PS 25 Aug., 10.
85 UCCLW Min., Fanø, 24–30 Aug. 1934, WCC.212.008, 51, ital. add. 'All groups', according to private minutes seemed to include even *Deutsche Christen*. British R. H. Crossman spoke as one 'who would have been a German Christian if he had been a German', PS 25 Aug., 11; and even Ammundsen noted 'truth ... behind the German Christian movement', namely 'that a great part of the people had been alienated from the church and must be brought back', PS 27 Aug., 3.
86 UCCLW Min., 51.
87 Ammundsen, PS 29 Aug., 3.
88 UCCLW Min., 51.
89 For Church Foreign Office opening, see 'Nazi Church Opens Foreign Office', *NYT*, 6 Mar. 1934, 8; for Heckel's 'brotherly' response at Fanø, PS 29 Aug., 3.
90 UCCLW min, 52; Heckel was speaking on behalf of the German delegation, which included Drs Krummacher, Simons, Wahl, Professors Wendland and Koch. See also Leiper, *The Church–State Struggle*, 26.
91 UCCLW Min., 59–64, for appointments. Bonhoeffer was at Youth Conference and WA meetings in the same hotel, and present at plenary joint sessions with UCCLW, but was not privileged to the private Council sessions; his co-opting to UCCLW applied to post-Fanø only.
92 Friedrich Wilhelm Krummacher joined the Nazi Party in 1933 and became part of the Church Foreign Office under Heckel in 1934. John Conway, *The Nazi Persecution of the Churches*, 37, places him on the steps of a Swastika covered church the Sunday after Müller's installation as Reich Bishop, heralding his call by the Nazi state to 'work for the creation of a unified German Evangelical Church'. Andrew Chandler, *British Christians and the Third Reich* (Cambridge: Cambridge University Press, 2022), 91–2, posits Heckel as a party member but not ideologue.
93 Leiper, *The Church–State Struggle*, 13.
94 PS 29 Aug., 3.

95 WA Minorities Commission, Fanø, 24–30 Aug. 1934, UCCLW.212.008.
96 Sally Coey to Parkes, 26 Apr. 1934, PP60/17/8/1.
97 The ISS refugee committee headed by Parkes included Kotschnig, Tatlow, appointees from France, England, United States and the World Union of Jewish Students; for *JTA* coverage, 3 May, 13 Aug. 1933; 17, 26 Mar. 1934.
98 Parkes's concern about joining the permanent staff was that the high salary of the HC was paid from refugee funds; see James McDonald, *Advocate for the Doomed: Diaries and Papers of James G. McDonald, 1932–1935*, ed. Richard Breitman, Barbara McDonald Stewart and Severin Hochberg (Bloomington: Indiana University Press and USHMM, 2007), 134, 143, 146–7, 198, 213, 215. Greg Burgess, *The League of Nations and the Refugees from Nazi Germany* (London: Bloomsbury Academic, 2018), 75, 191, n.28, credits Parkes with instigating a voluntary change in McDonald's salary.
99 For press on the Bavarian conference, *JTA*, 15, 24, 31 May; for ISS withdrawal, *JTA*, 13 Aug., *Manchester Guardian*, 18 Aug. 1934.
100 For Geneva letters on police occupation of Parkes's flat, attempted murder, injury, medical treatment, judge and articles from more than 25 newspapers, PP60/31/28.
101 James Parkes, *The Conflict of the Church and the Synagogue: A Study in the Origins of Antisemitism* (London: Soncino Press, Oct. 1934), esp. 33, 42–3, 95, 160–1.
102 Ibid., 375–6.
103 'Address by Dr Conrad Hoffmann', *Jewish Missionary Intelligence* (Jul. 1935), 76–7, published in abbreviated form.
104 Ibid.
105 Hoffmann, 'A Survey, Report and Forecast, 1930–35', delivered in London, 10–13 July, in New York, 25–26 Sept. 1935, IMC.261203.
106 Ibid., 3–14; for example of provocations, 'Jewry's failure or deliberate refusal to acknowledge any guilt on the part of even certain German Jews for provoking anti-Semitism'; 'the "chosen people" include the uncouth, unscrupulous ... underselling neighbour who causes real estate values to depreciate and threatens the business man's existence', 8, 28.
107 Ibid., 14, ital. add.; for other 'leavening the mass of Jewry', 11, 25, 27.
108 Hoffmann, DR, 4–5, 7–10, 14, 31; ICCAJ min., 10–13 July 1935, esp. 8, 10, 11; summary discussion, 1, 3; reports from Romania and Switzerland, IMC.261203.
109 *CATJ* (1927), 19, 38–9.

110 Hoffmann, DR Mar. 1931, 21–2, 26; ICCAJ min., 13–14 June 1932; DR Jul. 1935, 6, 19; ICCAJ min., 10–12 Jul. 1935; Forgács, 'Reformed Church of Hungary'; IMC.261202, 261203, 261205.
111 High Commission Report, 17 Jul. 1935, 11.
112 Webster, *IRM*, 1918 and 1925.
113 Anglican Bishop of Jerusalem MacInnes to ICCAJ, 27 Dec. 1929, IMC.261230.
114 High Commission Report, 9–15; Hoffmann, DR Jul. 1935, 10–12.
115 Ibid., see also Hoffmann, DR 1936, 2; IMC.261203.
116 Parkes Cadman, 'Germany's Christian non-Aryans', add.7d, Jul. 1935, IMC.261203.
117 Hoffmann, 'Confidential report concerning the condition of non-Aryans in Germany', 1 Sept. 1935, WCC.42.0038.
118 DR, July 1935, 28; Henriod, confid., 2–5 June 1936, citing a report from Adolf Keller, WCC.301.4307.
119 McDonald letter of resignation to League of Nations, 27 Dec. 1935, Ann., 3, 33.
120 Karl Schleunes, *The Twisted Road to Auschwitz* (Urbana: University of Illinois, 1990), 21, 92–132; *Legislating the Holocaust* (Boulder: Westview Press, 2001), 153–80.
121 Hoffmann's claim of 2–3 million non-Aryan Christians can be compared to McDonald's 'tens of thousands' in his letter of resignation. Figures from the Reich Interior Ministry in April 1935 showed 'non-Aryans to be 2.3 percent of the German population', 'Religious Jews' (475,000), 'Jews not of the Jewish faith' (300,000), Mischlinge 1st and 2nd degrees (750,000), re Doris Bergen, *Twisted Cross* (Chapel Hill: University of North Carolina Press, 1996), 83–4. The 1936 assessment of Rudolf Hess was that 4–500,000 fit the legal concept of 'Jew' and 300,000 the concept 'Jewish Mischling', Schleunes, *The Twisted Road*, 128–9.
122 ICCAJ min., July 1935, 11; Hoffmann to ICCAJ, 19 Feb. 1936; correspondence with van Nes, Pernow, Sloan and others, Jan.–Apr.; ICCAJ min., 28–29 Apr.; Hoffmann to comm., 15 Jul. 1936; WCC.261202, 261203, 261204.
123 UCCLW min., Chamby, 21–25 Aug. 1936, appointments, 59–60, WCC.212.008.
124 The Reich church delegation was made up of General Superintendent Zoellner, Bishop Heckel, Professor F. Brunstäd, Dr H. Wahl; Confessing delegation was Karl Koch, Otto Dibelius, H. Böhm and Bonhoeffer; Dr Hanns Lilje represented Lutherans; also from Germany were Dr E. Stange and Professors Deissmann and M. Dibelius, heads of the Oxford theologian commission.

125 UCCLW min., Chamby, 67–68; Bell to Eidem, 8 Sept. 1936, also in Boyens (1967), 343–6.
126 Ibid., min., 67–9.
127 Ibid., also admin. min., 20–25 Aug. 1936, 4–5, WCC.212.008.
128 Ibid., 68; 5.
129 Oldham to Hoffmann, 17 Sept.; Oldham to ten Boom, 18 Sept.; Hoffmann to Oldham, 28 Sept.; Hoffmann to Graham-Brown, 29 Sept.; NAICCAJ min., 29 Sept.; Hoffmann to ICCAJ comm., 17 Nov; IMC. 261201, 261203.
130 Hoffmann to ten Boom, Danby and others, 13 Nov.; 1, 4, 30 Dec. 1936; IMC. 261203.
131 Schleunes, *The Twisted Road to Auschwitz*, 92–132, and *Legislating the Holocaust*, 153–80; for more on cultural ministries, Sylwia Grochowina and Kątarzyna Kącka, 'Foundations of Nazi Cultural Policy and Institutions Responsible for its Implementation in the Period 1933–1939', *Kultura i Edukacja* 6 (2014), 173–92.
132 By 1940 there were six Nazi institutes in Germany, and by 1944 eleven more in occupied Poland (Cracow, Lodz), France (Bordeaux, Paris, 2), Italy (Ancona, Milan, Florence, Triest, Bologna), Hungary (Budapest). See Max Weinreich, *Hitler's Professors* (New York: YIVO, 1946); Patricia Papen-Bodek, 'Scholarly Antisemitism During the Third Reich', PhD, Columbia University, 1999; Alan Steinweis, *Studying the Jew* (Cambridge: Harvard University Press, 2006); Susannah Heschel, *The Aryan Jesus* (Princeton: Princeton University Press, 2008).
133 Hoffmann to Kohnstamm, 23 Feb. 1937, WCC.261203, ital. add.

3

Antisemitism, refugees and war: 1937–1939

Antisemitism on the Vienna stage

What had begun in 1935 as a collaboration with UCCLW on antisemitism became instead a fortuitous opportunity for ICCAJ to consult the 1937 Oxford conference that would usher in the World Council of Churches (WCC). When the awaited study was unveiled in Vienna between 28 June and 2 July 1937, ten days before Oxford convened, ICCAJ was described in a publicity report as being made up of 'men whose day to day lives were spent in wrestling with human distress and destitution in their bitterest form'.[1] The sixty-eight Protestant conferees, eight of whom were actually women, included fifty-seven from the Netherlands, Denmark, Norway, Sweden, England, Ireland, Scotland, Switzerland, Germany, Czechoslovakia, Austria, Poland, Hungary, Romania; seven from the United States and Canada; four from Palestine and Syria.[2] The commission orchestrating the study was chaired by Dr Willem ten Boom, a Dutch Reformed pastor who posthumously acquired fame as brother or son to Corrie, Elizabeth and Casper ten Boom, all of whom were named Righteous Among the Nations in the decades after the Holocaust.[3]

Ten Boom, who was secretary of the Central Bureau of Jewish Missionary Societies in Holland, had earned a doctorate at University of Leipzig for his dissertation on racial antisemitism.[4] His Dutch Reformed colleague, Philip Kohnstamm, a physicist by training and Extraordinary Professor of Pedagogy at University of Utrecht, was a gifted academic who would come to be known as founder of empirical educational science in the Netherlands. As a socialist-leaning intellectual of German-Jewish heritage who had been raised agnostically, he had joined the Reformed church in 1914 at the age of 42 and subsequently published in the postwar period on antisemitism, secularisation and the spiritual dangers of National Socialism.[5] The other half of the commission – William Paton and Conrad Hoffmann – was charged with oversight of both the study and the conference.

A first critical point is that there was nothing simple about the multilayered study, its process of drafting, the beliefs informing it or the statement unanimously adopted after its deliberation. The underlying perspective was that the issue of antisemitism and the Church was of such complexity that its description required 'as a presupposition hardly less than a complete theology, anthropology and sociology', as well as 'partners in discussion' who were familiar with its assumptions.[6] The materials collected for the study were thus largely based on commonly held understandings of views already in play in the ICCAJ milieu. Twenty-five country reports on Jewish missions and the socio-cultural aspects of antisemitism were solicited from associates in Great Britain, Austria, Belgium, Czechoslovakia, Denmark, Egypt, Finland, Germany, Greece, Hungary, Italy, Netherlands, Norway, Palestine, Poland, Portugal, Romania, South Africa, South America, Spain, Sweden, Switzerland, United States and Syria. While the data did not appear per se in the study, it was used interpretively as evidence of increasing antisemitism and its dangers to the Church.[7] A manuscript, informed by these and other select materials, was drafted by ten Boom and Kohnstamm, then circulated to associates in Austria, Poland, Romania, England and the United States for discussion and comment. The final version, which was edited and presented by Kohnstamm, was a thirty-one-page paper with seventy-three pages of appendices, one acknowledged as a resolution of diverging opinions.[8]

The contours of 'The Church of Jesus Christ and Antisemitism in the Age of Secularization' were shaped in two strategic ways to support, legitimise and advance the socio-theological needs for Jewish conversion. First, it argued on cultural grounds that 'the question of the secularized Jews must be placed at the centre' of considerations for decades to come.[9] The presumption for the claim was that natural enmity between unlike peoples was common, but three 'extenuating' factors had increased historical discord between Jews and non-Jews. (i) The 'destiny' and 'chosenness' of the Jewish people created a socio-cultural friction 'to an extent unparalleled' in the world; (ii) friction was added by Jewish 'peculiarities' that made Jews 'different';[10] and (iii) Jewish emancipation brought with it 'the first time in history' that persecution was directed against 'secularized' rather than religious Jews. Here, in reference to the 'secularized' factor, an appended paper by Hoffmann was invoked which effectually incorporated his racial-identity theory into the study. Citing 'facts' about antisemitism in America, the argument was repeated that Jews demanded full equality while insisting on the right to remain different, but that the difference demanded was increasingly based on race and nation. The take-away claim from this part of the study was that the racially and nationally conscious Jews in the United States had 'ceased to be' a religious community, and the situation was 'not so very different in West and Central Europe'.[11]

The theological contours of the study built on these cultural 'facts' by way of a Catholic document emanating from Vienna. By far the weightiest of the appended materials, it made its way into the study through the Delitzschianum, which had been transferred from Leipzig to Vienna by Dr Hans Kosmala in December 1935. ICCAJ member Kosmala became the Hebrew instructor of Fr Johannes Oesterreicher, a Catholic priest of Jewish descent whose Vienna activities had been followed by ICCAJ since 1934. Oesterreicher was co-founder of the Jewish mission Pauluswerk and publisher of its bi-monthly journal, *Die Erfüllung*.[12] At the time of his Hebrew instruction in the fall and winter of 1936, he and Catholic colleagues were developing a treatise on the Jewish question while Kosmala was collaborating on the ICCAJ study. When 'The Church of Christ and the Jewish Question' appeared in Oesterreicher's journal in February 1937, it carried the support of fourteen Catholic signatories from eight European nations, as well as 'outstanding religious and noted Catholic political leaders' who chose to remain anonymous for reasons of safety.[13] By choosing to append the treatise to the ICCAJ study, the Vienna commission was calling upon the weight of that concurrence. The other part of the decision was based on the belief that it presented a model of the gospel that treated the 'whole subject' of antisemitism from the 'same standpoint' as ICCAJ.[14]

On this landscape of theological agreement, the Vienna study pointed to the 'deeper' theological significance of Nazi racial antisemitism while quoting liberally from the Catholic document. As a religion, and more precisely a neo-pagan 'racial heresy', Nazi racial antisemitism was seen as 'the deadly enemy' of the Church, threatening 'to rend in pieces the mystic body of Christ'.[15] Referring to racial antisemitism alternately as a 'struggle against the true Israel' and a 'bitter life and death struggle against everything that first took visible form in Israel', the study went on to argue that it was thus only 'natural' that it would be 'directed not only against the *true* Israel, but also against the Israel which has fallen from God'.[16]

It is crucial to recognise the *reversal* of focus and conceptual transformation taking place here. Christianity, the 'true Israel', was being posited as the central object of antisemitism, while 'fallen Israel' was relegated to an 'also' secondary object. The way in which the significance of 'fallen' Israel' was being framed is also crucial, for the argument of both documents was that the Church had never forsaken 'belief in the final and indissoluble election of Israel'. Yet this theologically important claim was not in any way a denial of supersessionist belief about Israel's divinely imposed suffering. It was rather a theological clarification about the reason for the 'terrible tribulations' that 'must come over Israel'. Both treatises refuted claims about the eternal damnation of Jews by arguing that their divinely imposed suffering signified instead that God was pleading 'to win His people'.[17] Moreover, the more that 'fallen Israel' opposed God's pleading to become part of the 'true Israel', the 'fiercer' the pleading became.

> For this reason one may see in the terrible events in Central Europe since 1933 not only a warning of God to His people, without however trying to condone them in the least, but a warning, too, to a Christendom grown indifferent ... . No one can approach the Jewish question of our day without disappointment and sorrow that by and large Judaism did not see in the persecutions of recent years ... a reason for self-examination and conversion to God *and* His anointed.[18]

Not only was there no remitting of 'fallen Israel's' divine suffering in this shared theological position, Nazi persecution of Jews since 1933 was predicated as somehow being part of God's 'pleading'. While this was not an everyday showcased feature of ICCAJ argumentation, it was not a stranger either. It had appeared at the 1932 constitutional meeting in London, where antisemitism was explained as an anti-Christian force used as 'God's scourge' until Jews turned to Christ.[19] Other variations circulating in the milieu included one by Martin Niemöller of the Confessing church, which was being published and promoted by ecumenical leaders in a collection of sermons 'destined to take their place with the Theses of Martin Luther'. There, he invoked 'God's curse' of Jewish suffering as 'the unforgiven blood-guilt' for the crucifixion, going so far as to equate the racial emphasis that caused Jews to become the object of 'God's curse' with Nazism's 'Positive Christianity'.[20] This of course was in line with Hoffmann's equation of modern Jewry's racial emphasis with that of Hitler, a claim being made by other ecumenists as well. Bishop Ammundsen, vice-chair of UCCLW, for one, had noted in a private session at Fanø that the Jewish national religion 'was in principle the same thing as national socialism',[21] and Professor Willy Staerk at Jena, member of the Confessing church and ICCAJ (1932–1935), equated Judaism with Nazism while positing both as 'narrow-minded nationalism exalted to a political religion'.[22] Charles Clayton Morrison, editor of *Christian Century* and delegate to the upcoming UCCLW conference at Oxford, was another, arguing in two editorials in June 1937 that the Jewish 'idea of an integral race with its own exclusive culture' was 'the prototype of Nazism'.[23]

Yet another version was appended to the Vienna study by Willem ten Boom, soon to be vice-chair of the executive ICCAJ. In language that should be explained but not explained away, his 'Eight Propositions on Anti-Semitism' presented 'Jews as a "King nation" ... sore beset by demons', an insider expression meant to reveal the 'high calling' of fallen Israel, as well as the belief that it would be raised to its divine destiny through conversion. For ten Boom, and those advancing his theses, 'fallen' Israel's divine calling to Christian destiny was refutation of racial antisemitism and its claims about the unchangeable nature of Jews. By opening his 'Propositions' this way, he also revealed an accepted distinction between racial and non-racial accusations against Jews by asserting that antisemitism of the non-racial type was 'fully justified in so far as it distinguishes Jewish failings by name'.[24]

Once these distinctions were in place, ten Boom pointed to the 'Pharisaism' that had allegedly turned Israel into 'an arrogant people craving power', an attribute defined as a naturalistic 'universal urge' toward imperialism. Warning that this 'very Jewish universal impulse' was at its most dangerous when following 'secularist channels', he argued against the Zionism that made the 'biological pride' of modern Jewry the rallying point 'of its national policy'.[25] Having previously identified 'naturalism' as the 'universal impulse' in Zionism, nationalism, secularism and racial antisemitism, he argued in a second conference paper that Zionism and racial antisemitism were branches of the same universal thirst for power.[26] Ten Boom's conclusion in the 'Eight Propositions' was much the same, namely that racial antisemitism and secularist Zionism operated from the same nationalistic ideals.[27]

To line up these ideas informing the Vienna study is to stand faced with a powerful set of transnationally shared beliefs about the place and role of Jews in world society. First, 'the Jews' were implicated culturally as a provoking irritant. Second, the alleged secularised racial-national emphases of modern Jewry was equated in varying ways with the racial emphases of Nazism. Third, 'the Jews' were implicated theologically as under the 'suffering' judgment of God and subjected to antisemitic persecution. Indeed, as framed by Kohnstamm, conversion of 'millions of secularized Jews' was the only way to turn the tide of antisemitic backlash, for a people in possession of 'nothing but Zionism or Socialism' could not go on existing without provoking 'such horrible hostility'.[28]

Yet in a sweep of conversionary benevolence the ICCAJ study emphasised the need to seek God's mercy for Jews rather than stressing 'His blood be on us and on our children'. It was a summary way of affirming the infrangible election of 'fallen' Israel while insisting that God's continual pleading to Jews was necessarily related to the command to bring Israel to its destiny. In this way, so it was argued, the Christian duty to combat antisemitism was 'inextricably linked' to the divine call to Jewish missions and, to such a degree, that 'the two problems' were inseparable. At the deepest theological level it also meant that the duty of combating racial antisemitism was indivisibly tied to defending Christianity against the racial heresy targeting the 'true Israel'.[29]

This was made strikingly clear in the unanimous Vienna resolution by sixty-eight delegates from eighteen nations. First, it established that among forms of persecution and hatred the one being most vigorously protested was the one that created 'more crucial issues for Christianity':

> We desire to record our conviction that in contemporary anti-Semitism we face an extraordinary menace against which all Christians must be warned. All forms of hatred and persecution must be deplored by Christians, and their victims must be succoured; but there exists today a type of racial anti-Semitism and anti-Semitic propaganda inspired by hatred of everything springing from Jewish sources; and this creates more crucial issues for Christianity than ordinary outbursts of race feeling.[30]

Second, it defined the 'type' of racism causing the 'more crucial issues' for the Church as one that masked its anti-Christ nature:

> Realising that enmity to the Jews has now become a cloak for the forces of anti-Christ, and conceals hatred for Christ and His Gospel, the Christian Church must reject anti-Semitism with complete conviction.[31]

Third, reasons for warning Christians of its dangers were complementary to this understanding, for both silence *about* and involvement *in* antisemitism were held as acts of personal agency in undermining the Church, and both carried the penalty of God's severe judgment:

> Christian churches must be warned that they cannot be silent in the presence of this propaganda, still less connive at or participate in the extension of its errors and falsehoods, *without* betraying Christ, undermining the basis of the Church, and incurring the most severe judgment of God.[32]

Fourth, it warned of the 'potential danger for all mankind'. Racial antisemitism advanced 'theories regarding the value or non-value of different peoples or racial groups', it denied and abrogated 'human rights and privileges', and distorted 'prevailing ethical concepts and principles.[33]

What was missing from the resolution were the dangers of racial antisemitism to Jews themselves. Dangers were either particularised as relevant to the Church, or universalised as relevant to 'all mankind', while Jews were at best implied as being part of humanity. Indeed, beyond stressing that this 'type' of racism was 'inspired by everything springing from Jewish sources' and that 'enmity to the Jews' was 'a cloak for the forces of anti-Christ', Jews were not mentioned at all except in the context of Jewish missions, and there Jews were named three times:

> To realize its true nature and to vindicate its right to the title of the 'Body of Christ', the Church must preach the Gospel and open its fellowship to men of all races, including *Jews*. Our mission to the *Jews* cannot consistently be carried on without at the same time combating anti-Semitism among Christians, and giving more tangible evidence than has yet been given of our sympathy with *Jews* and Hebrew Christians in their present distress.[34]

While the Vienna resolution was clearly a vigorous repudiation of racial antisemitism, it is important to recognise that its series of denunciations were *foremostly* concerned with defence, preservation and advancement of the Church. This first use of the term 'antisemitism' in an official ICCAJ statement was forceful in asserting that Christianity had to reject racial antisemitism 'with complete conviction', but it was equally strong in urging that the combating of racial antisemitism was an act of defending the Church and vindicating the title of the Body of Christ. The statement was clear that the form of racism causing the 'more crucial issues for Christianity' was not just a conflicting ideology. The anti-Christian heresy of racial antisemitism was understood as a fully felt threat to the Church, and it was more fully felt the more it was recognised that it was nesting in the churches.[35]

All of this was driven home in the official letter to the UCCLW Oxford conference that accompanied the Vienna resolution. It summarised the problem that racial antisemitism posed to the Church in three broad strokes. First, racial antisemitism constituted 'one of the principal denials in modern life of the Christian doctrine of man'. Second, while acknowledging that the 'human misery' created for its objects was 'difficult to estimate', it asserted that the *'graver'* problem was 'the poisoning of the spirit, the drying of sympathy and warping of judgment' in those under its 'influence'. Third, having entered the Church from without, racial antisemitism worked as 'an evil within' and wherever it manifested Christianity no longer existed 'except in vain form'.[36]

On these grounds the Vienna conference asked the Oxford conference 'to do two things', and two things only. First, recognising that it could 'make its voice heard widely among churches of all lands', it 'begged' the Oxford conference 'to speak out clearly on the dangers of anti-Semitism to the Church *itself* and to recognise openly the total impossibility of a Church tainted with this form of racial absolutism bearing any valid witness to the word of God in the world'.[37]

The second had to do with protecting the turf that had been so arduously groomed over the ten years since the Budapest–Warsaw conferences. ICCAJ's self-image, and the one it wished to imprint upon the Oxford conference, was that it was something new and distinct from centuries of failed attempts to Christianise Jews. It thus offered its expertise, knowledge and abilities should antisemitism be included in any further study on 'the great problems that confront the Church in the modern world'.[38]

As a way of fortifying that image in the period before Oxford, ICCAJ publicity reports hailed the fact that 'unlike many conferences' it had 'its own permanent secretaries and regional groups who are able to take up matters and carry them through to the stage of action'. The point emphasised was that ICCAJ was capable of locating itself in the centre of problems to be dealt with, just as it had located its conference in Vienna, where it was 'in closer touch, so to speak, with the Jewish problems of Poland, Germany and the eastern countries of Europe'.[39]

Racial antisemitism at Oxford

When the Oxford assembly convened ten days later on 12 July 1937, according to a direct radio broadcast, the medieval British streets were filled with the 'drama' of a Church stacking itself up 'against a world of war and preparations for war, economic injustice, racial persecution and national bigotry'.[40] There was also pomp and continuity as the event was hailed as successor to the 1925 Stockholm conference that launched into existence the first centralising body of the ecumenical movement. With nearly a thousand in attendance from mainstream Protestant and Orthodox bodies in forty-five countries – 'every major communion in Christendom' and 'more of the Christian Church than have thought or acted together for half a millennium' – it was widely proclaimed as the 'most representative and carefully prepared church council of modern times', even though the German Evangelical and Roman Catholic churches were missing from the line-up.[41]

Yet Oxford was understood as something far greater. In the opening address, Archbishop of Canterbury Cosmo Lang proclaimed it a 'wholly new fact in Christian history'. The point repeated throughout the two weeks of meetings was that the historic event, evolving as it had since 1925, was manifestation of a unified Christian body transcending all 'barriers of race and nationality'. By the closing day of the conference a critical distinction between ecumenism and internationalism had been captured: 'international' pointed to mankind's division into separate nations, while 'ecumenical' began 'with the fact of unity in Christ'. The Christian Church was international in so far as it operated in a divided world, but it was ecumenical where Christians worked together to manifest the supranational, supraracial, supra-denominational essence of the *Una Sancta*. Everything in the official Oxford report was understood as fitting within these parameters.[42]

The first aim of the conference was to expand the idea of unity recognised in the 1930 Nobel Peace Prize to late Archbishop Söderblom for advancing national brotherhood through the creation of UCCLW. The second was to see what could be achieved through his vision of the Council as a Christian 'mouthpiece' on social issues bearing on the 'Christian understanding of life'. The idea was not that every jot and tittle had to be agreed but, rather, what a large body of diverse Christians could 'say *together*' on the most crucial issues of Church, Community and State.[43] Nearly three years of planning and research had preceded under the direction of Joseph Oldham, a feat involving as many as 300–400 scholars, 250 study papers, and innumerable drafts in English, German and French.[44] Key issues had been worked into memoranda by committee chairmen and delivered as a pre-conference package to the 425 main delegates assigned by choice to one of five committees. Each committee was tasked with the development of a specified report, and each was debated in plenary sessions under the gavel of John Mott. The final versions in the Oxford volume were understood as a compendium of well-sieved ecumenical thinking at a time in history when Christianity was in a 'life and death struggle' with advancing secular ideologies and world forces.[45]

Antisemitism was not among the topics of Oxford research. All possibility of its inclusion had been removed when Oldham bowed out of the joint study with ICCAJ in September 1936, but the withdrawal did not preclude its introduction by ICCAJ. Oxford delegate Professor Walter Horton, an acclaimed theologian of Oberlin College and member of NAICCAJ, presented the Vienna statement, and William Paton, general secretary of IMC, *ex officio* of ICCAJ and an Oxford officer, argued its case. By the time the latter took the podium on the third day, the plenary assembly had already heard a 'burning and searching' paper on racial discrimination against 'coloured peoples' in the churches. Paton followed by enjoining the assembly to consider 'the terrible relevance of the Jewish problem', emphasising that Jewish converts were also subjects of racial bias in the churches.

The case being argued in both addresses had to do with racial barriers between Christians *and* Christians *in* the Church rather than with people of colour or Jewish descent *outside* the Church. In treating antisemitism as a type of racism, Paton thus focused on the dangers of racism to the Church itself. His universalist argument was simple but powerful. The presence of discrimination within the body of Christ not only eclipsed Christianity's claims of universality, it emptied them to the point of extinguishing Christianity. Conversely, the universalism at the core of the Church placed it in the frontline of battle wherever attempts were made to raise racial or national barriers within the body of Christ.[46]

Viewed in this light, and it was indeed the light in which it was viewed at Oxford, antisemitism was weighed and measured as a form of the broader category of 'racism'. What was deliberated and agreed by the Oxford delegates constituted a strong universalist refutation of racism. Although what was said was contextually woven into various reports, there was a clear synthesis of thought on race and nation, and it significantly emanated from four of the five committees as well as the conference message.[47]

Three points were repeatedly brought to the fore in these contexts: the divine gift of race and nations; the sins of racial and national pride; and the Christian duty to be 'the leaven' by which Christ transformed society and nations. In brief, the synthesis entailed that racial and national distinctions were part of God's plan for enrichment of the world, that all races and nations shared equally in God's love and compassion, and that all were created with the divine intention of becoming part of the supraracial supranational Body of Christ.[48] The discussion at issue was thus not simply that all races and nations were equal parts of a humanity but, rather, that all races and nations were equal parts of a humanity created by God to come together in the Christian Church. The overarching and repeated concern was that racism in any form denied and thwarted the universality and hence missionary purpose of the Church.[49]

In terms of existing racial problems and the work of repair, the Oxford list was long. As citizens of world society and members of the universal body, each Christian was to bear responsibility for applying Christian principles to the solution of racial issues. In the civic realm, Christians had to ensure that public policies recognised and protected the value of each human being by way of rights to the essential conditions of life. In the spiritual realm, Christians were to cultivate the mind of Christ toward other races while acting corporately with the Church to resist and refute racism. In the moral realm, the Church had to call members to repent and 'confess their share in the common guilt of mankind' for any 'pride of race or nation' that created or embittered racial and national divisions in the past or present.[50] The three areas of responsibility were linked by the Christian duty to proclaim 'that the disintegration of society had one fundamental cause' and one remedy, namely, separation from God and reconciliation in Christ.[51] The Church was said to be 'under obligation' to never lose sight of that commission and, as such, all members of the supraracial and supranational body were to manifest 'costly concern for the outcast, the underprivileged, the persecuted and the despised'.[52]

All refutations of antisemitism, as a form of racism, were framed in this overarching context of the universal Church and its divine commission. In order of appearance in the conference volume, the first captured clearly that antisemitism was understood as a part of the larger problem of racism (a sub-category in parenthesis), and that racism was a major symptom of the greater problem of disintegrating society:

> The recrudescence of pitiless cruelty, hatreds and race discriminations (including anti-Semitism) in the modern world is one of the major signs of its social disintegration. To these must be brought not the weak rebuke of words but the powerful rebuke of deeds.[53]

The second came from the committee that formed the Oxford distinction between ecumenical and international, which included Paton, Horton and others associated in varying degrees with ICCAJ. Here, antisemitism as a type of racial division was repudiated from the standpoint of harming the ecumenicity of the universal Church:[54]

> The church dishonors its claim to ecumenical reality if it allows, even under the pressure of ... great and genuine difficulty, the presence of racial barriers within it. We call attention here to the acceptance of the color bar in certain churches and to the more widely diffused and less acknowledged evil of anti-Semitism, whereby not only have terrible sufferings been imposed upon the Jews by states historically Christian, but membership within the church denied or made difficult to those of the race to which our Lord belonged after the flesh.[55]

The third repudiation appeared in a list of ways in which the universal Church bore 'the heaviest guilt' and therefore had the 'greatest obligation' to transcend racial boundaries by making its anti-racial position clear to those both inside and outside the Church:

> Against racial pride, racial hatreds and persecutions and exploitation of other races in all their forms, the church is called by God to set its face implacably and to utter its word unequivocally both within and without its own borders. There is special need at this time that the

church throughout the world bring every resource at its command against the sin of anti-Semitism.[56]

While each of the three repudiations is of great significance, the last, with its presentation of racial antisemitism as a form of 'racial pride', was of great consequence in more than one way. The same wording in the first sentence, without reference to antisemitism, appeared in two other places and, additionally, 'racial pride' was coupled with 'national pride' and protested vigorously throughout the volume.[57] *All* forms of racial and national pride, egotism, superiority or deification of race and nation were disavowed as 'rebellion against God', as 'sin against the creator of all peoples', as 'idolatry' that led to 'increasing division and disaster'.[58] *All* attributions of 'divine status' or 'saving revelation' to one's own nation were refuted as 'utterly sinful', 'anti-Christian', and 'alien to the heart of the gospel'. *All* racisms and nationalisms were condemned as pseudo-religious components of the secularism that was causing disintegration of society – and *all* were to be 'irreconcilably opposed' by both individual consciences and the Church.[59]

This overall excoriation of racial and national pride added immeasurable weight to the Oxford protests against racial and national 'abuses' including that of racial antisemitism, but it must not go unrecognised that what was being excoriated applied equally to all. What was said about one race and nation, *ipso facto*, was being said about all others, such that protests against racial and national pride applied as much to Jewish nationalism as to German, Russian, Italian or Hungarian. The distinction is subtle but crucial, for the repudiations of racial and national abuses echoed many of the same claims that Conrad Hoffmann and other Protestant figures argued about the racial and national emphases of modern Jewry. Indeed, setting the face of the Church 'implacably' against modern Jewry's racial and national pride, as rebellion against God, was precisely what Hoffmann's racial-identity theory claimed to be doing.

While there were *no* such recorded claims at Oxford, there was broad transnational agreement on racial and national abuses and, in that critical sense, the Oxford excoriations of racial and national pride inadvertently revealed how they could *also* be used as support for transnational equations between modern Jewry and Nazism, such as those made openly by ICCAJ director Hoffmann, Bishop Ammundsen at Fanø, Niemöller in his 1937 published sermon, ten Boom in Vienna, and Oxford delegate Charles Morrison in *Christian Century* editorials, immediately before the conference convened.[60]

Restructure, antisemitism and non-Aryan refugees

If awareness of ICCAJ was raised at Oxford by Paton's plenary address on the Vienna resolution, it was enhanced even more by the restructuring of the ecumenical movement that the conference launched. Coined as a 'wholly new fact in Christian history', Oxford lived up to its image by ushering in the World Council of Churches in Formation (WCCIF). It was unanimously agreed that the two main ecumenical bodies concerned with the churches – UCCLW with social issues, WCFO with doctrine and worship – be merged into one body in order to 'facilitate more effective action of the Christian church in the modern world'.[61] Nine days after Oxford, WCFO stamped its own official seal at a parallel conference in Edinburgh. The constitutional drafting at Utrecht in May 1938 and its September ratification by WCFO joined the two councils into the World Council of Churches in Formation, which was to be housed in the same Geneva headquarters as the subsumed UCCLW.

What this meant in practical terms was that the same ecumenical leaders were moved into more complex and cross-linked roles with a significant shift in general secretariat power. Prior to Oxford, Henriod was general secretary of both UCCLW and the World Alliance, Visser 't Hooft was general secretary of WSCF, and Paton was general secretary of IMC and *ex officio* of ICCAJ. After restructuring, Henriod was left with the World Alliance, Visser 't Hooft was head of the WCCIF secretariat in Geneva, and Paton was co-general secretary in London as well as general secretary of IMC and *ex officio* of ICCAJ. To this, Henry Leiper of FCC was added as WCCIF associate secretary in America.

The European link between Paton and Visser 't Hooft was tightened when IMC and WCCIF took a first formal step toward collaboration on mutual concerns in December 1938. The following month Paton was made secretary of a new WCCIF-IMC Joint Committee under the chairmanship of John Mott, who was one of three vice-chairs of WCCIF as well as chair of IMC and *ex officio* of ICCAJ. While Paton remained based in London and Visser 't Hooft in Geneva, their cross-linked roles resulted in a mutually dependent and powerful relationship of multidirectional influence, one that moved the social issue and conversionary arms of the movement into closer proximities.

ICCAJ was undergoing changes as well, which brought Paton's position in the WCCIF structure not only in closer proximity but more central to ICCAJ planning and operations. In September 1937 Hoffmann was made head of Jewish Evangelization for the Presbyterian Board of National Missions in America. The plan was for him to remain director, increasing ICCAJ presence in America, but spend just three months a year in Europe. Dr Erwin Reisner, a German-Viennese advocate of the Confessing church, was nominated by Paton as associate director to bridge the nine-month gap. Concurrent with his appointment was the creation of an international committee on Jewish mission literature, whose main centre was to be in Vienna, with field offices in London, New York and Palestine. The decision to capitalise on ICCAJ's presence in Vienna was understood as a logical step of representative development in Europe. Of the twenty-three European nations associated with ICCAJ (Figure 3.1), the overwhelming majority of the mission resources were already being directed from west to east by 'sending' agencies in the United Kingdom, Scandinavia and Switzerland (Figure 3.1).

The Vienna office would centralise ICCAJ's presence on the Continent while emphasing expansion among the world's largest concentration of Jews in eastern Europe. It would work in conjunction with Hans Kosmala's Delitzschianum, which, like Reisner, was housed at the Swedish Mission to Israel. Within this web of associations, the Swedish mission was under the leadership of Birger Pernow in Stockholm, who with Willem ten Boom was the new co-vice-chair of the international ICCAJ. Kosmala was part of Reisner's international literature committee, as was Kenneth Grubb in London, and in turn Paton, Kosmala and Hoffmann were part

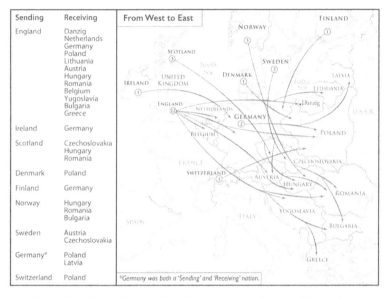

Figure 3.1 From West to East: European 'sending' and 'receiving' missionary nations

of Grubb's advisory team for a 'World Survey on Jewry and the Church', which was to be published in 1939.

Reisner's role as associate director in all of this underlines the fluidity with which ICCAJ principals moved in and among mainstream European Protestant circles. This was made clear in November 1937 in a report of his five-week itinerary in Czechoslovakia, Germany, Holland and Switzerland, which included arranged lectures in Prague, Berlin, Hamburg, Amsterdam and Basel, with additional meetings in each place as well as in Leipzig, Munich, Heidelberg, Rotterdam, Utrecht and Geneva. Among his discussants were Scotsman Robert Smith in Prague, who studied at Tübingen with Gerhard Kittel and translated his 1933 lecture on 'The Jewish Question' into English; Julius Richter in Berlin; Confessing church pastors and associates of Martin Niemöller at the home of Hans Asmussen; Hermann Maas in Heidelberg; Henriod and Keller in Geneva; ten Boom, Kohnstamm and van Neys in Holland; Karl Barth, K.L. Schmidt, Fritz Lieb and Adolf Köberle at University of Basel.[62]

The private and confidential, but well-circulated, report of his itinerary discussions included assessment of the most pressing issues facing ICCAJ in the two and a half-year wake of the Nuremberg Laws. The most 'urgent question' for Jewish missions was said to be the fate of non-Aryan Christians, but the 'most pressing danger' was seen as stemming from Jewish converts themselves. What was termed 'Hebrew Christian particularism' – a brew of Zionism, nationalism and legalism among converts who insisted on Jewish identity and 'Jewish' interpretation of Christian scriptures – was said to be gaining dominance in the Hebrew Christian church.[63] For Reisner, this was nothing less than 'the entry of false and ominous Jewish ideas … into the Church', and it had to be vigorously opposed, for wherever such emphasis existed, 'Jewish nationalism', the same in essence as German National Socialism, was lurking.[64] The 'danger' of bringing such converts into the Church had to be guarded against as a 'far more important' principle than bringing numbers of Jews to baptism. Such warnings were a critical part of his broader argument that 'the conversion of Israel is the work of God', and that suffering and powerlessness is a 'necessary condition' of 'real conversion'.[65]

Reisner's arguments for relations between powerless suffering and conversion were more emotively stated in a letter to Conrad Hoffmann four months later when Germany annexed Austria and began systematically excluding Jews under its harsh *Judenfrei* policy. Although clearly disturbed by the brutality with which Jews were being 'molested' in the wake of the *Anschluss*, Reisner nevertheless argued that God was 'quite openly' aiming at 'conversion of the whole people' and had thus 'permitted anti-Semitism among the races'. All earlier human attempts to bring salvation to the Jews now seemed 'laughable in the face of the elemental power of the present happenings'.[66]

One week after Reisner's appraisal of what was happening to Viennese Jews, he himself, an officer in the artillery reserve and 'a loyal German' who approved of the *Anschluss* while opposing harsh treatment of non-Aryans, was arrested and interrogated by the Gestapo. Papers and passport were confiscated and he was ordered on threat of imprisonment to cease all Jewish-related activities. What this meant for ICCAJ was that Vienna had become untenable as a European centre, and after only eight months its associate director was being forcibly exited. Hans Kosmala, who like Reisner was not of Jewish origin but understood that he could be next, was soon in planning with William Paton to move the Delitzschianum to London.[67]

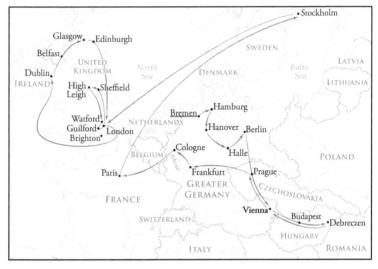

Figure 3.2 ICCAJ Director European itineraries in the wake of the *Anschluss*

Against this background of Nazi aggressions, apocalyptic assessments and unravelling plans for European expansion, Conrad Hoffmann sailed from New York in early July. When he arrived in Bremen, delegates from thirty-two nations were gathering in Evian (France) at the intergovernmental conference called by President Roosevelt to address the rapidly changing refugee problem in the wake of the *Anschluss*. Making his way through what was described as a nightmare of non-Aryan 'woe and torture of soul' in Germany, Austria and Czechoslovakia, Hoffman was sure that what he was witnessing nullified all of 'the marvellous achievements of the Hitler regime', and he now defied anyone seeing it to 'not come away haunted'.[68] The problem for the Church, as he saw it, involved two fronts of urgent responsibility. Non-Aryans, both Christians and Jews, were 'slowly but surely and inexorably being annihilated', and 'everywhere' – which meant Germany, Czechoslovakia, Austria, Hungary and Poland – the Church was 'involved in anti-Semitism'.[69] The burden on the Church to fight antisemitism while aiding and caring for its own refugees, however, was seen as greater than the burden placed on those at the Evian conference, for unless the Church spoke boldly and acted quickly it would 'seriously weaken its witness of Christ to the world, as well as its Christian calling'.[70] In his assessment there had never been such need, nor 'such opportunity to give witness of God's love to Jewry'.[71]

Although Hoffmann's series of reports between August and October 1938 were still marked by such conversionist thinking, they were significant in an unmistakable shift in language and attitude: thirty-seven pages with no implication that Jews were in part the cause of their own suffering. That did not mean, however, an unmistakable shift in belief. In late August at a national convention of the Reformed church in Debreczen (Figure 3.2), where Hungarian state adoption of its first anti-Jewish law on 29 May was being defended by church leaders as a solution to Hungary's Jewish problem, Hoffmann's increasing concern about what was happening to European Jews did not include abandonment of all blame. As an invited guest, with Bishop László Ravasz in attendance, he pointed out in deliberations on the Jewish problem that 'the Jews *alone*' were not solely responsible for antisemitism and that Christians too had to bear 'pangs of conscience' for not 'converting the Jews to Christianity'.[72]

Yet while Hoffmann's comments in Hungary still carried a level of Jewish blaming, the *denouement* of his obviously grieved reports was his pressing sense that he was being called to the refugee fields of Europe to work through a centralised agency that had not yet been created. To probe that absence, asking *why* there was no ecumenical relief structure for non-Aryan Christian refugees five years after the Aryan laws were enacted, it is necessary to look back to 1933 and see that a string of discomfiting efforts had in fact been attempted.

The most relevant began when American James McDonald was named High Commissioner for Refugees from Germany in October 1933. His conviction was that Christian churches had to be involved internationally in solving the refugee problem; and according to deputy Norman Bentwich that was also the emphasis of James Parkes, who sailed with him from America as one of his initial consultants. Both men stressed that Jews and non-Jews had to share in refugee relief efforts, but, as put by Parkes, Christians were not doing their part.[73] After returning to Geneva, Henriod sought Parkes's counsel on a UCCLW refugee fund for 'Christians of Jewish descent', and he urged the same. The churches had to be involved but 'not exclusively for Christian victims'. 'Emphasised discrimination' was not only contrary to the relief work of contemporary Jewish agencies, it was 'a pity' for the Church to distinguish in succour and aid.[74] Henriod forwarded Parkes's letter to chairman George Bell and by the year's end a UCCLW delegate had been appointed to the High Commission Advisory Council, but refugee funds were still being solicited 'with special interest for Hebrew Christians'. On that basis, appeals had been made in both October and December, but only 50 Swiss and 100 French francs respectively had been raised by the following March.[75]

As disparity increased between Christian and Jewish donations, both Parkes and McDonald urged from their respective lecterns that Christians in general and leaders in particular had to assume more responsibility for non-Aryan Christian refugees, while not abandoning support for Jewish victims. McDonald, in three consecutive High Commission reports between May 1934 and July 1935, entreated churches to prove the principle of Christian charity by assuming responsibility for all non-Jewish refugees.[76] Yet with few exceptions, namely the Society of Friends and the International Hebrew Christian Alliance, the dearth of Christian responses by mid-1935 was such that the High Commission published a special report on the plight of non-Jewish refugees, arguing in detail that mitigation of the non-Jewish refugee class was *dependent* upon the changed attitudes and actions of the Christian world.[77] That this pronouncement had to be made after the High Commission had been working behind the scenes for eighteen months to stimulate interest in an international Christian committee for non-Jewish refugees makes the lack of Christian responses all the more difficult to grasp and explain.

Walter Kotschnig, who joined the High Commission staff in early 1934, was assigned that task, but according to his confidential reports the first official steps toward organisation were not taken by the ecumenical movement until after the mid-1935 High Commission report appeared. Meeting in Chamby (Switzerland) under the World Alliance chair of Bishop Ammundsen, whom Kotschnig credited with initiating 'renewed Christian efforts on behalf of refugees', an official proposal for a central bureau for non-Jewish refugees was adopted by the World Alliance and UCCLW in August. A committee of four – Kotschnig, Henriod, Keller and Friedrich Siegmund-Schultze – held its first meeting three weeks after the Nuremberg Laws of 15 September were enacted. The goal was an international collaborative committee with a permanent office to serve as clearing house for the relief work of associated Protestant organisations. A proposed list of leaders was drawn up, and the goals of uniting Christian efforts, stimulating national committees and initiating united appeals were agreed. But owing to the amount of international travel and meetings that Kotschnig needed to solidify cooperative support, the first meeting of the International Christian Committee for German Refugees (ICCR) did not take place in London until 31 January 1936.[78]

The history from that point was as fraught with problems as had been its long and difficult birth. ICCR came into existence just as James McDonald resigned and the Office of High Commissioner as constituted was being liquidated, which meant that Kotschnig's acumen in planning and implementation was no longer available. The new initiative, which set up office in the same London building, had on paper four joint presidents from England, Yugoslavia, France and Sweden, as well as thirteen cooperating committees from nine western nations. Its supporters – including ICCAJ who was well represented with one executive member and four others on the national committees of England, Scotland and Sweden – endorsed and heralded the principle of duty to non-Aryan Christians, but financial responsibility was repeatedly cast back on the churches through organisational appeals that had abysmal results.[79] Although Jewish relief agencies were raising funds for Jewish refugees in multiple millions annually, the response to ICCR's modest appeal for £125,000 from British, Continental and American churches was only £9,000 from Britain by fall 1937.[80]

When ICCR's failing finances were presented by chairman Bell to the British sector of ICCAJ and CBMS that fall, all agreed that 'caring for non-Aryan refugees' was the duty of the churches. But when Bell suggested that the two bodies share the responsibilities, even if only secretarial duties, the answer was that it 'would be quite impossible' to do so. The best that could be offered was storage of files and papers if the ICCR office should have to close. By the time UCCLW was subsumed by WCCIF a year later in September 1938, the ICCR initiative was fundamentally bankrupt, having just barely held on by Bell's ingenuity in finding money to cover office expenses.[81]

Conrad Hoffmann's series of refugee reports in the same fall period were understood in the light of this five-year history. Meeting in London on 21 September, the British and European sectors of ICCAJ agreed to ask the American Presbyterian Board of National Missions to release Hoffmann for work on behalf of non-Aryan Christians in Europe. The following day in Geneva, a committee made up of Henriod (WA), Keller (Inter-Church Aid), and Visser 't Hooft (WCCIF) was created as a subgroup of Bell's ICCR to orchestrate aid for non-Aryan Christian clergy, with the promise that 'assistance and advice' would be sought from Hoffmann'.[82]

Six weeks later the *Kristallnacht* violence that erupted throughout Greater Germany – hundreds of synagogues desecrated and burned, thousands of Jewish businesses destroyed or damaged, thirty thousand Jewish men arrested and rounded into camps – triggered the realisation that refugee relief could not be limited to non-Aryan Christian clergy. Visser 't Hooft witnessed the violence first-hand on 9 and 10 November in Germany, and one week later the three-man subgroup issued a statement that called upon, but did not elaborate, the Oxford position on antisemitism. Pointing to 'the terrible persecution of the Jewish population in Germany and other Central European countries' as a time for the ecumenical movement to remember the stand it had taken at Oxford, it urged Christian prayer, increased immigration for non-Aryan refugees and church responsibility for non-Aryan Christians.[83]

Within weeks the Geneva subcommittee was referring to itself as the Ecumenical Committee on Aid to non-Aryan Christians. By January the Provisional Committee had moved to create a coordinating instrument for non-Aryan Christian refugees 'on behalf of the ecumenical movement', and by March the decision to establish a refugee office at Bloomsbury House in London to work closely with ICCR, which was being brought under the auspices of WCCIF for the 'sake of unity of action and authority', had been set into motion. The official announcement in mid-April, which named Bell, Paton and Visser 't Hooft as overseers, made clear that its purpose was to protect non-Aryan Christian interests while strengthening ecumenical representation with governments and relief agencies involved in the refugee crisis.[84]

Hoffmann's name as head did not become a matter of discussion until late in the process. In fact, a chief officer was not considered until a flaw in structural plans was noted by Sir Herbert Emerson, the new High Commissioner for Refugees. The initial plan involved only a secretary, and the man picked by virtue of availability and assets was Adolf Freudenberg, a 45-year-old German doctor of law who worked in the German Foreign Office before being ordained in the Confessing church. He was first employed by the Swiss Committee for Non-Aryan Refugees to work with British relief organisations in London, and the add-on plan was for him to represent WCCIF as well. Emerson, however, pointed out in February that it was unwise to use a man of German nationality as the face of an initiative for refugees fleeing from Germany. Over the next eight weeks, two non-Germans, one after the other, were offered the position of head officer. When the second candidate withdrew, Bell put forth Hoffmann's name on 14 April as one who 'has fire and is full of need'.[85]

Paton fastened on tenaciously, arguing up front that Hoffmann's defects were 'defects of his qualities' – a man who 'sometimes plunges ... when a more discreet man would take a different line' – but he was 'red-hot about the Jewish question' and had been 'deep' in the 'refugee business since the beginning of the Hitler regime'.[86] When Deputy Commissioner Gustave Kullmann warned that his 'missionary cause among the Jews would make Hoffmann's relationship with Jewish organisations impossible', Paton assured he had the ability to 'hold the affection of Jews while making no secret of his evangelistic position'. When American interests voiced reluctance to release Hoffmann from duties there, Paton was undeterred.

By early June he had rallied a second unanimous backing from the European and British sectors of ICCAJ on the grounds that Hoffmann would guard Christian interests as no other.[87]

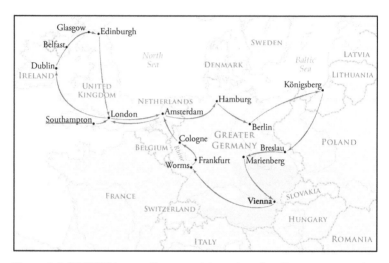

Figure 3.3 ICCAJ Director European itineraries after German occupation of Czechoslovakia

The remaining step was to gain the backing of key ecumenical and refugee relief leaders. At the behest of Visser 't Hooft, a list of the 'right people' was drawn for consultation in London. When the meeting convened on 3 August 1939, Paton presided over a group of twenty-two from England, Scotland, Ireland, Switzerland, Germany, Canada and the United States, including WCCIF Provisional Committee members Bell, Henriod and Leiper. Other consultants included Heinrich Grüber, head of the Church Relief Agency for Protestant non-Aryans in Berlin, Bertha Bracey, head of the Germany Emergency Committee, Kenneth Grubb, who would soon be immersed in the Religious Division of the British Ministry of Information, and a range of other affiliates, including Freudenberg, Kosmala and C.H. Gill, head of Church Mission to Jews and sitting chair of the international and British sectors of ICCAJ. Conrad Hoffmann was also present, with a carefully prepared report of twelve weeks of European itineraries since the March occupation of Czechoslovakia (Figure 3.3).[88]

Henry Leiper, who was there to protect both WCCIF and American interests, cautioned about taking too much of Hoffmann's time from his duties in the United States. It was one of the largest refugee-receiving countries and it bordered on Central and South America, which also absorbed refugees. It therefore had mission responsibility not only for itself but its southern neighbours as well, which created a problem in terms of following refugees into areas of emigration. There was also the issue of permanent refugees making their way to North America, as opposed to the more transient refugees on the Continent. Bell sympathised with all of the American concerns, but stressed that Christian non-Aryans 'were in need of a whole time ambassador'. Paton concurred with Bell that 'the American side of the problem' would be served by addressing the overall refugee problem. Moreover, he confirmed that Hoffmann would have the support of international church leaders, which would be 'secured by World Council officers'. Financial backing had already been secured from IMC, and European and British interests were waiting in the wings 'to pay' the rest of his salary and expenses.[89]

As Paton, Visser 't Hooft and Bell had hoped the consulting group affirmed the plan that ICCAJ and WCCIF had jointly pushed through. It was unanimously agreed as 'urgent' that a man 'already trusted by the churches', with the 'power to inspire others' and the ability to 'hold his own with government officials', should stand at the head of the refugee initiative. The official letter of 9 August requesting Hoffmann's release for a minimum of six months elaborated the degree to which he was thought to be that man.[90]

> The minds of many of those concerned with this problem have turned to Dr Conrad Hoffmann as the man ideally suited to be leader in this work. He possesses, in a unique degree, the qualifications required. He has himself frequently visited the areas from which the refugees come; he has shown himself able, in a remarkable degree, to gain their confidence; he is trusted by an increasingly wide range of the leaders of the Christian churches; above all, he has a passion of conviction, which he is able to communicate to others. It is the strong conviction, both of those who have worked with him in the sphere of missions to the Jews and those who have known him in refugee activity and of others of his friends in different Christian circles, that he has a power

of leadership, insight and ability to communicate enthusiasm which nobody else known to us possesses.[91]

What it had taken to get to this place of WCCIF–ICCAJ collaboration was as complex and convoluted as the path of Hoffmann's unanimous recommendation by the consulting group. The restructuring of UCCLW into WCCIF, the restructuring of ICCAJ aims and leadership, and the centralisation of joint efforts on behalf of non-Aryan Christian refugees had all coincided as concomitant developments, each of which had been affected by the accelerating aggressions of Nazi Germany. Planning and efforts in all three areas had moved through rapidly changing stages, spurred by incremental awakening to the refugee plight, as well as an increasing realisation of the need to protect Christian interests in the overall international refugee relief system that was developing.

The ardently devised plan was turned upside down on 1 September, however, when Hitler invaded Poland from the west, and Stalin invaded from the east sixteen days later. 'Who could have conceived', Hoffmann asked from New York on 19 September, 'the German–Russian alliance, the Russian–Japanese appeasement, and the carving up of Poland?' By the time the letter was written it was clear on both sides of the Atlantic that the refugee plan was no longer workable. Freudenberg was in Switzerland and Hoffmann was in America when Britain declared war on Germany on 3 September, and it was all but certain that the former could not re-enter England. The alternative plan in discussion was that Paton would head efforts in London and Hoffmann would work on American funding and refugee absorption.[92]

By early October Hoffmann was also being asked to consult Freudenberg, who was by now working from the Geneva office. An emergency committee had been formed and merged with the Ecumenical Committee on Refugees, under which relief work for non-Aryan Christians would function. The Emergency Committee of Christian Organizations (ECCO) had also been formed by the Geneva general secretaries of WCCIF, the World YMCAs, World Alliance, World Student Christian Federation and Central Bureau of Inter-Church Aid to coordinate ecumenical aid for emergency war needs.[93]

From this point on, emphasis on non-Aryan Christian refugees, which had occupied ICCAJ and WCCIF since the *Anschluss*, would have to be shared with prisoners of war and interned civilians. The landscape had already begun to shift as early as 12 September when Paton recognised POWs and internees as 'the biggest business' of wartime efforts. Five days later in a letter outlining WCCIF war plans Visser 't Hooft's thinking on POWs dominated to such degree that there was no mention of refugees at all. By early November, after permissions had been granted by British, French and German governments to organise POW work through the YMCA, Visser 't Hooft, in consultation with Max Huber of the International Committee of the Red Cross, had created a WCCIF Commission for Chaplaincy Service to Prisoners of War.[94]

What this meant for non-Aryan Christian refugee work, which had been up and running for only five months when war broke out, was that it would henceforth be in competition for emphasis and funding. Even Hoffmann, admitting as early as 10 November, had to 'confess' that he was 'restless' in regard to the POW service developing in Europe, where he had been so involved in the last war. He would 'much prefer', he said, 'to be over there …'.[95]

Declarations and war

At the outbreak of war the defence of ecumenical principles was invoked by WCCIF leaders as the primary task around which all other issues were to be approached. Undergirding that task, as framed by Visser 't Hooft to other core principles, was the idea that the reality of ecumenical unity 'must at all cost remain unbroken'. It was understood that no one 'can be really neutral in this war', but it was a question of 'how far ecumenical leaders can go without endangering the position of the Ecumenical Movement'.[96] It was an appropriate consideration for the general secretaries, particularly in the area of public statements that might be construed as 'political', for the tension between speaking out as an official body and keeping silence in order to avoid division was a fundamental aspect of the heritage that passed from UCCLW to WCCIF. To understand more fully what that might mean going into the war, it is necessary to grasp what it had meant up to that point, beginning with the Oxford conference that set WCCIF into motion.

Like the UCCLW resolution at Fanø in 1934, the 1937 Oxford conference message to the German church has been characterised as a solidarity with the Confessing church that stood against the Reich church. But archival evidence both before and after Oxford belies that this was the case. In August 1936, after the UCCLW administrative decision at Chamby to weight the 'rights' of German members against the need for an official statement on antisemitism, Wilhelm Zoellner, head of the Reich Church Committee, Hanns Lilje, and Reinold von Thadden were named to a Committee of Thirty Five, whose purpose was to advise the Oxford conference on unification of the ecumenical movement.[97] A united German delegation to Oxford was later formed under Lutheran Bishop Marahrens, which included Bishop Heckel of the Church Foreign Office *and* Confessing church members. In late January 1937, when all three groups came under fire in Germany and doubts were raised about whether the delegation could attend Oxford, Bell met with leaders of each group in Berlin.[98] When it became apparent between 3 and 16 June that the passports of three Confessing delegates had been withdrawn, Bell heard from each group that the decision was to send none if the full delegation could not attend. In the exchange of letters Bell's intention and Heckel's 'unaltered desire' for continuing ecumenical collaboration was made clear on both sides.[99]

That did not change during or after the Oxford conference, even though Martin Niemöller was arrested and imprisoned on 1 July, twelve days before Oxford convened. The conference message to the absent German church – which was orchestrated by Bell and should be read in full – was to the 'Evangelical Church in Germany' as a whole. It praised the fact that a joint German delegation to Oxford had been achieved, and noted that its absence created an even 'stronger sense of fellowship than before'. It importantly conveyed that 'we are greatly moved by the afflictions of many pastors and laymen who have stood firm ... in the Confessional church for the sovereignty of Christ and ... freedom of the Church', but it also expressed concern about the 'gravity of the struggle' for the Roman Catholic church as well. Moreover, it directed an Oxford delegation to deliver the work of the conference to the leaders of the German

Evangelical Church, which included the Reich church,[100] and then, in a concerted effort to maintain unity, the UCCLW Constituent Committee nominated at Oxford 'cordially welcomed' Bishop Heckel to its follow-up meeting in London one month later.[101]

In the period between the London meeting and spring 1938, Bell orchestrated planning for the Oxford delegation, which materialised in April, the month after Germany's *Anschluss* of Austria. In the official letter following the groundwork laid by Henriod, Lilje and Marahrens, Bell announced the delegation arrival for 20 April, stating plainly that its purpose was to discuss 'the ways and means' of maintaining and developing relations, including that of learning 'the standpoint and wishes of the Leaders of the German Evangelical Church'.[102] As it turned out, however, foreign press attacks on the *Anschluss* made a visit of the full delegation 'impracticable' for those in Germany, so only Bell and Alphons Koechlin from Switzerland went as scheduled. After three days of meetings, Bell was satisfied that each group expressed a 'strong desire' for ongoing relations, and that both Confessing and Lutheran leaders wanted to coordinate efforts through Bishop Heckel in the Church Foreign Office.[103] It was also the case the following month in Utrecht, at the UCCLW meeting that transitioned UCCLW into WCCIF, that NSDAP member Friedrich Krummacher was still a standing member of the Administrative Committee.[104]

As all of this should make clear, when the WCCIF constitution was drawn up in Utrecht in May 1938 and ratified by WCFO in September there was nothing even vaguely resembling a break with the Reich church. UCCLW sympathy for the Confessing church had not overridden its mandate for ecumenical unity, nor had accelerating German aggressions forced it into abeyance. The *Anschluss* had not prevented Bell from trying to maintain relations with all factions in the German church, nor did *Kristallnacht* deter WCCIF from picking up where Bell left off. As the heir to UCCLW's fractured history with the German church, what to say, when to say it, to whom it should be said and whether it should be said officially, openly or covertly was a gathering concern throughout WCCIF's first year. More specifically, what to say about Nazi aggressions, impending war, Jewish refugees and German claims against ecumenism were questions that merged into one increasingly complex deliberation that began in spring 1939 and continued up to the outbreak of war.

The Godesberg trigger

On 25 March 1939, ten days after Germany occupied the Bohemian and Moravian provinces of Czechoslovakia and proclaimed a 'Protectorate', eleven *Deutsche Christen* leaders of regional churches drafted a statement repudiating supranational, international and world bodies of churches as 'the political degeneration of Christianity'. It was the first of four theses of what came to be known as the Godesberg Declaration. The other three held respectively that Christianity 'is the unbridgeable religious opposition to Jewry', that the National Socialist fight against political church power is 'continuation and completion' of work begun by Luther, that the prerequisite for 'true Christian faith' in Germany is order and tolerance within the church structure.[105]

Visser 't Hooft was leaving Berlin after meeting with other church leaders when the Declaration appeared in the Gazette of the German Evangelical Church on 6 April. But it did not gain attention until Karl Barth urged response on 13 April. Writing to Paton, Temple, Bell and Boegner two days later, Visser 't Hooft assessed it as 'an aggressive statement against both the Confessional Church and the ecumenical movement', one of such 'anti-Christian character' that silence was not an option.[106]

Whether to speak officially about Nazi aggressions and impending war, however, were altogether different matters. When Barth pressed for a response to Godesberg, he also urged that if war were to come the churches represented by WCCIF should jointly declare that it was not a war against the German people. A different proposal from the Ecumenical Council of Sweden urged repudiation of German aggressions against small nations. While neither proposal was judged as cause for an official WCCIF statement, the internal deliberations for and against were part of the cumulative reasoning that informed the official response to Godesberg, which makes them highly relevant here.

In measuring responses to Barth's proposal for a WCCIF statement on the war, Visser 't Hooft summarised that such a statement would have to be 'very carefully worded' to make clear that other nations were 'not without responsibility' and that fellowship with all Germans 'who believe in the Lord Jesus Christ' was desired. Moreover, if such a statement were made, it could 'not be made by the Ecumenical Movement as such'. Paton and Temple agreed on the complexity of each point, particularly that WCCIF officers could not 'appear as agents' and that it could not come from the Provisional Committee, but Temple also doubted whether such a statement could even be made without coming off 'as hypocritical'. In a manner of summarising a veto, Visser 't Hooft added that neither individual nor joint statements of churches on the war would work, for in the former 'it would not make a strong impression' and in the latter it would give the impression of forming 'a block of democratic churches' encircling Germany.[107]

The second vetoed statement was the Swedish proposal to repudiate German aggressions. The five-part case was argued by Visser 't Hooft and backed by Paton, Temple, Boegner and Bell. First, an official refutation of Germany's aggressions 'would almost certainly' break 'relations with leaders of the German Churches'. Second, coming at the same time as the Godesberg response, it would appear as if WCCIF had started 'an anti-German campaign'. Third, if WCCIF 'made such a statement ... we would be playing right into the hands of those who look upon [it] as a semi-political institution'. Fourth, the authority of the Provisional Committee did not extend to issues not 'immediately connected' with its 'central purpose'. Fifth, Visser 't Hooft opposed using the term 'aggressions' in any official statement since it was a term of democratic nations and therefore 'resented not only in Germany but in Italy, Hungary, Yugoslavia and Bulgaria'. The only declaration he could envision, which was doubted 'worthwhile', was one that stated 'we have no common mind on the rights and wrongs of the international situation' but, nevertheless, believe 'in the absolute duty of Christians to maintain their unity in Christ and take a stand for peace and justice'.[108]

A third vetoed proposal arose as the WCCIF response to Godesberg was being drafted in Geneva, and the refugee office was being simultaneously launched in London. Visser 't Hooft called for an appeal to world churches that would draw attention to the ecumenical task 'implicit' in the refugee initiative. His reasoning was that 'the refugee question' could be used in a practical way to show 'that the Church is an ecumenical reality' and, as such, could counter the Godesberg claims attacking ecumenicity. Paton, who was lobbying Hoffmann for head of the refugee office at the time, was at first receptive, but then 'increasingly unwilling' to put 'the refugee business not only high up in the list of things that have got to be done, but absolutely first of all'. Paton's argument, to which Visser 't Hooft acquiesced for the present, was that it would make a 'very ambiguous impression on the churches of the world *if*, at a time when people are desperately seeking for the Word of God about war and peace, we come out with a very strong call about refugees'.[109]

In contrast to this battery of reasons for *not* making statements on impending war, German aggressions and non-Aryan refugees, the Godesberg Declaration required a response because it challenged the validity of ecumenicity. The period in which the Declaration was issued was part of that reasoning. International churches were making decisions about joining the new World Council, and doubt was being cast in some quarters about the legitimacy and efficacy of a structure of world churches. 'By far the biggest question' prior to Godesberg was the dearth of responses to WCCIF invitations for membership. Only two of eight Orthodox churches had joined and not a single Methodist or Baptist church had accepted the invitation. The strategy immediately before Godesberg was thus to counter misapprehensions by emphasising the *Una Sancta* implicit in the World Council, and to do so through the ecumenical press service as an 'instrument of ecumenical education and propaganda'. The strategic question *after* Godesberg was how to counter the German Christian claims against ecumenicity while emphasising to world churches that WCCIF was capable of protecting and advancing ecumenical Protestantism.[110]

That WCCIF chose to respond publicly rather than by private statement must be seen in this, as well as its theological, context. The goal was to answer each of the four theses with a counter claim that could not be construed as political. Both William Temple and Karl Barth constructed drafts that were 'harmonised' by Visser 't Hooft and then revised until agreement was reached by the four signatories: the two chairs of the Provisional and Administrative Committees (Temple and Boegner) and the two general secretaries (Paton and Visser 't Hooft). The decision to address the response to 'Christian churches of all countries', to publish it in the WCCIF international press service, and then circulate to both the religious and secular press, however, was far more provoking than had been bargained for.[111]

One hour after receiving word of its publication on 6 May, Bishop Heckel of the Reich Church Foreign Office issued a telegram demanding immediate retraction on grounds of 'intolerable interference in internal German affairs', charging WCCIF with exceeding its 'competence' and threatening future ecumenical relations.[112] The cable was followed by twenty-one pages of exchanges between WCCIF and Heckel without a single mention of Jews, the Jewish question, or the Godesberg thesis on Judaism, but it was not because WCCIF failed to address the Godesberg claim that Christianity was the 'unbridgeable religious opposition to Judaism'.[113] WCCIF stated clearly the traditional supersessionist claim that Christianity is the fulfilment of Judaism and that the Church rejoiced with those of 'the Jewish race' who accepted Christ. There was no further mention of Jews in the correspondence because Heckel's complaints to WCCIF had nothing to do with the content of its counterclaims. The German grievances against Geneva, according to WCCIF's own reports, were 'directed against the *form* that the statement had taken' and were 'in no way directed in *substance* to any of the expressions of opinion put forward'. The German criticisms rested solely on the WCCIF decision to enter the public arena, present their response as truth rather than opinion, and thereby imply that Christians in all countries adopt that position.[114]

The challenge thrown down by Heckel was that future ecumenical relations depended on the 'consciously responsible action' of withdrawing the issue from the public, and initiating discussion 'in brotherly confidence'.[115] Visser 't Hooft's initial response – each sentence of which was said to be 'weighed' in relation to 'further repercussions in Germany' – expressed appreciation for Heckel's willingness to approach the issue in a 'brotherly' spirit, while trying to convince him that the WCCIF decision to respond publicly should not be misinterpreted as interference in German affairs. The reason for the WCCIF response, as stated here by Visser 't Hooft and elsewhere by other core principals, was that the first Godesberg thesis could only be read as directed against ecumenism, with the other theses 'no less contrary' to underlying ecumenical principles.[116]

Heckel responded by asking Visser 't Hooft to come to Berlin as soon as possible. The four-hour meeting on 15 June, intense but friendly, included Eugen Gerstenmaier and NSDAP member Friedrich Wilhelm Krummacher from the Church Foreign Office, as well as Hans Schönfeld from WCCIF. The discussion was layered with German complaints and Visser 't Hooft's explanations of incidents like Archbishop Lang's speech about Germany's assault on Czechoslovakia on 20 March, William Temple's wartime liturgy distributed on 30 April, and WCCIF's public response to Godesberg on 6 May. *All* of this, Heckel summarised, made it difficult for the office entrusted with Foreign Relations in the German Evangelical Church to have a relationship with WCCIF. His terms for reconciliation included three WCCIF appointments: himself to the Administrative and Provisional Committees; a German juridical officer to the Provisional Committee; and a German secretaryship comparable to Leiper's in America. He also wanted approval of future WCCIF statements before they were made public. If these conditions were not acceptable, he concluded, it would be 'impossible to collaborate further with the Provisional Committee', and he would 'have to work against' it.[117]

To say that this degree of pushback was not only unexpected but contrary to the WCCIF intention to maintain relations with all groups in the German church would not be an overreach, but the *idea* of Heckel himself having a place in WCCIF was not new. The Provisional Committee had agreed at its St Germaine meeting in January that it was probably 'necessary and appropriate', and Visser 't Hooft had heard in Berlin in early April that some kind of request from Heckel would be forthcoming. At that point everyone involved – including leaders in both the Confessing and Lutheran groups – recognised that Heckel was the only one with 'a legally recognised position' in the German Evangelical Church and could 'do things for the Ecumenical Movement' that no one else could do. The crucial difference, in light of Heckel's pending threat, was that WCCIF had lost its leverage in negotiations.[118]

Writing privately, to WCCIF principals, Visser 't Hooft stressed the 'fact' that Heckel was 'in a strategic position in which maintenance of relations with the German church largely depend on him'. Still, he reasoned, WCCIF had to make certain it was not forced into a position where it was unable to work with other German groups or had to be mute in 'matters on which Heckel would want us to be silent'. Visser 't Hooft's suggested three terms for negotiation through which that might be achieved: i) WCCIF should not be 'forced' into any situation where it could be seen as 'responsible for ... breaking ... ecumenical relations with the German church'. ii) It should 'not give a purely negative response' to Heckel. iii) It should do everything possible to maintain relations with the other groups while ensuring that Heckel's office does not form a monopoly.[119]

Even before the terms could be mailed, however, Visser 't Hooft received word of yet another disturbing declaration emanating from the German church. Where Godesberg refuted Judaism as an 'unbridgeable' opposition to Christianity, this statement signed in Berlin on 31 May proclaimed that a 'responsible race policy is necessary for maintenance of the purity of nationality'. Moreover, it carried the signatures of Lutheran bishops, including August Marahrens of Hanover who was appointed by the Oxford conference as one of only ten Provisional Committee members who were part of both the Administrative and Committee of Fourteen. Copies were forwarded to Bell, Paton and Temple with two handwritten notes depicting it as a 'statement by Lutheran bishops attacking ecumenical universalism and supporting race policy', a 'sad document of compromise'.[120] Revealing somewhat more in a separate note to Paton, Visser 't Hooft lamented that no matter how we handle it, 'we will get into trouble' – to which Paton replied, 'things are just about as grave as they can possibly be'.[121]

Here was unequivocal public agreement with Nazi racial policy by a member of WCCIF's Provisional and Administrative Committees, but in the ensuing discussion there was no mention whatsoever of dismissing Marahrens, nor was anything said about the effect the statement might have on Christian attitudes toward Jews or on Jews themselves. The new declaration was seen as a 'kind of counterstatement' to the WCCIF Godesberg response – 'terribly serious', 'very distressing' and 'inspired either by pressure from the state or spontaneous agreement with the racial and national theories and plans of the German government' – but it was not something that WCCIF would respond to. As summarised by Nils Ehrenström in the Geneva study department, given that ecumenical statements 'might be, and have been, disparaged in Germany', the prevailing wisdom was that it would be better for Lutheran theologians outside Germany to deal with the matter.[122]

WCCIF attention was to remain focused on the 'ultimatum' issued by Heckel, one to be deliberated prudently, wisely and courageously so 'as not to spoil our last chance of keeping in touch with all groups in the Church of Germany'.[123] All who were involved agreed with Visser 't Hooft that separation from the German church was to be avoided and that it would be 'foolish' to return a negative answer to Heckel, but care had to be taken to satisfy the other groups in the German church as well.[124]

The decision of the Administrative Committee in Zeist, Holland on 21–22 July, after 'long and anxious thought', was that two additional places should be given to the German church, and that each of the two sectors of the Provisional Committee would be responsible for appointment of one. The conciliatory proposal to be set before Heckel in September was that he would be appointed by one sector, a member of the Confessing church by the other, and Bishop Marahrens's already established position would represent the remaining church group.[125] Bishop George Bell, who was unable to attend, hailed the solution as 'very wise', suggesting on 15 August that the next Provisional Committee meeting might possibly be held in Berlin to seal the appointments.[126]

This was the situation when Germany invaded Poland two weeks later and the question was raised as to 'how far ecumenical leaders can go without endangering the position of the Ecumenical Movement'.[127] In the six months leading up to that question, WCCIF principals had protested without hesitation when ecumenical integrity was challenged by the Godesberg Declaration, but abstained in silence when challenged by the racial alignment of Lutheran bishops with whom they were ecumenically involved. Core leaders had been able to see that the Lutheran statement was a 'sad document of compromise', but had been unable to view their own response in the same light. Moreover, the compromise was given legitimacy when Marahrens was allowed to remain on the Provisional Committee with his name on WCCIF letterhead. While the outbreak of war halted the appointment of Bishop Heckel, Marahrens stayed on in Provisional Committee capacity until he was replaced in October 1945 by Bishop Wurm of Württemberg, who was *himself* a signatory of the same 'sad document of compromise'.

If organisational conscience was uneasy about these decisions, the unease was lulled by an overriding concern for advancement of unified ecumenicity in the name of the new World Council. The diligence with which it was pursued was extraordinarily focused, and all the more so when viewed in the context of *known* worsening conditions for German Jews. By July 1939, when WCCIF made the decision to overlook German Lutheran agreement with Nazi racial policy, ten of the thirteen supplementary Nuremberg decrees had been imposed in the Reich, which with other racial laws were disenfranchising all categorised 'Jews' through deprivation of rights to citizenship, professions, wages, financial reserves, social access, property ownership, housing, transportation and personal possessions, including one's own name. The German Regulation of Name Changes Law in August 1938 required that all Jews within the Reich must have the first names 'Sara' or 'Israel', according to gender. By *Kristallnacht* two months later all remaining Jewish enterprises carried identifying marks, and all Jewish passports were stamped with the letter 'J'. In the last months before the war, while WCCIF core principals were moving back and forth between Geneva and Berlin in negotiations with Reich church Bishop Heckel, further decrees were issued on the confiscation of Jewish valuables, reduction of pensions and appropriation for forced labour.[128]

Yet whatever concerns were held about Nazi racial policy and worsening conditions for German Jews, they were held in abeyance and not in official statements about what was happening to Jews. WCCIF did, however, become more public about Nazi aggressions against Jews after the outbreak of war in a 1939 Christmas appeal for non-Aryan Christian funding. But it was James Parkes who voiced the first report to Christendom about Nazi war atrocities against Jews, even though the same information was in hand. What was known by Parkes in late fall 1939 was known by WCCIF European principals, and that was true of what was known by ICCAJ principals as well. All were being informed by reports flowing in and through existing refugee and mission networks, the earliest of which was circulating no later than fifteen days after Germany invaded Poland.[129]

The way in which Parkes responded to the more or less common cache of information was also strikingly different. His response was to publish a report in *Christian News Letter* on 6 December about the war's devastating effect on Jews, with emphasis on their deportation to a Nazi Jewish Reserve in Lublin (Poland) which was 'not intended to lead to anything but ... extermination'.[130] WCCIF's response later that month was to report on the same Lublin Reserve in an appeal for funds that would 'at least save our fellow Christians in Central Europe from being sent to this hell'.[131] ICCAJ's response was to launch an investigation into the effects of war on Jewish missions and begin postwar planning for mission reconstruction on the European Continent.

Yet, in pointing to these contrasts between Parkes's focus on Jews *as Jews*, WCCIF's focus on non-Aryan Christians who were classified as Jews, and ICCAJ's focus on Jews as a mission object, it should not be assumed that those were the only WCCIF and ICCAJ concerns. The attitudes of both sets of leaders to the plight and suffering of Jews were anything but indifferent, but it is precisely that which makes their fixed sets of aims all the more remarkable. The momentously changing events of the world had brought no corresponding changes in organisational mandates. WCCIF's focus after war began was powered as before by the advancement of ecumenical unity, while ICCAJ's focus remained driven by its mandate to advance God's call to Israel. Decisions about how to respond to unfolding conditions were never meant to be made solely on the basis of humanitarian needs but, rather, on the basis of humanitarian needs according to the precedence of organisational mandates. At the close of 1939, in the early months of World War II, it was not just a matter of responding, but responding in a way that advanced organisational mandates without losing sight of where they were headed.

Notes

1 Two press releases (IMC.261203) were drafted and distributed by BICCAJ member (Sir) Kenneth Grubb, British Controller of Overseas Propaganda, 1941–1946, president of the Anglican Church Missionary Society (1944–1969), chair of the WCC Commission of the Churches on International Affairs (1946–1968).
2 Five from the German Evangelical Church were prevented from travelling to the conference by the Nazi state.
3 The ten Booms were honoured as Righteous by Yad Vashem in 1967 (Corrie) and 2007 (Elizabeth and Casper).
4 Willem ten Boom, *Die Entstehung des modernen Rassen-Antisemitismus* (Leipzig: Institutum Delitzschianum, 1928).
5 Philip Kohnstamm, *Psychologie van het antisemitisme* (1934); *Het nationaal-socialisme als geestelijk gevaar* (1936).
6 Philip Kohnstamm, 'The Church of Jesus Christ and Antisemitism in the Age of Secularization', 1, IMC.261203.
7 Nineteen of the 25 reports dealt with Europe, 3 with the Middle East, 1 each with South Africa, South America and the United States. Of the European reports only three said antisemitism was 'practically non-existent' or 'hardly a public question' (Italy, Finland and Norway); the rest reported a rise in varying degrees. As to cause, 64% pointed to national socialist ideology or other political, economic, social and cultural conditions; 36% acknowledged antisemitism in churches; 7% said churches were openly opposed; 7% said churches assumed no responsibility for combating antisemitism. None of the reports associated cause with the Church per se, but 21% held that antisemitism was a 'phase of modern attack on religion in general' and that if Christendom failed to combat antisemitism 'its very existence would be endangered'. By the end of the conference the latter finding would be the prevailing theme of the 68 delegates.
8 The total conference package of 335 pages included country reports (123 pp), study and appendices (104 pp), related papers (108 pp), IMC.261203, 261204.
9 Kohnstamm, 'The Church of Jesus Christ and Antisemitism in the Age of Secularization', 30.
10 Ibid., 2–3; 'full-blooded' Jews were said to be different from non-Jewish Europeans and Americans in 'taste', 'speech', 'expression', 'temperament', 'colour', 'physical build', 'rhythm', 'humour', 'diseases' and 'crimes': added to this were 'peculiarities' that were

not characteristic of biblical Jews but developed over 'centuries of oppression'.

11 Ibid., 3, 5–6; 7–9; 13; more on de-religionised Jewry, 14, 22, 29; Hoffmann, 'A Few Facts Regarding American Jewry and Anti-Semitism', 2–4; see also Hoffmann to Kohnstamm suggesting this explanation, 23 Feb. 1937; IMC.261203.

12 For critical study of John Oesterreicher's anti-Judaism and his later role in *Nostra Aetate*, John Connelly, *From Enemy to Brother* (Cambridge: Harvard University Press, 2012). For Connelly's analysis of the Catholic treatise, 150–7; see also Elias Füllenbach, 'Shock, Renewal, Crisis: Catholic Reflections on the Shoah', *Antisemitism, Christian Ambivalence and the Holocaust*, ed. Kevin Spicer (Bloomington: Indiana University Press, 2007), 201–34. Both scholars view the treatise as early but flawed development in Catholic attitudes, but neither is aware of ICCAJ's use of it.

13 'The Church of Christ and the Jewish Question', *Die Erfüllung* (February 1937), was later published as *The Church and The Jews: A Memorial Issued by Catholic European Scholars*, trans., G. Feige (1937).

14 Kohnstamm, 'The Church of Jesus Christ and Antisemitism', 31.

15 Ibid., 12, 18–19, 20, 23, quoting from Catholic document, 15–16.

16 Ibid., 19, orig. ital.

17 Ibid., 18–19, 20–1, 23.

18 'The Church of Christ and the Jewish Question', 13–14, orig. ital. The passage went on, 'unfortunately most of them see in the happenings since 1933 nothing more than a materialistic, nationalistic self-determination. They persist in clinging to a God-forgetting humanitarianism. This ... has been encouraged by the attitude of many Christians who have kept silent in the face of injustice; all of this is, humanly speaking, regrettable'.

19 J. van Nes, 'Anti-Semitism on the Continent of Europe', 13–14 June 1932, IMC.261202.

20 Niemöller's quotation is from a 1935 sermon in the collection *Here Stand I* (Chicago: Willet, Clark & Co., 1937), a companion volume to *From U-Boat to Pulpit* (Chicago: Willet, Clark & Co., 1937), which carried a laudatory chapter by Henry Leiper. American and British editions of the former were published in fall 1937, with CC publicity on 21 July, 10 and 16 Nov.

21 Ammundsen, Minutes of Private Session, Fanø, 27 Aug., 1934, 3, WCC.24.248.

22 Uriel Tal, 'Modern Lutheranism and the Jews', *Religion, Politics and Ideology in the Third Reich* (New York: Routledge, 2004), 191–203,

argued that Staerk was but one of many Confessing church members to make equations between Jews and Nazism.
23 Charles C. Morrison, 'Jewry and Democracy', *CC*, 9 June, 735–6; 'What is Anti-Semitism?', *CC*, 7 Jul. 1937, 863.
24 Ten Boom, 'Eight Propositions on Anti-Semitism', prop. 1–3, IMC.261203. The text passed from Oldham to Paton without criticism in fall 1936, after which it circulated to commentators in England, Austria, Romania, Poland and the United States as points that could be expanded into 'a most valuable article'. None of the points, including the use of 'antisemitism' to describe valid criticism of Jews, were criticised; see Paton to Kohnstamm, 23 Oct. 1936, 11 Feb. 1937.
25 Ibid., prop. 4–8.
26 Ten Boom, 'Zionism', *IRM*, 19:2 (April 1930), 231–40; 'Naturalism is the Enemy' (1936), IMC.261201.
27 Ten Boom, 'Propositions', 4–8. These documents bring into question earlier beliefs about Willem ten Boom in regard to his family of Righteous Gentiles, namely, that the family supersessionism was not denigrating to Jews, that the ten Booms were sympathetic to Zionism, and that Willem's 1928 doctoral thesis on antisemitism was evidence of his anti-antisemitic position. For scholarly discussion, see Lawrence Baron, 'Supersessionism Without Contempt: The Holocaust Evangelism of Corrie ten Boom', *Christian Responses to the Holocaust* (Syracuse: Syracuse University Press, 2003), 119–31; Yaakov Ariel, 'Jewish Suffering and Christian Salvation: The Evangelical-Fundamentalist Holocaust Memoirs', *HGS* 6:1 1991, 63–78. Also Lawrence Baron, 'Evangelical Converts, Corrie Ten Boom, and the Holocaust: A Response to Yaakov Ariel'; Ariel, 'Reply to Lawrence Baron's Response, both of which are in *HGS* 7:1 (1993), 143–50.
28 Kohnstamm, 'The Church of Jesus Christ and Antisemitism', 29.
29 Ibid., 24–5; ICCAJ min., 12–13, Vienna, 28 June–2 July 1937, IMC.261206.
30 ICCAJ min., 'Resolution on Anti-Semitism and the Church', para. 1, 18–20.
31 Ibid., para. 1, 3.
32 Ibid., para. 1, 2, ital. add.
33 Ibid., para. 4–5.
34 Ibid., para. 2, ital. add.
35 Ibid., para. 2, 3.
36 Vienna conference, Letter to Oxford, ital. add., IMC.261203.

37 Ibid., ital. add.
38 Ibid.
39 'The Vienna Conference' was one of two press releases drafted and distributed by BICCAJ member Kenneth Grubb, IMC.261203.
40 Leiper, *Highlights of Oxford* (1937), 2 July, 12–26.
41 Ibid., 4; Oldham, *The Oxford Conference Official Report* (Chicago and New York: Willet, Clark & Co., 1937), hereafter OCOR, 2–3.
42 OCOR, 21–2, 152–3, 114–19.
43 OCOR, x-xii, 13–19, 17, orig. ital.; for Söderblom's vision, see Haberman, *Nobel Lectures*, 11 Dec. 1930.
44 For Oldham's critical role, Keith Clements, *Faith on the Frontier* (Edinburgh: T&T Clark, 1999); for other details, Leiper's 'Preface' and Oldham's 'Introduction', OCOR, vii-44; E.E. Aubrey, 'The Oxford Conference, 1937', *Journal of Religion*, 17:4 (Oct.), 379–96; Morrison, CC, 4 Aug., 967–9; 11 Aug., 991–4; 17 Nov., 1420–1.
45 OCOR, 2; also Adolf Keller, *Five Minutes Before Twelve: A Spiritual Interpretation of the Oxford and Edinburgh Conferences* (Nashville: Cokesbury Press, 1937).
46 OCOR, 21–4, 26; see also Vienna conference letter to Oxford.
47 OCOR, abbreviations for report citations hereafter in parenthesis: Message from the Oxford Conference to the Christian Churches (M), 45–52; Church and Community (C&C), 55–64; Church, Community and State in Relation to Economic Order (C&Ec), 75–112; Church, Community and State in Relation to Education (C&Ed), 113–50; The Universal Church and the World of Nations (UC&N), 151–71; Additional Report on Church and Community (C&C2), 172–233.
48 M, 46; C&C, 59–61; C&Ed, 116–17, 144; UC&N, 166–7; C&C2, 213–17.
49 Intro., 30; M, 45; C&C, 56, 63–4; C&S, 65–6; C&Ed, 115–16; C&C2, 187–8, 213–14.
50 UC&N, 166; C&C2, 215; C&C, 57.
51 C&C, 56–8; C&C2, 179.
52 C&C, 58, 62.
53 C&C, 62.
54 UC&N, Paton, Visser 't Hooft, Cavert, Henriod, Leiper, Basil Mathews and Horton were among the delegates who formulated this report.
55 UC&N, 167–8.
56 C&C2, 217–18.
57 The 'against racial pride' passage appeared first in C&C and was then adapted to the conference message. The third form with the tacked-on

reference to antisemitism was in C&C2, which was not submitted to the full conference. It was discussed and approved at the committee level in the last session, with the final revision by Sir Walter Mobley after the conference ended. Respectively, C&C, 60; M, 46; C&C2, 217–18.
58 M, 46; C&C, 59–61, 64; C&Ed, 121; UC&N, 166; C&C2, 209, 213, 214–15.
59 C&C, 59–60, 65; C&Ed 116–17; C&C2, 210, 211, 214.
60 Ammundsen, Private Session Min., Fanø, 27 Aug., 1934, 3, WCC.24.248; Niemöller, *Here Stand I* (1937); Morrison, 'Jewry and Democracy', *CC*, 9 June, 735–6; 'What is Anti-Semitism?', 7 Jul. 1937, 863.
61 *OCOR*, 261–7. The Committee of Thirty-Five, formed in autumn 1936, was the recommending body for unification at Oxford. Members directly related to ICCAJ were Mott, Paton and Cavert; other key figures included Oldham, Henriod, Brown, Bell, Visser 't Hooft and Temple.
62 Erwin Reisner, Private and confidential report, 14 Nov. 1937, IMC.261201, was later made public on request through *News Sheet* (Jan.–Feb. 1938), 5–6.
63 Ibid., 12; 8–9, 10. Reisner lectured on Hebrew Christian Zionism to the theological faculty of Basel, with further discussions in Basel, Geneva and Holland, where ten Boom urged that non-Aryan Christian refugees had to be placed in Aryan congregations 'to avoid the danger of setting up a sect of Hebrew Christians', IMC. 261201.
64 Ibid., 12; 3, for a second 'Jewish parallel to German Nazism'.
65 Ibid., 7, 9; the role of suffering in conversion continued in *Missions Korrespondenz* No. 3 (May 1938), 4–7, IMC.261201.
66 Reisner to Hoffmann, 5 May 1938, went on to portray German nationalism and Jewish internationalism as two anti-Christian 'demons' in opposition, IMC.261216; this letter also appears in Eberhard Röhm and Jörg Thierfelder, *Juden-Christen-Deutsche* 2 (Stuttgart: Calwer Verlag, 1992), 190–5.
67 ICCAJ financial support for Reisner continued until spring 1939, during which he worked briefly with Grüber in Berlin and was then promoted for ecumenical jobs by Visser 't Hooft and Henriod; see Reisner to Baker, 12 Jan. 1939; Grüber to Baker, 27 Jan.; ICCAJ Min., 2, 6 Feb.; Statement on Reisner, 3 Feb., IMC.261207; Visser 't Hooft to Bell, 4 Feb., 16 Mar. 1939, Besier 1 (2015), 86–8, 92–4.
68 Hoffmann, Strictly private and confidential report, 5 Aug. 1938, IMC. 261201.

69 Reports after 5 August include: Preliminary report, 21 Sept., Refugee report, 15 Oct.; ICCAJ minutes, British and European sections, 21 Sept.; 'A Plan for German Refugee Relief', 15 Oct.; 'Homeward bound', 23 Oct. 1938; IMC. 261201, 261203, 261207.
70 Hoffmann, 15 October, 10–11.
71 Hoffmann, Preliminary Report, 21 Sept.; Homeward Bound, 23 Oct.
72 Moshe Herczl, *Christianity and the Holocaust of Hungarian Jewry* (New York: New York University Press, 1993), 95, ital. add.
73 Norman Bentwich, 'Notes on Interview', 10–13 Nov. 1933, AJC THR-15.
74 Parkes to Henriod after meeting on the 15th, 16 Nov. 1933, WCC.42.0064.
75 Henriod to Parkes, 18 Nov. 1933, WCC.42.0064; for London meeting, 19 Nov., Breitman et al., *Diaries and Papers of James McDonald*, 198; Paton to Henriod, 6 Feb.; Henriod to Paton, 8 Feb. 1934, IMC.261142; UCCLW Report of Action with Regard to Alleviation of Distress Among Refugees from Europe, 22 Feb. 1934, WCC.301.4310.
76 Reports of the Governing Body of the High Commission for Refugees (Jewish and Other) Coming from Germany, May 1934 (London: Office of the High Commission), 31; Nov. 1934 Report, 24; 17 Jul. 1935 Report, 15.
77 High Commission Report, *The Plight of Non-Jewish Refugees Coming From Germany* (London: Office of the High Commission, July 1935).
78 Walter Kotschnig, 'Confidential report on Christian appeal for non-Jewish refugees', 1 Nov. 1935; 'Conversation with Keller', 24 May 1934; 'Confidential report on trip to Austria', 5–6 Feb. 1935 in *James G. McDonald Papers*, Vol. 7, *Archives of the Holocaust*, ed. Henry Friedlaender and Sybil Milton (New York: Garland Publishing, 1990), 224–5, 152–6, 223–36; UCCLW min., Chamby, 18–22 Aug. 1935, WCC.212.008, FCC.B9F17.
79 ICCR presidents were Bishop Bell (Britain), Archbishop Eidem (Sweden), Bishop Iriney (Novi Sad), Marc Boegner (France). ICCAJ associate on exec. committee was Kenneth Grubb; on national committees, Birger Pernow and Göte Hedenquist (Sweden), Macanna (Scotland); Wm. Simpson (England) was added in fall 1938; WCC.301.4329.
80 CBMS min., 16 Sept. 1937; Ad Hoc Group on ICCR, 5 Oct., IMC.261229; Memo from Mcleish, Oct. 1937, CMJ.c104.
81 Ibid., quot, Memo from Mcleish, Oct. 1937, CMJ.c104.

82 ICCAJ Min., 21 Sept.; Sub Comm., 16 Dec. 1938, IMC.261203, 261207; quot., Memoire on Non-Aryan Pastors, 22 Sept. 1938, WCC.301.4330.
83 *Kristallnacht* statement, 16 Nov. 1938, *ICPIS* 49, WCC.301.4330, also in Snoek, 100.
84 Henriod, Report, 24–30 Nov. 1938; Provisional Comm. Min., 28–30 Jan. 1939; Aide-Memoires on Aid to Non-Aryan Christians, Dec. 1938, 11 Jan. 1939, 17 Feb., 20 Mar; Paton to Home Office Under Secretary of State, 3 Apr.; Freudenberg to Paton w/draft, 3 Apr.; Paton to Visser 't Hooft (hereafter VH) w/2nd draft, FB to Paton w/ Bell's comments, 18 Apr.; Paton to VH w/changes for final draft, 19 Apr.; memo on refugee problems. 19 Apr. 1939; WCC.301.43.30, 425.1.022, IMC.261142 & 44.
85 This account is based on letters and memoranda between Paton, Bell, VH and others between 4 Feb. and 19 Apr.: Feb (4, 8, 10, 14, 15, 27), Mar. (3, 11, 13, 16, 20, 28), Apr. (3, 13, 14, 15, 19) at WCC.301.4330, 42.007, IMC.261142. Highlights include Aide-Memoire on Aid to Non-Aryan Christians, 17 Feb. 1939; Paton to VH re first offer, 27 Feb., 3 Mar., 13 Mar.; VH to Paton, 11 Mar. 1939; Bell to Baud, re second offer, 28 Mar.; Bell to Paton, 13 Apr.; Paton to VH, via Standley, w/copy of Bell's letter, 14 Apr. 1939; see also Memorandum on refugee problems, Geneva, 19 Apr. 1939, WCC.425.1.022.
86 Paton to VH, 18 Apr., IMC.261142.
87 Paton to Bell, 9 May 1939; Private Min., ICCAJ British and European, 1–2 June 1939, IMC.261142, 261213.
88 VH to Paton, 12 June 1939; Paton to Bell, 28 July; VH to Bell, 28 June 1939; ICCAJ Min., Special Meeting, 3 Aug. 1939, WCC.310.008.
89 Ibid., Min., 3 Aug. 1939; also Paton to Bell, 9 May; ICCAJ Min., 1–2 June 1939.
90 ICCAJ Resolution, 3 Aug. 1939; Paton to VH, 9 Aug. 1939, IMC.261143.
91 Memorandum on Invitation of Dr Conrad Hoffmann, 3 Aug. 1939, IMC.261207.
92 Hoffmann to Paton, 19 Sept. 1939, IMC.261143.
93 Paton to VH, 4 Sept.; VH to Paton, 6 Sept.; Paton to VH, 7, 13, 15 Sept.; Paton to Hoffmann, 18 Sept.; VH to Paton, 19, 25 Sept.; Paton to VH, 2 Oct.; VH to Hoffmann, 8 Oct.; FB to Paton, 3 Nov.; VH to Paton, 24 Nov. 1939; IMC.261142, 43, 44.
94 Confidential 'Policy of the Provisional Committee in Time of War', 4 Sept. 1939; Strong to Mott, 6 Sept., Paton to VH, 12 Sept.; Bell to

VH, 16 Sept.; VH to Leiper, 17 Sept.; Strong to Mott, 18 Oct.; Mott to VH, 23 Oct.; VH to WCCIF Officers, 23 Nov.; Temple to VH, 4 Dec. 1939, IMC.261142, WCC.301.008, 42.0057 & 0077.
95 Hoffmann to VH, 10 Nov. 1939, WCC.42.0038.
96 VH to Temple, Mott, Boegner, Oldham, Archbishop Eidem, Bishop of Novi Sad, bishops Berggrav and Damgaard, 20 Sept. 1939, WCC.42.0077; VH to Paton, 5 Oct. 1939, IMC.261143.
97 UCCLW Min., Chamby, 21–25 Aug. 1936, 67–8, WCC.212.008; Report of the Committee of Thirty-Five, OCOR, 261–3.
98 Hitler was irritated with the 'intransigence' of the Confessing church, Zoellner was at odds with Reich Church Minister Kerrl, and Lutheran bishops Marahrens and Meiser were being attacked as disloyal for visiting America in December. See Bell, Memorandum on Trip to Berlin, Private and Confidential, 21 Jan.–1 Feb. 1937, and Bell to Lang, 12 Feb. 1937, in Chandler, *Brethren in Adversity*, 121–34, 135–6.
99 Pre-Oxford letters, 3–16 June between Bell, Henriod and the German church are at WCC.42.0007; also in Gerhard Besier, *Intimately Associated for Many Years*, vol. I (Newcastle: Cambridge Scholars Publishing, 2015), 45–55, for quot., see Bell to Heckel, 16 June 1937.
100 OCOR, 259–60.
101 Private and Confidential to members of the Constituent Committee and Alternates, Min., London, 19 Aug. 1937, WCC.301.005.
102 The post-Oxford letters between 3 March–12 April 1938 are at WCC.42.0007, and in Besier, *Intimately Associated*, 58–74; for official letter of arrival, Bell to Marahrens, 12 April. The proposed delegation consisted of Bell, Oldham, Koechlin (Basel), Bishop Fuglsang-Damgaard (Copenhagen), Bishop Ysander (Sweden).
103 Bell, 'On Trip to Berlin and Hanover', 20–22 Apr. 1938, in Chandler, *Brethren in Adversity*, 144–9.
104 Min., UCCLW Admin. Comm., Utrecht, 13 May 1938.
105 The version of the Godesberg Declaration to which WCCIF responded is different from that in Wolfgang Gerlach, *And the Witnesses Were Silent* (Lincoln: University of Nebraska Press, 2000), 176–86; there the claim about Judaism appears as thesis three, while it is thesis two in the WCC documents. There are also two WCC renderings of thesis two in English: Christianity is the 'unbridgeable religious opposition to Jewry', and 'the unbridgeable opposition to Judaism', WCC.301.008. For contextual analysis of the Declaration and the Institute for the Eradication of Jewish Influence that it announced, see Heschel, *The Aryan Jesus* (2008), 67–105.

106 Barth to VH, 13 Apr.; Bell to VH, 14 Apr.; VH to Temple, Paton, Boegner, Bell, Canon Hodges, 15 Apr. 1939. Unless noted documents for n. 106–26 are at WCC.301.008, 42.0077, IMC.261143.
107 VH to Temple, 15 Apr., 1 May; Temple to VH, 21 Apr., 1 May; Paton to Temple, 28 Apr.; to VH, 2 May; Paton to Ogilvie at BBC, 18 Apr.; VH to Paton, 6 May.
108 Ecumenical Council of Sweden to WCCIF, 21 Apr. VH to Temple and Paton, 26 Apr.; Paton to Temple, 28 Apr.; Temple to VH, 1 May; VH to Temple, 1 May; VH to Paton, 6 May.
109 VH to Paton, 6 May; also 26 Apr., 1 May; VH to Temple, 21 May; Memo on refugee problems, 19 Apr., WCC.425.1.022; Paton to Temple, 3 May; Paton to VH, 4 May.
110 VH to Paton, 24 Feb.; Paton to VH, 27 Feb., 8 Mar.; Douglas to Paton, 4 Mar.
111 WCCIF response to Godesberg, *ICPIS*, 6 May 1939. For discussion on press expansion, Paton to VH, 18, 26 Apr.; Temple to VH, 21, 27 Apr.; VH to Paton, 24 Apr., 3 May; VH to Temple, 26 Apr., 1 May; WCC.301.4331.
112 Heckel to VH, cable, 6 May.
113 Heckel to VH, signed by Wahl, 8 May; VH to Temple, Paton and Bell, 8 May; VH to Heckel, 11 May; VH to WCCIF, 'Private and Very Confidential', 20 June; Schönfeld, Memorandum to WCCIF, 'personal and strictly confidential', 6 Jul. 1939.
114 Schönfeld, Memorandum, 6 Jul., 1–2, emphasis in the original.
115 Heckel to VH, 8 May, 1–3.
116 Quot., VH to Temple, Boegner, Paton, 8 May; VH to Heckel, two letters on 11 May; also Paton to Leiper, 30 May; Paton to Schlunk, 20 June 1939.
117 VH to Admin., Confidential Memorandum, 20 June, 1–4. Other records of the meeting include Schönfeld to WCCIF, 6 Jul.; Krummacher, 19 Jul. 1939.
118 PC Min., St Germaine-en-Laye, 28–30 Jan. 1939, WCC.301.005; VH to Bell, Boegner, Temple, Paton, Canon Hodgson, 7 April 1939.
119 VH to Admin., Confidential Memorandum, 20 June, 1–4, 6–7.
120 VH to Bell, Paton, Temple, 21 June, w/Lutheran bishop statement signed in Berlin on 31 May, which included bishops Wurm of Württemberg and Hans Meiser of Bavaria. For contextual discussion of the statement, Heschel, *The Aryan Jesus*, 85–7. For VH's more favourable account of the Godesberg and Lutheran statements, which excludes background deliberations and makes no mention of racial

emphasis in the second document, or names of those who signed it, except Marahrens, VH, *Memoirs*, 93–8.
121 VH to Paton, 21 June; Paton to VH, 26 June.
122 Ehrenström to Paton, 22 June, ital. add; Paton to Ehrenström, 26 June.
123 VH to Bell, 21 June.
124 Ibid; Temple to VH, 27 June; Schönfeld to WCCIF, 6 July; Bell to VH, 18 July, who was more pessimistic that all groups would be satisfied.
125 Admin. Min., 21–22 July, Zeist, Holland, WCC.301.005; Paton to Bell, 28 July.
126 Bell to VH w/copy to Boegner, 15 Aug.; also Bell to Paton, 4 Aug. Unless noted documents for n. 106–26 are at WCC.301.008, 42.0077, IMC.261143.
127 VH to Temple, Mott, Boegner, Oldham, Archbishop Eidem, Bishop of Novi Sad, bishops Berggrav and Damgaard, 20 Sept. 1939, WCC.42.0077; VH to Paton, 5 Oct. 1939, IMC.261143.
128 Schleunes, *Legislating the Holocaust*, 154–73. The German Regulation of Name Changes took effect on 1 Jan. 1939.
129 Gertrude van Tijn, Dutch committee for Jewish refugees (Joodsche Vluchtelingen), Report of Visit to Berlin, 16 Sept., IMC.261143.
130 Parkes, 'The Fate of the Jews', *The Christian News Letter*, 6 Dec. 1939, Supp. 6.
131 The first record of WCCIF knowledge about the Lublin reserve is 3 November. 'The Jewish Reservation Near Lublin and the Situation of the Jews' was sent out in late December under a cover letter, WCC.301.4330. The account reflects the same information as Doc. 5, 22 Nov., in Jürgen Matthäus's collection of WJC and Jewish Agency documents, *Predicting the Holocaust* (Lanham: Rowman & Littlefield in assoc. USHMM, 2019). See also Freudenberg to Paton, 3, 27 Nov; to Hoffmann, 4 Nov; w/circulation of *Neue Zürcher Zeitung*, 9 Nov. article on Lublin; Paton to Freudenberg, 27 Nov. 1939; IMC.261143, 261144, WCC.42.0038.

4

Voices and silences in war: 1940–1944

The severely practical business

The spectres of war, the tones of war, and the effects of war-workers took many forms in the years of World War II. As early as January 1940 war conditions had already made clear that 'the Jews as a mission field' were 'facing deeper and more far-reaching changes than any other nation or religion'. Within the range of ICCAJ concerns was the need to provide aid to refugees that were moving in 'great crowds' to find refuge in France, Britain, Palestine, the United States, South America and the Far East. Refugee relief was seen as a major wartime task of Jewish missions, but from more than one perspective. Beyond the Christian duty of providing material and spiritual aid, refugees were 'a ready-to-hand cross section of Jewish life', affording incomparable 'opportunity for study of the Jewish problem'. The 'poverty' of the refugee plight was making Jews 'especially responsive to acts of Christian kindness', and further study was needed on the 'incalculable effect of the present catastrophe in transforming Judaism from within'.[1]

When the first of three conferences over eighteen months convened in London to take up these war-driven issues in June 1940, it was said to be of a 'severely practical' nature and time would not be spent on 'passing resolutions of sympathy with suffering Jewry', important as they were 'on appropriate occasions'.[2] Opening and closing with prayer, three addresses set the theoretical and theological tones for the sixty-five delegates from sixteen missionary and refugee agencies. In an absentia paper from New York, Conrad Hoffmann outlined the three major wartime tasks as 'Samaritan service to refugees', combating of antisemitism, and advancement of its 'cure' through evangelisation and conversion. William Paton, who agreed with Hoffmann that wherever the 'grisly head' of antisemitism was raised 'the real struggle' was about Christianity, emphasised that study on relations between the Jewish problem, antisemitism and Jewish missions was crucial to postwar planning for 'a new world order'. In agreement with both, Robert Smith, the newly appointed associate director, stressed that Jews were 'the first victims of German aggressions' in a struggle that was 'really directed against Christianity'. The combating of antisemitism from this expressly 'Christian point of view' was, for the three wartime leaders, inexorably linked to spiritual and material relief for non-Aryan Christian refugees, planning of postwar Jewish missions, and prayer for suffering Jewry.[3]

Surveying the damages to Jewish missions since the 1937 Vienna conference, Smith emphasised the difficulty of foreseeing what the map of Europe or 'the map of Jewry is going to be' in the postwar world.[4] Antisemitism and 'anti-Christian tendencies' had overtaken Germany and the twin menaces were spreading with the advance of German armies. Austria, Czechoslovakia, Poland, Denmark, Norway, Holland and Belgium, all of which were key to the mission framework, either as 'sending' or 'receiving nations', were now occupied by German troops, and 'driven before them' were streams of refugees, mission workers and Jewish converts. Work in Germany had been 'liquidated', little was possible in Romania, Hungary and the Balkans, and the Continental sector of ICCAJ was effectually on hold. According to Smith's report, the effects on Jews had also been disastrous. Early mission accounts of Nazi atrocities against Jews, which first 'seemed incredible', no longer needed proof, for it was now clear that 'something amounting to extermination' was going on in Poland. Smith also noted that increasing knowledge of Nazi atrocities was generating greater callousness toward Jewish suffering, for in the views of many 'the fate of the Jews' was small in 'comparison with the agonies of other nations who are our allies'.[5]

Yet in spite of setbacks the overall tenor of the conference was a 'spirit of refreshing detachment', one that accepted the wartime losses with determination to meet the new conditions as conversionary opportunities. Delegates took note that the 'spiritual background' of the war was changing Jews from 'gold-seekers into God-seekers', that the upheavals were rousing Jews from 'spiritual lethargy', and that the deficiencies of Judaism were making Jews 'wanderers in the spiritual as well as physical sense'. What was needed now, Smith rallied, was 'to direct the energies of missions into new channels and follow the Jews in their migrations'.[6]

The discussion as to what that meant and how to proceed in the face of rapidly changing conditions moved along three familiar lines: the need to imprint on churches that Jewish missions were inherent to Christianity, the need to harness full cooperation between world mission societies, and the need for ICCAJ's international expertise in the whole range of problems.[7] From these perspectives, the widespread changes in geographic distribution, mental attitudes and social structures of European Jews were discussed in the language of dislocated missions and projected reconstruction. 'Occupation' of re-drawn Jewish mission fields was set as the immediate postwar goal, with the understanding that it would depend on reliable wartime knowledge of refugee demographics and integrated planning. William Paton took the lead in terms of data, and by mid-August 1940 information was being sought from Gustave Kullmann, Deputy High Commissioner, about 'where the Jews are and how much the numbers in different countries have been affected by emigration and forcible removal'.[8]

To the problem of mapping shifting Jewish populations was added the problem of dividing Jewish mission fields equitably at a second conference eight months later. A pro tem draft of mediating principles had been drawn up by Smith and circulated in February.[9] The main issue was how to allocate postwar spheres of Jewish populations without infringing the rights of individual mission agencies. Pre-war territorial 'claims' in areas where Jewish missions had been established were already in existence, but formal agreements or mechanisms for adjustment of missionary outreach to 'shifting centres of Jewish populations' had never been attempted. The provisional guidelines in discussion at the April 1941 conference were thus aimed at cooperation in respecting the mission 'rights' of those who had already staked territorial claims, as well as equitable division of geographic areas that had not yet been staked. Geographical spheres not previously occupied, spheres that had to be abandoned due to war, and spheres in which work was still at the experimental stages were seen as more or less trouble free in terms of 'infringement'. The overall aim was to keep them that way by integrated planning that avoided breaches, controversies, and was subject to peer review.[10]

Retrospective analysis of the world Jewish mission field before the outbreak of war was seen as the first step. Three types of problems were isolated for wartime analysis: over-distribution of resources, as in Palestine; overlapping of resources, as in Central Europe and Poland; and unoccupied or inadequately occupied fields, as in South America and British Dominions. The study was facilitated by baseline data derived from Jewish sociologist Arthur Ruppin's *Jewish Fate and Future* (1940), as well as summaries by Smith on mission conditions and refugee numbers in occupied nations, Italy, Romania, Hungary, the Balkans, Baltics, South Africa, Australia, Great Britain, Canada, Egypt, Palestine, Iran, Abyssinia, Tunisia, Algeria, Morocco, Central and South America and the United States.[11] By September, three months after the 1941 German invasion of Russia and the potential for another five million Jews being brought under Nazi control, seven designated areas were being discussed for postwar allocations: southeast Poland, Slovakia, Ruthenia, Transylvania; central Europe and other parts of Poland; Palestine, Syria, Iraq, Iran, Egypt, Abyssinia; North Africa, Algeria, Tunisia, Morocco; Russia; South Africa; British Dominions (including Australia). The projections dealt only with geographic spheres that were not self-contained by Jewish home missions and thus did not include Scandinavia, Switzerland, Great Britain, or North and South America, the latter of which was considered a responsibility of the United States.[12]

In the same period, Smith, who was co-head of refugee relief for the Church of Scotland and would become a main voice of ICCAJ during the war, developed a set of guidelines for providing relief to increasing numbers of Jewish refugees. His concern was that humanitarian appeals to Jewish suffering would become confused with the primary duty of evangelisation. At issue was the 'risk of materialising the gospel' by allowing relief to substitute for evangelisation, thereby diverting 'energies from the task of dealing radically with the most profound needs of the Jewish people'.

While realising that refugee work had given opportunity for 'perhaps the most powerful influence on Jews in our generation', he yet warned that one of the 'grave moral dangers' was the problem of 'rice Christians', by which was meant 'an ostracised and persecuted people' who sought 'social and economic advantages'. In such cases, which were 'especially present among the Jews', conversion had to 'be made difficult if it is to be sincere'. Among the safeguards advised publicly in late summer 1941 were: i) postponement of baptism for 'destitute enquirers until ... self supporting', ii) relief funds to 'baptised Christians' only, except when Jews were refused elsewhere – keeping in mind that 'relief does not solve any ultimate problems' for 'the spiritual need of the Jews remains untouched'.[13]

The other major effort of this period was William Paton's formation of two groups of 'influential Christians', a dozen each of theologians, lay and technical experts, to study postwar Jewish issues from the standpoint of the Church. As general secretary of IMC and *ex officio* of ICCAJ, the first group was brought together to look 'radically' at Jewish missions and bring 'the whole Jewish question effectively before the churches'.[14] Among those involved were A.E. Garvie, principal of New College London and moderator of the Federal Council of Free Churches; W.F. Lofthouse, principal, Handsworth College, Birmingham; J.S. Whale, president of Cheshunt College, Cambridge; Edwyn Bevan, historian of comparative religion whom ICCAJ used frequently to defend Jewish missions; Alec Vidler, editor of *Theology* and future dean of King's College Cambridge.

As co-general secretary of WCCIF, Paton's second group was formed to study international order and postwar settlement. Among discussants were historian Arnold Toynbee, study director at the Royal Institute of International Affairs; Sir Alfred Zimmern, past deputy director, League of Nations' Institute of Intellectual Cooperation, and professor of international relations at Oxford; Sir John Hope Simpson, author of the Hope-Simpson Report on British Mandate Palestine (1930) and *The Refugee Problem* (1939). While the two discussion groups were widely different in types and purpose, Paton's stated aim with both was to use his positions in IMC and WCCIF to influence 'influential Christians' to the 'fact' that no aspect of the Jewish problem – postwar settlement, antisemitism or refugees – could be solved in isolation of their relations to the essential nature of Jewish missions.[15]

Running parallel to this set of developments was a series of events that would be seen by ICCAJ as a looming threat to the viability of Jewish missions. In the summer of 1940 talks between James Parkes, Rabbi Israel Mattuck and Kathleen Freeman led to the idea of a collaborative group of Christians and Jews to combat antisemitism, a group separate from the Society of Jews and Christians that Mattuck chaired and Parkes would soon co-chair with him.[16] The initial talks, along with Freeman's organisational skills, opened the way for an October meeting of six Christians and six Jews, with invitations issued by the Anglican Dean of St Paul's in London. The meeting had to be postponed, however, due to the onslaught of German bombings that began in September. Parkes was among the six Christians when the group finally met in July 1941, and so was William Paton. Second and third meetings were held on 27 October and 19 November, neither of which Paton was made aware.[17]

On 20 November Paton wrote to Parkes, asking if 'anything concrete' had come from the July meeting. Parkes's reply was that Henry Carter, secretary of Methodist Social Welfare and chair of the Christian Council for Refugees, had joined the group with other key figures, and that the last meeting had launched the 'first concrete step' of a British Council of Christians and Jews.[18] By the time Paton received Parkes's answer, he had already heard from Henry Carter, to whom he penned an excoriating letter. Charging that his exclusion was based on his work in Jewish missions, he indignantly reminded Carter that he held 'perhaps the most representative inter-church post in the country' and would not hesitate to take the matter public. Paton went on to fume that it 'would be calamitous' if only Jews dealt with the 'question of the Jews' in postwar considerations, but no less so if the only Christians were those accepting the 'Jewish' view of Christian missions. Carter struck back by denying the charges and making clear that he would gladly deal with the matter publicly.[19]

In the talks that continued into the first week of December, Paton smoothed the surface, as he often did, and continued his attack in the background. Writing to E.N. Cooper at the Home Office Department of Aliens on 10 December, he urged that 'anxiety' over antisemitism was resulting in a tendency to overlook fundamental differences between 'devout Jews and devout Christians'. Referring to the current British attempt to bring Jews and Christians together to combat antisemitism, Paton sceptically pointed out that such attempts always seemed to involve a Christian receding from Jewish missions instead of Christian insistence that 'the Gospel has no bounds'.[20] Twelve days later, in a letter to the new ICCAJ associate director, he urged Robert Smith to stand firm against joint meetings of Jews and Christians unless 'insistence' on the 'universal evangelistic imperative' was preserved in advance. Paton had no objection to 'Jewish–Christian collaboration on defined themes', so long as Jews understood the Christian position, but 'any kind of cooperation which tacitly annuls part of the Christian witness' must be eschewed 'as morally futile'.[21]

A month later Robert Smith applied the principle of protecting Christian prerogatives to the issues of freedom and justice at an Edinburgh conference on the 'Post-War Situation of Jewry'. As an offshoot of the London conferences in 1940 and 1941, the January 1942 event was dominated by ICCAJ views even though it was sponsored by the Church of Scotland General Assembly for Presbyterian Churches of Great Britain and Ireland. All four speakers were delegates to the earlier conferences, and three (including Smith) were ICCAJ members. The purpose of the convening, which had been in planning since Smith drafted the proposal for the division of postwar Jewish mission fields, was to consider what approach could be made to ensure postwar rights for Jews while safeguarding Christian liberty.[22]

The issue was laid out in three overlapping parts: the problem of restoring political rights for Jews, the problem of restoring religious freedom for Jews, and the problem of preserving rights and freedoms for Christians. The goal was not to affirm the need for restoration of human rights for Jews – delegates readily agreed to that – but rather to distinguish rights and freedoms so that evangelisation and conversion of Jews would not be impeded. Smith pressed those points in a complexly argued paper on 'The Problem of Securing Religious Freedom for the Jews'. Emphasing that religious liberty had to be viewed from the aspects of both 'freedom of worship' and 'freedom of missionary propaganda', he argued that freedom of worship was dependent upon the freedom to follow the leading of a higher revelation of truth, which was itself derived from the freedom of preaching.[23]

There were two mutually dependent freedoms at stake, in other words, and the second could not be abandoned in lieu of the first, as was the case in goodwill movements that brought Christians and Jews together in a non-proselytising environment. *If* 'human dignity' were to be secured for Jews, so Smith argued, Christian belief in a 'final and universal truth that reconciled all human differences' could not be silenced. It had to be robustly heralded as 'more solid than the rights of man, equal citizenship or any of the other slogans of the emancipation', for the question was not how to get justice and equality, 'but how to rescue the Jews from a spiritual ghetto'.[24]

Yet that did not mean that postwar rights for Jews were to be ignored. The conference made strikingly clear in the first part of a resolution adopted after Smith's paper that *all* human rights for Jews had to be secured in any postwar settlement. The resolution deplored denial of equal treatment or citizen status 'to persons of Jewish descent'; it urged repeal of all unjust legislation; it called for postwar restoration to 'the full status of human dignity'; and it urged British and Allied governments to provide a 'scheme of emigration for Jews who cannot find a home in Europe'. But the resolution also held that the right to propagate the Christian gospel must in no way be infringed upon by liberties granted to Jews. This protecting part of the resolution was captured in the language of essentiality, namely, that the 'liberty of conscience is an essential part of civil liberty' and that 'free exchange of religious convictions is a necessary condition of all understanding between races and nations'. On these grounds the resolution went on to urge that governments recognise 'the unfettered right of every individual to free choice in religious faith and to the public profession and preaching of it'. In stressing the unimpeded right to profess and preach, the resolution safeguarded the Christian right to evangelise Jews while satisfying the question of 'how to rescue Jews from a spiritual ghetto'.[25]

Without the papers and deliberations preceding it, however, this was not so obvious since the Christian-protecting aims were not the ones publicised. The resolution itself, which was widely distributed to Presbyterian and ecumenical circles as benevolent concern for Jewish rights, did not reveal the discourse behind it or the attitudes informing it. It gave no hint that Smith's paper on the problem of securing religious freedom for Jews contended that the Jewish 'racial religion' was 'bound up with birth and blood in much the same way as the Nazi religion'.[26] It failed to capture that Clephane Macanna, who would become a postwar chairman of ICCAJ, pointed to modern Jewry's insistence on national rights while preserving its racial and national identity.[27] It revealed none of the ways in which 'the Jewish problem' was framed in discussions: 'Jews from European countries were dispersing to go and start a Jewish problem elsewhere'; 'they exerted a dangerous secularising influence'; 'if we shot every anti-Semite tomorrow, the non-Christian Jew ... would create more anti-Semites by his own conduct'.[28]

The benevolent aspects of the widely quoted resolution on postwar Jewish rights gave no insight into any of this, nor did it reveal that it was an inseparable part of a larger discourse that was as much about defending a conversionary social structure as it was about postwar rights for Jews. The core point being defended, here and at all three wartime conferences, was that 'there was one solution and one solution only for the Jewish problem', namely, 'when the Jews were won to Christ'.[29]

The neutrality of silence

As ICCAJ positional lines were being trenched on proselytising rights and postwar Jewish missions, ecumenical lines of a different sort were also being drawn. In early May 1940, before German aggressions spread into Luxembourg, Belgium, Holland and France, Willem Visser 't Hooft issued a memorandum that would lead to an informal policy on wartime statements. It had been eight months since the outbreak of war and 'many Christian circles' were criticising WCCIF silence in the face of the present world struggles, with 'widespread conviction' that the ecumenical movement would fail if silence prevailed.[30] The Administrative Committee had ventured a statement in January in Apeldoorn, Holland, but it went no further than delineation of three positions: i) that a statement should be made against aggression and suppression of freedoms; ii) that a corporate statement about war issues could jeopardise unity and possible peace; iii) that the role of ecumenism was mediation and not public confrontation of issues.[31] Deliberations had been of no avail, in Visser 't Hooft's view, because the committee failed to see that the war was only one aspect of 'the great spiritual conflict' engulfing the world. His aim in 'The Ecumenical Church and the International Situation' was to break the stalemate by bringing home the reality of the 'war behind the war', one in which the Church could be neither silent nor neutral.[32]

Like the war behind the war, however, there were words behind the words that made them contextually stipulative to those in the wartime milieu of Geneva ecumenicity. As revealed in dozens of confidential minutes, a distinction between 'political' and 'spiritual' neutrality was being made by the Emergency Committee of Christian Organizations (ECCO), formed by ecumenical leaders at the outbreak of war. In brief, as one result of the probing discussions, it was unanimously agreed that there could be no such thing as 'spiritual' neutrality on issues conflicting with Christian principles, but it was 'neither our job nor our right' to make political statements or take sides in political aspects of the war. The wartime task for ecumenical organisations, as Visser 't Hooft framed it in November 1939, was to steer a narrow course between defending ecumenical principles and mitigating political barriers between Christians of belligerent and neutral nations.[33]

As a principal ECCO discussant, he employed the same neutrality distinctions in his memorandum the following May. It was divided into two parts: a seven-page argument on the 'anti-Christian forces' moving the world toward 'spiritual and moral nihilism', and a five-page warrant for what had to be done as 'great spiritual powers struggle for possession of the human soul'. In arguing 'the war behind the war' he held that the spiritual war was the 'real war' and world de-Christianisation by anti-Christian forces was the 'real question'. The military and economic war was 'only part and not even the most important part of the total war situation'. The role of WCCIF, as key representative of non-Roman churches in a time of 'life and death decisions for the

Church and civilization as a whole', was therefore to 'confess' the Church universal in four related ways. It had to speak against 'anti-Christian forces' so that silence did not turn into 'compromise'; it had to speak clearly about the supranational unity of the Church; it had to speak warning about threats to unity; and it had to speak order to the nations of the world. Moreover, it had to speak from the spiritual realm as *one* unified body that shared responsibility for Christianity's failure to make its presence a living reality in the world.[34]

Responses to the memorandum were divided. Robert Mackie, general secretary of WSCF and ECCO discussant, declaimed Visser 't Hooft's equivocation of 'aggressive anti-Christian elements' with the 'powers of darkness', on the grounds that it was 'dangerous to think or write' in terms of 'spiritual warfare'. He had no objection to the idea of 'a spiritual war in which no Christian can remain neutral', but the use of such metaphysical language failed to distinguish human agency, thereby implying that 'dark spirits' were in control of anti-Christian forces and ideologies. Such arguments, he warned, confused the spiritual demise of the world with 'actual warfare' and relegated issues of societal justice to the spiritual realm.[35] John Bennett of the Pacific School of Religion was 'convinced and stirred' by the need for a formal statement, but cautioned restraint, less pessimism and more fact-based distinctions, particularly in stating that invasion of a nation by a totalitarian force necessarily implied the destruction of Christianity.[36] Administrative chair Marc Boegner from France was concerned that voices from belligerent countries would lack authority, while others, including William Adams Brown, focused on the wartime difficulties of coming together to deliberate a statement. Paton in particular, as in fall 1939, was still 'doubtful' about a WCCIF statement on the war and, being cut off by its escalation, it seemed of little worth for a few 'in the World Council capacity' to say what was being said elsewhere.[37]

Archbishop William Temple's response was much weightier, and with it came his authority as chairman of the Provisional Committee. Drawing on the fact that WCCIF was still 'in formation' and would remain so until a full assembly of world churches ratified its constitution, he could see no way in which such a statement could be made without full ecclesiastical authority. Even an unofficial or quasi-official statement was inconceivable unless the Administrative Committee could meet, a possibility that was more and more dimmed by the war. More crucially, if WCCIF were to speak corporately on the war, it could erect 'fresh barriers', making it not only difficult but almost impossible for Christians from warring nations to reunite in a postwar body that had 'taken sides' or 'officially condemned, directly or by implication'. But, Temple went on to say, '*if we are silent because we have no authority to speak*', the churches from belligerent and neutral nations could reunite in WCCIF in the postwar period.[38]

To narrow the lens on what would become WCCIF working wartime policy, Temple was employing a strategic device set in place by the British Ministry of Information (MOI) in the early days of the war. As Diane Kirby has revealed in another context, the MOI strategy was to distinguish between official and unofficial statements so that Anglican leaders, 'acting in their *individual* capacities, and not as churchmen', could cooperate with the Religions Division of the Ministry without 'compromising ... ecclesiastical status or the Ministry's propaganda'.[39] By adopting the same strategy for WCCIF, its official voice could remain neutrally silent on divisive issues while allowing its constituent leaders to speak and act in their other capacities. Rather than speaking corporately on anything divisive, Temple's solution was for each to speak individually and to do so in a coordinated fashion so that 'the same message' of ecumenicity – orchestrated from Geneva – could be given 'with a variety of emphasis'.[40]

By the time Visser 't Hooft received and responded to Temple's directive on 6 June, Belgium, Luxembourg and Holland had fallen, the battle at Dunkirk had driven the British to evacuate by sea, and the last lines of French defence were about to be breached. With his own Dutch country now under Nazi control, Visser 't Hooft's concerns had deepened to despair about whether an ecumenical movement could even survive in a world in which the Church was fighting 'a life and death struggle'. His letter, which recognised the issues of making a corporate statement as well as the wartime difficulties of coming together, was an anxious response of 'buts' and 'howevers', which nevertheless reconciled with Temple's solution.

Yet, while acknowledging the wartime difficulties of coming together, he also cautioned of the hazards of *not* speaking out if leaders should come together while the 'foundations ... of the whole of civilization are shaking'. If that were to happen, he pointed out, it would be very difficult for 'people to feel that our Movement has any relation to the realities of the world'.[41]

Yet when Temple, Visser 't Hooft, Paton, Bell, Oldham, Leiper and Brown were brought together in London in April 1942, no attempt was made to find even a quasi-official word in the name of WCCIF. The occasion was Temple's inauguration as Archbishop of Canterbury, which could be argued as inappropriate or inconvenient for deliberations but, given the world situation and the previously stated urgings, such argument does not hold. Nor does it size with Visser 't Hooft's report of other war issues dealt with on the inaugural trip to London.[42] Moreover, at no point leading up to the 1942 gathering of WCCIF principals in London was a joint statement *in lieu of* an in-person meeting considered, even though they remained in constant contact not only by mail but courier and hand-carried documents between Geneva, London and New York. The reality was far more the case that the whole issue of corporate statements on the war flagged from exhaustion as acceptance set in that the safest and most unity-preserving position was to say that WCCIF did not have the ecclesiastical power or authority to make official pronouncements.[43]

Indeed, the adopted position was repeated so *ad nauseum* that Karl Barth broke out in harsh criticism of WCCIF in December 1942.[44] He deplored the fact that while memoranda, conferences and studies occupied Geneva, at no time was 'the Ecumenical Movement heard' on decisive issues, not from 1933 to 1938 when it was embodied in UCCLW, nor from 1938 to the present day when embodied in WCCIF. Barth was tired of hearing 'that the Ecumenical Council ... had no authority, no commission, and no power to speak publicly and authoritatively'. He found it not only 'deplorable' but 'tragicomic' that a 'discernible form' of ecumenism had finally been attained but was unable to act because it was 'engaged in some endless process of development'. He rejected the idea that a 'publicly binding utterance of a real Council of the Churches ... must ... have the character of a papal encyclical', and refuted as invalid any explanation of silence based on the unstable argument that WCCIF did not have ecclesiastic power to speak. Instead of waiting for churches to give such power by a formal vote of confidence, it 'should long ago, without asking leave, have given proof of spirit and strength even at the risk of being blamed for it'. If WCCIF continued to insist that it was incapable of speaking, Barth warned, history will view it 'as a friendly but impotent game like the League of Nations ... which also became morally bankrupt because nobody felt inclined to accept responsibility for endowing it with *power*'.[45]

The sting of Barth's criticism was deeply felt in Geneva but the silence on divisive issues remained unchanged.[46] Silence on some issues, however, did not mean silence on others. What was to be said and done within the parameters of neutrality was to use every available platform to herald the idea that ecumenical unity was emanating from Geneva in both theory and practice. As gauged at the outbreak of war, WCCIF would 'stand or fall' by what could be accomplished in brokering 'Christian understanding between the nations'. The more Europe was cut off by the aggressions of war, so it was added a year later, the more incumbent it was to 'reiterate emphatically that the Ecumenical Movement is a fellowship of Churches which cuts across all geographical, political, or racial divisions', avoiding 'even the slightest impression of a break in solidarity'.[47]

That WCCIF could be producer, distributor and in many ways controller of an ecumenical information network became central to this line of thinking. An extensive survey in 1938 had shown that the ecumenical *International Christian Press and Information Service* (*ICPIS*), published weekly in three languages to 405 religious journals and papers in 57 countries, could be used to great advantage. While circulation impact was greater on the European Continent, the reproduction of press items was such that 'hundreds of thousands of readers all over the world' made it a 'perfect instrument' of ecumenical coordination, 'education and propaganda'.[48] Recognising before the war that no mechanism was in place for saying what could not be said officially, Visser 't Hooft thus introduced the practice of planting articles, prefaced by the tag 'we have received the following from ecumenical sources'. One of the first planted stories, in fact, was an article on the reasons why ecumenical organisational statements on the war could not be made officially.[49]

The strategy, however, was not limited to *ICPIS* nor were forays with the British Ministry of Information limited to William Temple. Visser 't Hooft also collaborated with the Religions Division of MOI, headed by former ICCAJ exec Kenneth Maclennan. As revealed in seventeen letters from fall 1939 to spring 1942, he worked closely with MOI deputy chief Hugh Martin, ecumenical editor of SCM Press, to plant stories that advanced mutually beneficial religious issues in *ICPIS* and elsewhere, with assurances from both sides that connections would not be revealed. In January 1940 alone, for example, Visser 't Hooft oversaw the translation and placement of twelve copies each of MOI articles by Paton, Temple and A. E. Garvie in religious periodicals in Norway, Denmark, Sweden, Switzerland, France, Hungary, China and Japan.[50] He also introduced the concept of an ecumenical 'sieve group' for *ICPIS*, which was put into play by ECCO leaders in June 1942. The idea was to anonymously 'interpret' material on the churches of neutral and belligerent nations in ways that would counter negativity and disunity between them, while emphasising similarities in the spiritual challenges of the war.[51]

In these and other direct and indirect ways, ecumenicity as a cohering element flowing from WCCIF in Geneva to the non-Roman churches of the world was a continuous theme throughout the war. A crucial piece of the message was the need for re-Christianisation of the world. Although Robert Mackie remained averse to Visser 't Hooft's metaphysical language about the 'war behind the war', he and other leaders were united on what needed to be done to win the spiritual war: namely, to impress with renewed force that 'the Church holds the secret' to salvation.[52] It was thus recognised early in the war that the common mission goal could be used to advantage as a unifying element of the churches, such that by fall 1940 WCCIF was liaising for not only German but French and Dutch missions.[53] At the same time Visser 't Hooft was advancing the work of Dutch scholar Hendrik Kraemer who, jointly with Hoffmann, would lead the first WCC conference on Jewish missions in 1949.[54] Kraemer was an international expert on bonding churches and missions, and when asked to produce a volume for the 1938 IMC world conference in Madras, he had framed the 'obligation' to evangelise Jews not only 'as stringent' *but* 'even more stringent' than the 'rest of the non-Christian world'.[55] For Kraemer, like Hoffmann, Paton and Visser 't Hooft, Jewish missions was the litmus test of Christianity's efficacy to evangelise the world, and its inclusion in the WCCIF message, like other wartime efforts, was part of the overarching goal to harness and promote all aspects of the Church under the Geneva umbrella of ecumenicity.

The silence of neutrality

Even before the outbreak of war Visser 't Hooft voiced his intention to highlight the ecumenical task 'implicit' in the refugee initiative.[56] It was another way in which WCCIF could manifest ecumenical reality in a war-torn world. That ICCAJ director Conrad Hoffmann was named chief officer in August 1939 is highly relevant, even though the outbreak of war altered his appointment, for it signals clearly that relief efforts for non-Aryan Christians were rooted in the Jewish mission imperative. The small, but far from insignificant, office that developed in Geneva, which was perpetually underfunded, under-staffed and under-supported in contrast to ecumenical Protestant interest in POWs, must on all accounts be seen as a dedicated effort to provide material and spiritual relief to suffering refugees. But the complexly layered story is also a story of what was known about the Nazi assault on European Jews, and what was said privately and publicly about it. The many-dimensioned role of information was central in both respects, for what was known not only determined the location and extent of relief, it formed the basis for which moral and practical decisions were made on the need for interventional protests.

To understand the development of the refugee initiative, it is necessary to grasp its place within the framework of ECCO, as well as its relation to the International Committee of the Red Cross (ICRC). Chairman Max Huber – as implied by his nomination of Nobel Laureate Archbishop Söderblom in 1930, his chairing of the Committee on Church and State at Oxford in 1937, his *Good*

Samaritan, Reflections on the Gospel and Work in the Red Cross in 1945 – held an esteemed position in the ecumenical movement.[57] Huber's ICRC was the official coordinating body of national Red Cross societies, and ECCO, which was formed in consultation with Huber at the outbreak of war, followed in kind by joining in one body the Geneva leaders of the six major ecumenical organisations to function as a coordinating instrument for national Protestant agencies working in wartime ministry.

The informal agreement between the two committees was that wartime work would divide into the fields of relief and welfare in accordance with Articles 16, 17, 39, 78 of the 1929 Geneva Convention on POWs. Red Cross bodies would be responsible for relief in the areas of food, shelter, clothing and other basic needs of prisoners, internees and evacuated civilians, while each of the major ecumenical bodies would provide spiritual, moral and social welfare to specific groups, with the understanding that crossover would be inevitable: YMCA (male POWs and internees); YWCA (female POWs and internees); WSCF (student POWs and internees); ECB (churches and pastors); WA (POW chaplaincy); WCCIF (non-Aryan refugees and POW chaplaincy).[58]

The second common feature is that relations between the two organisations were structured in accordance with ICRC's 'well known policy of strict neutrality', as well as mutual agreement 'to pool information' where it could be helpful.[59] ICRC's neutrality policy functioned on the premise that no distinctions in suffering could be made, that aid had to be distributed equally to all belligerents, and that intermediaries like ICRC had to be governed by impartiality. As framed by Huber in a 1936 article that defended its refusal to release information to the League of Nations on Italy's use of chemical weapons in the invasion of Ethiopia, that included the obligation to treat information entrusted to it with discretionary measures that were 'free from every suspicion of partiality, political or other'.[60]

ECCO leaders agreed with ICRC neutrality policy, as well as Huber's belief that there could be no spiritual neutrality, but that did not prevent ongoing discourse about the moral, spiritual and political challenges of maintaining neutrality, and what it meant both organisationally and for the ecumenical movement as a whole.

There were thus levels and variations of neutrality thinking in these circles, as well as differences in organisational challenges. As noted previously, Visser 't Hooft was central to the idea of steering a course of ECCO neutrality, as well as a key proponent of cooperation with ICRC, but WCCIF was also its own entity with its own agenda and reasons for neutrality. The policy set by Temple's directive in May 1940 – that speaking on incendiary issues would erect barriers but neutral silence would allow churches of warring nations to reunite in WCCIF at the end of war – all but determined that its course of refugee action would be relief rather than interventional protest.

As the *only* ECCO body specifically designated to non-Aryan refugees, it is equally relevant that WCCIF became the principal ecumenical holder of Jewish refugee information. Collaborative sharing was robust from the onset of the war, and much of what was known in the early days came from mission and refugee sources through the vast networks connecting the official and unofficial national affiliates of the major ECCO bodies.[61] Their headquartered locations on the crossroads of Geneva in neutral Switzerland, home to the League of Nations and dozens of international and world organisations, including ICRC, allowed for a continuous current of privileged information between Geneva, London and New York. In addition to the vast networks of ECCO, information flowed from WCCIF constituency sources in Germany and all occupied and satellite countries, as well as unoccupied France, neutral Spain, Portugal and Sweden. Other streams included the Central Jewish Agency, World Jewish Congress (WJC) and the Relief Committee for the War Stricken Jewish Population in Geneva (RELICO); the High Commission for Refugees, British Ministry of Information and Royal Institute of International Affairs in London.

Information from these and other sources was the key determinant of refugee aid, the grounds on which appeals were made and funds distributed. The first information-driven task after the onset of war was collaboration with the Grüber office in Berlin to raise emigration funding for German non-Aryan Protestants threatened by deportation to the Jewish Reservation in Lublin, Poland. But even with the use of 'annihilation' in the 1939 Christmas appeal, donations barely trickled in. That focus began to shift after Visser 't

Hooft met with High Commissioner Herbert Emerson in March 1940. After Emerson reported that Nazi transports to Lublin had halted, he cautioned about further emphasis on Poland. His concern was that the Jewish Joint Distribution Committee had just reduced allocations for aid in Belgium, France and Switzerland in order to increase aid in eastern Europe, and that more emphasis on Poland would lead to more reductions in Jewish aid to central Europe and, thereby, increase antisemitism in the European countries bearing the brunt of the refugee burden.[62]

The second event influencing WCCIF focus came two months later with Germany's aggressions on France, the French–German armistice six weeks later with its line of demarcation leading across France to the southern Swiss border, and thousands of refugees fleeing to the unoccupied southern zone. In quick succession the first anti-Jewish law was issued by the Vichy government in unoccupied France on 3 October; a law of internment for all foreign Jews was passed the following day; and three weeks later 6,500 German non-Aryans from Baden and Saar were forcibly deported to internment camps in the unoccupied zone.[63] Public outcry and WCCIF appeals for ecumenical funding brought with it stipulated Swiss allocations, which allowed the Geneva office to engage in a relief and welfare service that became the primary (but not only) field of refugee activity. Beginning in late fall 1940 with later expansion, it assumed partial support for two French Protestant initiatives in the southern unoccupied zone, both of which were initially launched in the internment camp at Gurs: Aumônerie des étrangers protestants en France, a chaplaincy service headed by Rev. Pierre Toureille, and Comité Inter-Mouvements Auprès Des Évacués (Cimade), supervised by Madeleine Barot.[64]

ICRC pooling, 1941–1942

The welfare and relief work in the French camps gave WCCIF and ECCO access to first-hand refugee information. Both Barot and (to less extent) Toureille, along with other ECCO associates, moved back and forth between unoccupied southern France and Geneva with a steady stream of information. Visser 't Hooft's own trip in fall 1941, parts of which were included in a November confidential report on the church situation in Europe, gives insight to some of the ways in which information was understood, transmitted or held. The report was organised according to the parts that could be published without 'mention of origin', those that could be shared with discretion, and those that could not be published at all. Boundaries were drawn between what was transmitted to groups of ecumenical leaders and what they could pass along more publicly. Transmissible information included the spirit of reception in the camps where non-Aryan Christians were praising 'ecumenical' meals, shoes and literature received through WCCIF supported funding. A transmissible word on refugee conditions was 'tragic', but the more content-laden parts of the report could not be published in any form. The general facts of the camps – inhumane treatment by guards, 'very bad' overall conditions, 'cases of real cruelty', 'terrible things' happening during requisitions for labour – were not publishable at all on the grounds that it would 'make it impossible to continue the work'.[65]

The same report, which noted that 15,000 Berlin Jews and 10,000 from the Greater Reich had been deported to Poland, also revealed by way of omission that some non-publishable information was being kept within the circles of neutrality. More specifically, alarming information about Poland had already been transmitted to ICRC before the November report was issued.

Visser 't Hooft's memorandum to Carl Burckhardt and Max Huber on 29 October 1941 was the first of three such shared reports during a critical fifteen-month period. It was based in part on a confidential ECCO report of 22 October by a delegate from the Central Mennonite Committee on a German Foreign Office tour of Zakopane, Cracow, Radom, Lublin and Warsaw. Although the ECCO report included the ghettos of Cracow and Radom, both of which were in 'acute need',[66] the first part of Visser 't Hooft's 'Zur Lage in Polen' focused only on the Warsaw ghetto, where famine, typhus and a mortality rate of 26 per cent in children under 3 were said to be spreading. The second part, which was based on unacknowledged Jewish sources, summarised what was thought to be the 'beginning of the complete deportation of Jews and Christians of Jewish origin from the Reich and the Protectorate'. Transports from Berlin had taken place on 19–20 October, Jews from the

Rhineland were 'already there or en route', trains from Vienna were ongoing, and some 2,000 more Jews were being deported from Prague to what were thought to be hut camps in Litzmannstadt (Lodz).[67]

The stated reason for the WCCIF memorandum was not to condemn or intervene with the deportations – it had already been recognised in March that 'there was no practical way of stopping this'[68] – but rather 'to intervene on behalf of the persecuted' with relief that would mitigate the 'misery'. As self-understood, the refugee office could not launch its own relief programme but neither could it 'close its eyes', for the 'Jewish question' touched 'the centre of the Christian message', and neglect to raise a 'warning and protective voice' would be disobedience to God. The privately raised voice to ICRC was an appeal to investigate 'the most urgent needs' of 'Polish as well as Jewish populations' in the largest areas of the General Government and Warthegau.[69]

That appeal was followed nine months later by a note from Freudenberg to the ICRC Joint Relief Committee on the need for food and medications in the camps of Izbica and Piaski (near Lublin), Warsaw and Lodz; Riga in Latvia; Wilna and Kowno in Lithuania. Included was a short but sincere appeal to 'continue to relieve the fate of these unfortunate people'. Nothing more was put in writing to ICRC until the end of the year, by which time the situation in Poland was widely known and publicised to be that of extermination.[70]

In the interim period, a long-term associate of the World YMCA and delegate to the 1927 Budapest–Warsaw conferences was the principal source of information during the 1942 deportations of non-French Jews from the unoccupied zone of France. In the wake of the French–German armistice in June 1940, Dr Donald Lowrie set up office for the World Alliance of YMCAs in Marseilles and, under the approving eye of the Vichy Ministry of Interior, organised twenty-five national and world relief bodies into what became known as the Nîmes Committee.[71] As organiser and chairman, Lowrie had access to Vichy authorities including, at the onset of deportations, Marshal Philippe Pétain.[72] In addition to reporting on his 6 August meeting with Pétain, he wrote nine confidential first-hand reports, some twenty-six pages in all, which were widely circulated through the ecumenical channels of Geneva, London and New York.[73]

The Lowrie reports began immediately after the first known train left Gurs on 6 August at midnight. Ten thousand foreign Jews were to be deported within the month, the first 3,600 in shipments on 6, 8, 10 and 12 August. The destination, he alerted, was 'uniformly reported' as the Jewish reservation in Poland but, given that children and elderly, 'epileptics, palsied, insane and bedridden' were being taken, a 'need for labour' did not explain the deportations. The best that could be imagined was that Germany's plan for a new Europe involved 'purification' of all undesirable elements.[74] His further reports in August on the 'terror and suffering' being inflicted revealed that deportation numbers were increasing and that 15,000 more Jews were to be taken over the next month.[75] As the deportation net widened, Lowrie described in detail how exemptions were being reduced and categories 'altered almost daily to include more Jews', with no indication of abatement.[76] By the 17 September report 10,495 Jews had been deported, by early October 'about 11,000, and the 'revolting' conditions in which they were carried out was made starkly clear by Lowrie's depictions of the 'bestial violation of all principles of human dignity and respect'.[77]

In addition to these first-hand accounts of Nazi deportations from unoccupied France, WCCIF was receiving reports on measures being applied on the other end. A 'reliable German source with close relations to certain military and industrial circles' told of the arrival of trains in Poland from France, Holland and Belgium, partially filled with corpses used in the 'manufacture of soap, glue, and train oil'. The same report indicated that Nazi studies of 'methods of extermination and utilization of corpses' had been ordered. Another, written in code unravelled, reported that Jews used in heavy industry were the only ones exempt out of 600,000 in Warsaw, and that all others were being removed from the city to a rural area for mass killings.[78]

Killing centres and gas chambers were also made known through connections to Swedish diplomat Baron von Otter, who learned of Treblinka, Belzec and Sobibor from Kurt Gerstein, a Confessing church member who, in Visser 't Hooft's words, entered the SS 'in order to find out the truth'.[79] Visser 't Hooft himself had learned of the story by late August or early September, which agreed in essence with a report by Gerhart Riegner of the WJC. Riegner's report on the Nazi plan to settle the Jewish question by exterminating all Jews in occupied and satellite countries was known and discussed by WCCIF no later than 23 September as an 'extremely critical situation', and, as recorded three days later, it was understood that 'deportation means in many cases extermination'.[80]

So *why* – in the face of acknowledged extermination and a deepening pool of what was seen as reliable information – did WCCIF not respond until December? Two sets of archival documents offer some shadowed light. First, at an ECCO meeting in mid-February, Hugo Cedergren of YMCA War Prisoners Aid reported that the Quaker Centre in Berlin was urging 'that the less done by our organizations for non-Aryans not yet deported, the better'. The idea relayed was that no one was to 'write or speak about these people', 'for the sake of the people themselves', in order to not draw Nazi attention.[81]

The second set of archival documents are equally uncomfortable, for they reveal that WCCIF was immersed in Provisional Committee meetings on postwar reconstruction of European churches when the Riegner report was acknowledged. Marc Boegner and Samuel Cavert had been brought to Geneva to draft a reconstruction programme, with an attendant schedule of meetings, lunch and reception with Red Cross leaders on 24 and 25 September.[82] The meetings, as it turned out, took place right after learning of the Riegner report on the 23rd and just before acknowledging that deportation meant extermination on the 26th. The WCCIF minutes that day confirm that the 'extremely critical situation' had been discussed 'very fully' over the previous few days, but there was no talk whatsoever of a break in policy on public statements. Instead, the September 1942 decision was to increase aid to the refugee groups to whom WCCIF was already committed, particularly those in southern France.[83] This decision, it is important to note, was consistent with ICRC's own fall decision to stay its course of neutrality *sans* protest.[84]

At least three other reports on deportations and the worsening conditions for Jews in Belgium, France, Germany, Holland, the Protectorate, Hungary, Italy, Bulgaria, Latvia, Poland, Romania,

Serbia, Slovakia and Switzerland reached the WCCIF refugee office by the end of September or early October.[85] Whether or not all of this, as well as the Nazi occupation of southern France on 11 November, weakened the WCCIF decision is up for question. What is clear is that by the end of November the refugee office was aware that Riegner's report had been verified by the US State Department on 24 November, and that WJC president Rabbi Stephen Wise had announced it in a publicised press conference on the same day. The British section of WJC followed with a circular plea three days later to the archbishops of Canterbury, York and Wales, the Moderator of the Church of Scotland, the President of the Methodist Conference, and Cardinal Hinsley, a copy of which was directed to WCCIF. Emphasising that Nazi extermination of 'the entire Jewish population, men women and children' was in progress, the WJC letter begged church leaders to lend voices and aid 'to save the remnants of the Jewish people of occupied Europe'.[86]

When WCCIF at last responded on 3 December, it was again in a private letter to ICRC's Carl Burckhardt. 'Assuming' that he was already 'informed of the mass executions' of Jews, Visser 't Hooft's update on the 'persecution and misery of the Jews in Poland' was that a 'distinguished German', whose reliability was guaranteed, reported that in one location '6,000 Jews, men, women and children are being shot every day', that the 'executions are made in three groups ... of 2,000 persons' and that it had 'been going on for weeks'. The rest of the note repeated from his 'Zur Lage' of October 1941 that the 'Jewish question touches the centre of the Christian message' and thereby compels our voice to be raised 'on behalf of these people who are being threatened with extermination'. The request to ICRC was essentially the same as 'Zur Lage' – 'take urgent steps to send delegates to the areas in question' – but this time Theresienstadt in the Protectorate was also included.[87] Six days later on 9 December Freudenberg sent the update on daily mass exterminations of '6000' Jewish women, men and children to Cavert in New York, with a capitalised 'CONFIDENTIAL'. By the end of the month another thirty pages on the camps of Poland and Romania were part of WCCIF's deepening pool of information.[88]

The Bermuda Conference, 1943

It was not until the following March that a WCCIF statement moved beyond its information-sharing agreement with ICRC, and, when it did, it was coloured by internal and external controversy. On 8 April co-general secretary William Paton heard from High Commissioner Herbert Emerson that Visser 't Hooft had issued an Aide-Memoire with the World Jewish Congress.[89] That he would do so without consultation was an infuriating matter for Paton and, after reviewing the document, it was also a matter of avid dissent. 'Being somewhat an expert in the matter', he did not mince words in regretting that Visser 't Hooft 'had to some extent swallowed the Zionist proposals' and 'gone in so definitely' with the WJC.[90]

Paton's other main objection coincided with Emerson's, namely that the Aide-Memoire hinged on the claim that the most acute refugee problem was the 'deliberate extermination of the Jews'. Emerson, assuming (correctly) that the Aide-Memoire had been initially drafted by WJC, held that 'Jews made a great mistake in speaking only of Jews and in systematically disregarding ... that a very large number of refugees of all kinds are not Jews at all'. For him, as well as Paton, such singular attitude was a 'fostering cause' of antisemitism and Visser 't Hooft's involvement gave credence to the 'excessive Jewish propaganda'. The suggested 'rescue' in the Aide-Memoire – exchange of Jews for German civilians and en bloc admission into Allied countries – was unthinkable to Emerson and Paton, for antisemitism in Britain would only worsen if German civilians were exchanged for Jews instead of British prisoners. The idea of 'abrogating' security for en bloc admission of Jews was equally disdained as 'wildcat thinking'.[91]

To place this in the broader context of what was known and what was being said publicly, talk of systematic Jewish extermination and the need for international action was widespread by March 1943. Highly publicised statements condemning the Nazi extermination of Jews were issued in December 1942 by the exiled Polish government; the International Federation of Trade Unions; and the United Nations Joint Declaration of Belgium, Luxembourg, Holland, Czechoslovakia, Norway, United Kingdom, Northern Ireland, United States, Yugoslavia, Greece, Poland, Soviet Union and the French National Committee, which was announced in London, Washington and Moscow and then broadcast in twenty-three languages to all of Nazi-occupied Europe. One immediate result from Britain, stirred by pressure from church, synagogue and relief action leaders, was a January proposal from the British Foreign Office to the US State Department for an international conclave on the refugee problem, which came to be known as the Bermuda Conference.

Running alongside these public calls for action, however, was a strong undercurrent which held that Jews should not have preference in either refugee rescue or relief, one that reached into the ranks of Anglo-American diplomats organising the Bermuda Conference. The stated British position in January, that the refugee issue could not 'be treated as though it were a wholly Jewish problem', was matched in February by the American position that it could not be 'confined to persons of any particular race or faith'.[92] Both positions, with which Emerson and Paton agreed, were made public in March when American Secretary of State Cordell Hull released the memoranda to the American press.[93] In response to this widely publicised devaluation of Nazi efforts to exterminate European Jewry, the WJC attempted with varying degrees of success to engage co-signing partners to urge Bermuda Conference officials to give more consideration to Jewish rescue, one of which was the Aide-Memoire with Visser 't Hooft.[94]

As to why Visser 't Hooft thought he could act without consulting Paton, it is clear that strong personalities, neither of which were overburdened by humility, were at play. But so was Visser 't Hooft's enlarging sense of his own role in determining what could and should be said from Geneva. His preoccupation with integration of all aspects of ecumenicity under the WCCIF umbrella was also a major factor. That he aspired to a role in international decisions on postwar issues, including that of refugees, is clear, as was his emphasis on the 'ecumenical value' of interventional acts that demonstrated WCCIF efficacy.[95] There was also the continuing issue of silence and the gauntlet thrown down by Barth. Just days before engaging in the Aide-Memoire, he had written to Paton that Barth was 'on the warpath' again over the silence issue, and he was now wondering if WCCIF had too readily accepted its 'reasons for silence'.⁹⁶ Moreover, two days later there was another brief but harrowing report from Riegner: 15,000 Berlin Jews and partners of mixed marriages had been taken to 'assembling centres in Berlin' between 26 February and 2 March, with several hundred shot.⁹⁷

Yet while all of this was playing out and likely combined in his decision to act independently of Paton, it did not affect his measured approach. The Aide-Memoire was a private appeal for Allied actions that were already being called for publicly in many forms. The draft that developed from a WJC text was pared down by WCCIF by at least a third, and sections that might be construed as political – such as WJC and WCCIF having possession of the British and American memoranda – were removed from the form sent to Allied diplomats and the High Commissioner.⁹⁸ To add to the many complexities of Visser 't Hooft's involvements, within months of jointly stating in the Aide-Memoire that the most urgent problem was 'deliberate extermination of the Jews', he turned around and argued to Temple, as a number one moral issue, that if the bombardment of German cities continued, it would be 'the Allies who have killed far more civilians than the Nazis ever succeeded in killing'.⁹⁹

Hungarian Jewry, 1944

There was only one known instance during the course of the war when WCCIF stepped fully outside its self-imposed boundaries to publicly and officially protest against Nazi atrocities against Jews. Issued in late June 1944, fifteen months after the Aide-Memoire, it stands not only as a break in neutrality policy but as substantiation of WCCIF's intended course of refugee aid rather than protest. The situation prompting the exception was the destruction of the only remaining intact community of European Jewry. It did not, however, come about quickly. Two days after Nazi occupation of Hungary on 19 March, Gerhart Riegner cabled an urgent request for Protestant and Catholic leaders to launch a world appeal to the Hungarian nation to not accept the Nazi policy of Jewish extermination.¹⁰⁰ Visser 't Hooft and Freudenberg cabled Temple and Bell in London right away, urging support while pointing out that 'numerous Christians' were among the

800,000 Jews whose destiny was in danger, but, keeping with policy, WCCIF itself made no public statement.[101]

Over the next ninety days three reports comprising 107 densely packed pages on the rapidly deteriorating conditions of Hungarian Jewry reached the WCCIF refugee office on or about 30 April (22 pp), 19 May (50 pp), 5 June (35 pp). The details, stunning in compound nature, catalogued the systematic enactment of antisemitic laws and decrees before and after the Nazi occupation. This included official Hungarian statements on the Jewish question being 'liquidated once and for all'; public notices on segregation, transport and ghettoisation of Jews in Hungarian territories; notices of transfers and 'de-fortunization' of Jewish businesses, homes and holdings to national interests and 'honest Christian hands'. Other news accounts on implementing the ghetto scheme, town by town, with increasing restrictions on Jewish movement, left no doubt that separation and insulation were being carried out 'relentlessly', especially in Budapest where Jews were being moved to areas of Allied bombing that disallowed the evacuation of even Jewish children. All of these worsening conditions, as well as official notices that 300,000 Jews from Transylvania and northeast Hungary had been 'put into concentration camps so far', were strikingly clear by the first report on 30 April. The May and June reports, which held publicised promises by Hungarian state secretaries László Endre and László Baky that 'no compromises' would be made on the Jewish question, included ongoing accounts from Hungarian newspapers as Jews were segregated and 'resettled' into designated ghettos, factory internment zones and 'concentration camps'.[102]

Yet it was not until two further reports on extermination and numbers reached WCCIF that the scale tipped enough to step outside its non-protest policy. The first was an abridged version of a 32-page report by two Slovakian escapees, known later as the Auschwitz Protocols, which described in detail a systematised process of deportation, selection, gas chambers and crematoria, with numbers and nations of 1,715,000 Jews killed at Birkenau between April 1942 and April 1944. The second report on Nazi operations in occupied Hungary documented the deportation of 335,000 Jews between 14 May and 10 June 1944. The combined numbers in black and white were chilling: Poland (900,000); France (150,000); Holland (100,000); Belgium (50,000); Germany (60,000); Slovakia (30,000); Bohemia, Moravia, Austria (30,000), Yugoslavia, Italy and Norway (50,000); Greece (45,000); mixed foreign Jews from Poland (300,000); Subcarpathia (106,000), Transylvania (94,000), Northeastern (75,000), Southern (25,000) and Upper Hungary (35,000).[103]

The WCCIF break in policy came on the heels of these reports, three months after Riegner's cable urged immediate protest by church leaders. The statement was published in the ecumenical press service *ICPIS* at the end of the last week of June 1944:

> The Ecumenical Commission for Refugees exists in order to give material and spiritual aid to refugees of all faiths. Its main task is therefore to relieve the suffering of the refugees rather than to protest against the treatment meted out to them. But there are situations in which the only aid we can give is in the form of a solemn and public protest. To-day this is the case.
>
> Trustworthy reports state that so far some four hundred thousand Hungarian Jews are deported in inhuman conditions and, in so far as they have not died on the way, brought to the camp of Auschwitz in Upper Silesia where, during the past two years, many hundreds of thousands of Jews have been systematically put to death.
>
> Christians cannot remain silent before this crime. We appeal to our Hungarian Christian brethren to raise their voice with us to do all they can to stop this horrible sin. We appeal to Christians of all countries to unite in prayer that God may have mercy on the people of Israel.[104]

While this 'solemn and public' protest, much heralded by WCCIF in Geneva, was laudable and needed, it was late and unexceptional in the broader picture of international protests being made. Just days before, the US Legate in Bern had summarised in a press statement on 26 June that 'individuals, groups and organizations, private and public officials of all kinds' had been 'vainly protesting and seeking to express indignation at this outrageous and unspeakable conduct'.[105] Moreover, as detailed in the extensive Hungarian reports, press items on the rapidly changing conditions of Hungarian Jews had been appearing in Swiss newspapers since 23 March – *Tribune de Genève, Gazette de Lausanne, Basler Nachrichten, La*

Suisse, Neue Zürcher Zeitung, Israelitisches Wochenblatt – and by 24 June the Auschwitz Protocols were being reported as well. The 'evidence is overwhelming', argues historian Randolph Braham, that the Protocols reached Switzerland by 19 and 20 June, creating a flurry of diplomatic activity.[106] The earliest date indicating that WCCIF would protest was Saturday 24th, but the issue of *ICPIS* in which it appeared was not published until the following week, and would not have been mailed until the 29th or 30th at the earliest.[107] By that time letters and cables urging Hungarian interventions in the deportations had been issued and publicised by Pope Pius XII (25th), President Roosevelt (26th), and King Gustav of Sweden (30th), to name a few of the notables.[108]

Even though the WCCIF protest was not exceptional in the bigger picture, or 'first' as Visser 't Hooft reported to Temple and Cavert shortly afterwards, it was exceptional in its unbroken line of silence and in essence as well.[109] The private memoranda to ICRC in 1941 and 1942 were grounded in claims that the Jewish question touched 'the centre of the Christian message' and that an unraised voice constituted disobedience to God. In contrast, the protest in late June 1944, which was visibly touched by something more deeply human than a question and a message, was shorn of all such reasoning even though framed in a Christian context. As Visser 't Hooft revealed to Temple and Cavert in July, 'the revelations about the fate of the Jews deported from Hungary made a deep impression ...'.[110]

Yet in the same memorandum Visser 't Hooft reiterated the importance of the WCCIF non-protest policy. More precisely, he praised administrative chairman Marc Boegner for handling the issue of Allied bombing 'in the truly ecumenical fashion', namely by refusing 'to make any public protests on the question'.[111] It was also the case, in keeping with the aim of not drawing negative attention to the German churches, particularly in the area of German church silence, that the most powerful sentence in the WCCIF protest – 'Christians cannot remain silent before this crime' – was *removed* from the German edition of *ICPIS*.[112]

The decision to exclude those words, like other incongruities colouring or shadowing what was happening in and around WCCIF wartime statements, is not inconsequential. What was not said (and when) is as critical as what was said when trying to understand motivations, policies and how they played out as European Jewry was being systematically disenfranchised and murdered. The presences and absences of voices and words, however, have to be seen within the fuller picture of what the refugee initiative was doing. While it remained relatively small in terms of numbers aided, funds collected, staff and resources expended, it was indispensable in effect to those who received succour and aid. It provided vital funds to both Cimade and Aumônerie in southern France between 1940 and 1945, as well as funding for shorter periods to Protestant refugee groups in Switzerland, Italy, Shanghai, Hungary, Poland, and (briefly) Portugal and Spain.

But the fuller picture must also include the inconvenient layers, like the stated 'missionary importance' of the refugee work. While the intended focus on non-Aryan Protestant refugees remained wherever possible, the complex mix of refugee populations in internment camps made such differentiation more difficult as time went on. One result, hailed by Freudenberg to ICCAJ leaders three months after WCCIF's protest against the murder of Hungarian Jews, was that European Jews 'from all classes of society and of all shades of belief' were being brought into contact with the 'loving witness' of the Church through relief services funded by WCCIF. Such interactions, described as 'living contacts between the ecumenical movement and the Jews', were breaking down 'ancient enmity and deep-rooted mistrust' so that 'a freer hearing of the message of Christ' was possible. By providing the 'connection and dialectic between relief work and Jewish missions', the work of the refugee office was understood to be paving the way for 'close cooperation' between WCCIF and ICCAJ in the postwar areas of refugee relief and Jewish evangelisation.[113]

The sobriety of tracking

Two weeks after the WCCIF protest against the murder of Hungarian Jewry at Auschwitz, Visser 't Hooft urged forty ecumenists from twelve countries that an equitable postwar solution of the 'Jewish question' involved more than humanitarian concerns or 'love for one's neighbour', for the Church was 'little by little recovering consciousness of the unique links which bind it in the history of salvation to the people of Israel'.[114] What this meant was made more clear four months later in his edited collection of documents on the struggle of his Dutch Reformed Church under Nazi occupation. In what was presented as a 'positive teaching' on the 'significance of the Jewish people', a supersessionist pastoral letter urged that the Jewish people, who had once been 'Israel' and the *'symbol of God's free grace'*, must remain the object of Christian prayer, even though they were now 'Jews' and *'a sign of human hostility to the Gospel'*. The point being made was that the Church, whether under occupation or not, was duty bound to pray and work for the salvation of Jews – for 'the Jew remains a Jew in the bitter sense ... and ... cannot free himself from himself so long as he does not come to Christ'.[115]

At the time those words were published, and through the remaining months of war, ICCAJ's role in advancing the 'consciousness' to which Visser 't Hooft referred was clear in concept but hazy in form. At the outbreak of war both he and Paton had understood that postwar planning would have to focus on Christianisation and re-Christianisation of the war-torn world. But it was Paton who was the undeterred force behind initiatives to advance the Jewish mission agenda and bring ICCAJ structurally closer to WCCIF. When George Bell suggested Hoffmann as head of the refugee office, Paton was the man who pushed the nomination through its rounds of approval. When Hoffmann's installation as chief officer was stymied by German aggression and the onset of war, Paton became the engine behind wartime planning that kept ICCAJ relevant to Geneva.

In addition to study groups on the Jewish question and involvements in BICCAJ projects on geographic data, division of territorial spheres and allocation of mission resources, Paton orchestrated three projects aimed at increasing church-wide support of Jewish missions. Beginning in fall 1940 he vigorously pursued theological colleges at Cambridge, Oxford, Edinburgh and Manchester to establish a lectureship for Hans Kosmala, who had fled Vienna with remnants of the Delitzschianum after the *Anschluss*.[116] Kosmala's focus on so-called Jewish 'causes' of troubled Christian–Jewish relations was the first of three projects to explicate modern Jewish problems in relation to the fundamentals of Christian faith. His lectures on antisemitism and the Jewish question to Cambridge theological faculty and students in early 1941 served as the basis for a co-authored book with ICCAJ associate director Robert Smith in March 1942, which in turn served as grounding for a Christian Institute for Jewish Studies in 1943. Paton's aim in all of this was to bring the credibility of scholarship to Jewish missions, develop universal argumentation for theological validity, and counter tendencies of 'goodwill' Christian attitudes that eschewed or put in abeyance the divine commission to evangelise Jews.

Concurrent with these projects was a retreat from the ranks of ICCAJ that bore significantly on the 'goodwill' issue, and set into motion a series of related events. The resignation of W.W. Simpson from the British and executive ICCAJ is significant not only in this respect but because his eight-year involvement with ICCAJ challenges the current understanding of scholarship.[117] Contrary to the belief that the first general secretary of the British Council of Christians and Jews was a pioneer advocate of Christian–Jewish relations *sans* Jewish missions, his appearance on the conversionary landscape marked the entry of British Methodist church involvement in Jewish missions.[118] Simpson was hired by the Methodist Missionary Society in April 1933 to work under the British Society for Propagation of the Gospel Among the Jews, specifically for the development of a Christian apologetic for modern educated Jews.[119] After introducing himself by letter to James Parkes, announcing his conversionist 'convictions', and asking to no avail for help with Jewish contacts in London, he moved into the realm of ICCAJ by way of his supervisor, Rev. Frank Exley, who was a member of BICCAJ.[120]

Simpson worked in the ICCAJ milieu from July 1934 to November 1941, first as an appointed member of BICCAJ, and then as British appointee to the executive ICCAJ. Parkes sensed that he was 'slowly coming round' to a revised position in mid-1936, but that was also the year he was appointed to the executive ICCAJ.[121] That he would remain in that role for the next five and a half years asks more than can be addressed here, but evidence suggests it was a matter of avoiding conflict and seeking benefit from both sides of the Jewish missions issue. Both before and after his international appointment, he served on ICCAJ conference committees, presented papers and engaged in recorded discussions, and nowhere was his dissent registered. Yet it was also the case that he was being incrementally influenced by Parkes, that he was growing weary of hindrances placed on Christian–Jewish relations by overt declarations of mission intention, and was increasingly displeased with traditional methods of evangelising Jews. When Simpson resigned in November 1941, Paton tried to reason with what was deemed his 'wobbly' theological position, but did not dissuade him from resigning. He learned later that Simpson had resigned to become co-secretary of the emerging 'goodwill' Council of Christians and Jews, from whose formation meetings he himself had just been excluded.[122]

By the time word of these events reached America and Hoffmann's response made its way back, it was spring 1942. Arguing that goodwill councils 'undercut' evangelistic efforts, Hoffmann ordered the British sector of ICCAJ to launch a counter programme in British churches to forewarn of the dangers of goodwill initiatives to Jewish missions. Simpson learned of the call to action and forwarded the news to James Parkes instead of getting directly involved himself.[123]

For Parkes, whose patience with Hoffmann had run out, this act of initiating 'sabotage' of Christian–Jewish efforts to collaborate and combat antisemitism constituted a 'show-down'.[124] He began with William Temple on 16 April, the newly installed Archbishop of Canterbury who had been named chair of the emerging Council of Christians and Jews two days before, asking him to stand against 'official missionary attitude to Judaism' by refusing patronage to Anglican Church Mission to Jews. Although Temple had not yet been approached for patronage, he made it clear that his interest in 'Christian–Jewish friendship' did not preclude 'equal interest in attempting to convert Jews' and, if choice had to be made, the latter would 'take precedence'. Temple's position, like that of Paton and Visser 't Hooft, was that Jewish missions were an indispensable 'Christian obligation'.[125]

Ten days later Parkes put into circulation a memorandum intended to challenge Jewish missionising policy.[126] His core argument was that official missions to Jews defeated the efficacy of collaboration that was necessary for Christians and Jews to come together to combat the antisemitism that was so valuable to Hitler. For his respondents, however, the issue of antisemitism was unrelated to Church attitudes and policies on Jewish missions. The first rejection came from Canon John McLeod Campbell of Canterbury Cathedral, secretary of the Anglican Missionary Council and soon to be member of the British ICCAJ. While granting that Parkes was an expert in antisemitism, he rebuked him for getting involved in 'controversial historical and theological issues' of Christian–Jewish relations, labelling his arguments as 'emotional reaction to the dangers of antisemitism'.[127] Edwyn Bevan, a Fellow of the British Academy and New College at Oxford, shared Parkes's concern about the 'horrors' of antisemitism and 'wrongs' that Christians inflicted on Jews historically, but it did not equate to a 'viable' case for change in policy on Jewish missions.[128] Paton, who dismissed Parkes's claim that collaboration between Jews and Christians could only be effective in the absence of missionary attitudes, roundly rejected that Christians had to approach Jews on a basis of equality. For Paton, that could never be a factor, for Christianity was in possession of what Judaism both lacked and needed.[129]

Two other versions of the memorandum were circulated between May and October, with no visible change in attitudes toward Jewish mission policy.[130] But Parkes's persistence, coupled with formal announcement of the British Council of Christians and Jews in October as well as his appointment to co-chair the Society of Jews and Christians with British Rabbi Mattuck, crystallised for Paton that doubt about the place of Jewish missions was gaining ground.[131]

It was at this point that Paton's aims began to take shape in the form of a Christian institute to emphasise the biblical and theological bases for Jewish evangelisation. The steps put into motion six weeks later, however, should not be seen as wholly reactive. An institute for theological validation and training on Jewish missions had been in discussion since the 1927 Budapest–Warsaw conferences, with renewed emphasis when Kosmala fled Vienna with the Delitzschianum after the *Anschluss*, and again after the outbreak of war. Paton, like other ICCAJ principals, held that the only hope for both Jews and society was the diluting and corrective effects of Christianity. As framed in his 1942 foreword to Kosmala and Smith's book, *The Jew in the Christian World*, Christians had failed to probe the depths of the Jewish problem historically by refusing to face the religious questions that juxtaposition of Christendom and Jewry necessarily raised. An institute, like the orchestrated book, would cast theological light on relations between the realities of the Jewish problem, the issues of Christian–Jewish coexistence, and the imperative of Jewish evangelisation.[132]

There was another critical factor here as well. An institute for theological validation of ICCAJ initiatives was directly in line with postwar planning for re-occupation of European mission fields. As summarised in a demographic chart extracted from Joint Distribution Committee data and discussed on 4 December, some 5,083,330 European Jews were thought to be accounted for, with some 87 per cent (4,460,000) located in Greater Germany, the General Government and other eastern European areas (Figure 4.1).[133] While it was understood that these were not final numbers, distribution percentages were not expected to shift dramatically, and as such the areas of densest population fitted well with the proposed institute staff of Hans Kosmala, whom Paton heralded as an 'expert' on German Jewish questions, and Lev Gillet, who was promoted as an 'authority' on the Jews of eastern Europe.[134]

The proposal for the institute was formalised three months after discussion of the December 1942 data. That it was adopted at the same time as Visser 't Hooft's engagement with the Aide-Memoire in Geneva (and Paton's criticism of it) is significant, for it reveals two very different responses from the WCCIF secretaries to mounting information on what was happening to European Jews. In addition to numbers of Jews in Poland's ghettos, as shown in the December chart – Warsaw (530,000), Lodz (150,000), Lvov (120,000), Bialystok (80,000), Otwock (60,000), Lublin (40,000), Czestochowa (20,000), Kielce (20,000), Cracow (11,000), Bochnia (5000) – the United Nations Declaration of 17 December affirmed in graphic language that the ghettos were being 'emptied' by way of 'cold-blooded extermination'. Moreover, on 12 March Paton and the British sector of ICCAJ had in-person confirmation from Harold Beeley of the Royal Institute of International Affairs that there was 'no doubt about Hitler's determination to exterminate the Jews'.[135]

Country	Citizens	Refugees
Greater Germany	305,000	
(Austria, Bohemia-Moravia, Slovakia, Luxembourg)		
Hungary	800,000	
(Sub-Carpathia, Transylvania, Banat)		
Rumania	297,000	
Poland	2,100,000	
Polish Jews in (Asiatic) Russia		600,000
Vichy France	110,000	70,000
Spain		1,300
in transit 1/41–5/42		2,000
Portugal		12,400
in transit 1/41–5/42		13,000
Switzerland	18,000	6,300
Yugoslavia	68,000	7,000
Italy	40,000	7,000
Sweden	7,000	2,000
North Africa		7,800
(Algiers, Tunisia, Morocco)		
Turkey		200
Iran		800
Shanghai		22,000
Japan		4,500
Philippines		1,200
Argentina	300,000	55,000
Bolivia	150	5,000
Brazil	85,000	25,000
Chile	13,000	12,000
Colombia	4,000	2,850
Cuba	8,000	6,000
Dominican Republic	10	1,100
Ecuador	1,000	2,700
Uruguay	30,000	7,000
Other Central South American areas	24,065	4,955

Figure 4.1 ICCAJ estimated 'Distribution of Jewish Population', December 1942

That the proposal was adopted five days after Beeley's confirmation underlines the degree to which evangelisation and conversion were seen as the only viable solution for surviving Jews. The Christian Institute for Jewish Studies would meet the 'fundamental changes' in world Jewry and the attendant 'grave problems' for the Church through courses on Jewish questions for theological colleges and missionaries, apologetic literature, and workshops on Jewish missions. Its main focus, however, was to be biblical scholarship and theological argumentation that would move Jewish evangelisation to a new level of scholarly sophistication. Combating antisemitism would be a 'collateral aim' but, unlike 'goodwill' bodies, it would be fought on religious rather than humanitarian grounds. In Paton's words, the institute would meet the need for sound theological argumentation, while diffusing the 'vaguely syncretistic position' that was expected from the Council of Christians and Jews and other 'goodwill' organisations.[136]

Paton's sudden death on 21 August had no effect on the October 1943 launch of the institute. The yields of his vigorous campaign to overcome internal doubts, gain prominent support, gather organisational strands, and standardise institutional aims were handed to Robert Smith as administrative overseer. The early financial backing of the Anglican Church Mission to Jews, Church of Scotland, Presbyterian Church of Ireland and Swedish Missionary Council was incrementally followed by other church and mission agencies, including WCCIF in Geneva. As Paton intended, the London-based institute was to be international in scope, staffed by Kosmala and Gillet, and governed by a board of mission principals and theological scholars from Oxford, Edinburgh, Manchester, Birmingham, Cardiff, Bangor and Cambridge, the latter of whom was a member of the WCCIF Provisional Committee.[137]

In the five months between the institute proposal and Paton's death, the widely reported Bermuda Conference of 19–30 April revealed that little could be expected from the Allied rescue of European Jews, while the Warsaw ghetto uprising, which began the same day, revealed that more than 55,000 Jews could be shot, burned or forcibly deported to labour or death in one month of Nazi violence.[138] In the midst of this, on 10 May, Hoffmann announced his return to full-time work on Jewish missions. Up to this point his wartime efforts had been split between combined work for the Presbyterian Board of Missions, ICCAJ, and POW work for YMCA War Prisoner Aid, including some 3,000 German and Austrian non-Aryan refugees sent by Britain to internment camps in Canada and Jamaica, where he saw at first hand that 'the current universal distress of Jews' had made them 'responsive and appreciative of Christian sympathy and interest'.[139] His work would now refocus on Jewish evangelisation, and his time would be divided between ICCAJ and the Presbyterian Board of Missions.

In a change of guard memoranda between Hoffmann and associate director Robert Smith, three main areas of accelerating concerns were set out. One, the Bermuda Conference had brought with it the realisation that Allied liberation of Europe was the most effective means of Jewish rescue. As such, agitated concern over European Jews had 'died down' among mission constituents and in its place attention was turning to postwar relief, with the belief that the churches would have to 'Christianise the impact'. Two, because little help came from the Bermuda Conference, Jewish emphasis on Zionism was increasing 'the strategic importance of Palestine as a centre for missionary work'. Three, along with rising Zionism was increasing antisemitism and anti-Jewishness, both within and without the churches. A great deal thus depended, so it was reasoned, on having the right machinery in place so that Jewish missions and related work could resume on the Continent and elsewhere at the earliest possible postwar moment.[140]

The issue on the table just before Paton's death was the 'exact form of the machinery' for placing ICCAJ in Europe while increasing collaboration with WCCIF. Having a man in Geneva would ensure protection of ICCAJ interests while advancing Paton's idea of a 'total scheme for Jewish work', particularly that of a coordinating office under the new WCCIF department of reconstruction.[141] With Paton's death, however, came the loss of his influential cross-linked roles and the burden of shoring up what was already conceptually in place with WCCIF, a task that both Hoffmann and Smith pursued vigorously through the remainder of the war.[142]

In these and other related tasks, both before and after the decisions of Bermuda, the nature of ICCAJ planning remained very much the same as in 1940: 'severely practical'. It was especially so in the matter of postwar reoccupation of European mission fields, which meant knowing where Jews were on the geographic landscape. Before Paton's death he had urged constituents to have 'plans ready to put into action when the appropriate time comes', and leaders in turn now urged that constituents stay abreast of shifting Jewish populations and plan accordingly.[143] The difficulty, as outlined in the December 1943 *News Sheet*, under 'Where shall we find the Jews?', was that there was 'still no means of estimating how many' European Jews 'will survive or where they will be when the war ends'. Constituents therefore had to 'be prepared to follow the Jews' from the camps and ghettos as they were liberated by the Allies, for their 'present whereabouts' gave no indication of 'their eventual place of settling'.[144]

What this meant to constituents like Canon John Campbell of Canterbury Cathedral, who was now part of the executive ICCAJ, was that the 'recent dispersion' of 'the international race *par excellence*' would have to be followed 'in many new directions'. Writing as chair of the Missionary Council, in a June 1944 book advertising forty-two new positions for Jewish missionaries in eastern Europe, Palestine, Transjordan and North Africa, he went on to preview what was a new refrain of ICCAJ apologetics, namely that 'the tragic experiences of Jews', 'reaching their climax under Nazi tyranny', make it ever more 'incumbent' on the Church to honour its 'long neglected debt to the Jews'.[145]

For James Parkes, whom Campbell had rebuked for confusing theological issues with emotionalism about antisemitism, the most pressing concern about known ICCAJ work in Britain was deprecating mission literature emanating from the Christian Institute for Jewish Studies. After the institute's *Bulletin* appeared in March 1944, with a board of prominent Christian scholars on the masthead, he sent a twelve-page memorandum to fellow Christians in the British Council of Christians and Jews. Parkes was well aware that Jewish missions could be neither promoted nor refuted in the context of collaborative Council work, yet he urged that Christian members of the Council could and should voice concern about the denigrating ways in which missions to Jews were being promoted. Institute publications were creating negative and false impressions of Jews and Judaism in the context of the 'superior merits of Christianity and the solution of conversion'. Kosmala especially, though Smith was not 'exempt', injudiciously used selectively interpreted Hebrew passages to highlight unfavourable aspects of Judaism and Jewish history. As one example, the book by Kosmala and Smith, with a foreword by Paton, equated the Jewish commonwealth in Ezra with Nazi racial legislation, labelling Israel as 'a kind of Herrenvolk'. The negative tone of the authors, the misuse of Hebrew texts out of context, and the persistent attempts to 'expose' ingrained negative attitudes of Jews to Christians and Christianity occurred all too frequently to be anything less than deliberate. The effect on uninformed Christian readers, Parkes stressed, could be nothing less than the creation and feeding of hostility and dislike. His concern, although doubtful that 'conscious antisemitism' was at play, was that the stream of literature emanating from the institute was doing 'more to create an atmosphere friendly to antisemitic propaganda than anything else in the country'.[146]

Two months later Parkes followed with a more challenging thesis than had sparked the five-month debate in 1942, which he sought to publish in both Jewish and Christian journals. 'A Christian Looks at the Christian Mission to the Jews' criticised the ecumenical movement for failing to recognise that a 'full "ecumenical" attitude' involved the righting of relations between Christians and Jews, including correction of Christianity's historical misrepresentation of Judaism and its relation to Jesus. Second, he challenged the idea of any group believing it was in possession of all of God's truth. Third, he argued appositely that Judaism remained a living religion that represented 'aspects of truth' that Christianity missed altogether.[147]

The manuscript was accepted by *Metsudah* but rejected by World Dominion Press, who was working with ICCAJ on a world survey of Jews and Jewish missions. *Theology* editor Alec Vidler, who was part of the early Paton group that looked 'radically' at relations between the Jewish question and Jewish missions, agreed to publish it with the stipulation that a response from the Christian Institute appear alongside in the fall issue.[148]

The opportunity for the Institute 'to answer' Parkes was welcomed by Robert Smith, who, citing the late Paton, saw him as 'a dangerous influence'. While granting that Parkes was a 'clever fellow' whose criticism of older mission tactics was somewhat right, he regarded him as an unbalanced thinker who 'sometimes goes badly off the rails' and was determined to undermine distinctions between Christianity and Judaism. Yet Smith also realised that Parkes could not be ignored. He had tried to counter him in the July 1944 *IRM*, but, in his words, Parkes argumentation was 'so radical' that it could not be adequately addressed without re-examining the 'foundations of the missionary approach'.[149] His 'revolutionary' claim that 'God needs the Jews *as Jews* and that it is not His will they should be converted' negated the very grounds of the missionary enterprise. For Smith, like the late Paton and other ICCAJ principals, Jewish evangelisation was the litmus test of the whole mission movement of the Church. Moreover, as Smith argued in *IRM*, the Christian imperative to evangelise Jews was a crucial answer to the 'dangerous challenge posed to the Christian faith' by Nazi racial doctrine. Those 'basic facts' about the 'fundamental question of the Church and its relations to Israel', he insisted, underlay all other 'concern about the sufferings of the Jews and their political destiny'.[150]

As these starkly opposing views continued to play out in the pages of *Theology* and *IRM* in the summer and fall of 1944, it was clear to all involved that the so-called 'goodwill' versus 'evangelisation' issue was not *just* a British problem playing out on British soil.[151] As framed by Hoffmann in a December report beginning with the words 'the Eternal Jew is still with us', the Church was 'slowly but surely being split into two camps' in answering the question, 'What Shall We Do With the Jews?' It was a question that would be asked over and over in the postwar years, one repeated so often it would become a major topic at the 1948 founding assembly of the World Council of Churches.[152]

Notes

1 Letters to and from Foreign Office, 9, 11 Jan.; Gerhardt to Paton, 12 Jan.; BICCAJ Min., 12 Jan.; letters of Standley, Gill, Hoffmann, Baker, 19, 20 Jan., 7, 11 Mar.; CBMS, 4 Apr.; quot., Robert Smith, 'Missionary Problems from Wartime Conditions', Feb. 1940. Unless noted documents for n. 1–15 are at IMC.261201, 261207, 261229.

2 Report of United Conference on the Christian Approach to the Jews, 11 June 1940.
3 Hoffmann Remarks, 11 June 1940; also 'Confidential: In Germany', July 1939. Paton, 'The Jewish Situation and the Christian Message', 11 June 1940, and 'Conference of Refugee Pastors and Missionary Leaders', London, 31 May–1 June 1939. Smith, editorial report of conference, *News Sheet* (Jul.–Aug. 1940), 2.
4 Smith, 'Summary of Wartime Difficulties', 3.
5 Smith, 'Effect of the War on Jewish Mission Work', 2–3.
6 Report of United Conference on the Christian Approach to the Jews, 5, 8, 9; Smith, editorial report, *News Sheet* (Jul.–Aug. 1940), 2.
7 Ibid.; also C.H. Gill, 'Points for Possible Action', 26 June; Smith to Paton, 3 July; 'Notes of Sub-Committee on Jews Conference', 11 Jul. 1940.
8 Paton to Kullmann, 21 Aug. 1940. Data on relocated Jewish refugees had the added value of providing their 'whereabouts' to missions still operative in areas where 'migrating' Jews were moving; see CBMS min., Committee on Work among Jews, 9 Oct. 1940. For Paton's tracking through official and semi-official channels, Emerson to Paton, 25 June 1941, FCC.B9F19; Harold Beeley to Paton, 27 Nov. 1941; Paton to Beeley, 28 Nov. 1941, WCC.301.4331.
9 Smith, 'On Jewish Missionary Cooperation', 3 Feb. 1941; Proposed conference, 5 Feb.; CBMS min., 5 Feb.; Hoffmann to Standley, 9 Jul. Minutes of the 29–30 April 1941 conference did not survive the war but pre and post documents summarise proceedings and outcomes.
10 Smith, Memoranda, 3 Feb. 1941.
11 Summaries from Arthur Ruppin, *Jewish Fate and Future* (London: Macmillan and Co., 1940) were drawn as early as June 1940 in Smith's 'Effect of the War'.
12 BICCAJ min., 10 Sept. 1941.
13 Smith's guidelines were published in *News Sheet*, XI:4 (Jul.–Aug. 1941), 6–7.
14 Quot., CBMS min., 9 Oct. 1940; Paton, Memo of Sub-Group, 20 Nov. 1941.
15 'Points for Possible Action', 26 June 1940; Notes of Sub-Committee, 11 Jul.; CBMS min., 9 Oct. 1940; Standley to Hoffmann, 5 May 1941; Hoffmann to Standley, 9 Jul.; BICCAJ min., 10 Sept.; Paton, Memo of Sub-Group, 20 Nov.; Paton to VH, 23 Nov. 1941; IMC.261207, 261142.
16 Parkes had been involved in forming study groups of Jews and Christians since 1929, four of which in 1929–1930 were overseen by

Herbert Loewe at Cambridge. Since February 1940 he had also been working to form a group of Jewish and Christian leaders from the Board of Jewish Deputies, Royal Institute, Society of Friends Peace Committee, and Bishop George Bell; PP.60/15/14, 60/17/31.
17 Letters and invitations, Aug.–Oct. 1940 and May–July 1941, WCC.301.4331.
18 Paton to Parkes, 20 Nov.; Parkes to Paton, 22 Nov.; Paton to Parkes, 26 Nov. 1941, PP.60/17/8/2.
19 Paton to Carter, 26 Nov., 7 Dec.; Carter to Paton, 21 Nov., 4 Dec. 1941, WCC.301.4331.
20 Paton to E. N. Cooper, 10 Dec. 1941,WCC.301.4331.
21 Paton to Smith, 22 Dec.; Smith to Paton, 17 Dec. 1941, WCC.301.4331.
22 The 25-page conference report, 28 Jan. 1942, includes texts of keynote speakers, proceedings and resolution. Unless noted, n. 22–9 are at PP.60/17/10/2.
23 Ibid., Robert Smith, 'The Problem of Securing Religious Freedom for the Jews', in 'Conference on Postwar Situation of Jewry', 20–3.
24 Ibid., 20–3.
25 Ibid., resolution, 25.
26 Ibid., Smith, 22.
27 Ibid., Clephane Macanna, 'The Problem of Securing Political Rights for Jews', in 'Conference on Postwar Situation of Jewry', 10–14.
28 Ibid., 10, 15, 18.
29 Ibid., 18.
30 VH, 'The Ecumenical Church and the International Situation', written in late April, issued early May 1940, WCC.301.008.
31 WCCIF Admin. confidential min., Apeldoorn, 7–8 Jan. 1940, WCC.301.005. See also VH to Cavert, 20 Jan.; Cavert to VH, 20 Feb., WCC.42.0015; VH, 'The Genesis of the World Council of Churches', Ruth Rouse and Stephen Charles Neill, *A History of the Ecumenical Movement* (Geneva: WCC, 1954), 708–10; VH, *Memoirs* (1973), 119–20; Marc Boegner, *The Long Road to Unity* (London: Collins, 1970), 140–3, where he speaks of Temple and Bell's 'anxiety' to mention no one by name and 'to judge nobody'.
32 VH, 'The Ecumenical Church and the International Situation', May 1940.
33 ECCO minutes, esp. 7, 24 Nov., 11 Dec. 1939, WCC.425.1.022.
34 VH, 'The Ecumenical Church and International Situation', 5, 8–9, 10–12.
35 Mackie to VH, May 1940, WCC.301.009.

Voices and silences in war: 1940–1944 209

36 Bennett to VH, 16 May, WCC.301.009. See also Cavert to VH, 15 May, who agreed without elaboration that some statement along the lines suggested was in order, WCC.42.0015.
37 Paton to VH, 3 June; for reports of Brown and Boegner, VH to Paton, 18 May, 6 June; VH to Temple, 6 June; WCC.42.0077, IMC.261143.
38 Temple to VH, 20 May 1940, ital. add.; this document is missing from WCC.42.0007 but appears in part in VH, *Memoirs*, 123.
39 Diane Kirby, 'The Church of England and Religions Division During the Second World War', *Journal of International History* 4 (2000), 10–11. Emphasis in the original.
40 Temple to VH, 20 May 1940, in VH, *Memoirs*, 123.
41 VH to Temple, 6 June 1940, WCC.42.0077.
42 For VH work agenda in London during the inauguration, ECCO min., 22 June 1942, WCC.425.1.022.
43 VH's exclamation in *Memoirs*, 'if only one could have talked this out with Temple!', 123, must be compared to his account in 'Genesis of the World Council of Churches' twenty years earlier in 1954, where no such concern was expressed, 710–11. Temple's instructions were noted as a fact that needed no explanation, but by 1973 in *Memoirs* the policy and silence were being explained apologetically.
44 Karl Barth, 'The Churches of Europe in the Face of the War', 12 Dec. 1942, and later in *The Church and The War* (New York: Macmillan Co., 1944).
45 Ibid., 46–9, orig. ital.
46 For evolution of VH account of Barth's criticism: VH to Cavert, 27 Nov. 1942, where Barth is charged with an 'unhistoric and unrealistic conception' of the ecumenical movement, FCC.B9F19; *Memoirs* (1973), where he agreed with Barth that WCCIF should have spoken out, but 'could not disregard the conviction of our most responsible leaders (especially William Temple)', 134–5.
47 Quot., Paton to VH, 13 Sept. 1939; VH, Strictly Confidential, 'Future of Ecumenical Work in Europe', Jul. 1940; Notes on Meeting, 8 Sept. 1940, WCC.301.005.
48 'First Results of an Enquiry on ICPIS', Aug. 1938; 'Report on the Future of ICPIS', 24 Feb. 1939; VH to Paton, 24 Feb. 1939; WCC.301.005.
49 VH to Temple, 1 May 1939; draft of planted story, WCC.301.005.
50 Series of 17 letters, WCC.42.0076.
51 ECCO Min., 30 June 1942, WCC.425.1.022. Monthly reporting included Scandinavia (Ehrenström), Holland (Visser 't Hooft), France–Belgium (Guillon, de Dietrich), Germany (Freudenberg and

Schönfeld), German Switzerland (Freudenberg), French Switzerland–Italy (Henriod), Czechoslovakia–Poland (Lowrie), Hungary (Beguin); eastern Orthodox nations (Weymarn).
52 Mackie to VH, May 1940, WCC.301.009.
53 VH to Paton, 13 Sept. 1939, 18 Jul. and 18 Sept. 1940; Paton to VH, 1 Nov.; VH to Paton, 29 Nov.; WCCIF Prov. Comm., Jul.–Dec. 1940; WCC.301.005, FCC.B23F1.
54 VH to Hoffmann, 4 Feb.; to Paton, 4 Feb., 27 Mar.; to Mott, 10 Apr. 1941, WCC.42.0038, 42.0057.
55 Hendrik Kraemer, *The Christian Message in a Non-Christian World* (London: Edinburgh House Press, 1938), 227.
56 VH to Paton, 26 April, 1 May, 6 May 1939, IMC.261142, WCC.301.008.
57 Max Huber, *The Good Samaritan: Reflections on the Gospel and the Work of the Red Cross* (London: Victor Gollancz, 1945), was written during a period of convalescence in November 1942; includes a 10-page introduction by Adolf Keller in Nov. 1943 and a foreword by Archbishop William Temple in Sept. 1944.
58 For ECCO formation in consultation with ICRC, ECCO min., Nov. 2, 6, 7, 10, 13, 16, 20, 22, 24; Dec. 6, 7, 11, 21, WCC.425.1.022; VH to Paton, 4 Sept.; Strong to Mott, 6 Sept.; VH to Leiper, 19 Sept.; Strong to Mott, 18 Oct.; Mott to VH, 23 Oct.; IMC.261142, WCC.42.0057, 301.008.
59 Strong to Mott, 6 Sept., 18 Oct.; ECCO min., 16 Nov., 6 Dec. 1939.
60 Max Huber, 'Red Cross and Neutrality', *International Review of the Red Cross*, No. 209 (May 1936), in Sandoz, 'Max Huber and the Red Cross', *European Journal of International Law* 18:1 (2007), 171–97, esp. 187–8.
61 Number of official and unofficial national affiliate bodies represented in the ECCO network included: YMCA (66 nations); YWCA (57); WSCF (43); ECB (25); WA (33); WCCIF (50), ECCO min., 14 Mar. 1940.
62 VH to Freudenberg (hereafter FB), 15 Mar. 1940, IMC.261244.
63 Michael Marrus and Robert Paxton, *Vichy France and the Jews* (Stanford: Stanford University Press, 1995; 2nd edn 2019).
64 For Toureille's complex relations and controversies with WCCIF, Tela Zasloff, *A Rescuer's Story: Pastor Pierre-Charles Toureille in Vichy* (Madison: University of Wisconsin Press, 2014).
65 'Confidential: Situation of the Church in Europe', Nov. 1941, WCC.301.4329.
66 Report of Visit to Poland, ECCO min., 22 Oct. 1942, 4–5; WCC.425.1.022.

Voices and silences in war: 1940–1944　211

67　VH to Burckhardt and Huber, 'Zur Lage in Polen', 29 Oct. 1941, WCC.301.4331. The second part of the memo reflects the same 20 Oct. Jewish Agency report that appears in Matthäus, *Predicting the Holocaust*, 149–51.
68　Freudenberg report on '*judenrein*' plan, ECCO Min., 14 Mar. 1941, WCC.425.1.022.
69　'Zur Lage in Polen', 29 Oct.
70　Freudenberg to Joint Relief, 3 June 1942, also in Snoek, 272. For more on exchanges with ICRC on medical needs, 'Confidential Report on Refugee Work in Wartime', Jan. 1942, 3, 10–11, 12, WCC.425.1.022.
71　The Nîmes Committee included American Friends of Czechoslovakia, American Friends Service Committee, the Belgian Office, Polish Red Cross, Swiss Aid for Children, Polish YMCA, French Red Cross, French Student Christian Association, French YMCA and YWCA, French Committee in Aid of Jewish Refugees, French Protestant Federation, Cimade (joint relief agency of French Protestant youth organisations), Unitarian Service Committee, Catholic Centre d'Accueil, delegate for Cardinal Gerlier, World Alliance of YMCAs, International Migration Service, European Student Relief. Six agencies were Jewish: American Joint Distribution Committee (JDC), OSE (Jewish children's relief agency), ORT (Jewish technical education organisation), HICEM (Jewish emigration society), Central Jewish Committee of Relief Organizations, RELICO (Jewish agency for health and medical service).
72　Lowrie, 'Confidential Notes on Interview with Pétain', 6 Aug. 1942, WCC.301.4329, FCC.B9F19.
73　Confidential Lowrie reports to Tracy Strong (Geneva), John Mott and Paul Anderson (NY), were issued on 10, *c*. 20, 24, 25, n.d. Aug.; 17, 19 Sept.; 7, 27 Oct. 1942. Five of the nine were titled and numbered 'Memorandum on Measures Applied to Foreign Jews in non-Occupied France'. WCC.301.4329, 425.1.022; PP60/15/57/2; FCC.B9F19. Marrus and Paxton (1995) cite copies in British PRO and AFSC. Also Donald Lowrie, *The Hunted Children* (New York: W.W. Norton, 1963).
74　Lowrie to Strong (hereafter L to S), 1st Memo, 10 Aug. 1942.
75　L to S, *c*. 20 Aug., 25 Aug.
76　L to S, 4, 17 Sept.
77　L to S, 17 Sept., 7 Oct.
78　Report fragments labelled 'Notes', 22 Sept. 1942; WCC.301.4331.
79　VH, 'WCC Action at Time of Extermination', 3 Mar. 1965 WCC.301.4331. For more on Gerstein, Saul Friedländer, *Kurt*

Gerstein: The Ambiguity of Good (New York: Knopf, 1969); see also Rolf Hochhuth, *The Deputy* (New York: Grove Press, 1964).
80 Riegner to Freudenberg w/copies to VH, Boegner, Cavert, Henriod, Weymarn, 23 Sept.; quot. in confidential Prov. Comm. min., 26 Sept.; VH, 'Notes for PC', 26 Sept., re 'news of killing'; WCC.301.005. For more on Riegner, Walter Laqueur and Richard Breitman, *Breaking the Silence* (New York: Simon & Schuster, 1986); Christopher Browning, 'A Final Hitler Decision for the "Final Solution"? The Riegner Telegram Reconsidered', *HGS* 10:1 (1996), 3–10.
81 ECCO min., 12 Feb. 1942, 8; WCC.425.1.022.
82 For planning, event schedules, reception invitations, guest lists, WCC.42.0015.
83 Confidential Prov. Comm. min., 26 Sept.; WCC.301.005.
84 Jean-Claude Favez, *The Red Cross and the Holocaust* (Cambridge: Cambridge University Press, 1999), 64–7, 293–4; on the ICRC decision to not act with WJC, Gerhard Riegner, *Never Despair: Sixty Years in the Service of the Jewish People and the Cause of Human Rights* (Chicago: Ivan R. Dee in assoc. with USHMM, 2006), 233.
85 'Sur le processus d'extermination des Juifs d'Europe', *c.* 30 Sept.; 'Report on deportations and conditions', *c.* 30 Sept.; 'Eastern Refugees Arriving in Switzerland', 8 Oct. 1942; WCC.425.1.022.
86 Easterman and Barou, 27 Nov. 1942, WCC.301.4331.
87 VH to Burckhardt, ICRC Joint Relief Committee, 3 Dec. 1942, WCC. 301.01, 425.1.022; also in Snoek, 272–3.
88 FB to Cavert, 9 Dec. 1942, FCC.B9F19. Further reports include: 'Confidential Nouvelles De Pologne', 8 Dec.; 'Bericht über Rumänien', and 'Die Lage der Juden in Rumänien', Dec. 1942; WCC.425.1.022.
89 Emerson to Paton, 7 Apr. 1943, which Paton received on the 8th, WCC.301.4331. Unless noted documents for n. 89–92 are at WCC. 301.4331.
90 Paton to Emerson, 9, 16 Apr.
91 Ibid., Paton to Carter, 16 Apr.; Carter to Paton, 19 Apr.; Paton, Notes on Conversation with Sir Herbert Emerson, 20 Apr.; Paton to Carter, 20 Apr., w/copies to Temple and Bell; Paton to Temple w/copy to Bell, 14 May 1943.
92 US Secretary of State to British Ambassador in response to British Aide-Memoire of 20 Jan., 25 Feb., was given to Riegner by LON Sec. Erim and passed to WCCIF; Riegner to VH, 14 Apr. 1965.
93 Monty Penkower, 'The Bermuda Conference and Its Aftermath', *The Nazi Holocaust: Bystanders*, Pt. 8, Vol. 1, ed. Michael Marrus

(De Gruyter Saur, 1989) 413–31; David Wyman, *Abandonment of the Jews* (New York: Pantheon, 1984); Lipstadt, *Beyond Belief*.

94 Riegner, *Never Despair* for other attempts to partner proposals, 67–9.
95 See for example VH to Cavert, where the 'ecumenical value' of relief for Greece is weighed, 16 Oct. 1942, FCC.B9 F19.
96 VH to Paton, 6 Mar. 1943, IMC.261142.
97 Riegner's reports, *c.*8 and 9 March, were followed by telegrams to Temple and Cavert to 'back Allied rescue efforts' and support proposal for 'exchange against German civilians'; WCC.301.4331.
98 The Aide-Memoire is in four graduated forms: WJC text for first draft, 9 Mar.; draft, with editing in handwriting of both VH and FB; form submitted to Norton, 22 Mar.; summary form to Foreign Office, with pencil notation by VH, 24 Mar. The latter appears in VH's *Memoirs*, 168–9, but Snoek's *Grey Book* mistakenly used the earlier draft, 275–7. For discussion of forms, Norton to Riegner, Riegner to Norton, 24 Mar. 1943; WCC.301.4331.
99 VH to Temple, 15 Dec. 1943, WCC.42.0077. Reports in 1943 on worsening conditions of Jews after the Aide-Memoire included 'Strictly Confidential', 4 June; 'Confidential Juive En Belgique', n.d. June; 'Location of Lager', 14 Sept.; 'Leitsätze für die Behandlung der Judenfrage im Deutschland der Nachkriegszeit', Dec.; WCC.425.1.022.
100 Riegner cable to Silverman, w/copy to WCCIF, 21 Mar. 1944. Unless noted documents for n. 100–13 are at WCC.301.4330, 4331, 4329.
101 VH and FB to Bell and Temple, 23 and 30 Mar. 1944.
102 'A Concise Summary of the Situation of Hungarian Jews', 30 April; 'Recapitulation and Second Report on the Situation of Hungarian Jews', 19 May; 'Third Report on the Situation of Hungarian Jews', 5 June 1944. All three are datelined Geneva.
103 The abridged version of the Auschwitz Protocols and the report on Hungarian Jews are in German, untitled, undated and marked 'not mention source'.
104 WCCIF Ecumenical Commission for Refugees, *ICPIS* No. 26 (June 1944).
105 US Legate quoting Sec. of State Hull's press conference, M 153, 26 June 1944. For major associated protests, see Wyman, *Abandonment of the Jews*, 235–54.
106 Randolph Braham, *The Politics of Genocide: The Holocaust in Hungary* (New York: Columbia University Press, 3rd revd edn, 2016), argues in 'The Conspiracy of Silence' that one set of reports reached Switzerland on June 19th and a second on the 20th, 961–79.

107 A cable to Cavert and Temple indicates that decision to protest was made on 24 June. In a separate action initiated by Karl Barth the Auschwitz reports were also sent to ecumenical leaders under signatures of Barth, Emil Brunner, Paul Vogt and Visser 't Hooft, but it did not begin until 4 July.
108 Wyman, *Abandonment of the Jews*, 235–54.
109 VH to Temple and Cavert, Jul. 1944.
110 Ibid.
111 Ibid., ital. add.
112 Hartmut Ludwig, 'Christians Cannot Remain Silent About This Crime: On the Centenary of the Birth of Adolf Freudenberg', *Ecumenical Review*, Vol. 46, No. 4 (1994), 475–85; in a 1974 interview Freudenberg 'could not remember why the phrase was left out of the German edition'.
113 Freudenberg to Pernow, Smith, Hoffmann, 4 Oct. 1944.
114 'Conference of Collaborators', Geneva, 7–9 July 1944, FCC.B23 F1.
115 VH, *The Struggle of the Dutch Church: Documents Collected and Edited by W.A. Visser 't Hooft* (Geneva: WCC, October 1944), 28, 35–6 orig. ital.
116 Paton to Flew, 15 Nov. 1940, was one of 58 letters between Nov. 1940 and April 1941 detailing Paton's promotion of Kosmala, IMC.261213.
117 For the standard view that Simpson and his youth council were not missionary in intention, see Marcus Braybrooke, *Children of One God: A History of the Council of Christians and Jews* (London: Vallentine Mitchell, 1991), 8, whose study relied mainly on Simpson and CCJ papers, limiting Simpson's early years in London to one paragraph on the period 1933–1938.
118 Simpson's involvement with ICCAJ is drawn from extensive documents in IMC.26120, 261219, PP60/17/8/1, WSP.66/1/3/4, as well as eight years of BICCAJ and ICCAJ minutes, reports and correspondence from multiple archives. Documents on the early missionary aims of the youth council include 51 letters and reports between 1934 and 1936. For outline, see Carolyn Sanzenbacher and Tony Kushner, 'When Knowledge Comes, Memory Comes Too, Little by Little', *Common Ground*, Autumn 2022, 28–32.
119 E.W. Thompson, Methodist Missionary Society, to Frank Exley, British Society for Propagation of the Gospel Among the Jews, 22 Apr. 1933; Thompson to Simpson, 22 Apr. 1933, WSP.66/1/3/4.
120 Simpson to Parkes, 15 Nov. 1933. Parkes answered the same day that he stood 'on the other side of the hedge' and would not advise contacts for a purpose he deeply regretted; PP.60/17/18/1.

121 Parkes to Parbrook, 16 Jun. 1936, PP. 60/17/18/1.
122 Standley to Hoffmann, 4 Dec. 1941, IMC.261201; Kosmala to Paton, 2 Jan., 21 May 1942, IMC.261213.
123 Hoffmann to Macanna, 5 Mar.; Simpson to Parkes, 15 Apr. 1942. Documents for n. 123–32 unless noted are at PP.60/17/10/2; 60/16/449.
124 Parkes to Temple, 16 Apr.
125 Temple to Parkes, 19 Apr., 11 May.
126 Parkes, 'Christianity and Judaism: Conversion or Cooperation?', 29 April 1942.
127 Campbell to Parkes, 8 May; Parkes to Campbell, 11 May, 30 Jun. 1942.
128 Bevan to Parkes, 12 May 1942.
129 Paton to Parkes, 12, 15, 19 May, 2 Oct.; Parkes to Paton, 14, 18 May, 20 Jun.
130 While Temple's position on missions remained unchanged, he credited Parkes with indirectly convincing him that new methods of Jewish evangelisation were needed; Temple to Parkes, 11 May, 5 Oct. 1942.
131 The CCJ announcement draft was circulating in October, but the member list was not to be published before 5 Nov., WCC.301.4331. Parkes was elected co-chair of the Society of Jews and Christians on 8 Oct. 1942, PP.60/15/76/5.
132 Paton, 'Foreword', Hans Kosmala and Robert Smith, *The Jew in the Christian World* (London: SCM Press, 1942), 5–7; for extensive correspondence on Paton's orchestration of the book, IMC.261213.
133 'Distribution of Jewish Population', 4 Dec. 1942, addendum to BICCAJ min., was extracted from American Jewish Joint Distribution Committee reports for use in postwar planning, as well as wartime references on refugees in transit. Data showed that some 35,000 refugees had moved through Spain, Portugal, or Casablanca since 1939, marking a trend to be referred to missionary agencies in those areas. Refugee settlement patterns in Central and South America were also discussed, with the aim of alerting area churches to the numbers of Jews 'in their midst'; IMC.261201.
134 Rev. Lev Gillet was a French priest in the Russian Orthodox Church, working for the Mildmay Mission to the Jews in London. For discussion on the need for an eastern European expert on Jewry, Macanna to Paton, 22 Dec. 1942; Paton to Macanna, 28 Dec.; Paton to Fisher, 18 Jan. 1943; Paton to Cedergren, 5 Feb. 1943; Fisher to Paton, 16 Apr. 1943; WCC.261213.

135 Report by Harold Beeley, BICCAJ min., 12 Mar. 1943, clarified that physical extermination was underway and 'economic extermination' was complete, IMC. 261207. Unless noted documents for n. 135–8 are at IMC.261207, 261213.
136 Memorandum on Proposed Christian Institute for Jewish Studies, 17 Mar.; BICCAJ min., 17 Mar., 16 Jul. 1943; Kosmala to Paton, 2 Jan. 1943.
137 Professor Newton Flew, host of Kosmala's lectures in 1941, was on the WCCIF PC.
138 Israel Gutman, *Resistance: The Warsaw Ghetto Uprising* (New York: Houghton Mifflin, 1994). Also *News Sheet*, 4 (Oct.–Dec. 1943); 1943 Survey on Jews, *IRM*, 33:1 (Jan.–Mar. 1944).
139 Hoffmann, Report on the Christian Approach to the Jews, 25 Mar. 1941, IMC.261229.
140 Hoffmann, Memorandum on the Christian Approach to the Jews, 10 May; Smith, Memorandum, 5 Aug. 1943, IMC.261201, 261213.
141 BICCAJ min., 12 May 1942, 30 Sept. 1943; CBMS min., 7 June 1943; IMC.26213, 261207, 261229.
142 For ongoing discussion of ICCAJ-WCC postwar collaboration, BICCAJ min., 4 Dec. 1942; CBMS min., 7 June 1943; BICCAJ min., 30 Sept. 1943, 8 Feb. 1944; Smith to VH, 17 Jul.; VH to Smith, 12 Sept.; Freudenberg to Pernow, Smith, Hoffmann, 4 Oct. 1944; Smith to VH, 18 Oct.; WCC.301.4331, 425.3.175, IMC.261207, 261213, 261229.
143 For Paton quot., CBMS Min., 7 June 1943, IMC.261229.
144 'Where shall we find the Jews?', *News Sheet* (Oct.–Dec. 1943), ital. add.
145 J. McLeod Campbell, *Manpower in the Twentieth Century Church* (London: Missionary Council of the Church Assembly, June 1944), orig. ital., 81. Campbell is noted on the title page as 'Chaplain to the King'.
146 Parkes, 'Confidential, CCJ and the Christian Mission to the Jews', Mar. 1944, PP.60/17/8/2.
147 Parkes, 'A Christian Looks at the Christian Mission to the Jews', PP.60/9/5/15, 60/7/10/3.
148 Macleish to Parkes, 22 May; Parkes to MacGregor, 27 May; series of letters between Parkes and Vidler, Jul.–Oct. 1944; PP.60/17/10/3, 60/9/5/15.
149 Smith to Gillet, 26 July 1944, IMC.261213.
150 Smith, 'New Dimension in Evangelism', *IRM*, Vol. 33, No. 3 (Jul. 1944), 304–11.

151 James Parkes, 'A Christian Looks at the Christian Mission to the Jews', *Theology, A Monthly Review*, Vol. 47, No. 292 (Oct. 1944), 218–24. For Institute response, Lev Gillet, 'Remarks on Dr Parkes' Article', 224–7; both are at PP.60/9/5/15, 17/10/3.
152 Hoffmann's report on 1 December from New York was written five days after the War Refugee Board report of the Auschwitz Protocols appeared in all major American newspapers, IMC.261207. For details on press accounts of the WRB report, Lipstadt, *Beyond Belief*, 263–7.

5

More than one guilt in the embers: 1945–1948

Guilt and reconciliation

The ecumenical crisis over German guilt in World War I, which played such a crucial role in shaping official responses to Germany and its policies in the Nazi years, bore heavily on reconstruction of relations with the German church at the end of World War II. The unity-threatening memory, its fractures, implications and hovering history, pushed to the fore again in early 1945 as claims of German collective guilt spewed from both sides of the Atlantic. Reports about the 'overstated' or 'exaggerated' acts that had peppered world news in the early years were replaced by the 'impossible to exaggerate' crimes of the German nation as a whole.[1] As outcries intensified with the unfolding of Nazi atrocities at Buchenwald, Bergen–Belsen and death march carnages in and around the historically Christian towns of Germany, few in the waking public were left untouched; and it is clear that the WCCIF Provisional Committee meeting in London on 26 April was not among them.[2] The 'most difficult problem' of ecumenical postwar business was understood to be that of Germany, and it would take six full months to solve the issue of how to restore official relations with the German church while dealing with undeniably valid questions about German guilt.[3]

Karl Barth had set the tone for ecumenical debate in a series of lectures printed and critiqued in the Swiss and English press in the first four months of the year. While holding that 'collective guilt' was an untenable concept, Barth argued for 'collective responsibility' of the whole German nation. His concern was not so much 'with guilt itself', or admittance of actual 'crimes committed', but with admitting that 'they all took the road leading to those crimes, either in the form of actions or negligence, direct or indirect participation, explicit or tacit consent, unequivocal, active or pro forma party membership, political indifference' or 'political errors and miscalculations'.[4]

Like Barth, Willem Visser 't Hooft argued for co-responsibility at the London meeting on 26 April but, unlike Barth, it was more narrowly rooted in a vision of ecumenism and more broadly distributed. As chairman of the sub-committee on the Christian attitude to war at the 1937 UCCLW Oxford conference, its three-point finding on mutual responsibility for war and continuing wars was central to his thinking. War had to be condemned in principle as manifestation of the 'power of sin'; the Church had to call its members to confession and repentance for commissions and omissions in past wars and the spirit of war; and if war broke out the Church had to remain 'the Church' in one unified spiritual body.[5]

When war overtook two years later, he and other leaders understood that WCCIF would stand or fall on its success in brokering these principles. The clearly stated goal was to do so while avoiding any hint of bias or 'even the slightest impression of a break in solidarity'.[6] As such, there was never a time during the war when Visser 't Hooft did *not* argue a form of co-responsibility for the outbreak and continuation of war, nor was there a time when the German churches were not seen as part of the reconciled postwar structure. The WCCIF safeguard based on Temple's 1940 directive guided what could and could not be said corporately on the issues of war, while the orchestrated message from Geneva aimed at reuniting the belligerent and neutral churches after armistice.

In memoranda before and during the war, Visser 't Hooft urged the Oxford principles as well as co-responsibility for Christianity's failure to be enough of a 'living reality' to prevent the war.[7] Specific claims of failure included the injustice of the war guilt clause at Versailles, western concessions that enabled Hitler, and the failure of western Allies to support German resistance groups.[8] As organisational attention turned to postwar reconstruction in 1942, so did the focus on relations between co-responsibility, repentance and postwar reconciliation. Memoranda in January and May 1943, as well as Provisional Committee critiques in July, stressed that the role of the Church was to call the nations 'to repentance for their common guilt and work for their reconciliation'.[9] The core idea was that the universal 'message' of the Church was dominated by an acute consciousness of the sin and guilt of all humankind, and that postwar 'confession of universal guilt' by all involved would eliminate the 'sole guilt' of any one nation, while not excluding national confessions of 'injustices and crimes'. The wartime task of WCCIF, so it was argued, was to create the atmosphere in which such confession, repentance and reconciliation could become possible.[10]

In the same period of stressing co-responsibility and universal guilt, Visser 't Hooft argued against unilateral condemnation of Germany and public criticism of the German church. In private censure of Provisional Committee chairman William Temple, who criticised the Confessing church in a January 1943 sermon for having made 'no specific protest against the treatment of Jews and Poles', he warned that such statements could have 'real bearing' on relations with the German churches, and that public correction was needed. While agreeing that the Confessing church had not 'spoken out as clearly as it should', he urged that a stand had been made on 'euthanasia and the persecution of Jews' and the 'chief thing' was that they had been made, even if not publicly. In a second private censure of Temple, for warning of a 'penal element' against Germany in another sermon, Visser 't Hooft argued that punishment beyond that 'implied in the course of historical events' was not in order.[11]

Both arguments appeared again in a confidential report of December 1943 in which Temple was not named. In what can be seen as a counter-argument against German church inaction and silence, he advocated for a 'concentration of forces' gathering in Germany as a 'bulwark' against Nazi ideology and the 'victory of totalitarianism'. Arguing that this group of men under Bishop Theophil Wurm *could* be 'among the most trustworthy and active supporters of a complete overhauling of national life', Visser 't Hooft warned that their 'readiness' to collaborate would be largely contingent on the way in which Germany and the war guilt question were treated at the time of armistice. From their standpoint, and his, it would have to be a common recognition of guilt and 'not a unilateral condemnation of the German nation alone'.[12]

Behind these arguments were behind the scenes engagements. Ten months after the December memorandum, the group gathering around Bishop Wurm laid out plans to remain 'part of the ecumenical movement'. That this was part of an ongoing discourse with Geneva was made clear by annotations indicating that documents were being sent for a second time, one of which was 'The Joint Action of the Churches of the Ecumenical Movement under Reconciliation'.[13] The 'strictly confidential' plans, an English translation of which was ordered by A.C. Craig, pro tem co-secretary of WCCIF since Paton's 1943 death, included the 'Life and Struggle of the German Evangelical Church' (1943–1944); an outline of church restructure, administration and function; and an eight-point plan for self-aid at the end of war. That a discussion of guilt was already in progress is clearly evident. The 'unification movement' under Bishop Wurm was self-described as a repentant church rising from its struggle, strengthening in spirit and structure while recognising the failures that led to its 'responsibility and complicity' in the 'horrid developments of a totalitarian war with all its brutal implications'.[14]

Three weeks later on 6 November 1944 at a Provisional Committee meeting in London, with Craig in attendance, Visser 't Hooft confirmed 'continuous contact' with German church leaders, stressing that they would do 'whatever they could' to stay in 'close touch with the ecumenical movement'.[15] As was typical of his orchestrations, however, not everything was revealed to the larger group. On 19 February, after meetings in France, Holland and Belgium, Visser 't Hooft confided to Robert Mackie that 'satisfactory understanding for our concerns' had been reached about the 'place of the German church after the break-down of National Socialism', but the issue bristled with such difficulty that it had to be 'treated in a most confidential manner'. Four days later he emphasised the same confidentiality to George Bell while adding that those around Wurm 'want us to go ahead'.[16]

As all of this strongly implies, the issue of war guilt at the 26 April Provisional Committee meeting in London had nothing to do with whether official relations with the German church would be restored. Indeed, even before the issue of war guilt was broached it was agreed by all that the first postwar meeting of the full committee would include Germany. The question on the table was what could be said officially to German church leaders, when and how it should be said, and what it would mean in ecumenical consequences. The deliberations began with Visser 't Hooft's argument for a message of 'spiritual influence and significance', which was based on a memorandum by German members of his Geneva staff. He proposed that any such message to Germany should recognise the 'true and living' German church as well as its 'communion of repentance' when raising the issues of guilt and sin. 'Crimes committed in the name of the whole German nation, murder of Jews, Russian prisoners of war, innocent hostages, extermination of whole villages' should all be included, *but* so should recognition of German church protests 'against persecution', as well as the failures of British Christians to recognise the danger of Nazism and support resistance groups in Germany. Broad categories of German crimes could be stated in an official message to the German Protestant churches, in other words, so long as the praiseworthy attributes of German churches *and* the failings of Allied nations were simultaneously acknowledged.[17]

While the wartime nucleus of the Provisional Committee was familiar with Visser 't Hooft's 'common guilt theology', it was far from agreeing with his proposal for a message to the German churches. The responses were of two distinct types. The first was a volley of rejections to 'put on the same level the sin of the Allied nations and that of the German nation'. There could be no return to the ameliorating solution of the World War I guilt problem by equating the actions of Allies with those of Germany. While admitting that errors in Allied judgments 'contributed' to Nazi power, those mistakes were not on the same level as Germany's guilt and could not be equated. The other type of response, however, captured the overall desire for postwar reconciliation by calling attention to the committee's reluctance to raise 'controversial' or 'delicate' issues. Any attempt to name crimes in order to stimulate a statement of German church repentance could provoke 'undesirable reactions' in churches that were victims of Nazi aggressions, and thereby defeat the postwar aim of reconciling the Protestant churches.[18] In lieu of alienating one group or the other, it was thus decided, with Visser 't Hooft's acquiescence, that no official message 'should be sent at least for the present', but that as many 'bilateral conversations' as possible should take place with German church leaders and that a delegation should be sent to Stuttgart as soon as possible.[19]

The bilateral conversations

The first set of bilateral talks after Germany's surrender on 8 May began in early June when Eugen Gerstenmaier, who had served under Wurm on the Reich Advisory Council while liaising with German resistance, arrived in Geneva with an ICRC delegation. But, like the behind-scenes discussion on postwar reconciliation with the German church, this too had a wartime history. In response to the eight-point German plan for self-aid in October 1944, WCCIF produced an eight-point response drafted by Hans Schönfeld in February.[20] Meetings in April with Hutchinson Cockburn, new senior secretary of reconstruction, resulted in a pledge for German church relief with the promise of a proposal 'as soon as personal contact' could be made.[21] Gerstenmaier was in Geneva as Wurm's representative to consult on the needs of the churches in preparation for Schönfeld and Freudenberg's upcoming tour of Germany.

The two WCCIF German staffers left Geneva on 15 June with plans to meet Gerstenmaier again two weeks later. By 26 June they had made one trip through the French and American zones of central and southwestern Germany, and were helping Wurm in Frankfurt am Main and Wiesbaden with Allied permissions for German church leaders to convene a conference in Treysa. Gerstenmaier had arrived and was preparing for their joint trip to the Rhineland, Ruhr, Bremen, Hamburg, Lübeck and Hanover. The other German travelling with them was Eduard Waetjen, attorney and former *Abwehr* agent for the German consulate in Zurich who liaised with German resistance groups during the war.[22]

During the two weeks of travel through bombing devastation and the early stages of Allied occupation, Freudenberg and Schönfeld met with churchmen in Freiburg, Karlsruhe, Heidelberg, Mannheim, Weinheim, Eisenach, Naumburg, Weimar, Leipzig, Göttingen, Halle, Kassel, Bad Nauheim and Marburg, including, in addition to Bishop Wurm, Otto Fricke, Martin Niemöller and Hans Asmussen. Prominent among items discussed on the physical, spiritual and moral issues of reconstructing the German churches was that the Confessing church was well aware it needed to put its household in order. While there is no indication of who broached which topics recorded in the reports, it is clear that issues discussed included the necessary removal of 'unsuitable' church leaders who 'bowed down to Nazism'; an 'imperative' to inform the nation of the 'plain and unvarnished truth' about what had happened; and the need to 'stir the nation's conscience and lead the people to true repentance'.[23]

The second set of 'bilateral conversations' were far more orchestrated and targeted. Within days of Freudenberg's return to Geneva on 19 July, Visser 't Hooft reported to Bell that contact with Dibelius in Berlin had been made and that Stewart Herman, who had just arrived in Geneva, was being sent there.[24] Herman had been pastor of the American church in Berlin until the outbreak of war, and was then with OSS intelligence in London until recruited by Visser 't Hooft, the proposal for which was discussed with OSS Swiss director Allen Dulles as early as October 1944.[25] Bell had learned two full months before the 26 April meeting in London that Herman was being brought in to help with 'the whole German situation'. As confided by Visser 't Hooft, Herman's 'usefulness' would 'largely depend on the discussions' with German church leaders, but 'officially' he would work as a secretary in reconstruction.[26] His update to Bell on 24 July was that Herman's immediate task, beyond reporting on relief needs in eastern Germany, was to determine when and how WCCIF could send 'more important delegations' to German church leaders, and then 'prepare the way'.[27]

When Herman crossed into Germany on 30 July he carried two documents bearing the imprint of the WCCIF position.[28] The first was a letter from Visser 't Hooft to Bishop Otto Dibelius, dated 25 July, which assured that WCCIF would 'do all we can to restore the fellowship', but that 'obstacles have to be overcome'. More pointedly, 'a fraternal conversation' with the churches that suffered under Nazi occupation would be 'required', one facilitated by speaking of both the Nazi crimes and 'the sins of omission of the German people, including the church'.[29] The second document was Herman's version of the same message, stating in a less direct way that his 'visit of reconciliation' to the German churches on behalf of WCCIF was in the spirit of Christian brotherhood and 'universal repentance', and that Christian 'witness' from each nation 'emerging from conflict' was 'essential to Christendom's complete confession'.[30]

Over the next five weeks, via Visser 't Hooft's orchestration, Herman established himself with US military officials in Höchst, Heidelberg and Berlin, requesting priority permission for a delegation to enter Germany. WCCIF was presented as representative of 'virtually the entire Protestant and Orthodox communions', willing and ready to use its resources to aid in the spiritual reconstruction and stabilisation of Europe. As lobbied by Herman, WCCIF was acting in the conviction that, despite 'a Nazified minority of pastors and priests', the German churches constituted the only German agency that had not fully succumbed to Nazism, one that was 'probably the strongest single agency for rehabilitation that the bankrupt nation possesses'. The WCCIF aim was to bring 'the German churches back into the fellowship of ecumenical Christianity' and assist in the role they would play 'as architects of a new nation' – while insisting they 'accept their due share of responsibility for Adolf Hitler and his activities'.[31]

Herman was no less straightforward with church leaders in Freiburg, Karlsruhe, Heidelberg, Wiesbaden, Frankfurt, Stuttgart and Berlin. The issues of guilt, responsibility and admission were repeatedly broached. Of points raised, the 'interest' of the World Council 'in preserving a common Evangelical front in Germany' was urged on Martin Niemöller.[32] To Otto Fricke in Frankfurt he stressed that 'churches outside Germany expected some sort of declaration of responsibility for the events of the last decade'.[33] In Stuttgart he emphasised to Bishop Wurm and Oberkirchenrat Wilhelm Pressel 'the necessity of making some declaration' on church 'responsibility for the Nazi regime and its actions'. To Bishop Dibelius and the Berlin Bruderrat three days later, he made clear that WCCIF wanted 'to aid the German churches as far as possible, but ... the help of the giving churches would be *inevitably conditioned* by the sense of responsibility expressed by the German churches for the Nazi regime'.[34]

Herman also made himself useful to church leaders, carrying invitations from Fricke (in Frankfurt) and Wurm (in Stuttgart) to

Dibelius and associates in Berlin, then arranging for a German delegation from Berlin to be flown to the western zone for a major church conference in Treysa. When the conference convened between 27 and 31 August, Herman was seated directly in front of Wurm and Niemöller, and was given the floor to extend official greetings from WCCIF.[35] Equally significant is that Wurm himself reported directly from Treysa to Geneva to inform that factions in the church had united and he had been unanimously named to head a governing council for the Evangelical Church in Germany (EKD), with Niemöller as vice-chair and Gerstenmaier as deputy of church aid.[36] As Visser 't Hooft relayed to Bell, everyone in Geneva was 'very pleased with the Treysa results'.[37]

In the two weeks after Treysa a critical part of Herman's task in Germany was to determine the 'most convenient' date for a WCCIF delegation to meet with the new EKD Council and then make the 'necessary preparations'.[38] He had further meetings with military officials in the British zone, as well as with churchmen in Schleswig-Holstein, Lübeck, Hamburg, Bremen, Hanover, Oldenburg, North Rhine-Westphalia (including Detmold) before meeting with church and military officials in Frankfurt and Berlin.[39] When he returned to Geneva on 20 September to meet with Visser 't Hooft, Koechlin, Cockburn, Freudenberg and S.C. Michelfelder, he carried tentative dates for the EKD Council meeting, with confirmation of 18 October the following week.[40] Military permission for a WCCIF delegation into Germany, however, remained an issue until early October, even though Herman assured officials that 'we are ready to fit our own caravan', if necessary, rather than using military motor fuel, rations and billets.[41]

When Herman went back into Germany on 9 October to Wiesbaden, Frankfurt and Berlin, it was for the express purpose of coordinating 'communication between church authorities in the eastern and western zones' and making the 'final arrangements for an ecumenical delegation to attend the Council of German church leaders at Stuttgart'.[42] The culminating details of his eleven-week effort are a critical part of the end-to-end orchestration that resulted in the formal moment of postwar reconciliation so robustly sought by WCCIF. They also stand in refutation of stubborn memories surrounding what became known as the Stuttgart Declaration of

More than one guilt in the embers: 1945–1948

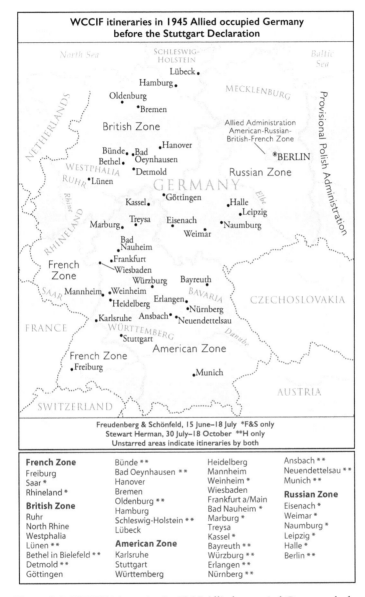

Figure 5.1 WCCIF itineraries in 1945 Allied occupied Germany before the Stuttgart Declaration of Guilt (shaded areas in the ledger indicate regional itineraries)

Guilt, namely, that there was *no* pre-discussion between WCCIF and German church leaders, that the EKD council did not know the Geneva delegation was coming, and that upon arrival in Stuttgart the delegation merely 'heard' that 'there would be a special service in the Markuskirche' that evening. Archival reports from multiple sources belie such memories by rendering an altogether different picture of what was taking place in the three days of meetings and receptions.[43]

The Stuttgart Declaration

On 15 October Visser 't Hooft, Cavert, Koechlin and Michelfelder were met at the Swiss–German border by Colonel Marcel Sturm, head of the French Protestant chaplaincy, and were taken to Baden-Baden where they were joined by Pierre Maury, who was representing Marc Boegner of the French Protestant Federation. As the overnight guests of General Pierre Koenig, commander of the French zone, they were received by administrative General Émile Laffon for discussions on the role of the German churches in the postwar restructure of Germany.

On the morning of 17 October, after a night at Hotel Graf Zeppelin in Stuttgart, they met with Eugen Gerstenmaier to discuss material aid for the German churches. In mid-afternoon, Stewart Herman, who had been meeting with Paul Althaus (in Erlangen) and Hans Meiser (in Munich) joined the delegation to attend, in his words, 'the special meetings from which the Stuttgart Declaration emerged'. The WCCIF group was with Bishop Wurm when Herman arrived.[44] At 7:30 that evening, 'everyone went to the opening service in the Markuskirche', where they were joined by Hendrik Kraemer from Holland for addresses and sermons by Wurm, Niemöller and Dibelius.[45] It should also be noted that the US military escort for Dibelius reported that, according to military order AG30014L-10, dated 11 October, the purpose of his trip was to attend the EKD Council and 'make possible a meeting with the Ecumenical Council'.[46]

On the morning of the 18th, the EKD Council met in closed session while the WCCIF delegation worked on reconstruction with Gerstenmaier and associates.[47] In mid-afternoon both groups were guests at a tea hosted by the military governor of Württemberg. After Hans Meiser arrived, both groups gathered in closed session around a table described and sketched by Herman. Although George Bell and Dr Reidar Hauge from Norway had not yet arrived that did not delay the 'fraternal conversation' which had brought the delegation and EKD Council together. The recorded time of the private session by Dibelius's military escort was one hour, and that included discussion of church problems in east Germany, Silesia and Sudeten as well as WCCIF plans for aid to eastern Germany.[48] Later that evening, after the EKD Council met a second time and Bishop Bell arrived, Wurm and his wife hosted a dinner at their home in Bell's honour.[49]

That all of this could take place in occupied Germany without advance planning, mutual knowledge and military permissions is as contradictory to evidence as the claim that the statement read the next morning was a spontaneously rendered declaration of guilt. Any admission that has been pre-requested, pre-discussed and is expected is not in any sense a product of spontaneity, even if those requesting would like it to seem that way. Yet that is what Visser 't Hooft recorded the following week, vis-à-vis that he, Cavert, Koechlin, Michelfelder and Maury had agreed that, while a statement on acts 'committed in the name of the German nation' was needed, it could not be said conditionally for it 'would not have the character of true spontaneity'. What he went on to record about the 60-minute meeting, however, was in fact conditional. Opening on behalf of WCCIF, he conveyed gratitude for the Confessing church struggle against Nazism, as well as hope that official relations could be restored, but in so doing he reiterated what had been said multiple times and what everyone around the table knew: there were 'obstacles to be removed and questions to be answered'. Speaking on behalf of the EKD Council, Hans Asmussen responded that it was understood that 'the ecumenical delegation would like to have a definite declaration from the Council of the German Church'.[50]

The formal moment of reconciliation came the next morning on 19 October in a second closed session of the two groups. Reading from a unanimously agreed EKD Council statement to the WCCIF delegation, Asmussen spoke of suffering, guilt, struggling, accusing and cleansing in that order. Neither the German Council delivering, nor the World Council receiving it, spoke of the suffering of Jews, of guilt for Germany's crimes against Jews, nor were 'antisemitism' or 'Jews' mentioned. Such specificity had been neither sought nor expected since the 26 April Provisional Committee meeting in London, so there was no expression of regret by any member of the delegation that anything was missing from the declaration.

A WCCIF press release to twenty-five newspapers and the international *ICPIS* news service one week later helps to explain why it was not only unquestioned but praised as a 'truly Christian message' that restored ecumenical unity. The widely distributed release, announcing that the 'new' Protestant church of Germany had become the 90th participating body of the World Council, framed the now historic document as 'a *formal entente* between the German churches [that] survived the Nazi terror and churches in recent enemy nations'. The hailed achievement in the opening paragraphs of the publicity report was not presented as a declaration of German guilt but a reconciliatory repair of the breach in unity between the non-Roman churches of previously warring nations. The EKD Council declaration was the means by which the formal entente had been reached, as clarified in the publicised account of what had taken place:[51]

> The delegation told the German leaders that it hoped to arrive again at fully fraternal relationships but that there were obstacles which had to be removed. The German leaders said they wished to express their implication in the guilt of the German nation, in which the Church had shared, and presented a statement signed by eleven German members present.

The actual admission of guilt, which followed in block quotation in the press release, was captured in 115 words, a good part of which (indicated by italics) had to do with the suffering and struggles of the German church itself. Yet this was enough to satisfy the WCCIF delegation, for the part that dealt with German church guilt met the general conditions for recognition, admittance and repentance, and it did so within the context of recalling that the German church had struggled against Nazism.

... we know ourselves to be with our people in a great company of suffering, but also in a great solidarity of guilt. With great pain do we say: through us has endless suffering been brought to many peoples and countries. What we have often borne witness to before our congregations, that we declare in the name of the whole Church. *True we have struggled for many years in the name of Jesus Christ against a spirit which has found its terrible expression in the National Socialist regime of violence*, but we accuse ourselves for not witnessing more courageously, for not praying more faithfully, for not believing more joyously and for not loving more ardently.[52]

The WCCIF publicity release went on to say that the new German church, risen from its struggles, was 'cleansing' itself 'from influences alien to faith', and reuniting with the Christian principles from which it had strayed.[53] With guilt and cleansing declared, and the formal entente in place, the repair of the breach between the church of the country that produced Nazism and churches of countries that suffered due to Nazism could resume ecumenical relations, and each could play its needed role in the Christian healing of the postwar world.

This unequivocal relationship between the Stuttgart Declaration and the advancement of official ecumenism was hailed unambiguously by Visser 't Hooft in February 1946 at the Provisional Committee meeting in Geneva, with newly appointed Niemöller and Wurm in attendance. The declaration of 'solidarity in the guilt of the German people' was said to have cleared the way 'for full participation of the German church in the World Council'.[54] Some 27 years later the stakes of that relationship were stated more pointedly as essential to the 1948 founding assembly that transformed WCCIF into a World Council of Churches:

It was *due* to the Stuttgart meeting that the ecumenical movement could now go ahead and turn to the future. If that meeting had not been held or if it had not succeeded in restoring fraternal relations, it would have been *impossible* to create the necessary spiritual conditions for the inauguration of the World Council at Amsterdam in 1948.[55]

That Visser 't Hooft actually meant that WCCIF could not have proceeded to the founding assembly without the Declaration does not have to be taken at face value.[56] It is evidently clear that the causes and processes of ecumenism's fractured history were so etched in organisational memory that reconciliation was deemed requisite to circumvent a repeat of the divisiveness over Germany's war guilt in World War I. Reconciliation was in this way part of the broader pursuit for ecumenical unity, with roots reaching back and certitude of purpose moving it forward. Any breach, but especially a major breach with the Reformation nation, would not only diminish but wound the efficacy of a unified supranational ecumenical message. Moreover, just days before the WCCIF delegation traveled to Stuttgart, Visser 't Hooft distributed a confidential memorandum to Provisional Committee members, elaborating the 'profound significance' of the wartime emergence of 'confessional theology' from 'confessing churches', which could serve 'as pioneering bodies for the whole ecumenical movement'.[57]

All of this has a bearing on how we view and interpret the Stuttgart Declaration, whose origins most certainly lay in the WCCIF orchestrated requests for a German church statement. While it remains critically important to the histories of the *Kirchenkampf*, postwar German Protestantism and Protestant Christianity as a whole,[58] the broadening and deepening of context from the perspective detailed here reveals the extraordinary degree to which it was pursued in principle as a reconciliatory ecumenical aim, with far-reaching implications. It also explains the otherwise unexplained issue of why WCCIF would be the urging, receiving and publicising body of a German Declaration of Guilt.

That the formal entente was also mutually beneficial must not be ignored. Of its eleven signatories, nine were placed in key positions for the WCC 1948 founding assembly in Amsterdam. In addition to their Provisional Committee appointments, Bishop Wurm was named to the Committee of Fourteen and Committee for Reconstruction and Inter-Church Aid, while Niemöller was made vice-chair of the steering committee for a new ecumenical training centre, vice-chair of the Commission on the Church's Witness to God's Design, and member of the Message Committee. Hanns Lilje became chair of the Commission on the Universal Church in God's Design, chair of the Press Committee and part of the editorial board for a new ecumenical journal. Hans Asmussen was appointed to the Commission for Chaplaincy to POWs and the Arrangements Committee. Rudolf Smend and Gustav Heinemann were named to the Commission of Churches on International Affairs, Hans Meiser was placed with the Committee on the Church and the Disorder of Society, and Otto Dibelius was made vice-chair of the Commission on the Church and International Disorder. Dibelius, Niemöller, Lilje, Meiser and Wilhelm Niesel were then appointed to the Central Committee of the World Council.[59] Even more directly relevant, Niesel was named to a landmark Committee on the Christian approach to the Jews, while Asmussen and six other EKD churchmen were named alternates or consultants to a parallel committee, the two of which would formulate the WCC founding statement on Jews, antisemitism and Jewish missions.

Guilt and reparation

Five days after the Stuttgart Declaration was received by WCCIF, Dr Otto von Harling, senior member of ICCAJ, and Dr Karl Rengstorf, term member from 1932 to 1935, issued a resolution from the Lutheran Evangelical Committee for Mission to Israel that work would resume as soon as conditions permitted, 'hopefully, within the year'. Rengstorf and von Harling also wrote to Conrad Hoffmann in New York, urging him 'to come as soon as possible for counsel and help', a plea being heard from other parts of Europe including Britain, Sweden, Holland and Switzerland.[60] Hoffmann, who recognised that 'spiritual isolation' during the war had left German colleagues with 'little conception of the radical changes that had taken place in Jewry', had just returned from the first of twelve Atlantic crossings in three years in order to answer those calls, but had got no further than Britain and Geneva due to entry restrictions.

The purpose behind both calls and crossings was reconstruction of Jewish missions in the rubble of European devastation and changing world Jewry. In his October summary of concerns, one-third of all Jews in the world had been exterminated, Jewish survivors were physically and spiritually ravaged, and the 'goodwill and religious tolerance' movement was endangering Jewish missions.

There was also the ongoing issue of increasing Zionism, which was being fuelled by increasing antisemitism, both of which were increasing division in the churches. On one side were Christians who agreed with political Zionists on the need for a Jewish state in Palestine, and on the other were those who opposed it, many of which yet granted that Palestine should be an area of refuge. All of this, according to Hoffmann, was in the purview of postwar Jewish missions, ICCAJ's prominence in it, and the need to reconstitute the mission impetus on the Continent as quickly as possible.[61]

The reconstitution being sought, however, had new postwar meaning. Varying levels of discussion about ICCAJ collaboration with WCCIF had been in play since organisational attention turned to reconstruction in 1942. After Geneva signalled that cooperation with the 'various aims' of ICCAJ was indicated in October 1944,[62] Samuel Cavert in New York chaired a reorganisational meeting of NAICCAJ in November, where Hoffmann was 'unanimously' named to an IMC commission on reconstruction of Jewish work on the Continent, 'Near East, Great Britain, North and South America'.[63] Efforts from both sides of the Atlantic to dovetail his first European trip with Visser 't Hooft's April meetings in London were not successful, but consultations were held in Geneva shortly thereafter. Following Hoffmann's return to New York, the North American sector of ICCAJ resolved that 'every effort' should be made to ensure that Church responsibility for Jews became an integral part of the WCCIF postwar agenda. Within days intentions to that effect were set out in a letter to Samuel Cavert on 3 October, who by that time was en route for a six-month WCCIF appointment in Geneva, and would be part of the delegation receiving the Stuttgart Declaration.[64]

As these interorganisational efforts unfolded over the next nine months, two forms of WCCIF–ICCAJ alliance came into focus. The first was the appointment of a joint secretary in the WCCIF department of reconstruction. Göte Hedenquist, head of Swedish Missions to Jews in Vienna from the *Anschluss* through 1940 under the direction of ICCAJ vice-chair Birger Pernow, was well received in Geneva in February 1946, but his joint agency for ICCAJ remained unsettled for some time.[65] Both WCCIF and ICCAJ agreed that, while his work on reconstruction in central and eastern Europe could not be 'exclusively on behalf of Jewish missions', the 'interests' of ICCAJ could be kept in view. Hutchinson Cockburn, head of reconstruction, however, was concerned about WCCIF overt identification with Jewish missions so soon after the war. While he was 'personally' in favour of Jewish evangelisation and felt sure 'we would not have the Jewish problem we have today' if it had been pursued earlier in history, he conditioned that Hedenquist could not 'in any way implicate' reconstruction or WCCIF while representing ICCAJ. The caution was necessary, he advised, due to the 'nature and problems' of Jewish missions which often involved 'not only Church tensions but political tensions as well'.[66]

When pressed by ICCAJ associate director Robert Smith in March to elucidate the 'kind of tensions' he wished to avoid, Cockburn pointed to the 'situation of World Jewry today and the political reactions which it inevitably brings'.[67] In May, however, he confirmed that the 'closest relationship' was indicated until official policy was settled, and that he and Freudenberg would do everything in their power to help in the prosecution of ICCAJ work.[68] By August Freudenberg and Hoffmann were discussing the coordination of trips into Germany in order to present a 'common basis and policy' that would ensure 'a solid front' between the two organisations.[69]

The other kind of alliance unfolding concurrently was more complex. WCCIF's work as wartime liaison between IMC and European missions was increasingly understood as a step toward integration of the mission and church arms of the ecumenical movement.[70] Three formal resolutions in that direction were adopted during a ten-day period of administrative meetings in Geneva in February 1946. The WCCIF–IMC Joint Committee resolved that the two would seek areas of 'closer cooperation and relationship';[71] the Ad Interim Committee of IMC 'offered' ICCAJ to WCCIF for collaboration on 'the witness of the Church to the Jewish people';[72] the Provisional Committee passed a resolution put into motion by FCC's department of evangelism, stating that missions should be considered an area of 'special concern' in its organisational structure.[73] The resolution was introduced by Walter Horton, notably, a member of NAICCAJ as well as its sitting chairman.

The following month IMC New York secretary John Decker predicted that ICCAJ would be one of the first agencies brought under joint auspices of IMC and the World Council.[74] Three months later in June the announcement was made that 62-year-old Hoffmann would return to full-time work with ICCAJ to advance that collaboration. Two layers of organisational appropriation were being sought: structural changes that would move ICCAJ under the joint auspices of the two councils, with shared administrative and financial authority, and WCCIF adoption of ICCAJ's aims and principles. The basis for both was that collaboration would ensure fuller use of ICCAJ's 'missionary dynamic' while availing of the 'evangelistic opportunity' in the constituent nations of the World Council. More pointedly, the targets of missionary aims were in the 'territory of the churches ... directly related to the World Council', and collaboration would open 'vast new opportunities for evangelistic approach ... to the suffering Jewish people in Europe and elsewhere'.[75]

Although Hoffmann's salary and pension were to be paid by the Presbyterian Board of National Missions as its contribution, the immediate obstacle in mid-1946 was money. Henry Leiper, who was involved with the New York decision to pursue collaboration, now informed that there was no means in WCCIF's administrative budget, for it had nearly doubled with increasing staff and expanding facilities in Geneva. After consulting with IMC and Hoffmann in August and November, Visser 't Hooft placed the issue on the agendas of the Administrative and Provisional Committees, which confirmed in April 1947 that a department of evangelisation that included Jewish missions would be considered. In the interim, ICCAJ was authorised to apply for funding through WCCIF reconstruction.[76]

Two months later, in June, an ICCAJ conference of 61 delegates from 14 countries convened in Basel to rule on structural changes that would advance formalised ICCAJ–WCCIF collaboration. The constitutional changes, informally agreed by ICCAJ, IMC and WCCIF prior to convening, allowed for a 36 per cent expansion of the Continental European, British and North American sectors, which meant an increase from seven to eleven members in each region, three of which were to be assigned by WCCIF. With allotment power of nine places, in other words, 27 per cent of each regional sector could now be appointed by the World Council.[77]

The upshot of this series of formalised actions is that, while not yet under its auspices, ICCAJ had moved to a new level of relations with WCCIF by mid-1946, after which all plans proceeded on the assumption that collaboration on Jewish issues would be the norm. By the following November, the month after Hoffmann resumed full time work with ICCAJ, the programme committee for the WCC founding assembly confirmed that the 'question of Israel' would be on the agenda and he would be assisting.[78] By early December Hoffmann had penned two of a number of memoranda that would ultimately inform the assembly statement on Jews.

What is perhaps most remarkable about the first, which was structured around 'the Order of God and Present Disorder of Man', is his attempt to place and sensitise ICCAJ arguments within the context of the 1948 assembly theme, thereby marking the Jewish people (rather than the Nazis who almost succeeded in their extermination) as a symbol of the 'disorder of man'. More specifically, 'We believe that the Jews as a people are a symbol as to other people of the disorder of man both in the past and in the present'.[79] Yet the Jews as a people were also a 'mysterious' factor in God's design for mankind, as well as the 'most universal neighbour' of the Church. As such, it was only as the Church immersed itself in the practice and profession of the faith that the 'disorder of man so widespread and continuous in relation to the Jews has any hope of solution'.[80] The same type of claims were elaborated in the second memorandum by arguing that the Church was confronted in three distinct forms with the 'inescapable question', '*What are you going to do with the Jews?*' in regard to Zionism? in regard to antisemitism? in regard to Jewish missions?[81]

This of course was the same set, howbeit *reset*, of claims that had been in play since Macdonald Webster's 'Jewish Problem' appeared in *IRM* in October 1925.[82] The perceived issues facing the Church in the aftermath of World War II were thus the same as those in the aftermath of World War I, with one crucial difference. The Church now had to deal with the questions not only in the wake of war itself but in the aftermath of 'Hitler's madness', wherein 'more than six million Jews were liquidated'. Within that realm of difference, however, was an element that Hoffmann believed should shape the ways in which the Church approached the same (but different) issues of Zionism, antisemitism and Jewish missions.

> Had the voice of the Christian world through the Churches been loud and vigorous enough, perhaps the great modern tragedy of Israel might have been prevented. Christendom, especially the Christian Church, must be both penitent and humble in confessing its great failure to be 'the brother's keeper' in this time of greatest need of Jewry.[83]

The humility, confession and penitence being called for, however, did not extend to self-critique of Hoffmann's vigorous warnings about Jewishness and Judaisation on both sides of the Atlantic before the war, nor did it include ICCAJ's postwar insistence on the need for evangelisation of surviving Jews. Conversely, in a reorganisation of rationale, the failure of the Church to raise its voice sufficiently was rallied as cause for compensatory expansion of Jewish missions. The argumentation for Jewish evangelisation in the wake of exterminations was thus *solutionary* in terms of solving the 'disorder of man so widespread and continuous in relation to the Jews', and *compensatory* in terms of reparation for Church failure to prevent the murder of six million Jews – and it was this that Hoffmann set out to imprint through memoranda and intercontinental itineraries.

The first step in concrete planning was the 'realistically and tragically statistical' survey that defined the range and areas of the surviving Jewish population. While it was impossible to determine precise figures, it was clear by the end of the war that the European and North American continents had reversed in terms of population numbers. The majority of world Jewry, some 5 million, now lived in the United States and Canada. Of the pre-war European population of 9.8 million, only 3.6 were thought to have survived the twelve-year Nazi onslaught, and of those only 1.5 to 1.6 million were thought to be outside Soviet European territories. Numbers in individual countries could only be approximated but the earliest reports indicated drastic changes in numbers and densities throughout the Continent. Adding to the complexity were the indeterminate numbers of surviving Jewish refugees migrating from Russia, Poland and other eastern European countries to the western Allied zones of occupied Germany, who were now labelled as 'displaced persons' that were unable or unwilling to return to their former national homes.[84]

In the face of such indeterminate numbers and continental shifts in Jewish populations, the best hope for success on the changing mission field was thought to be the parish approach, meaning the inclusion of Jews in the ministry of each local church on each continent. The initial aim for educating and rallying Protestant 'forces' in America was 115 cities with 2500 or more Jews, and by March 1946 Hoffmann had held training courses in Seattle, San Francisco, Los Angeles, Chicago, Minneapolis, St Paul, Atlanta, Philadelphia and Montreal.[85] With the same message he embarked a rigorous six-month itinerary in Europe that October, moving back and forth between London and the Continent in a stream of invited meetings and consultations: Geneva, Bern, Amsterdam, Stuttgart, Frankfurt, Heidelberg, Munich, Ludwigsburg, Pasing, Wetzlar, Friesen, Bad Arolsen, Bad Salzuflen, Hanover, Kloster Loccum, Celle, Hamburg, Edinburgh, Glasgow, Belfast, Dublin, Paris, Copenhagen, Oslo, Stockholm, Uppsala, Gothenburg, Malmö and Lund.[86] Everywhere on these itineraries leading to the June 1947 Basel conference that revised the ICCAJ constitution, Protestant groups were rallied to confess, repent and evangelise the Jews in their vicinities while providing support and aid to non-Aryan Christian survivors.[87]

This was not a matter of trying to convince an unconvinced audience. In addition to interorganisational backing by IMC and WCCIF leaders, Hoffmann's newly mandated work was supported by geographic swaths of troops on the ground. It was a point brought home repeatedly in itinerary reports. In these early postwar accounts, in which he referred to himself as 'the Wandering Jew', much was made of the 'almost endless travel' that was the 'lot of the Director', while referencing the 'keen interest' and 'almost grim determination' of mission groups to launch out anew. While he was not, of course, of Jewish descent, such labelling was accepted in mission circles, for it was understood that 'the Wandering Jew' required Christian conversionists to track after him with the gospel.[88]

Outside of these circles, however, there was growing unpopularity toward Jewish evangelisation and Hoffmann was clear-eyed in realising that it would not hold unless the Church as a whole was convinced of its 'urgency'.[89] Wherever he spoke on the twelve-country sweep to solidify European support, his stated intention was thus to lobby for churchwide adoption of official policy and IMC-WCCIF auspices of ICCAJ's outreach, with emphases on 'duty', 'responsibility' and 'change'. That a new form of appeal was needed in the wake of the exterminations was a central tenet of argumentation, and he did not hesitate to advantage Cold War sensitivities by arguing that the 'centre of gravity' in Jewish population had shifted, and 'the future trend, if not destiny, of world Jewry' would most likely be determined by Russia or America.[90] But the major foci for reconstruction and expansion of Jewish missions remained linked to claims about Christianity's failure to solve antisemitism and prevent extermination of European Jews.

Within these contexts, antisemitism was repudiated as a form of the disorder of man and irreconcilable with the Christian faith. It went hand in hand with claims about the validity and prerogative of Christian evangelisation of Jews. Yet, as stressed in his opening address at the June 1947 Basel conference, it was only by way of penance and contrition that one could hope for the forgiveness and liberty to proclaim that prerogative to surviving Jews.[91] The resolution unanimously passed by the sixty-one delegates from fourteen countries mirrored faithfully Hoffmann's call for unity in the rapidly changing conditions of the postwar world, and it did so in the context of confession and reparation.[92]

> The Church as a whole must confess that its witness and protest were not vigorous enough to prevent the barbaric persecution of the Jews in Europe. Its indifference to the moral and spiritual needs of the Jews is equally blameworthy. The best *reparation* it can make is to recognise evangelisation of the Jews as the responsibility and task of the whole Church, and in all its denominations it must organise and equip itself to carry out this task.[93]

A French 'Message' and a German 'Word'

By early 1948 two other streams of ecumenical thinking on postwar repentance and reparation had opened. The first emanated from the Geneva research department on the upcoming founding assembly theme, 'Man's Disorder and God's Design'. Four commissions were appointed between August 1946 and June 1947 to research specific aspects of the theme and produce pre-assembly volumes for delegates. In early February the Commission on the Church's Witness to God's Design, headed by Dutch theologian Hendrik Kraemer and Anglican Bishop Stephen Neill,[94] circulated a confidential document entitled 'A Message for Israel'. The nine-page study looked at surviving European Jewry from the standpoint of the theological duty of the Church, assessing its postwar plight as less tragic than during the war but more desperate because hope had been extinguished by homelessness, ill-treatment and antisemitism, which was provoking the ongoing 'evolution of Zionism'.[95]

The theological argument was that the Church, as the 'New Israel', could not 'remain indifferent' or tolerate the rising persecution of surviving Jews, but the proper attitude was not to be derived from 'pitying the Jews'. Instead, Christians had to recognise that Jewish and Christian salvation and destinies were bound together, and that attacks against Jews were attacks against the 'mystery of the Incarnation of the Word of God'.[96] Yet while the Church was bound in solidarity with Jews, it was also bound by the divine imperative to proclaim the gospel to Jews, which meant that sensitive theological issues could *not* be avoided in order to spare Jewish feelings, but Christians had to be sensitive to the inherent danger.[97]

> A Jew who has been stricken in body and soul by the trials of the last few years will tend to make no difference between an anti-Semite like Hitler, who declared he was fulfilling the will of the Almighty by annihilating the Jews, and the men who explain or even excuse the persecutions by saying they are God's answer to the cry of the Jewish people, 'His blood be on us, and on our children'.[98]

To remove such misunderstanding the 'Message' called for a more balanced explication of the causes and consequences of 'the curse'.

While it was true that the deicidal 'curse' was invoked in the name of 'the whole Jewish people', it was equally true that Christ was condemned by Pilate 'in the name of all Gentiles' and that Jesus had asked God to forgive both.[99] It therefore had to be made clear, as 'a message of repentance and hope', that the crucifixion was *not* the reason why Jews were divinely reproached.[100]

> To the persecuted people, the Church must say that their sufferings are not God's vengeance for the death of Jesus, but an appeal to conversion and to turn from their unfaithfulness.[101]

The 'Message' went on to say that it was 'very hard to use this language to the survivors of the Nazi massacres', but that Christians could not proclaim the gospel unless they began by explaining that Jewish 'unfaithfulness consists in their refusal to recognize' Christ as the Messiah. Yet it was also made clear that the 'unfaithfulness' of the 'persecuted people' could never justify antisemitic attitudes or actions by those who fashioned themselves as 'instruments' of punishment. Antisemitism was self-administered justice and never an instrument of God, which meant that antisemites who 'attacked God's people' were also condemned. Moreover, antisemitism was a deterrent to Israel's conversion, for so long as Jews think that Christians are antisemitic they will run from the gospel.[102] Distinctions therefore had to be made between antisemitic intention to negate or extinguish Jews and the divine Christian imperative to convert Jews. More precisely, distinctions between the radically different natures of antisemitism and Christian anti-Judaism were requisite because each carried the intention of 'destruction'. But unlike the malevolent destruction of antisemitism that sought annihilation of Jews, the benevolent intention implicit in the Christian summons to Jewish conversion sought only the 'spiritual destruction of Judaism' – and only for the purpose of leading Jews to their spiritual destiny.[103]

Two of the responses to this WCC 'Message for Israel' are of particular relevance. The first by Conrad Hoffmann in March 1948 is significant for its agreement with the essence of the paper. The only theological point on which he disagreed was the distinction between the 'destruction' of antisemitism and the 'destruction' of anti-Judaism, and there he rejected the claim that evangelisation of Jews is a form of destructionist anti-Judaism, stating in a single sentence that Christianity is the fulfilment of Judaism and not its opposition. As for the other theological arguments, however, he expressed no concern about the stated cause of Jewish suffering or the stated need to tell 'survivors of the Nazi massacres' that Jewish suffering was God's appeal to conversion. His only other criticism centred on form and degree of emphases, namely, that the paper should take a 'realistic' rather than theological approach, with more attention to Jewish missions and less self-righteousness. He also wanted 'the guilt of certain Jews in provoking anti-Jewish attitudes' to be addressed, with emphasis on 'joint responsibility' for antisemitism, while avoiding generalisations.[104]

James Parkes, in contrast, rejected the 'Message for Israel' in its entirety. His contention was that its 'whole complicated and difficult argument' was invalid because it hinged on the false premise that the aim of conversion was 'the spiritual destruction of Judaism'. Such claims could only mean that God's revelation at Sinai had 'no present validity' except as viewed with a Christian lens through the 'revelation of Calvary', which Parkes rejected. His refutation, summed in a single introductory sentence and elaborated over five pages of criticism, was that Judaism was still 'operative' and that it was part of God's design for it to exist in *its own right*. The argument, which was a summary of his Charles William Eliot Lectures at the New York Jewish Institute of Religion in 1946–1947, was that Sinai and Calvary were not 'alternative schemes of salvation', and that it was not God's design that one choose or accept 'either the one or the other'. Both Judaism and Christianity were included because humankind was in need of both. For Parkes, instead of missions to Jews, what today's world needed 'above all else' was a 'spiritual conversion' to the moral and social revelations of Judaism at Sinai, 'a whole way of life, a whole habit of thought, a whole relationship to God'.[105]

It is important to point out that Parkes was not solicited for comment as was Hoffmann. After learning of the 'Message' from William Simpson, he wrote to Bishop Stephen Neill for consent to comment, making clear that it would reflect a 'radically different' position.[106] His letter was forwarded to Geneva by WCC associate secretary Oliver Tomkins in London, with a note that Commission II would benefit from his input. Permission was granted within a few days, but Parkes's comments, or for that matter Hoffmann's, had little influence on the 'Message for Israel'. With just minimal editing and the removal of four sentences on Zionism, it was issued to assembly delegates in June 1948 as part of the pre-assembly Commission II volume, *The Church's Witness to God's Design*. The only other significant difference was that the title was changed to 'The Approach to Israel' and the author was revealed to be the French Protestant Federation Committee on Witness to Israel.[107]

The respondent comments, however, were sent to the other stream of thought informing the WCC founding assembly on Jews. This second line derived from a February 1948 decision to appoint four assembly committees on 'Concerns of the Churches', one of which was initially named 'Committee IV on the Christian Attitude to the Jews'.[108] That Hoffmann would be involved as architect and key provider of materials was substantiated by Visser 't Hooft's agenda notes in March, confirming that the 'document is to be prepared by Conrad Hoffmann'.[109] George Bell also affirmed on 30 April that 'our relations to the Jews' is on the agenda and ICCAJ 'has the question of preparing for it in hand'.[110]

Earlier in February Visser 't Hooft's new assistant general secretary, Herbert Newell, had written to Hoffmann for 'cutting edge' material related to Jewish evangelisation, and Hoffmann, convinced as he was that ICCAJ was already the source of cutting edge thought, sent documents reinforcing his 1946 memoranda to Visser 't Hooft.[111] Two new memoranda on the Church and Israel, along with Basel conference resolutions, were among other ICCAJ materials sent between March and May.[112]

To these Newell added two sources, the first of which was the British Council of Christians and Jews. Hutchinson Cockburn, head of the WCCIF Reconstruction Department, and Henry Carter, chair of the Ecumenical Commission for Refugees under that department, were founding members of CCJ and in 1946 they appointed its general secretary to the Ecumenical Commission. In these dual roles, William Simpson was part of a WCCIF round table on the Christian Approach to the Jews in February 1947, where, under Visser 't Hooft's chairmanship, the group was brought to a consensus that basic differences between Jewish missions and goodwill approaches often 'centred around methods rather than principle'.[113] As secretary of CCJ, one who did not insist that Jewish missions were inconsistent with goodwill, Simpson was viewed as holding a middle position and, as such, was solicited for CCJ resolutions and later appointed as participant in the assembly committee on Jews.[114]

The last source for Newell's assembly material was 'A Word About the Jewish Question' issued by the EKD German Brethren Council on 8 April. To understand the complexity of this inclusion, it is necessary to look first at two statements that proceeded it. The ICCAJ Commission on the Church and Relief to Hebrew Christians at the June 1947 Basel conference urged WCCIF to give special attention to the postwar plight of Christians of Jewish descent.[115] In turn, the WCCIF Ecumenical Refugee Commission under the Committee for Reconstruction, of which German Bishop Theophil Wurm was part, passed a resolution of 'atonement' on 28 February 1948 for having failed Christians of Jewish descent, who 'equally with Jews [had to bear] the grievous persecution of the Nazi regime'. The point emphasised was that the church had failed to receive Christians of Jewish descent 'whole-heartedly' in the Nazi years, and that henceforth they should receive 'preferential treatment' in postwar aid. According to the resolution, all spiritual and material relief bodies in Germany were to coordinate with the Geneva refugee division to that end.[116]

The following week Bishop Wurm issued an EKD Council 'Statement on the Question of Reparation', which was signed and forwarded to Geneva on 5 March. In speaking to the 'question of general reparation and special care for the Jews who have been persecuted by the Third Reich', the statement stressed that the German nation has a 'special duty of reparation towards its Jewish members'. 'The guilt ... committed against the Jewish people by our nation' was a 'special one, the weight and size of which demands a special atonement'. As such, the statement invoked on behalf of the EKD Council a 'special understanding' of reparation duty that distinguished its material and spiritual aspects. Material reparation could be made by 'sacrifices in care' through Aid for the Racially Persecuted in Stuttgart, which was in 'contact with the Committee on the Christian Approach to the Jews in London and New York'. But spiritual reparation, in accord with 'the special understanding of the Church', required a 'special responsibility to meet the members of the Jewish nation as brothers, and proclaim to them the Gospel'.[117]

When the EKD Brethren Council issued 'A Word About the Jewish Question' a month later on 8 April, it was seen in Geneva as having set out the theological basis for the evangelising reparation in the EKD Council statement. Like the French 'Message', the German 'Word' of April 1948 relied on injunctions of scripture to supply the theological foundation for action in the wake of 'all that has happened'. Unlike the French 'Message', however, the stated impetus in the German 'Word' was guilt and sorrow for having stood in silence during the war and failing to make admission in the three years afterwards. The failures were explained as a result of having abandoned the theological tenets about Israel's election, which were now being reclaimed. The German 'Word' was thus both an admission of wrongs against Jews, and an explication of the theological tenets to guide the 'right' approach to individual Jews, Jewry and 'the Jewish question' in the postwar era.[118]

The guilt being admitted in the German 'Word about the Jewish Question' was that Christians in Germany had withdrawn from the divine injunction to be 'a saving witness to Israel', justifying it 'by speaking of the curse laid on Israel'. They had forgotten that God's judgment followed 'Israel even … in her state of rejection', and that 'Israel under God's judgment' was 'unceasing evidence' of God's truth and faithfulness, as well as 'unceasing warning to His people'. 'The tacit lesson of the fate of the Jews' was to stand as warning that 'God is not mocked', a warning to Christians to return to the divine injunction, and 'an admonition to the Jews to turn to the One in whose Name alone their salvation is to be found'.[119]

When Newell pulled all of the sources together in an assembly memorandum, the ICCAJ material and the German 'Word' constituted some 80 per cent of the text. The rest was comprised of extracts from CCJ resolutions and one piece from Parkes's refutation of the 'Message for Israel', which was attributed to an anonymous theological position.[120] The memorandum of excerpts and comments went through two circulated drafts as 'The Christian

Attitude to the Jews', but, after reaching Visser 't Hooft in June, its title as well as the assembly committee name were changed to 'The Christian Approach to the Jews'.[121]

Other changes were taking place as well. On 18 and 30 June James Parkes received letters from the WCC study department indicating that he would be a member or visitor of Commission II at the founding assembly, but that either way he was expected at a pre-assembly conference on 18–20 August. Two weeks later on 13 July he received an apology from WCC assistant general secretary Oliver Tomkins, explaining that, when he was allowed to submit comments on the French 'Message', it was assumed he would serve with Commission II and Committee IV on Jews. The 'situation', however, had changed. The 'number of consultants' had been completed and 'the official ruling at another level was that no one else could be added'.[122] Within a month, in other words, Parkes had been included and excluded from the founding assembly without mention of even visitor status, even though such seats were added as late as the opening day of committee deliberations on 25 August. The last, it should be noted, was a member of Hoffmann's North American sector of ICCAJ, who would become its chairman in 1952.[123]

Guilt and the founding statement

Committee IV on the Christian Approach to the Jews was a complex configuration of eighty-two appointees from twenty countries: delegates (22), alternates (34), consultants (17), fraternal delegates (3), observers (2), visitors (2), assembly officers (2). All categories except visitors were allowed to deliberate the issues, but only delegates and alternates were allowed to rule on the content of an assembly statement. The group was split into delegate and alternate sections which met separately but simultaneously to deliberate identical agendas. The presiding officers were from the main delegate section and as such carried significantly more weight. American Episcopal Bishop Angus Dun was chair, Conrad Hoffmann was secretary, Göte Hedenquist was coordinating liaison. Dr Otto Fricke of the EKD and American Presbyterian

Rev. Charles Arbuthnot headed the alternate section as chairman and secretary respectively. The liaison circulated between the two groups and at the end of each day's parallel sessions officers from both sections coordinated the findings and made the required adjustments in the next day's agenda. This was followed for four consecutive sessions during the first week of the two-week assembly that convened on 22 August.

On the first day of deliberations, chairman Angus Dun outlined the published version of Newell's memorandum and the Commission II 'Message for Israel' while cautioning against 'outside' materials and views from 'special interest' groups.[124] It was agreed in the opening session that 'Israel' was a specific case in the general design of God, but there was no consensus about the 'unique and specific element'. Was the Jew a 'minority problem' to be considered from social and political aspects, or a 'purely theological problem'? Did the term 'the Jew' designate the race regardless of faith adhered to or was it limited to the Jewish religion?[125] More specifically, 'what is the Jew?' 'to us'? 'to himself'? 'to God', 'to the non-Christian world'? These and other questions would be considered in this order: the theological place of the Jew in God's design; the role of Jewish missions in God's design; sociological aspects of the Jew in society; and the emergence of Israel as a state.[126]

The theological deliberations on Jews in God's design were dominated by German and French members of the committee, both of whom were involved with the Stuttgart Declaration: Dr Wilhelm Niesel from the EKD and Rev. Pierre Maury from the WCCIF delegation. Both were also involved in the materials assembled by Newell. Niesel was part of the Brethren Council issuing the German 'Word About the Jewish Question', and Maury was part of the French committee responsible for the 'Message for Israel'. Each now argued in agreement that the Jewish problem required a 'strong theological' basis.

Niesel, invoking the Brethren 'Word' while voicing the language of the EKD Council statement on 'Reparation', argued that the Church was imbued with 'a special responsibility', which meant 'it was not enough to assist the Jews like any other needy people'. It was only in the light of theology that the place of Jews in God's design could be understood, and only after recognising that the history and vocation of Israel was completed with Christ's incarnation that the 'right attitude' toward Jews could be found.[127] To the objection that theology was not sufficient for all issues, as in the case of 'moral and social justice',[128] Niesel argued that a 'purely theological approach' included social actions for Jews, which were always intended as 'a witness for Christ'.[129] To claims that 'the Jew was a witness to God' and that during the Hitler years 'the Jewish problem meant fighting for the true revelation, the true ethos, the true God', there were no challenges, but it was suggested that the 'same radical stress on the theological issue' was not necessary in the changed postwar conditions.[130] Maury, in support of Niesel, countered that the divine emphasis on the theological basis for Christian–Jewish relations was unchanging, and that the Church had to stress 'that the Jews were the chosen people of God'.[131] The consensus reached, and cited in accordance with the Brethren Council 'Word', was that 'the election and designation of Israel had been fulfilled in Jesus Christ', that the scriptures were very much concerned with the Jews, and that 'God had a very special dealing with them'.[132]

On these grounds Hoffmann posited as a fundamental tenet that 'the Gospel was to be preached to every man and woman', including Jews, to which no objection was raised, even from CCJ William Simpson, who later suggested that the assembly statement should begin that way.[133] This across-the-board agreement on relations between the theological place of the Jews and the imperative of Jewish missions allowed discussion to move to the problems of evangelising Jews. Among those raised were lack of Christian education;[134] failure to distinguish Jewish 'types' such as the 'modern communistic Jew of Palestine' and 'capitalist Jew in the West';[135] differing geographical conditions;[136] Jewish exclusivity that created 'barriers of suspicion and hatred';[137] and baptism, whereby many Jews were 'only trying to escape the stigma of their race'.[138] While varying views were held on how such problems would be overcome and when God's design for Jews would be fulfilled, it was nevertheless agreed that the task of the unchanging Church was to carry out its Jewish mission.[139]

On the question of Christian–Jewish cooperation, however, the Committee was initially split. There were those, like Simpson, who held that Jewish missions could be put in abeyance when aligning with Jews against issues like antisemitism, but there were also those who warned about the dangers of doing so.[140] Niesel argued that such alliances were 'based on the dangerous assumption' that Jews and Christians shared a common understanding of 'justice' and 'liberty', whereas such concepts and terms could only 'be understood through Christ'. He rejected that the divine imperative could be left in abeyance while pursuing alliance with Jews, insisting that Christians 'were not allowed to deprive Jewish brethren of Christ's message'.[141] Pierre Maury, in agreement, argued that once such precedent was set the Church would have to 'collaborate in the same way with all other religions as well'.[142] The open-ended compromise between the two positions was that Christian cooperation with Jews could be of value so long as it did not affect 'religious matters'.[143]

There was also agreement and disagreement on the other sociological issue. Wilhelm Niesel captured what was seen as a 'strong formulation' of antisemitism by defining it as 'anti-Christianism' whose fight 'against the elected people is fighting against God's design'; and Hoffmann added that where antisemitism thrives the Church cannot survive.[144] Within this area of agreement, however, three very different arguments arose. One held that any accounting of antisemitism had to include Jewish causes, citing Jewish hatred of Arab Christians in Palestine as current example.[145] A second held that any discussion of guilt had to consider historical insistence on 'the crime of Israel' in Christian theology.[146] The third, from Hoffmann, insisted that postwar approaches to Jews 'had to be preceded by admission of guilt' for Church failure to solve antisemitism, prevent annihilation and provide rescue for survivors – and he tied it to the 'crisis in Palestine', by which was meant the declaration of the state of Israel on 14 May, the subsequent Arab attack, the war over territories and rights, and a gathering Palestinian refugee problem.[147]

Hoffmann's argument, here and in memoranda leading here, was that Christianity's failure to provide rescue to Jews during and after the Nazi years had enflamed an 'aggressive political Zionism', with serious consequences not only for Jewry but for the Church and the world.[148] To make clear what was meant, he had summarised in a report circulated just ten days earlier that, regardless of what attitude one held on Zionism, Palestine and the establishment of Israel, it involved a re-birth of Jewish nationalism, and that creation of a Jewish state was akin to 'a destroying of God's purpose for Israel'. Emphasising that 'God's design for Israel … alone matter[ed]', he went on to assert that some were even asking 'if there is any other *raison d'état* for preservation of the identity of the Jewish people than on the religious plane'.[149]

As these issues continued to overlap, the bishop of Worcester charged 'big nations' who closed doors to Jews with responsibility for the Palestine crisis, arguing that the first task of the churches, rather than acknowledgment of guilt, was to find 'homes for the dispossessed Jews of Europe'.[150] When Hoffmann raised a second time that Church failure to provide rescue had exacerbated the crisis in Palestine, WCC secretary Herbert Newell firmly countered that the Committee could *not* say 'that the situation of the Jews was caused by failure of the churches'. He also vetoed the idea of issuing an emergency call for nations to provide temporary homes to Jewish displaced persons, on the grounds of its unfairness to the majority of displaced persons who were *not* Jews.[151]

But it was not just these who disagreed on what could and could not be said about antisemitism, Palestine and the state of Israel. Indecisiveness and caution had been the hallmark since opening day when chairman Dun informed that 'the Palestine problem' would not be part of the deliberations. Reference to the state of Israel could be made so long as it had 'bearing on the general Jewish problem', but if more had to be said it would have to go before the assembly commission on international problems.[152]

For reasons unexplained the policy was amended the following day, but the issue remained laden with caution and conflict. That Israel had not been recognised by all nations,[153] that its founding would fortify barriers against missions,[154] that Jewish Christians were expecting some kind of pronouncement, and that 'rights' had to be assessed not only from political but spiritual aspects, were all matters of stated concern.[155] When an assembly officer tried to summarise that the World Council could only say that it *could not* make a political statement but that it viewed 'with horror' the displaced persons situation exacerbating the Palestine crisis, Rev. Charles Westphal vigorously contended that 'right and justice' demanded not only a political statement but 'recognition of the State of Israel'.[156]

The unsettledness of issues, if not impasse, led to consultation with Section IV on the Church and International Disorder, headed by former BICCAJ member Kenneth Grubb, director of the WCC Commission of the Churches on International Affairs, and his assembly vice-chair, Otto Dibelius of the EKD.[157] The ruling at that higher level was that it was 'most inappropriate for the World Council to take position on a political issue', but if reference had to be made on 'the moral issue underlying the situation' it should state that the question of Palestine 'could only be settled satisfactorily on an international and truly impartial basis'. Any solution 'had to give justice to the rights of all three parties', while clarifying that Christian churches 'had a particular interest in the preservation of the Holy places', as well as 'duty and opportunity' to care for 'refugees of all parties'.[158]

The drafted statement

Three critical points should be made before looking at the statement drafted at the end of these layered deliberations. First, while consultants were not allowed to vote on statement content, they dominated all categories of committee influence: materials (100%), officers (60%), deliberations (66%).[159] Second, because the theological place of the Jew in God's design was seen as intrinsic to the divine imperative to evangelise Jews, the theological and practical issues of Jewish evangelisation were given far greater place than any other topic, receiving as much as three times more emphasis than even the most debated issue on Palestine and the state of Israel. Third, the team of nine selected to draft the statement was overwhelmingly composed of men involved with evangelisation or related Jewish issues, and its curious mix should not go unmentioned.

Hoffmann of course was director of ICCAJ, Hedenquist would become his assistant in 1949, and Charles Arbuthnot, WCC representative of the Presbyterian Church (USA) in Geneva, would become a WCC appointee to ICCAJ in 1951. Dr Otto Fricke, a *Deutsche Christen* pastor who supported the Führer principle, gave the 'fire speech' at the 1933 book burning in Frankfurt and later joined the Confessing church, was one of five EKD delegates to

More than one guilt in the embers: 1945–1948   253

the 1947 Basel conference who was denied permission to travel.¹⁶⁰ Dr Karl Hartenstein, who also hailed Hitler's rise and settled into the Confessing church, was director or delegate to the Basel Mission from 1926. Dr Regin Prenter, a professor of Lutheran theology in Denmark, was a working advocate of the Danish Israel Mission who had just published a series of articles on *Jewish* causes of Christian hatred of Jews in its postwar periodical.¹⁶¹ Rev. Charles Westphal was a French member of ECCO involved in the relief and rescue of non-Aryan Christians and Jews in southern France, and would be posthumously honoured by Yad Vashem as Righteous Among Nations.¹⁶² Of the two not directly involved with Jewish matters, Rev. Alexander Clark was the WCC delegate for Scottish Baptists, and American Anglican Bishop Dun was a newly appointed member of the WCC Central Committee.

What the noteworthy mix had in common was abiding belief. Each point of their five-part statement, which was penned by Hoffmann, was framed around justification for postwar evangelisation of surviving Jews. As William Simpson suggested, the commission to preach the gospel to the Jewish people was the first theological point made.¹⁶³ The second, 'the special meaning of the Jewish people for Christian faith', was more complex. Following from an introductory claim that Christians and Jews were bound together in 'a special solidarity' that linked destinies, the supersessionist theology discussed in Committee sessions was summarised in the proclamation: 'The Messiah for whom you wait has come'. The argumentation moved beyond theological justification, however, by asserting that Israel's divine destiny was the only way to explain the continuing existence of Jews after Israel's heritage was passed on to the Church. The passage, in essence, was a stronger restatement of Hoffmann's earlier claim that there was no other *'raison d'état* for preservation of the identity of the Jewish people' except for their divine destiny, one that moved from the subject of 'identity' to that of 'existence'.¹⁶⁴

> For many the continued existence of a Jewish people which does not acknowledge Christ is a divine mystery which finds its only sufficient explanation in the purpose of God's unchanging faithfulness and mercy.¹⁶⁵

'Barriers to be overcome' before that destiny could be fulfilled was the matter of the third point. Here, important admissions were made of Christianity's failures. The failures 'to manifest Christian love', to 'will for common social justice', and to fight antisemitism 'with all our strength' were all acknowledged, as were the attitudes of past churches that 'helped to foster an image of the Jews as the sole enemies of Christ'. But they were also acknowledged as 'high barriers' to fulfilling the divine commission to bring Israel to its destiny. Churches were soberly called to denounce antisemitism as 'irreconcilable with profession and practice of the Christian faith', but at the same time that antisemitism was denounced as 'sin against God and man' it was posited as the predominant postwar barrier to bringing Jews to their destiny. More precisely, it was 'only' as churches gave 'convincing evidence' that these barriers were being overcome that it would be 'possible' to share 'the best which God has given us in Christ'.[166]

The fourth point on 'the Christian witness to the Jewish people', constituting a third of the text, was the familiar ICCAJ argument for Jewish evangelisation to become intrinsic to the mission outreach of every world church. Attendant appeals for WCC church constituencies to 'recover the universality' of the divine commission 'by including the Jewish people in their evangelistic work' and for WCC to 'stimulate and assist' in carrying out the missions, were tied together by the often repeated recommendation for WCC and IMC to bear 'joint responsibility for the Christian approach to the Jews'.[167] Even the fifth and final part on 'the emergence of Israel as a state' had mission implications when viewed from the standpoint of Committee concerns about potential negative bearing on Jewish missions.

The plenary debate

When chairman Angus Dun presented the Committee report to the plenary assembly near the end of the two-week conference, the section on Israel was also the only one that required revision. There was no challenge to the opening claim that 'the establishment of the state "Israel" adds a political dimension to the Christian approach to the Jews and threatens to complicate antisemitism with political fears and enmities'.[168] The issue that arose was the same that led to consultation with the Commission on International Disorder, namely, that WCC could not express judgment 'on the political aspects of the Palestine problem'. Dr W.F. Golterman, secretary of the Dutch Ecumenical Council, argued that the statement as a whole would be unacceptable unless it stated 'more definitely the right of the Jews to live in their own country'. There was also dissent from within Committee IV itself. Canon Henry Baines, Church of England, who spoke on behalf of alternates, argued that, even though WCC could not make political statements, the assembly would fail 'in its bounden duty' if it did not make clear that 'the problem' was more than political.[169] His amendment, accepted by the assembly, was to add a sentence to the original text, italicised in brackets below, which affirmed Grubb's Commission IV ruling while recontextualising the issue 'of a Jewish state' to that of a moral and spiritual question.

> On the political aspects of the Palestine problem and the complex conflict of 'right' involved we do not undertake to express a judgment.
>
> [*Nevertheless, we appeal to the nations to deal with the problem not as one of expediency, political, strategic or economic, but as a moral and spiritual question that touches a nerve centre of the world's religious life.*]

The rest of the original text on 'the Palestine problem', which was uncontested, followed Grubb's cautious guidelines by stating that 'whatever position may be taken towards the establishment of a Jewish state and towards the "rights" and "wrongs" of Jews and Arabs' or Hebrew and Arab Christians, the churches were 'duty bound to pray and work' without discrimination for justice and relief of 'the victims of this warfare'.[170]

Beyond the debate and amended wording on Palestine there was also praise and condemnation for the evangelistic emphasis of the statement. Dr B.E. Mays of the Northern Baptist Convention in America praised the clear intention 'to bring the Jews into full Christian fellowship here and now', while Dr Heering of the Remonstrant Brotherhood in Holland condemned it for the same reason. Speaking both personally and for the Brotherhood, Heering argued that for those who took to heart Jewish sufferings, it must seem 'impossible to preach to a people' who had gone through so much even before they had been given the 'opportunity of living'. Heering went on to propose that the whole statement be 'dropped' on the grounds that it was 'hypocritical' and 'quite unacceptable', but the motion was not adopted. Nor was a motion from Anglican pastor Allan de Vere to send a message of sympathy to the Jewish community of Amsterdam, where, as cited in the introduction, 'no less than 100,000 Jews were taken and murdered only five years ago'. In response, chairman Dun reported that Committee IV was 'of the opinion that once they began expressing sympathy with special groups, they would not know where to stop'. When the issue was raised a second time, Dun 'expressed doubts' as to the wisdom of such a message, 'particularly as the trials of the Jews had already been mentioned in the body of the report'.[171]

In the end the decision was left to the plenary assembly, who, while accepting the statement as a whole, did not approve the motion for a message of sympathy to surviving Jews. The accepted statement, which called attention to the 'continued existence of a Jewish people which does not acknowledge Christ', was unequivocal in its conviction that God's design for Jews was acquiescence to Christianity.[172]

To look briefly at what that meant in the broader foci of the overall assembly, it is important to recognise that the statement was accepted in the context of the constitutional mission-function of the founding World Council adopted earlier that same week.[173] The evangelising tone was set on the opening day by John Mott's successor to the chairmanship of IMC, Dr John Mackay of Princeton Theological Seminary. Mackay was also chair of assembly Section II on the Church's Witness to God's Design, whose conference volume of the same name included the renamed French 'Message for Israel'. After urging in his keynote address for WCC to never 'sell its missionary birthright' and to uphold the 'universal *right* and obligation of Christian missions',[174] Mackay's Section II, the vice-chair and secretary of which were Martin Niemöller and Bishop Stephen Neill, drafted the basic tenets of evangelisation that were 'unanimously received' in plenary before the statement on Jews was presented. In reduced form, the fundamental task of the Church was to make 'Christ known' to all by confronting each individual 'with the necessity of a personal decision', a 'yes or no' on the 'life and death' matter of the gospel.[175] The Committee IV statement, debated after this, was not intended to reflect anything other than agreement as it applied to God's design for Jews.

Second, it is important to recall that the WCCIF priority postwar task of acquiring a German church statement of 'solidarity in the guilt of the German people' was an acknowledged requisite step toward postwar unification of ecumenical churches. It made possible, in Visser 't Hooft's words, 'the necessary spiritual conditions for the inauguration of the World Council', thereby allowing the German Protestant church to play a prominent role in the deliberation and drafting of the founding statement on Jews.[176] Indeed, of the twenty countries represented on Committee IV, only Britain and the United States had more places than the nine assigned to the EKD, and two of those had places on the nine-man drafting subcommittee. While this is not to imply that German input was theologically exceptional, it is to say that Niesel's assertive argumentation was influential in deliberations, and that his arguments consciously invoked the Brethren Council 'Word about the Jewish Question', which was selectively included as a major source of Committee IV material. Moreover, the Brethren 'Word' and the renamed French 'Message', which were in agreement on basic tenets with ICCAJ, were published by WCC again sixteen years later. At the time the founding statement was formulated in 1948, and in the decade and a half following, both documents were viewed by WCC leaders as two national expressions of theological truths on Jews that Protestant churches of postwar nations were urged to come to terms with. That could not have been put more clearly in the preface to the German 'Word' in the 1964 publication: 'this emphasis now dominates and guides the thinking on this issue'.[177]

Last, in analysing the theological convictions inherent to the assembly statement, it is impossible to do so sufficiently without the twenty-year post-Budapest–Warsaw history that led to replication of ICCAJ aims and views. From its title 'A Christian Approach to the Jews' to the closing recommendations, there was no part of the report that did not bear the ICCAJ imprint. Passages were taken either verbatim or paraphrased from Hoffmann's postwar memoranda, conference findings or earlier foundational papers. Indeed, except for references to extermination in the introduction and part five on the new state of Israel, points made in every section were paraphrased forms of findings from the 1927 Budapest–Warsaw conferences, each of which had become fundamental to ICCAJ argumentation in the twenty years thereafter. That does not mean unanimous or even partial agreement on all of the ICCAJ arguments that have been tracked in this book, nor that every aspect found place in the statement, but it does mean that the fundamental conversionary tenets that ICCAJ was mandated to carry to Protestant churches were received by the WCC founding assembly.

All positions in the 1535-word statement – received by the voting electorate of a 1200-person assembly of 147 churches from 44 countries – were circumscribed around 'the special meaning of the Jewish people for Christian faith', with no hint that Jewish existence had other significance. It was not the case that all of those formulating and voting on the statement looked at Jews solely in that narrow theological light but, rather, that official profession of the theological position took precedence over the sentiments of concern expressed in the deliberations. Each point was hinged on the Christian responsibility and need to evangelise surviving Jews and not, as James Parkes had argued since 1930, the Christian responsibility of allowing Jews to exist as Jews while making the world safe for them to do so. As such, there was little if any difference between the pledge of the 1927 conferences to bring 'Israel to her destiny' and the 1948 proclamation 'the Messiah for whom you wait has come', even though some six million Jews had been exterminated in the interim.[178]

Notes

1 Lipstadt, *Beyond Belief*, 267–8.
2 Daniel Blatman, *Death Marches* (Cambridge, MA: Belknap Press, 2011); Harold Marcuse, *Legacies of Dachau* (Cambridge: Cambridge University Press, 2001), 47–54; Yehuda Bauer, 'The Death Marches, January–May 1945', *Modern Judaism*, 3:1 (Feb. 1983), 1–21.

More than one guilt in the embers: 1945–1948 259

3 PC min., Strictly Confidential, 26 Apr. 1945, 7; WCC.301.010.
4 Barth's lectures, published as *The Germans and Ourselves* (London: Nisbet & Co., 1945), were followed by a piece for *Manchester Evening News* in April, and then combined in *The Only Way: How to Change the German Mind* (New York: Philosophical Library, 1947), quot. 34.
5 *OCOR* (1937), 'The Church and War', 162–6; 47–8.
6 Quot., Paton to VH, 13 Sept. 1939; VH, Strictly Confidential: 'The Future of Ecumenical Work in Europe', Jul. 1940; Notes on Meeting, 8 Sept. 1940; WCC.301.005.
7 VH, in 1939: 'The Church as an Ecumenical Society in Time of War' (Apr.); 'Summary of Issues in Relation to International Problems' (Jul.); 'The Church and the International Crisis' (Aug.); 'Confidential Notes on the Attitude of Christians to this War' (Nov.). In 1940: 'Responsibility of the Church for the International Order' (Jan.); 'The Ecumenical Church and the International Situation' (Apr.); 'The Ethical Reality and Function of the Church' (Jul.); WCC.301.005, 301.008, 301.009.
8 VH, 'Considerations Concerning the Post-War Settlement', Mar. 1941, w/letters to and from Temple; 'The Church and the New Order in Europe', co-drafted with Bonhoeffer, Aug.–Sept. 1941. Also 'Strictly Private and Confidential' by Adam von Trott zu Solz, carried by VH to London for Temple's 1942 inauguration, arguing the same points on German resistance, w/Bell's follow-up letters to Eden between 18 June and 17 Aug.; VH to Dulles, Conversation with von Trott, 11 Jan. 1943; WCC.42.0077, 301.009.
9 This set of memoranda was sequel to 'Reconstruction of Christian Institutions in Europe' (25 Sept. 1942); for quot., VH, 'The Church and International Reconstruction: Analysis of Agreements and Disagreements on the Message of the Church and a Just and Durable Peace', Jan. 1943, 7–8. Elaboration appears in 'The Post-War Task of the World Council of Churches', May 1943; Confidential PC min. on Postwar Memo, 8 Jul. 1943; WCC.301.005, 301.010. These should be read in combination with two letters in which common guilt was discussed: Hans Asmussen to VH, 13 Dec. 1942, Freudenberg to Asmussen, 11 Jan. 1943, in Martin Greschat, *Die Schuld der Kirche* (Munich: Chr. Kaiser, 1982), 25–8.
10 Quot. VH, 'The Church and International Reconstruction', Jan. 1943, 7–8.
11 VH to Paton, 27 Jan., VH to Johansson, 6 Apr. 1943, w/copies to Paton and Cavert, WCC.301.4331, IMC.261142, FCC.B9F20.

12 VH, 'The Situation of the Protestant Church in Germany', Dec. 1943, was sent to Temple, Dulles, Paton and other PC members; VH to Temple, 15 Dec., WCC.301.1.03, 42.0077.
13 English translations of the German plans, letters between Craig and translator, and list of partial distribution are at WCC.301.110; quot., Annot.10.
14 Ibid., 'Life and Struggle', introductory note, 1.
15 PC Min., Strictly Confidential, London, 6 Nov. 1944, FCC.B23F1.
16 VH to Mackie, 19 Feb.; VH to Bell, 23 Feb., WCC.42.0008; also Gerhard Besier, ed., *Intimately Associated for Many Years* (Newcastle: Cambridge Scholars, 2015), vol. 1, 267–70, 271–3.
17 PC min., Strictly Confidential, 26 Apr. 1945, 7; WCC.301.010.
18 Ibid., 7–8.
19 Ibid.
20 Schönfeld, 'Das Selbsthilfewerk der Deutschen Evangelischen Kirche', WCC.301. 4314.
21 Cockburn, 'Statement on Relief Work for Lutheran Churches', Apr. 1945, WCC.301. 4317.
22 'Confidential', Schönfeld to Tomkins, 26 June 1945,WCC.301.110. For more on Gerstenmaier, see Paton's distrust in 'Confidential Notes on a Visit to Copenhagen October 1939', WCC.301.008; for more on Waetjen, Richard Doerries, *Hitler's Intelligence Chief* (New York: Enigma Books, 2009), 142, 168.
23 Freudenberg, 'Impressions Gained During a Visit to Germany', 15 June–18 July; 'Notes on Church Conditions in Germany in July 1945', WCC.301.43. 30.
24 VH to Bell, 24 Jul. 1945, in Besier, *Intimately Associated*, vol. 1, 275–80.
25 Herman's position with WCCIF was confirmed at a PC meeting in New York on 18 May; he arrived Geneva on 18 July.
26 VH to Mackie, 19 Feb., VH to Bell, 23 Feb. 1945, WCC.42.0008.
27 VH to Bell, 24 Jul.
28 The collected Herman reports are in Gerhard Besier, 'Ökumenische Mission in Nachkriegsdeutschland: Die Berichte von Stewart W. Herman über die Verhältnisse in der evangelischen Kirche 1945/46', *Kirchliche Zeitgeschichte*, May 1988, 151–87; Oct. 1988, 316–52; May 1989, 294–358; Clemens Vollnhals, *Die evangelische Kirche nach dem Zusammenbruch: Berichte ausländischer Beobachter aus dem Jahre 1945* (Göttingen: Vandenhoeck & Ruprecht, 1988).
29 VH to Dibelius, 25 Jul. 1945, in VH, *Memoirs*, w/out notice that it was hand carried by Herman, 190.
30 Herman, 29 Jul. 1945, Besier (May 1988), 164–5.

31 Herman to Heath, USGCC, Berlin-Dahlem, 13 Aug. 1945, Besier (May 1988), 184–6. Vollnhals, 106–8.
32 Herman, Niemöller, 31 Jul. 1945, in Vollnhals, *Die evangelische Kirche*, 76.
33 Herman, Fricke, 31 Jul. 1945, Vollnhals, *Die evangelische Kirche*, 70.
34 Herman, Wurm 6 Aug. 1945, ital. add.; diary on Wurm (6/8), Dibelius (9/8), in Besier (May 1988), 153, 177–179. For Herman contacts in Berlin, 7–15 Aug. 1945, Vollnhals, 93.
35 Herman, report Jul. 1945–Jul. 1946, Besier (May 1989), 351–2; Memo to Dulles, 1 Sept. 1945, Besier (Oct. 1988), 316–18; Conference at Treysa, 18 Aug. 1945, WCC.301.1.10.
36 Wurm to WCCIF Reconstruction, 31 Aug. 1945, WCC.42.0084.
37 VH to Bell, 10 Sept. 1945, WCC.42.0008, Besier (2015), 287–9.
38 Ibid.
39 Herman, Jul. 1945–Jul. 1946 report, Besier (May 1989), 352.
40 VH to Bell, 27 Sept. 1945, WCC.42.0008, Besier (2015), 291. Herman knew by 20 Sept. that the council would meet between 10 and 20 Oct., the 18th was confirmed the next week. S.C. Michelfelder from the American Lutheran World Convention was on assignment in Geneva.
41 Herman to Heath, USGCC Hq. Berlin, 18 Sept., Besier (Oct. 1988), 329–30.
42 Herman, Jul. 1945–Jul. 1946 report, Besier (May 1989), 352.
43 The source of the belief is apparently VH, *Memoirs* (1973), 189–94, which states that the EKD council was unaware the delegation was coming. Yet this was contradictory to his own 23 Oct. 1945 report, which said that 'Wurm was not aware that such a large delegation was coming', WCC.301.103. The Bell report a few weeks later said 'they knew we were coming', Vollnhals, 224–33; Besier and Sauter (1985) said that 'Wurm knew very well' but had not expected such a large group, 29; the Koechlin report, Vollnhals 204–23, said that Wurm knew from authorities that a visit 'was imminent'.
44 Herman, interviews w/Althaus (14 Oct.), Meiser (16 Oct.), Besier (Oct. 1988), 341–4; quot., Report of Activity, 352, Besier (May 1989).
45 Herman diary, 18 Oct., Besier (May 1988), 156.
46 Karl Arndt to Major Knappen, USGCC Religious Affairs, Vollnhals, 191–3. Eberhard Bethge travelled with Dibelius.
47 Arndt to Knappen, 24 Oct., Vollnhals, 191–3; VH report, 23 Oct., WCC 301.103.

48 Arndt to Knappen, Report of Stuttgart Meetings, 17–19 Oct., Vollnhals, 193. VH, report on delegation, 23 Oct., WCC.301.103; Bell report, Vollnhals, 224–33.
49 Michelfelder, Herman, Bell and E. G. Rupp (Bell's translator) were at the dinner, with Asmussen, Niemöller and wife joining afterwards, Vollnhals, 341–4.
50 VH, report, 23 Oct. 1945, WCC.301.103.
51 WCCIF press release, ital. add., 1; for drafts, recipients, correspondence, 26–29 Oct. 1948, WCC.301.110.
52 Ibid., ital. add.
53 The publicity release closed with announcement that Bishop Marahrens of Hanover had been removed from the Prov. Comm. and replaced by Wurm and Niemöller.
54 *World Council of Churches: Its Process of Formation*, 21–23 Feb. 1946 (Geneva: WCC, 1946), WCC.301. 006.
55 VH, *Memoirs* (1973), 193–4, ital. add.
56 See also VH, 'Genesis of the World Council of Churches', *HEM* (1954), 714–15; Robert Bilheimer, head of credentials for the founding assembly, stressed the same relevance in 'The Significance of Amsterdam', *ER*, 40:3–4 (Jul.–Oct. 1988), 326–44.
57 VH, 'Confidential, The World Council of Churches: Its Nature, Its Limits', Sept. 1945, FCCB23F2.
58 For example, in addition to Greschat (1982), Besier and Sauter (1985) and Vollnhals (1988), John Conway, 'How Shall the Nations Repent? The Stuttgart Declaration of Guilt, October 1945', *Journal of Ecclesiastical History* 38:4 (Oct. 1987), 596–622; Victoria Barnett, *For the Soul of the People: Protestant Protest Against Hitler* (Oxford: Oxford University Press, 1992); Wolfgang Gerlach, *And the Witnesses Were Silent: The Confessing Church and the Persecution of the Jews* (Lincoln: University of Nebraska, 2000); Matthew Hockenos, *A Church Divided: German Protestants Confront the Nazi Past* (Bloomington: Indiana University Press, 2004).
59 Dibelius was elevated to WCC joint presidency in 1954, followed by Niemöller in 1961.
60 'Beschluss zur Wiedergründung des Zentralvereins vom 24.Oktober 1945, Evangelisch-Lutherischer Zentralverein für Mission Unter Israel', *Die Kirchen und das Judentum: Dokumente von 1945 bis 1968*, ed. Rolf Rendtorff and Hans Henrix (Munich: Bonifatius-Druckerei, 1989), 529–30; see Hoffmann to Standley, 22 Dec. 1945, IMC.261201.
61 BICCAJ Min, 16 May, 27 Sept.; IMC Ad Interim, 30–31 Oct. 1945; IMC.261201, 261207.

More than one guilt in the embers: 1945–1948

62 Freudenberg to Pernow, vice-chair of ICCAJ, 4 Oct. 1944, WCC.301.4331.
63 NAICCAJ Min., 3 Nov. 1944, appointment made by FCC, HMC and FMC delegates, IMC.261207.
64 NAICCAJ Min., 3 Oct. 1945, IMC.261207.
65 The budget for ICCAJ's share of Hedenquist's salary and expenses was agreed by 9 May, but by June it was being discussed as part of a larger package of shared expenses, one that eventually included WCC funding for an ICCAJ assistant director, a position filled by Hedenquist in 1949.
66 Cockburn to Smith, 28 Feb.; S to C, 21 Feb. 1946; WCC.425.3.175.
67 Cockburn to Smith, 15 Mar.; S to C, 9 Mar. 1946; WCC.425.3.175.
68 Cockburn to Smith, 2 May, IMC.261208; BICCAJ Min., 9 May 1946, IMC.261207.
69 Freudenberg to Hoffmann, 25 Aug. 1946. WCC.425.3.175.
70 WCCIF Report on Activities, July 1943–July 1944, FCC.B23F1.
71 WCCIF–IMC Joint Comm. Min., Geneva, 14–16 Feb. 1946, A–B, 44.
72 IMC Ad Interim Comm. Min., Geneva, 16–19 Feb. 1946, 11.
73 PC Min., 21–23 Feb. 1946, 67.
74 BICCAJ Min. 5–6 March 1945, IMC.261207.
75 Decker to Goodall, 10 June 1946, WCC.420038.
76 Decker to Warnshuis, w/c to Goodall, 12 June 1946; VH to Goodall, 8 Jul.; BICCAJ min., 17 Jul.; Smith to Decker, w/c to VH, 19 July; Standley to Goodall, 23 Jul.; Hoffmann to VH, 28 Oct.; BICCAJ min., 6 Dec.; CBMS min., 6 Dec. 1946; PC min., April 1947; BICCAJ min., 19 May 1947; IMC.261203, 261207, 261208, 261229; WCC.42.0038, 301.007.
77 ICCAJ min., Basel, 4–7 June 1947, IMC.261206. Discussion on constitutional changes began in Dec. 1946: Hoffmann to VH, 29 Dec., w/c to Goodall and Decker; Hoffmann to VH, 18 Feb. 1947, WCC.42.0038, 42.0077. The revisions expanded the executive committee to 36 members, allowing 11 each in 3 sectors, plus co-opting as needed. Each regional sector was to have appointees by IMC (7), WCC (3), HCA (1).
78 CBMS Min., 6 Dec.; BICCAJ Min., 6 Dec. 1946, IMC.261208, 261229.
79 Hoffmann to VH, 'The Christian Approach to the Jews', 9 Dec. 1948, WCC.42.0038.
80 Ibid.
81 Hoffmann to VH, 'The Church and the Jews', dated 20 Nov. but not posted until 9 Dec. w/c to Ehrenström and Neill, WCC.42.0038.

82 Webster, 'The Jewish Problem: Some Newer Aspects', *IRM* (1925), 598–607.
83 Hoffmann, 'The Christian Approach to the Jews', 9 Dec. 1946.
84 'The Jews', Survey, *IRM* 35:1 (Jan. 1946), quot., 47–9; Hoffmann, Dec. 1946 memoranda; 'Travel Diary', 22 Oct. 1947–12 Mar. 1948, IMC.261222. See also 'Statistics of Jews' and 'American Jewish Committee 39th Annual Report', *American Jewish Yearbook* (1946–47), 599–633, from which some of Hoffmann's data was extracted and interpreted.
85 Hoffmann, 'Conferences on the Parish Approach to the Jew', Nov. 1945, IMC.261201.
86 Hoffmann's itineraries, were supplemented by the European itineraries of Birger Pernow (vice-chair of ICCAJ) and Hedenquist, who argued the same.
87 The European itinerary included England, Scotland, Ireland, Sweden, Norway, Denmark, Holland, France, Switzerland, Czechoslovakia, Hungary, the British and American zones of occupied Germany.
88 Quot., 'The Wandering Jew', *News Sheet*, 2 (Jan.–Mar. 1947); for wartime use by ICCAJ constituent, David McDougall, *In Search of Israel* (Edinburgh: Thomas Nelson and Sons, 1941), 28.
89 Quot., 'The Jews', *IRM*, Vol. 36 No. 1 (Jan. 1947), 64.
90 Hoffmann, 'The Church and the Jews', 9 Dec. 1946, prev. cit.
91 Hoffmann, 'A Changed World Demands Cooperation', Basel, 4–7 June 1947, IMC. 261206.
92 Basel delegates were from England, Scotland, Sweden, Norway, Denmark, Holland, Switzerland, France, Czechoslovakia, Hungary, Romania, South Africa, Palestine, United States. WCCIF delegates included Alphons Koechlin, who had been part of the Stuttgart delegation; Dr Werner Wickstrom of Reconstruction; Göte Hedenquist, ICCAJ's representative to the WCC secretariat; Professor Walter Horton, chair of NAICCAJ working in Geneva with the WCC Commission on God's Design and Man's Witness. Freudenberg, who had been pivotal to discussions between ICCAJ and WCC, was commissioned for a keynote paper, which was given by Hedenquist. The five Germans who could not secure visas were Professor K.H. Rengstorf, Dr Erwin Reisner, Revs Otto Fricke, Hermann Maas, F. J. Plotke.
93 'Resolution on the Church and Methods', ital. add., ICCAJ min., Basel, 4–7 June 1947, IMC. 261206.
94 Anglican Stephen Neill was appointed to the WCC Study Department in early 1946, in place of Hans Schönfeld, who was let go at the end

of the year. Neill's missionary career in south India began in 1924. He was bishop of the Tinnevelly diocese from 1939 until his hushed dismissal in 1945 for sexual anomalies. He was involved with WCC from 1946 to 1961, editing with Ruth Rouse in 1954 what is still the standard work on *A History of the Ecumenical Movement*. For circumstances around his dismissal, see Dyron Daughrity, *Bishop Stephen Neill: From Edinburgh to South India* (London: Peter Lang, 2008); Bishop Richard Holloway, 'The Mystery of Stephen Neill', *Church Times* 6717 (8 Nov. 1991); Donald Coggan, 'Stephen Neill's Thorn in the Flesh', *Church Times* 6718 (15 Nov. 1991).

95 'A Message for Israel', Commission II on 'God's Design and Man's Witness', Study 47E/230 (B), for private circulation only, n.d. Dec. 1947, but not issued for comment until Feb. 1948, PP 60/17/10/4.
96 Paras 1–4.
97 Paras 5–7.
98 Para. 8, referring to Matthew 25:27.
99 Para. 11.
100 Paras 13, 16–18.
101 Para. 19.
102 Paras 17, 19, 21–5.
103 Para. 26.
104 Hoffmann to Nils Ehrenström, 9 Mar. 1948, 'Comments on Study 47E/230 (B): A Message for Israel', 'God's Design and Man's Witness', WCC.420038.
105 Parkes, 'Comments on A Message for Israel', Assembly Commission II on 'God's Design and Man's Witness', Study 47E/230 (B), 30 April 1948, PP60/17/10/4. The Eliot Lectures were expanded and published as *Judaism and Christianity* (Chicago: University Chicago Press, 1948).
106 For letters between Simpson and Parkes, Parkes and Tomkins, WCC and Parkes between 9 Mar. and 20 May 1948, PP60/17/10/4.
107 With no further editing 'The Approach to Israel' was later published in the final version of the official Assembly Series on Man's Disorder and God's Design, Vol. II, *The Church's Witness to God's Design: An Ecumenical Study Prepared Under the Auspices of the World Council of Churches* (London: SCM Press, 1948), 190–9.
108 Committee IV was made up of four parts, initially named: a) Life and Work of Women in the Church; b) Christian Attitude to the Jews; c) Significance of the Laity in the Church; d) Christian Reconstruction and Inter-Church Aid.
109 VH, Agenda for Assembly Committees, 16 Mar. 1948, in Besier (2015), 404–5.

110 Bell to Levison, 30 Apr. 1948, in Besier (2015), 409–10.
111 Newell to Hoffmann, 14 Feb.; Hoffmann to Newell, 31 Mar. 1948, WCC.42.0038.
112 Papers to Newell included: Basel resolutions on 'Church and Evangelisation', 'Church and Methods', 'Church and Hebrew Christians', 4–7 June 1947; 'Findings of Conference on the Christian Church and the Jewish People', 7 Oct. 1947; 'The Church and Israel', Mar. 1948; 'The Church and Israel *or* The Christian Approach to the Jews', 20 May 1948; at WCC.301.4329, IMC.261206, 261207, 261208.
113 Documents for the round table are at IMC.261206; for quot., Hoffmann to VH, 18 Feb. 1947, WCC.42.0038.
114 Simpson, 'The Jewish Problem: Notes for the Committee on Concerns of the Churches', 26 May 1948, PP60/17/10/4.
115 ICCAJ Min., Basel, 4–7 June 1947, 17, IMC.261206.
116 Refugee Commission, Appendix D, 28 Feb. 1948, WCC.425.3.175.
117 Wurm, EKD Council, 'Regarding the Question of Reparation', 5 Mar. 1948, WCC.42.0084, ital. add. This newly discovered document complicates rather than offering light on Wurm's personal letter in January, which Hockenos (2004, 150–5) and Heschel (2010, 54–5) find as a disparaging antisemitic response to a draft of the Brethren Council statement. For more on the relief body cited by Wurm, see 'Report on Christian Relief Work for Victims of Racial Laws', May 1946–April 1947, by BICCAJ member Herman Newmark, WCC.425.A18.
118 An English translation of 'A Word about the Jewish Question', 8 Apr. 1948, was widely circulated from Geneva, and published almost immediately in ICCAJ's *News Sheet* (Mar–-Apr. 1948). The 1948 translation at WCC.301.4330 is different from that published by WCC in 1964.
119 Ibid., 'A Word about the Jewish Question', 8 Apr. 1948.
120 Parkes was never made aware of the anonymous use of his text.
121 Newell, 'The Christian Attitude to the Jews', first and second drafts; Newell to VH, 3 June 1948, WCC.301.4330.
122 WCC Study Depart. to Parkes, 18, 30 June; Tomkins to Parkes, 13 Jul.; P to Tomkins, 17 Jul. 1948, PP60/17/10/4.
123 Bilheimer to Hoffmann, 25 Aug. 1948, confirming Charles Leber had been added, WCC.31.005.
124 These previously undiscussed minutes are at WCC.31.005; quot. Session 1, hereafter S-1, etc. Speakers are noted as: D=delegate, C=consultant, A=alternate, O=observer. Newell's published materials appeared in *Memoranda on Concerns of the Churches* (Geneva: WCC, 1948), 3–14.

More than one guilt in the embers: 1945–1948 267

125 S-1, 2, Hedenquist (C).
126 S-2, 1.
127 S-1, 2–3, Niesel (D), EKD.
128 S-1, 3, Dr Regin Prenter (C), Church of Denmark.
129 S-1, 3, S-2, 2, Niesel went on to say about the theological need that: 'even Hitler in "Mein Kampf" was aware of the fact that there was some kind of connection between the Jews and Christ, and even [as] enemies of God the Jews were regarded as indirect witness for Christ'.
130 S-1, 3, Professor Haitjema (D), Dutch Reformed Church; S-2, Reverend Charles Westphal (C), Reformed Church of France.
131 S-1, 3, S-2, 2, Maury (C), French Reformed; others agreeing were Rev Charles Westphal (C), French Reformed, Rev. Elio Eynard, Italian Waldensian.
132 S-2, 1–2, Professor Henri Clavier (C), French Reformed; Hoffmann (C).
133 S-2, 2, Hoffmann (C); S-4, 2, Simpson (O), British Methodist.
134 S-2, 2, Simpson (O).
135 S-2, 4, Stanley Morrison (C), Church of England; Prenter (C).
136 S-2, 3, Prenter (C), Hedenquist (C), Dr Carl Ihmels (C), EKD.
137 S-2, 2, Hoffmann (C).
138 S-2, 4, Hoffmann (C).
139 S-2, 1, Clavier (C).
140 S-3, 1–2, Simpson (O), Aubrey (C), Westphal (C) from different perspectives.
141 S-3, 2, Niesel.
142 S-3, 2, Maury (C); Morrison (C) agreed, citing 'dangerous tendencies'.
143 S-3, 2.
144 S-3, 2, Niesel (D).
145 S-3, 2, Morrison (C).
146 S-3, 3, Clavier (C).
147 S-2, 1; S-3, 3, Hoffmann; the crisis was understood to have begun with the November 1947 UN Resolution to divide Palestine into Jewish and Arab states.
148 S-2, 1; S-3, 3, Hoffmann (C).
149 Hoffmann, DR, 15 Aug., circulated then delivered to ICCAJ Stockholm conference, 14–19 Sept. 1948, IMC.261203.
150 S-3, 3, Bishop of Worcester (D).
151 S-4, Newell (C).
152 S-1, 1; S-2, 1.
153 S-4, Bishop of Worcester.
154 S-4, Dun (D).

155 S-4, Denis Baley (C), Church of Scotland; Morrison (C).
156 S-4, Baley (C); S-4, Westphal (C), French Reformed.
157 Grubb was director of the Commission of the Churches on International Affairs, created in 1946 under the joint auspices of WCC and IMC.
158 S-4, Morrison (C), a member of Grubb's commission, reported the consultation.
159 Of 62 recorded comments and arguments: 41 (C), 14 (D), 7 (O).
160 Junginger (2017), 89; Hans-Walter Schmuhl, *The Kaiser Wilhelm Institute for Anthropology, Human Heredity and Eugenics* (New York: Springer, 2008), 159–60. Fricke became an EKD Council member in 1948.
161 Martin Schwarz Lausten, *Jews and Christians in Denmark* (2015), 260–1.
162 Charles and Denise Westphal were honoured by Yad Vashem in 2004.
163 Report of the Committee on the Christian Approach to the Jews, *First Assembly of the World Council of Churches* (New York: Harper & Brothers, 1949), 160–6, pt i, 'The Church's commission to preach the Gospel to all men'.
164 Hoffmann, DR, 15 Aug. 1948, IMC.261203.
165 Report of the Committee, pt ii, 'The special meaning of the Jewish people for Christian faith'.
166 Ibid., pt iii, 'Barriers to be overcome'.
167 Ibid., pt iv, 'Witness to the Jewish People'; Recommendations 1 and 2.
168 Ibid., pt v, 'The emergence of Israel as a state'.
169 Ibid., plenary debate, 164–6. Dr. Ernest Perkins (D) of the British Methodist church expressed similar concern, urging that the cultural and social issues were greater than the political. He also criticised insufficient emphasis on Christian–Jewish cooperation and the need to address the causes of antisemitism, but neither was considered for revision.
170 Ibid., pt v.
171 Ibid., plenary debate, 164–6.
172 Ibid., 'The special meaning of the Jewish people for Christian faith'.
173 Ibid., WCC Constitution, Article III.vii, adopted on 30 August 1948, 198.
174 Ibid., 26; Mackay's keynote, 'The Missionary Legacy to the Church Universal', was published in full in *IRM* (Oct. 1948), quot. 369, ital. add.
175 Ibid., Report of Section II, 'The Church's Witness to God's Design', 64, 70.

176 VH, *Memoirs* (1973), 193–4.
177 *The Relationship of the Church to the Jewish People: Collection of Statements Made by the World Council of Churches and Representative Bodies of Its Member Churches* (Geneva: WCC, 1964).
178 Budapest I.ii, *CAJ* (1927).

6

The Jews as a problem

Some conclusions

In Uriel Tal's 1970 critique of Hitler era Protestant protests in Johan Snoek's *The Grey Book* – the introduction to which he was invited to write – he asked pointedly 'are there any pronouncements of the Church that offer a Christian–Jewish relationship other than of conversion?' One of his concerns was that among postwar statements condemning antisemitism he could find *none* that acknowledged 'the right of Judaism to exist on its own terms'.[1] Citing a statement by a group of twenty theologians to the second assembly of the World Council of Churches (WCC) in 1954, he pointed out that even though 'composed years after the wholesale extermination of the Jews', they 'could find no solution' but to hope as a group for the conversion of Jews. He went on to say that 'when these circles in the Church desire for reasons of conscience and remorse to express "the grievous guilt of the Christian people towards the Jews throughout the history of the church", they find no better way ... than to revert to "Findings ... of the American Committee on the Christian Approach to the Jews"'.[2]

Tal was referring to a resolution from an NAICCAJ conference held just before the second WCC assembly, which restated its mandate that 'the Church cannot rest until the title of Christ is recognized by His own people according to the flesh'.[3] What he was not aware of was the pre-conference volume published by ICCAJ, WCC and IMC shortly before the second WCC assembly, which elaborated the 1948 founding belief that 'the continued existence of a Jewish people which does not acknowledge Christ is a divine

The Jews as a problem 271

mystery which finds its only sufficient explanation in the purpose of God's unchanging faithfulness and mercy'. As framed by now familiar figures in *The Church and the Jewish People*, Bishop Stephen Neill explained 'the survival of the Jewish people [as] a mystery, a challenge and a problem' for any 'Christian who takes his religion seriously'.[4] Robert Smith summarised as a consensus of spokesmen from 'all denominations' that the world had 'no category' to which Jews 'belong', that they are 'a people with a divine destiny which they themselves cannot fully understand', and that it is only 'from the Christian standpoint' that Jews can be understood and explained to the world.[5] For Professor Karl Rengstorf, in speaking of 'the Jewish Problem and the Church', 'the existence and the form of the Jewish people *post Christum natum*' created multiple theological problems for the Church, all of which lay 'in the shadow of the Cross'.[6]

This widely ploughed theological conception of the continuing existence of the Jewish people as 'a problem' for the Church has been the central theme of this book. That these Protestant versions survived Nazi extermination of two-thirds of European Jewry with such force of expression stands in answer to Tal's question as it pertains to this book. In and among the ardently held transnational beliefs revealed about the place, role and destiny of Jews in world society, Jews existing *as Jews* was never a theological consideration in the purview of ICCAJ and its collaborative partners. At every stage, over and above all other cumulative factors, the predominant informing solution to all issues and questions about Christian–Jewish relations was the unchanging vision of benevolent conversion.

The question here is what more can be said that will enlighten what has already been said of the certitudes held by one group about the place, role and destiny of another. The origins and aims of ICCAJ have been analysed from four perspectives – people and organisations who created, supported and collaborated; methodologies, strategies and tracking; discourse and dissemination; a parallel plane of opposition – and problematisation has made clear that each aspect was struck through with historical complexities, intrigues, contradictions, ambivalences and incongruities. Any attempt to force the pieces into a seamless picture of black or white conclusions ultimately fails, for the duality of the benevolence vision at the core of the initiative contradicts and refutes any open and shut view.

Summary points that further problematise facile conclusions while isolating some of the most critical findings, however, can be made. What has been described is a framework of Protestant aspirations for global expansion of Jewish evangelisation around which supersessionist beliefs were constructed and disseminated in the years before, during and after the Nazis' attempted extermination of European Jewry. The use of the modern Jewish problem as a matter of urgency to the Church and world society was central to the theoretical substratum of that framework. The empirical wedding of supersessionism to the modern Jewish problem, which began with Macdonald Webster's IMC call for Christian experts in 1925, drew the attention of 104 mainstream Protestant bodies and branches from 26 countries on four continents in 1927. The 175 men and women from a wide swathe of international Protestantism, who undoubtedly held a plurality of views, were nevertheless able to unanimously agree about relations between the historical failure of the Church to convert the Jews, the emergence of a universal Jewish problem, and the societal need for Jewish conversion. The series of transnational conference findings, the unanimity of which was publicly stressed, formed the basis of what would become the widely dispersed discourse at the centre of this book. None of this emanated from the periphery, nor was it based on peripheral beliefs. Both the views and factors that set into motion and sustained the creation of ICCAJ as a planning and lobbying initiative for world expansion of Jewish evangelisation arose from within mainstream Protestantism.

These interrelated facts cannot be overstated when trying to assess the developing structure, dimensions of outreach and questions of who influenced whom. Grasping the role of discourse and dissemination is equally crucial. ICCAJ was a mandated initiative in need of evangelising forces to carry out the transnational aspirations. The rallying of 'troops' to the 'duty' of Jewish missions was the most crucial course of strategy, for the success of globally expanded missions hinged on success of recruitment. By 1932 education on the 'right' Christian attitude toward Jews was a critical part of the outreach. The rallying and education, as understood, predefined that audiences would be predominately Protestant. Populations were for the most part related to the network of bodies that made up the ecumenical movement of the period, but not exclusively so. Not all among the multidenominational, multinational, multilingual groups exposed to ICCAJ were directly or even indirectly related to the ecumenical movement, nor can it be said that all were Protestant. What can be said is that many were both, and that over time its sphere of operations expanded within the multidimensional movement as disseminator of views on Jewish issues.

This general identification of audience becomes all the more significant when it is recognised that the 'troops' to whom ICCAJ discourse was directed were part of the greater anonymous mass that was later charged by scholarship with a general silence and indifference to the twelve-year Jewish plight during the years of the Third Reich. By reconstructing ICCAJ discourse and outreach, this study has complicated that indictment by revealing an international Protestant initiative that was anything but silent and indifferent. It has brought into sobering relief the complex and paradoxical ways in which a broad international toleration of traditional anti-Judaism allowed or encouraged, under a banner of Christian benevolence, a public discourse of incendiary antisemitic ideas, claims and concepts wrapped in conversionary language.

Yet, as illustrated throughout the study, ICCAJ was more than its discourse, and its discourse included components that were not anti-Jewish, antisemitic or incendiary. The initiative was the sum of all its parts, and some important parts were made up of components that vigorously protested against racial antisemitism, advocated for Christian support of non-Aryan Christian refugees, and urged Christian justice for Jews. A question at issue is thus whether or not the incendiary aspects of the discourse can be balanced out by the facts of the latter. Some would undoubtedly argue that case, but it is not the argument here. The deeper issue is whether or not it caused *harm*. The fact that incendiary claims were widely dispersed under a banner of conversionary benevolence forces the question of when, if ever, intended benevolence can become unintended maleficence. Can the aims and goals of perpetrator harm be furthered by the benevolent intentions of others? Is everything that ensues from the context of declared benevolence necessarily benevolent? Does it make it more so if it is born, executed and sustained within the environs of prayer?

The evidence of this study argues 'yes' to the first question, on the grounds of arguing 'no' to the latter two. The consciously developed and widely dispersed discourse of a proclaimed moral authority, with stated intentions to educate and influence the 'right' Christian attitude toward Jews, had consequences that cannot be glossed over in lieu of benefit that may or may not have derived from protests and advocacy for non-Aryan Christian refugees. Major claims of the ambiguously layered discourse provided legitimacy to the language, concepts and claims of Nazi antisemitism, on one hand, while functioning as claims of moral suasion from a proclaimed moral authority, on the other. The *harm* of legitimising and the *harm* of moral suasion were directly linked to the incendiary elements of the discourse *and* the ways in which it was woven into patterns of benevolent concern.

In traditional ways ICCAJ discourse was a continuation of the centuries-long discussion about how and where Jews fit into the metaphysical schemata that governed Christian theology. The developing claims centred around a specific view of God's design, Jewish dissent from it, and a divine commission to help change the course of dissent through conversion. In its most reduced form, Jews were insinuated into metaphysical explanations and conclusions about the purpose of human existence, which bore directly on the understanding of actual people, issues and events in human history. Those who placed their faith in the metaphysical schemata became self-appointed educators who sought to explain, on an international level, how concrete Jews in concrete spaces were to be understood and approached. The incorporation of a universal Jewish problem as an explanation for evangelising expansion took on its darkest overtones precisely because it was developed and dispersed internationally at the same time that Nazism was seeking its own 'solution' to an alleged universal Jewish problem.

The discourse was *inordinately* concerned with the movements of Jews in western society, and the concern was directly linked to claims about a collective Jewish threat to Christendom. Beginning with the call for Christian experts on the Jewish problem and then

The Jews as a problem 275

formalised in the findings of the Budapest–Warsaw conferences, the movements of Jews into political, economic and intellectual spheres of society, along with stated movements toward secularism, Zionism, nationalism, atheism, were framed as developments of 'great danger to the world, unless ... directed into Christian channels'.[7] The epigraph for this study bears repeating for its summary of the same threatening concern in 1935. 'The Jew' had to be won to Christ 'to save the Jew from becoming a problem and even a menace to the Christian faith': 'The need was never greater than today in view of the geographical dispersion of the Jews to the ends of the earth, his racial pride, his aggressiveness.'[8]

This line of argument peaked in the rapidly changing atmosphere of Hitler's early rule and the corresponding increase in propaganda about the threat of 'Jewishness'. Both before and after the 1935 Nuremberg Laws, ICCAJ director Hoffmann targeted with frequency a 'renaissance of Jewishness' rooted in racial and national aspirations. The purported dangers of increasing 'Jewishness', Jewish involvement with nationalistic or antireligious movements, and increasing numbers of atheistic Jews, were framed as an 'undeniable entrenchment of Jewry in opposition to Christianity'. The 'entrenchment' was said to pose a three-way challenge to 'the Christian mission of the Church', 'the reality of our faith', and 'the doctrines on which Christendom is so largely based and established'.[9] International Protestant audiences were urged to find, love and evangelise the Jews in their regions, on one hand, and rallied and 'educated' on the dangers of an increasingly atheistic, nationalistic and racially conscious Jewry, on the other.

The elaboration of these ideas into theory included the 'vicious circle' schemata that causally linked the provocations of modern Jewry to rising antisemitism, and it did so in the context of race. The idea at root was that Judaism was a conveyor of racial advancement and breeder of racial traits that provoked non-Jews to antisemitic backlash. The initial contention was that Nazi antisemitism provoked racially motivated Jewishness that provoked antisemitic backlash, and vice versa, in a deadlock pattern, but the 'vicious circle' was later applied to Jewish persecution through the ages. The theoretical presumption in all cases was that antisemitism would disappear *if* did Jewishness, but that antisemitism would sustain so long as Jewishness persisted. Jews had to choose between preservation of Jewishness and consequential persecution *or* the assimilated disappearance of 'Jew' and consequential toleration. In framing this dilemma for Jews as a critical issue for Christendom, Hoffmann incorporated concepts and language deeply imprinted with the Nazi brand. Urging in 1933 that Christians had to develop 'convictions' on the issue, he warned that 'Jewry will Judaise the world' if Christianity does not 'Christianise Jewry'.[10] The image of Jewish assimilation *without* conversion was forebodingly conveyed the next year when posing the question in *IRM*: 'shall Jewry disappear in humanity, like salt in a solution, no longer existent as Jewry, but permeating all mankind with Jewish spirit and influence?'[11]

The potentiality of these consciously placed statements about the threat of Judaisation to Christianity must not be ignored.[12] As a pejorative for dangerous Jewish influence, the ancient term 'Judaise' became part of 'the language and literature of every Christian people', preserved in biblical, conciliar, patristic, exegetical and popular texts that passed through the centuries into modern times.[13] That the term and concept were central to the Nazi project has been made clear by Steven Aschheim's probing analysis of 'Judaiser' and 'Judaisation' as they moved from ancient Christianity into modernity, through the Reformation, Enlightenment and Emancipation periods to the Third Reich. First as a metaphor for heresy, then as a symbol for dissent, Jews were cast into the universalised role of subversives who exercised Judaising influence to the detriment of the Church, culture, society, institutions and nations. By the Nazi period, Aschheim argues, Hitler's 1925 *Mein Kampf* could be 'read as a treatise on both the moral and physical "Judaisation" of the world and a ruthless dynamic program for radically solving the problem'.[14]

The moral force of ICCAJ director Hoffmann's disseminated threat in the same language and in the same period cannot be whitewashed as something less serious than it was. Conscious contributions to the known atmosphere of antisemitic claims – the threat of Jews Judaising the world unless Christianity can Christianise the Jews, *stated in the context of the need for disappearance of 'Jew' and 'Jewishness'* – cannot be seen as innocent no matter how much ill-intent is denied. Every claim about the threat of modern Jewry

The Jews as a problem 277

to Christendom carried the potential of legitimising similar Nazi claims about the Jewish threat, and it was not only the words but the impression of what was being said that carried the weight of the message. When the same message is repeated over and over, an impression is raised and it is raised incrementally more when the message is that of a threat. How much more is the power of impression raised when the threat is purportedly of divine significance?

Christian claims about the threat of Jews Judaising the world are not only legitimising statements but statements of moral suasion. In considering that power, presentation to international Protestant audiences cannot be overlooked. Conflation of proclaimed benevolence and conversionary self-interest was a hallmark of ICCAJ discourse from the beginning. Argumentation in both written and spoken texts was an exceedingly complex mix of theological and theoretical validation for global expansion of Jewish evangelisation, declarations of Christian love, denigration of modern Judaism, remorse for past Christian failings, protests and repudiation of Nazi racial antisemitism, warnings about the effects of Jewish thought and influence on Christianity and world society, advocacy for non-Aryan Christian refugees, and prayers for suffering Jews. Such conflationary thinking and presentation confuses and masks the dissemination of incendiary ideas with the face of good intentions, complicating, if not blocking, conscious awareness of the transmissible effect that professed benevolence can have on advancing dangerous ideas about Jews.

Uriel Tal, who has masterfully analysed Christian and anti-Christian aspects of antisemitism,[15] addressed the issue of conflated statements in Protestant protests in his introduction to the 1970 *Grey Book*. After studying the decontextualised collected statements (some of which were by ICCAJ), as well as omitted parts, he concluded that 'protest of the Church against the persecution and annihilation of the Jews was an inseparable part of its general protest against the inhumane and anti-Christian character of modern anti-Semitism' – and not just a protest on behalf of Jews.[16] The excerpted texts were 'clear confirmation of the Church's repudiation of Nazi doctrines, not only when directed against the Jews but, first and foremost, when they threatened the very existence of the Church itself'.[17] Tal's concern, which is a concern here as well, was that 'by concentrating on only one aspect of the interrelationship between Christianity and Judaism during the period of the Holocaust', a collection of such sources could 'confuse the reader into thinking that protest was the prime characteristic and policy of the church regarding antisemitism, persecution of the Jews, and their extermination'. As critically assessed, 'a collection of sources on the protest of the Church did not preclude the fact that there existed other positions among Christians', namely, 'the position of cooperation with antisemitism, whether active or passive, direct or indirect, with knowledge or without, voluntary or through coercion'.[18]

To Tal's point, ICCAJ protests against Nazi racial antisemitism were persistent and they were determinedly tied to preservation and advancement of the universality of the Church, in general, and defence of the Church against an anti-Christian racial heresy, in particular. Nazi racial antisemitism was understood as something that created more crucial issues for Christianity than 'ordinary' racism. It was a cloak for the anti-Christ, and Christians were repeatedly warned that they could not remain silent without undermining the Church and betraying Christ. The Christian duty to combat antisemitism was also linked in various ways to the duty of Jewish evangelisation. Christians were warned that involvement in antisemitism hindered Jewish mission efforts, while opposition to antisemitism advanced the efficacy of missions by offering evidence of Christian sympathy for Jews. Each of these arguments against racial antisemitism gained ground as Nazi antisemitic persecution of Jews increased. That they were made with the utmost sincerity cannot be denied, but neither can the concomitant attendant claims of the same discourse that gave legitimacy to Nazi claims being levelled at Jews.

Historian Todd Endelman, a scholar in modern Jewish history, has asked in regard to the post-World War I diffusion of antisemitic ideas *why* they appealed to 'some social groups more than others'. The question within the question, which I take as my own, was not that antisemitic ideas had to be sought out, but 'what people do with the beliefs and slogans that are available to them'.[19] The claims, concepts, images and language discussed here, some of which were shared with Nazi antisemitic theory, constituted a powerful set of ideas about Jews in the service of a proclaimed conversionary benevolence. While this is not to equate Hoffmann's discourse with Nazi antisemitism, it is to point out that the power of antisemitism lives in its universalisation of ideas, and that the discourse of *both*, for vastly different motivations and reasoning, were drawing from the same cache of historically familiar ideas embedded in western culture about Jews as a threat and problem.

Ideas depend upon human agency for cultural existence and each agent has the choice as to whether she or he will advance and sustain them. That Hoffmann consciously chose to use historically powerful universalised ideas about Jews to advance a transnationally mandated conversionary solution to 'the Jewish problem' cannot be easily overlooked, nor can it be easily explained. That no refutation or challenge by other international members of ICCAJ can be found increases the complexities of explanation, while strongly indicating (not just implying) that the discourse carried collective agency, whether by agreement or conciliatory acquiescence in part or whole. That there is no recorded recant of any aspect further indicates not only collectiveness but the representative role of ICCAJ. Hoffmann was not in any sense an original or against the grain thinker; he was called to represent ICCAJ, and ICCAJ was created to represent a wide swathe of international Protestant interests in the global expansion of Jewish evangelisation. *Any* idea that appeared in his considerable part of the discourse indubitably thrived first in the mainstream Protestant populations he represented.

Ideas and beliefs do not have to be strictly monolithic in order to have an accepting effect, particularly in a working collective whose aim was to advance a corporate purpose believed to be of a higher order. A widespread familiarity with traditionally shared anti-Judaic supersessionism, the driving force of ardent belief in its metaphysical core, and willing interactive affirmation of universalised ideas about Jews opened the way for expanded and unchallenged claims, whether by agreement, acquiescence or toleration, so long as they were argued in a Christianised context within a familiar range of commonly held assumptions.

The complexities in explaining the toleration of incendiary elements increase when trying to distinguish between moral agency for development and dispersion of the discourse *and* the concentric circles of people and organisations who fostered ICCAJ into existence, supporting and promoting its development. Indeed, the line of unanswered questions grows longer as the evidence is considered, and nowhere is it more complex than in the social issue trajectory with which ICCAJ collaborated, where expression of anti-Jewishness was *not* pronounced. Explanation of toleration in this respect lies in the nature of international collaboration, wherein various sets of beliefs and aims are brought together with the willingness to overlook, underweight, or look away on some points in order to advance a higher collective purpose. This held true for both ICCAJ and the UCCLW–WCCIF social issue trajectory, as well as collaborative efforts between them. In each case decisions on official responses to unfolding Jewish issues were ultimately subordinate to the precedence of organisational aims and mandates. For ICCAJ it was advancement of God's call to Israel, for UCCLW–WCCIF it was advancement of ecumenical unity as a manifestation of the *Una Sancta*. These overarching motivations, as in any collective effort, played a pivotal role in guiding organisational responses, over and above personal views and sympathies with and for Jews.

In reconstructing and tracing the relations that led to ICCAJ's architectural role in the 1948 WCC founding statement on Jews, it became evident that the divisive war guilt crisis of World War I had bearing on the mandated task of advancing ecumenical unity, and that historical contextualisation would be required to understand official UCCLW and WCCIF responses to Nazi persecution of Jews. The resulting analysis in this book, without setting out to do so, now challenges the prevailing image of WCCIF, as set by Armin Boyens's document-heavy *Kirchenkampf und Ökumene* in 1969 and 1973.[20] His main summary argument – that WCCIF was an 'almost powerless' body without authority to speak, who nevertheless did all within its power to be 'the mouthpiece of the persecuted Jewish people in Europe' – has remained unquestioned for almost five decades. While not disputing the documents in Boyen's important two-volume collection, the evidence presented here argues that the interpreted image does not bear up to the challenges of extended investigation.

The Jews as a problem 281

By widening and deepening the documentary base and extending chronology back to the origins of its antecedent body, a surfeit of inescapable questions have been raised about what WCCIF did and did not do 'within its power'. In this longer-range view reaching back to 1914, WCCIF, which did not exist before 1938, became the *conscious* inheritor of a moral and political history that bore directly on official responses to increasing Nazi aggressions against Jews. When that requisite background is brought to the forefront and documentation is sufficiently contextualised, human agency is restored to WCCIF's 'powerlessness' and an altogether different image of consensus politics *opting* for 'neutral silence' comes into focus.

UCCLW, which was forged from the fires of bitterness over the war guilt issue and then recognised by the 1930 Nobel committee as a platform of Christian unity between nations, was charged with 'the duty' to represent, study and promote supranational unity under the banner of ecumenicity, while functioning as a 'mouthpiece' of Christian conscience.[21] The commitment to that end was severely tested after Hitler came to power. Within a matter of nine months threats of German withdrawal were reignited by ecumenical protests over Germany's handling of its Jewish problem, Nazi Aryan laws affecting both Jews and Christians of Jewish origin were being viewed as an attack against Christianity, the adoption of the Aryan clause by the Prussian Synod and the subsequent launch of the Confessing church against the state-church faction were being explained as a representative fight on behalf of the Church universal. Within these contexts, UCCLW decisions on what could and could not be said officially about unfolding Jewish issues were tempered and shaped by tightly strung tensions between dissuasion of ecumenical division, preservation of Council unity, maintenance of relations with the German church, and carefully measured caution about collateral damage.

Reconstruction and analysis of these internal dynamics, much of which took place in closed door meetings and confidential memoranda, revealed again and again that the driving priority behind official responses was preservation and advancement of the Council mandate. The *only* official statement voicing 'anxiety and distress' about German actions against Jews per se was sent to German church president Hermann Kapler in May 1933 for pre-approval, and then revised to Council concern about 'Jews *and* restrictions on church freedoms' – before being shelved by Kapler's request to not publish it in any form. The same 'twinning' was used at Novi Sad in September by refocusing concern about 'Jews' to persons of Jewish origin *and* church liberty, while making clear that Christians of Jewish heritage were intended. By August 1934 neither Jews nor Christians of Jewish origin were mentioned in the Fanø resolution that censored the autocratic rule of the Reich Bishop and threatened Church liberty. In the same pattern of subordination, the August 1936 conference at Chamby (Switzerland) overruled an official statement condemning antisemitism on the grounds that it would infringe the 'rights' of opposing German members.

As inheritor of UCCLW in 1938, WCCIF kept to the same path of measured caution while trying to balance the tensely strung wire of unity with all factions of German Protestantism including the Reich church. Concern over what to say, when to say it and whether it should be said openly or covertly, was a fixed part of that legacy. Indeed, after its *Kristallnacht* statement reminded Protestant churches of the ecumenical stand taken against antisemitism at the 1937 Oxford conference and elsewhere, there was *no* other official WCCIF protest against antisemitism in the period leading up to and throughout the war.[22] As shown in detailed analysis of the internal dynamics leading up to the war, WCCIF leaders protested without hesitation when ecumenism was overtly challenged by German Christians at Godesberg, but abstained in silence when faced with the racial alignment of German Lutheran bishops with whom they were involved. Official condemnation of German state policy on Jews, or German church silence about it, was not in the WCCIF pre-war purview.

At the outbreak of war, the first line of action was said to be the defence of ecumenism, with the belief that unity 'at all cost' must remain unbroken.[23] The policy set in 1940 – that speaking on incendiary issues would erect barriers but silence would allow churches of warring nations to reunite at war's end – determined that the path of official WCCIF response would be refugee relief rather than public protest. That policy was rigorously guarded, even though

The Jews as a problem 283

boundaries were skirted in 1943 when Visser 't Hooft, without consulting co-secretary Paton, joined with Riegner of the WJC in issuing the internally and externally criticised Aide-Memoire on Jewish refugees. But it was not until after the graphically detailed Auschwitz Protocols were received in late June 1944 that a clear break was made in the form of a 'solemn and public protest', before resuming the 'truly ecumenical fashion' of 'refusing to make public protest' on divisive issues.[24]

To consider, first, how Boyens arrived at such a completely different image and, second, how the conflation against which Tal warned culminated in Boyens's claim that 'again and again the World Council of Churches tried to be the mouthpiece of the persecuted Jewish people in Europe', it is instructive to look at three ways in which that point was made in two summary articles.[25]

> The ecumenical fellowship of the churches became manifest in a special way in the work of the WCC and its member churches, not only for the Christian non-Aryans but for all persecuted Jews in Europe.[26]
>
> The reaction of the churches of the WCC in Europe was one of protest, in varying degrees.[27]
>
> The member churches of the WCC and the staff of the WCC raised their voices in protest against the persecution of the Jewish people. In almost all of the churches there were small minorities, brave men and women, who took up the fight for the rights of the persecuted and who tried to help the refugees. In some instances whole churches protested publicly and thereby resisted Hitler's policy of extermination by their word and deed.[28]

As these claims make clear, the idea ultimately expressed was that WCCIF was coterminous with its ecumenical constituency and the two functioned as a protesting unit on behalf of European Jewry. That was achieved in the summary articles by fusing a wide array of actors in a wide array of acts across wide geographic divisions, ranging from refugee aid, cooperation with resistance movements, fund-raising and donations, pastoral sermons, hiding and smuggling of Jews across borders, letters to the Red Cross, speeches in the House of Lords by Anglican leaders, transfer of information and so on. As such, the undefined manifestation of the 'ecumenical fellowship of the churches' becomes fused with the concrete WCCIF body, creating a web of blurriness that can be stretched and applied to any number of individuals in any number of WCCIF constituent churches. The equivocal result is that all correspondence between the generalised claim about WCCIF and the particular acts 'on behalf of the persecuted Jewish people in Europe' as they actually occurred has been lost. Such equating of many into a single identity confuses actors and acts, obscures differences, and creates misinterpretation of reality about the moral voice of WCCIF itself.

Yet in a critically important sense, the creation of a such an image is what was envisioned and set into practice by WCCIF general secretary Visser 't Hooft, a brilliant strategist who understood the value of proactive propaganda – a term used freely when speaking of ecumenical education. One of the primary wartime goals, as seen in Chapters 3 and 4, was to use every available platform and means to advance the idea that the spirit and force of ecumenism was emanating from WCCIF in Geneva. As part of that project, primary source collections offering evidence of ecumenism in protest began to be issued in early 1942.

The first in an *Ecclesia Militans* series was distributed as evidence of an ecumenical militant church at work, conscious of its 'essential unity' and 'ready to pay the price in suffering and persecution' as guardian of God's will in state, nation and society. The collection of forty statements from ten countries was a conflation of excerpted statements against Nazi aggressions, the anti-Christian nature of racial–national ideology, state interference with the Church, anti-Jewish decrees and actions, and attempts to usurp the Church as guardian of conscience.[29] A second decontextualised collection on attitudes of Anglo-Saxon churches to the 'Jewish question' was published in 1944, comprising excerpts from not only recognised bodies of the ecumenical movement but a wide range of individual and joint statements by church leaders from various countries in varying contexts.[30] The 1942 stated purpose for these and other WCCIF collections, which played a pre-emptive role in shaping not only postwar explanations but memory as well, was to illustrate the essential unity of the Church in action while arguing that 'there is only *one* history of the Church because there is only *one* Church of Jesus Christ'.[31] The additional recorded aim in 1944 was to preserve an account of joint ecumenical witness increasing in strength and desire 'to really help persecuted Israel in brotherly love', a unified effort 'to succour the victims of persecution and combat the fundamental evil of anti-Semitism'.[32]

This was still the atmosphere of emphasis when Boyens served as a WCC secretary during 1961–1967 while researching the PhD that became the published study. His 1969 volume on ecumenism and the *Kirchenkampf* was the first collection of WCC source documents that did *not* bear a WCC imprint, and it was followed by the 1970 *Grey Book* of protests collected and edited by Johan Snoek, executive secretary of the WCC Committee on the Church and the Jewish People, the renamed entity that evolved from ICCAJ after it was subsumed by WCC in 1961. Both Boyens and Snoek were working in the archives in the same period, as was Visser 't Hooft, who was collecting documents for his *Memoirs*, published in 1973. That there was cross-thinking between the three is apparent in references, document interpretation, and multiple archival documents with notes in Visser 't Hooft's handwriting: 'for Boyens'.

Armin Boyens was the first researcher to make extensive use of the WCC archives and his two-volume collection of documents is still important, but his use and interpretation of the documents is only part of the story that is still being unearthed. Boyens's interpretative summary articles, however, must be challenged as inadvertently contributing to a conflationary myth about WCCIF's protesting voice on behalf of Jews. Historiography is no longer content with one-dimensional litanies of conflated Church responses, nor should it be if we are to understand how Nazi antisemitism got to the point where it was able to exterminate six million Jews in the midst of Christianised Europe, and why it was tolerated at every earlier point in its eight-year public development.

Requisite questions such as these are not encouraged by laudatory, apologetic or condemnatory conflation of acts and actors. In considering who was and was not a 'Christian mouthpiece' for the persecuted Jews of Europe – if indeed there was one – distinctions have to be made between the official actions of WCCIF and the actions of its wide and layered constituency. Distinctions must also be made between its official actions as an agency and individual unofficial actions of leaders for, as this study has shown, prominent UCCLW and WCCIF leaders protested as individuals while abstaining from doing so collectively. WCCIF, as a unit moral agency with moral authority, did not emerge as a bold and unequivocal moral voice on behalf of Jews. Instead, as shown in contextualised archival detail, a consciously adopted organisational pattern of neutral silence illustrates how individuals and collectives could be disturbed by Nazi anti-Jewish atrocities yet reticent to speak against them as a corporately identifiable body of moral authority.[33] If the evaluative premise is that WCCIF relief actions were bigger than words then the relationship between what was known and what was protested becomes for some less important, but if we take soberly the scholarly claim that the Nazi assault on European Jews could not have been sustained without the silence and complicity of bystanders, then the issue of what was known in relation to silence and protest becomes a non-negotiable point of inquiry.

Distinctions must also be made between the WCCIF of the bitter war years and the more richly endowed, enlarged and staffed WCCIF of the early postwar years as it transitioned to WCC. But it is important to stress again that the history discussed in this study is not the whole WCCIF or WCC story of the period.[34] Of the paths explored here, all are the result of following trails of evidence that help to explain how a conversionary initiative rose in status as ecumenical expert on the Jewish question during the Nazi years to become architect of the WCC founding statement on Jews.

The landscape of interactions leading from one point to the other was complexly peopled with two different sets of moral agents and organisational agendas and policies, such that what can be said about one cannot necessarily be said about the other. Yet ICCAJ, which was anything but silent in its layered discourse of benevolent and incendiary elements, and the UCCLW–WCCIF social issue trajectory, which favoured a policy of increasingly measured neutrality, intersected and ultimately merged on the issue of world evangelisation of Jews.

Hoffmann's postwar co-responsibility argumentation, which was in line with Visser 't Hooft's 'common guilt' theology, was contoured to the WCCIF priority of unifying world churches through its constitutional founding, with efforts directed toward structural changes that would bring ICCAJ under the joint auspices of WCC and IMC. After it was determined that ICCAJ would be involved with the founding assembly, he lobbied vigorously in North America and twelve European nations stressing that the failure of the Church to prevent Nazi extermination of European Jews required *unity* in humility, confession and evangelising reparation, which subsequently led to the highly orchestrated WCC statement on Jewish conversion in August 1948.

Its life expectancy was shortened after Hoffmann retired, however, when the second assembly in 1954 refused to include ICCAJ's conversionary passage. By the third assembly in 1961, when IMC and ICCAJ were brought under the WCC banner, Hoffmann and many of his wartime principals had died and the post-Holocaust thinking of a relatively new group was moving toward dialogue as the principal mission to Jews. On this changing landscape, in which Martin Niemöller followed Otto Dibelius as one of WCC's six honorary presidents, Visser 't Hooft was featured on the cover of *Time Magazine* as orchestrator of a 'Second Reformation' based on Church unity,[35] and ICCAJ was renamed, followed by a second rechristening ten years later, leaving it with a past remembered differently from the extensive archival evidence presented here.

The case of WCCIF, like that of ICCAJ, is remarkably complex, not easily summarised, resistant to generalisations and difficult to label. Tracking the people who tracked the Jews has thus complicated rather than simplified bystander questions about the 'good people' who, in the words of sociologist Helen Fein, were co-present while Jews were 'labeled, stripped, isolated, stored and shipped' from the protection of European societies before being systematically murdered.[36] Yet, in that very sense, this study substantiates generally what historian Robert Ericksen has argued specifically about the German Protestant church for decades: namely, that some of what we knew about the responses of the churches is true, but *not* exclusively true, while much of what we thought we knew is far more shadowed, layered, complex and inconvenient.[37]

The work of differentiating the amorphous mass of bystanders has been a matter of slow discovery, of finding and uncovering layer by layer the masks of anonymity and what lay behind them.

The Christian Church was at every corner of the field, so to speak, by virtue of the fact that the global 'Church' appeared in every geographic schematic, overlapping in time and place in all Nazi-occupied, satellite, Axis, neutral and Allied countries. The controversial issues surrounding the question of what it meant to be a bystander has produced a scholarship of increasing complexity and problematisation. The term itself has been under critique since the late 1980s, with ongoing efforts to rename, redefine and re-understand by way of taxonomies, typologies, continuums and models of interaction between perpetrators, bystanders and victims.[38] The central inquiry has been how *if at all* those under study contributed by way of silence, indifference, legitimisation or enablement to the Nazi ability to disenfranchise and exterminate six million Jews. As scope, depth, nuance and sophistication of research increased, historians have shifted from viewing bystanders as simply passive and inactive, probing more deeply the question of fluid rather than static boundaries between the categories. Within this probing expansion the circle of perpetrators, circle of complicities and, to a far lesser extent, circle of rescuers have been enlarged,[39] which in turn has deepened and broadened discussions on relations between perpetrators, bystanders and victims.

The moral issues that make these relations a magnetic point of inquiry, as framed by Norman Geras in *The Contract of Mutual Indifference*, are the fundamental questions of human to human responses: how we respond to the tragedy of others, how and why we look on, how and why we look away, how and why we tolerate or refuse to see the wrongs of others.[40] To this I would add how and why we fail to consider whether our own responses are harmful, and I do so on the basis of one of the most profound findings in this study: that physical extermination did not, and does not, constitute the only form of Jewish destruction in Jewish eyes.

'*Let me raise a voice of solemn protest on behalf of the Jewish people against the campaigns of aggression which Protestant churches are waging against the Synagogue*' was part of an eloquent plea to ICCAJ in 1933 to cease the harmful conversionary discourse aimed at the spiritual destruction of Judaism and Jews.[41] That it was published in *IRM* as part of ICCAJ's portrayal of its more open attitude to hearing Jewish complaints must be balanced by the facts that it appeared only with a commissioned rebuttal, and that at no point in the breadth of this study was this or other such Jewish voices actually heard as anything more than defensiveness and denial of Jewish destiny in Christ.

What were these *unheard* voices trying to convey?

Rabbi Samuel Cohon, who was writing on behalf of nine American Rabbis while voicing concerns of other Jewish leaders in America and Britain, wanted ICCAJ to understand that its conversionary discourse was inflicting *harm*. In addition to fomenting 'strife and ill will', feeding 'the flames of prejudice, hatred and persecution', the 'organised campaigns' predicated 'the inferiority of both Judaism and the Jewish people'; and it was not just 'the Crucifixion story' that fed the flames. The whole conversionary attack 'to prevent the Jew from remaining a Jew' was circumscribing the Jew as 'an inferior, spiritual and moral being' and 'a vessel marked for destruction'. But even worse than 'maligning the Jewish people', Cohon went on, was the denigration of Judaism and what that meant for the Jewish people as a whole. While allowing that ICCAJ leaders were 'too human to endorse persecution of the Jewish people', he wanted them to hear and see that their claimed 'irenic and sympathetic' attitude did not prevent them from engaging in work aimed 'at the destruction of Judaism, which is the soul of the Jewish people and without which it cannot possibly live'.[42]

At the time this plea for the right to Jewish self-determination was published and throughout the period of study, those gathering around ICCAJ heard in it just that which was already believed, namely, as framed by Robert Smith early in the chapter, that Jews are 'a people with a divine destiny which they themselves cannot fully understand'.[43] This metaphysical *certitude* about the place, role and destiny of Jews never faltered, and at no point can evidence be found that the conversionary discourse associated with it was ever recognised as harmful. The *belief* of benevolent intentions self-persuaded that it was neither negative nor harmful, and it was sealed with such certainty that it precluded self-critical consideration and analysis. In the early postwar period there were multiple calls for confession of Church failure to prevent annihilation – with compensatory expansion of Jewish missions *as reparation* to surviving Jewry – but at no point throughout the period under study was there recorded confession, acknowledgement or even hint of sustained awareness that tensions existed between ICCAJ's proclaimed benevolence and the targeted campaigns that Jewish leaders repeatedly protested as harmful and destructive to the Jewish people.

Why is a question that keeps historians awake at night, and, in this case, it joins with other unanswered questions to suggest we are not at the end of our understanding of the ways and degrees to which negative ideas about Jews were embedded in the fabric of Western culture as normalised attitude during the Holocaust years. ICCAJ discourse was not the result of a single view but rather a multidimensional flow of transnational Protestant beliefs and commentary. Its broad base of consensus about a universal Jewish problem and need for a Christian solution, ease of agreement across denominational and language lines, and lack of recorded challenges to anti-Jewish claims, concepts and images point to something far greater than just unacknowledged permeation of harmful anti-Jewish elements in ICCAJ conversionary discourse. The ideas and concepts isolated here – 'Jewish problem', 'Jewish influence', 'Jewishness', 'world Jewry', 'Judaising threat', 'eternal Jew' – had no apparent barriers or limits to connotations that could be packed into the terms, or ways in which they could be interpreted and used in the marketplace of ideas to rationalise, justify, explain or advance any of a number of sundry causes and policies related to 'the Jews'. They were active ingredients for vastly different reasons in both ICCAJ discourse and Nazi antisemitic ideology, and similar widespread use and tolerance of the same ideas and concepts is found in mounting studies of not only international Protestant[44] but Catholic[45] and Orthodox churches[46] as well as the liberal democracies.[47]

The uncomfortable reality is that the 'Jewish question' and its attendant universalised ideas did not reach a peak of notoriety during the Hitler years just because it was a question to which Nazi Germany was seeking a 'final solution'. The evidence of this study, in the light of that broader picture, points to permeation, pattern, and the staying power of embedded beliefs.[48] An essential quality of an embedded or perdurable idea is its universalisation and, hence, versatility to be adapted without losing fundamental meaning while moving and diffusing back and forth between varying modes of

The Jews as a problem 291

thought, both religious and secular, across time. Ideas that perdure over time do so precisely by retaining universalised elements that remain familiar even when other elements have been changed, added or removed. More specifically to the point of this study, the universalised ideas analysed here were part of the nineteen-century portrait of two identity-bearing groups – divinely established Christians bearing salvation to the world and divinely condemned 'dissident' Jews bearing witness to deicidal crime – long before they were modernised and adapted as key elements of Nazi antisemitic ideology. Universalisation, as James Parkes isolated in his 1934 classic on the origins of antisemitism, was the core building block of foundational supersessionist theology that codified 'the Jews' as *not only* a problem for Christian theology.[49]

Notes

1 Uriel Tal, 'Introduction', *The Grey Book: A Collection of Protests Against Anti-Semitism and the Persecution of Jews Issued by Non-Roman Catholic Churches and Church Leaders During Hitler's Rule*, ed. Johan Snoek (New York: Humanities Press, 1970), xxiii–iv.
2 'Statement on the Hope of Israel' (1954), containing the NAICCAJ finding, was signed by 24 theologians associated with WCC, inclu. Martin Niemöller, Pierre Maury, Alphons Koechlin, Marc Boegner, Oliver Tomkins. It was appended to the second WCC assembly *Evanston Report*, ed., Visser 't Hooft (London: SCM Press, 1955), 327–8.
3 'Findings of the Pre-Evanston Conference of the American Committee on the Christian Approach to the Jews', 8–11 Aug. 1954, Lake Geneva, IMC. 261205.
4 *The Church and the Jewish People* (London: Edinburgh House Press, 1954), a collection of 12 essays edited by Göte Hedenquist, who became ICCAJ director after Hoffmann retired in 1951; Neill, 11–25, quot., 14.
5 Ibid., Smith, 'The Christian Message to Israel', 189–200, quot., 195.
6 Ibid., Rengstorf, 'The Jewish Problem and the Church', 27–62, quot. 27–8. Two papers by Rabbi Leo Baeck and Hans Schoeps argued on behalf of Judaism and, in the case of Baeck, asked 'Questions to the Christian Church from the Jewish Point of View'.
7 *CATJ*, Findings of Budapest, 36.
8 Hoffmann, *Jewish Missionary Intelligence* (Jul. 1935), 76–7.

9 Hoffmann, as example, DR, July 1935. IMC.261203.
10 Hoffmann, DR, 'Modern Jewry and Christian Responsibility', Sept. 1933, 2–5, 20. IMC.261207.
11 Hoffmann, 'Modern Jewry and the Christian Church', *IRM* (April 1934), 190–4.
12 For analysis of term, concept, and threat of Judaisation from Christian inception to the Nazi solution of dejudiasation, Carolyn Sanzenbacher, *Early Christian Teachings on Jews: A Necessary Cause of the Antisemitism that Informed the Holocaust*, MA, UNCG 2010, esp., 45–88, 89–125, 126–69.
13 For 'Judaising' and Jewish influence in Christian texts from antiquity to Reformation, see the classic work of Newman, *Jewish Influence on Christian Reform Movements* (1925), quot. 1, 2.
14 For contemporary analysis, Steven Aschheim, 'The Jew Within: The Myth of "Judaisation" in Germany', *Culture and Catastrophe: German and Jewish Confrontations with National Socialism and Other Crises* (New York: New York University Press, 1996), 45–68, quot., 67.
15 For Tal's major work, *Christians and Jews in Germany: Religion, Politics, and Ideology in the Second Reich, 1870–1914* (Ithaca: Cornell University Press, 1975).
16 Tal, 'Introduction', *The Grey Book*, vii.
17 Ibid., i, xx–xxiii, xviii–xxv; xxiv–xxv.
18 Ibid., xxv–xxvi.
19 Todd Endelman, 'Comparative Perspectives on Modern Anti-Semitism in the West', in *History and Hate*, ed. David Berger (Philadelphia: Jewish Publication Society, 1986), 100; for his important work on Jewish conversion up to and including pre and post-WWII periods, see *Leaving the Jewish Fold: Conversion and Radical Assimilation in Modern Jewish History* (Princeton: Princeton University Press, 2015).
20 Boyens, *Kirchenkampf und Ökumene, 1933–1939* (1969), *1939–1945* (1973).
21 Söderblom, Nobel Lecture, 'The Role of the Church', 11 Dec. 1930, *Nobel Lectures, Peace 1926–1950*, ed. Haberman.
22 *Kristallnacht* Statement, 16 Nov. 1938, published in *ICPIS* 49, WCC.301.4330.
23 VH to Temple, Mott, Boegner, Oldham, Archbishop Eidem, Bishop of Novi Sad, bishops Berggrav and Damgaard, 20 Sept. 1939, WCC.42.0077; VH to Paton, 5 Oct. 1939, IMC.261143.
24 Confidential memorandum from Visser 't Hooft to Temple and Cavert, shortly after the WCCIF protest against extermination of Hungarian Jewry in late June 1944, WCC.301.4330.

25 Boyens, 'The Ecumenical Community and the Holocaust', *Annals of the American Academy of Political and Social Science*, Vol. 450 (Jul. 1980), 140–52, quot. 144; 'The World Council of Churches and Its Activities on behalf of the Jews in the Nazi Period', *Judaism and Christianity Under National Socialism*. (Jerusalem: Historical Society of Israel, 1987), 453–69, quot. 458.
26 Boyens (1987), 467; (1980), 140, 152.
27 Boyens (1987), 464; (1980), 149.
28 Boyens (1987), 467; (1980), 140, 151–2.
29 *The Church Speaks to the World* (Geneva: WCC, Feb. 1942), includes excerpted statements from Germany, Norway, Sweden, Finland, Netherlands, France, Switzerland, Great Britain, Scotland, United States, and four excerpts from Popes Pius XI and XII.
30 *The Church and the Jewish Question: Attitude of the Churches and of Christian Leaders in Anglo-Saxon Countries* (Geneva: WCC, Fall 1944).
31 *The Church Speaks to the World* (1942), intro, 1–2, orig. ital.
32 *The Church and the Jewish Question* (1944), preface.
33 Scholarship will at some point have to compare the WCCIF neutrality of silence policy with the neutral silence of the Vatican, as, i.e., in David Kertzer, *The Pope at War: The Secret History of Pius XII, Mussolini, and Hitler* (New York: Random House, 2022).
34 See, for example, Gerhard Besier, '80 Years of the World Council of Churches: Theological, Political and Societal Ambiguities', *Kirchliche Zeitgeschichte*, 30: 2 (2017), 294–311; Klemens von Klemperer, *German Resistance Against Hitler: The Search for Allies Abroad, 1933–1945* (Oxford: Clarendon Press, 1992) for Visser 't Hooft's involvement with German resistance. For his role in advancing unity and internationalism, Michael Kinnamon, *Unity as Prophetic Witness: W.A. Visser 't Hooft and the Shaping of Ecumenical Theology* (2017); Jurjen Zeilstra, *Visser 't Hooft, 1900–1985: Living for the Unity of the Church* (Amsterdam University Press, 2020), *European Unity in Ecumenical Thinking* (Utrecht: Boekencentrum, 1995); Lucian Leustean, *The Ecumenical Movement and the Making of the European Community* (Oxford: Oxford University Press, 2014).
35 The *Time Magazine* cover story on 8 December 1961, 'The Ecumenical Century', 76–80, was supplemented by a special on Visser 't Hooft as 'The Chief Fisherman'.
36 Helen Fein, *Accounting for Genocide: National Responses and Jewish Victimization during the Holocaust* (Chicago: University of Chicago Press, 1979), 33.

37 Robert Ericksen, *Complicity in the Holocaust: Churches and Universities in Nazi Germany* (Cambridge University Press, 2012); 'Protestants', *The Oxford Handbook of Holocaust Studies* (Oxford University Press, 2010); *Theologians Under Hitler* (Yale University Press, 1985). See also 'Resistance or Complicity? Balancing Assessments of German Churches under Nazism', *Kirchliche Zeitgeschichte* 28:2 (2015), 246–61.
38 For example, Michael Marrus, *The Holocaust in History* (Hanover: New England University Press, 1987); David Cesarani and Paul Levine, ed., *Bystanders to the Holocaust: A Re-Evaluation* (London: Frank Cass, 2002); R.M. Ehrenreich and Tim Cole, 'The Perpetrator-Bystander-Victim Constellation: Rethinking Genocidal Relations', *Human Organization* 64:3 (2005), 213–24; Tom Lawson, *Debates on the Holocaust* (Manchester: Manchester University Press, 2010); *Bystanders, Rescuers or Perpetrators? The Neutral Countries and the Shoah*, ed. C. Guttstadt et al. (Berlin: Metropol, 2016); Victoria Barnett, *Bystanders: Conscience and Complicity during the Holocaust* (Westport, CT: Greenwood Press, 1999); 'The Changing View of the "Bystander" in Holocaust Scholarship: Historical, Ethical, and Political Implications', *Utah Law Review* 4:1 (2017), 633–47.
39 For recent rescue research, Christopher Browning, 'From Humanitarian Relief to Holocaust Rescue: Tracy Strong Jr, Vichy Internment Camps, and the Maison des Roches in Le Chambon', *HGS* 30:2 (2016), IMC. 21146.
40 Norman Geras, *The Contract of Mutual Indifference* (Manchester: Manchester University Press, 2020), 11.
41 Cohon, 'The Jew and Christian Evangelization', 470–80 ital. add.
42 Ibid. Rabbi Professor Samuel S. Cohon, Chair of Theology at Hebrew Union College, was writing on behalf of nine other American rabbis, including Solomon Freehof, Reform Congregation Chicago, and Professor Meyer Waxman, Hebrew Theological College. Other Jewish leaders who expressed similiar concerns in the period of the study were Central Conference of American Rabbis; Louis Marshall, head of the American Jewish Committee; New York Board of Rabbis; Roger Strauss, co-chair of the National Conference of Jews and Christians; Herbert Goldstein, head of Association of Jewish Orthodox Communities; Louis Newman, a founder of the Jewish Institute for Religion; Israel Mattuck, head of Liberal Judaism in Great Britain; Herbert Loewe, scholar of Semitic languages at Oxford and Cambridge; Claude Montefiore, Hebrew, Rabbinic and New Testament scholar and president of University College Southampton.

43 Smith, 'The Christian Message to Israel', *The Church and the Jewish People* (1954), 189–200.
44 For example, in addition to Ericksen, Doris Bergen, *Twisted Cross: The German Christian Movement in the Third Reich* (Chapel Hill and London: University of North Carolina Press, 1996); Steven Koblik, *The Stones Cry Out: Sweden's Response to the Persecution of the Jews, 1933–1945* (New York: Holocaust Library, 1988); Martin Lausten, *Jews and Christians in Denmark* (Leiden: Brill, 2015); Anders Gerdmar, *Roots of Theological Anti-Semitism: German Biblical Interpretation and the Jews, from Herder and Semler to Kittel and Bultmann* (Leiden: Brill, 2009); Susannah Heschel *The Aryan Jesus* (Princeton and Oxford: Princeton University Press, 2008); Richard Steigmann-Gall, *The Holy Reich: Nazi Conceptions of Christianity, 1919–1945* (Cambridge: Cambridge University Press, 2003); Milton Shane, *A Perfect Storm: Antisemitism in South Africa, 1930–1948* (Johannesburg and Cape Town: Jonathan Ball, 2015). For studies that address both Protestant and Catholic churches in Hungary, Moshe Herczl, *Christianity and the Holocaust of Hungarian Jewry* (New York: New York University Press, 1993); Paul Hanebrink, *In Defense of Christian Hungary: Religion, Nationalism and Antisemitism, 1890–1944* (Ithaca: Cornell University Press, 2006); Randolph Braham, 'The Christian Churches of Hungary and the Holocaust', *Yad Vashem Studies* 29 (2001), 241–80.
45 For example, Derek Hastings, *Catholicism and The Roots of Nazism: Religious Identity and National Socialism* (Oxford: Oxford University Press, 2010); Dariusz Libionka, 'Antisemitism, Anti-Judaism, and the Polish Catholic Clergy during the Second World War, 1939–1945', *Antisemitism and Its Opponents in Modern Poland*, ed. Robert Blobaum (Cornell University Press, 2005), 233–64; Michael Phayer, *The Catholic Church and the Holocaust, 1930–1965*. (Bloomington: Indiana University Press, 2000); Ronald Madras, *The Catholic Church and Antisemitism: Poland, 1933–1939* (London and New York: Routledge, 1994); Hermann Grieve, 'Between Christian Anti-Judaism and National Socialist Antisemitism: The Case of German Catholicism', *Judaism and Christianity Under the Impact of National Socialism*, ed. Otto Dov Kulka and Paul Mendes-Flohr (Jerusalem: Historical Society of Israel and Zalman Shazar Center for Jewish History, 1987), 169–79.
46 For example, Ionut Biliuta, '"Christianizing" Transnistria: Romanian Orthodox Clergy as Beneficiaries, Perpetrators, and Rescuers during the Holocaust', *HGS*, 34:1 (2020), 18–44; Ion Popa, *The Romanian Orthodox Church and the Holocaust* (Bloomington: Indiana University Press, 2017); William Pearce, 'The Romanian Orthodox Church

during World War II', PhD, University of California Riverside (2014); Paul Shapiro, 'Faith, Murder, Resurrection: The Iron Guard and the Romanian Orthodox Church', *Antisemitism, Christian Ambivalence, and the Holocaust*, ed. Kevin Spicer (Bloomington: Indiana University Press, 2007), 136–70; Jean Ancel 'The "Christian" Regimes of Romania and the Jews, 1940–1942', *HGS* 7:1 (1993), 14–29.

47 Tony Kushner has argued since the 1990s that where there is expressed concern about Jewishness, Jewish differences, and Jewish behaviour in liberal democracies, *anti-Jewishness*, which is central to all types and forms of antisemitism, is often harbouring, even among those who proclaim against antisemitism; see as example, *The Holocaust and the Liberal Imagination: A Social and Cultural History* (Oxford: Blackwell Publishing, 1994). Also David Nirenberg, *Anti-Judaism: The Western Tradition* (New York: W.W. Norton, 2013), who reconstructs and analyses the ways in which the threat of Judasim is 'encoded' into 'some of the basic concepts of Western thought' (459); Alon Confino, *A World Without Jews: The Nazi Imagination from Persecution to Genocide* (New Haven: Yale University Press, 2014), who finds that 'ideas of Jews and Judaism in the Third Reich were part of a rich familiar symbolic universe' (23), and that 'modern racial antisemitism took shape within the contexts of memories, habits and beliefs inherited from Christian anti-Judaism' (126).

48 For important recent scholarship calling for greater attention to patterns and recurring elements of images, language and concepts in antisemitism, see Dan Michman, 'The Jews as a Problem for Modern European Political Logic', *Confronting Antisemitism in Modern Media, the Legal and Political Worlds*, Vol. 5, eds. Armin Lange et al. (Berlin: De Gruyter, 2021), 27–43.

49 Parkes, *The Conflict of the Church and the Synagogue: A Study in the Origins of Antisemitism*, esp. 33, 42–3, 95, 160–1, 375–6.

Select bibliography

Note: Select bibliography does not include archival materials cited in notes.

Archives

American Jewish Committee Archives
Bodleian Library University of Oxford
    Church Mission to Jews
Duke University David M. Rubenstein Rare Books and Manuscripts
    Henry Leiper Rare Books
Franklin D. Roosevelt Presidential Library
Harry Truman Presidential Library
    World War II Era Archives
Hebrew Union College Jewish Institute of Religion Klau Library
    Periodical Collections
Jacob Rader Marcus Center of American Jewish Archives
    Rabbi Marc H. Tannenbaum Collection
Lambeth Palace Library
    Archbishop Lang Papers
Leo Baeck Institute
    High Commission for Refugees from Germany Collection
Pennsylvania State University Special Collections
    Henry Leiper Rare Books
Presbyterian Historical Society (Philadelphia)
    Federal Council of Churches Archives
    Papers and Correspondence
      Parkes Cadman
      Samuel McCrea Cavert
      John Conning
      Conrad Hoffmann
      Adolf Keller

Henry Smith Leiper
Charles Macfarland
Presbyterian Board of Jewish Missions Archives
United Nations Commission on Human Rights (UNCHR)
United Nations Economic and Social Council (UNESCOSOC)
United Nations Relief and Rehabilitation Administration (UNRRA)
University of Albany Special Collections
   Walter Kotschnig Papers
University of Illinois at Urbana-Champaign Speical Collections
   Donald A. Lowrie Papers
University of Minnesota Special Collections
   Donald A. Lowrie Papers, Kautz Family YMCA Archives
University of North Carolina Chapel Hill
   WWII Microfilm Collection
University of North Carolina Greensboro
   WWII Microfilm Collection
University of Southampton Special Collections
   Anglo-Jewish Archives
   Council of Christians and Jews
   Institute of Jewish Affairs
   Rabbi Israel Mattuck Papers
   James Parkes Papers
   Charles Singer Papers
   Rev William Wynn Simpson Papers
World Council of Churches Archives (Geneva)
   General Secretariat Correspondence
   World Council of Churches in Process of Formation
   World War II Era Records
   Organisations
      Conference of Missionary Societies in Great Britain and Ireland
      Ecumenical Institute
      European Central Bureau for Inter-Church Aid
      International Christian Social Institute
      International Committee on the Christian Approach to Jews
      International Missionary Council
      International Student Service
      Universal Christian Council for Life and Work
      World Alliance for Promoting International Friendship through the Churches
      World Alliance of YMCAs
      World Student Christian Federation
   Papers and Correspondence
      George Bell

Marc Boegner
William Adams Brown
Parkes Cadman
Samuel McCrea Cavert
Norman Goodall
Kenneth Grubb
Adolf Freudenberg
H.L. Henriod
Conrad Hoffmann
Adolf Keller
Alphons Koechlin
Hans Kosmala
Henry Smith Leiper
Donald Lowrie
Charles Macfarland
William Paton
Hans Schönfeld
William Temple
Willem Visser 't Hooft
Yale University Divinity Library Special Collections
International Missionary Council
International Committee on the Christian Approach to Jews
John R. Mott Papers
William Paton Papers
World Student Christian Federation
YIVO Institute for Jewish Research

Primary source document collections

Besier, Gerhard, ed. *Intimately Associated for Many Years: George K.A. Bell's and Willem A. Visser 't Hooft's Common Life Work in the Service of the Church Universal, Correspondence*, Parts 1 and 2, 1938–1949; 1950–1958. Newcastle: Cambridge Scholars Publishing, 2015.

Besier, Gerhard. 'Ökumenische Mission in Nachkriegsdeutschland: Die Berichte von Stewart W. Herman über die Verhältnisse in der evangelischen Kirche 1945/46', *Kirchliche Zeitgeschichte*, May 1988, 151–87; Oct. 1988, 316–52; May 1989, 294–358.

Besier, Gerhard, Hartmut Ludwig and Jörg Thierfelder, eds. *Der Kompromiß von Treysa: Die Entstehung der Evangelischen Kirche in Deutschland (EKD) 1945*. Weinheim: Deutscher Studien Verlag, 1995.

Chandler, Andrew, ed. *Brethren in Adversity: George Bell, the Church of England and the Crisis of German Protestantism*, Woodbridge: Boydell Press, 1997.

Friedlander, Henry, and Sybil Milton, gen. eds. *Archives of the Holocaust: An International Collection of Selected Documents*, Vol. 7, *James G. McDonald Papers*, ed., Karen Greenberg. New York: Garland Publishing, 1990.

Greschat, Martin. *Die Schuld der Kirche: Dokumente und Reflexionen zur Stuttgarter Schulderklärung vom 18./19.Oktober 1945*. Munich: Chr. Kaiser, 1982.

Matheson, Peter, ed. *The Third Reich and the Christian Churches*. Grand Rapids: William B. Eerdmans Publishing Company, 1981.

Matthäus, Jürgen. *Predicting the Holocaust: Jewish Organisations Report from Geneva on the Emergence of the 'Final Solution', 1939–1942*. Lanham: Rowman & Littlefield in association with USHMM, 2019.

McDonald, James G. *Advocate for the Doomed: Diaries and Papers of James G. McDonald, 1932–1935*, eds., Richard Breitman, Barbara McDonald Stewart, and Severin Hochberg. Bloomington: Indiana University Press in association with USHMM, 2007.

Mendelsohn, John, ed. *The Holocaust: Selected Documents in Eighteen Volumes*. New York: Garland Publishing, Inc., 1982.

Raina, Peter, ed. *Bishop George Bell: House of Lords Speeches and Correspondence with Rudolf Hess*. Bern: Peter Land, 2009.

Rendtorff, Rolf, and Hans Hermann Henrix, eds. *Die Kirchen und das Judentum: Dokumente von 1945 bis 1968*. München: Verlag Bonifatius-Druckerei Paderborn und Chr. Kaiser Verlag, 1989.

Röhm, Eberhard and Jörg Thierfelder. *Juden-Christen-Deutsche*, Band 1 1933–1935 (1990), Band 2 1935–1938 (1992). Stuttgart: Calwer Verlag.

Snoek, Johan M., ed. *The Grey Book: A Collection of Protests Against Antisemitism and the Persecution of Jews Issued by Non-Roman Catholic Churches and Church Leaders During Hitler's Rule*. New York: Humanities Press, 1970.

Solberg, Mary M. *A Church Undone: Documents from the German Christian Faith Movement, 1932–1940*. Minneapolis: Fortress Press, 2015.

Vollnhals, Clemens, ed. *Die evangelische Kirche nach dem Zusammenbruch: Berichte ausländischer Beobachter aus dem Jahre 1945*. Göttingen: Vandenhoeck & Ruprecht, 1988.

World Council of Churches. *The Relationship of the Church to the Jewish People: Collection of Statements made by the WCC and Representative Bodies of Its Member Churches*. Geneva: WCC Commission on Faith and Order and Committee on the Church and the Jewish People, 1964.

World Council of Churches. *The Church and the Jewish Question: Attitude of the Churches and of Christian Leaders in Anglo-Saxon Countries*. Geneva: WCC Secretariat for Refugees, 1944.

Wyman, David, ed. *America and the Holocaust: A Thirteen Volume Set Documenting the Editor's Book, Abandonment of the Jews*. New York: Garland, 1989–1991.

Published primary sources

Arendt, Hannah. 'Organized Guilt and Universal Responsibility', *Jewish Frontier* (Jan. 1945), 19–23.
Aubrey, E.E. 'The Oxford Conference, 1937', *Journal of Religion* 17:4 (1937), 379–96.
Barth, Karl. *Against the Stream: Shorter Post-War Writings, 1946–1952*. New York: SCM Press, 1954.
Barth, Karl. *The Only Way: How Can the Germans Be Cured?*, trans. Marta K. Neufeld and Ronald Gregor Smith. New York: Philosophical Library, 1947.
Barth, Karl. *The Church and The War*, trans. Antonia H. Froendt, Introduction by Samuel McCrea Cavert. Mimeograph, 1942. New York: Macmillan Co., 1944.
Barth, Karl. *The Christian Cause: A Letter to Great Britain from Switzerland*. New York: Macmillan, 1941.
Barth, Karl. *The German Church Struggle: Tribulation and Promise*. London: Kulturkampf Association, 1938.
Bell, G.K.A. *The Kingship of Christ: The Story of the World Council of Churches*. Westport, CT: Greenwood Press, 1954.
Bell, G.K.A. *A Letter to Friends of Refugees from the Bishop of Chichester*. London: Church of England Committee for Non-Aryan Christians, 1944.
Bell, G.K.A. *Humanity and the Refugees*. London: Woburn Press, 1939.
Bell, G.K.A. *The Stockholm Conference, 1925: Official Report of the Universal Christian Conference on Life and Work in Stockholm, 19–30 August, 1925*. London, 1926.
Bereczky, Albert. *Hungarian Protestantism and the Persecution of Jews*. Budapest: Sylvester, 1945.
Bethge, Eberhard. *Dietrich Bonhoeffer: Theologian, Christian, Contemporary*, trans., Eric Mosbacher, Peter and Betty Ross, Frank Clarke, William Glen-Doepel, ed., Edwin Robertson. London: Collins, 1970.
Bevan, Edwyn. 'Considerations on a Complaint Regarding Christian Propaganda Among Jews', *IRM*, Vol. 22:4 (October 1933), 481–99.
Black, James. *The Validity of the Christian Approach to the Jews*. New York and London: International Missionary Council, 1931.
Black, James, ed. *The Christian Approach to the Jew: A Report on the Conferences Held at Budapest and Warsaw in April 1927*. London: Edinburgh House Press, 1927.

Boegner, Marc. *The Long Road to Unity: Memories and Anticipations*, trans. Rene Hague. London: Collins, 1970.
Bonhoeffer, Dietrich. *London: 1933–1935*, Vol. 13, *Dietrich Bonhoeffer Works*, trans. Isabel Best, ed. Keith Clements. Minneapolis: Fortress Press, 2007.
Bonhoeffer, Dietrich. *The Way to Freedom: Letters, Lectures and Notes, 1935–1939*, Vol. II, *Collected Works of Dietrich Bonhoeffer*, trans. Edwin H. Robertson and John Bowden, ed. Edwin H. Robertson. London: Collins, 1966.
Bonhoeffer, Dietrich. *No Rusty Swords: Letters, Lectures and Notes, 1928–1936*, Vol. I, *Collected Works of Dietrich Bonhoeffer*, trans. Edwin H. Robertson and John Bowden, ed., Edwin H. Robertson. New York: Harper & Row, 1965.
Brown, W.A. *Toward A United Church: Three Decades of Ecumenical Christianity*. New York: Charles Scribner's Sons, 1946.
Brown, W.A. *A Teacher and His Times*. New York and London: Charles Scribner's Sons, 1940.
Brunner, Emil. 'Secularism as a Problem for the Church', *IRM*, 19:4 (1930), 495–511.
Campbell, J. McLeod. *Manpower in the Twentieth Century Church*. London: Press and Publications Board, 1944.
Carter, Henry. *The Refugee Problem in Europe and The Middle East*. London: Epworth Press, 1949.
Cavert, Samuel McCrea. *The American Churches in the Ecumenical Movement, 1900–1968*. New York: Association Press, 1968.
Cavert, Samuel McCrea. 'Preview of Amsterdam', *IRM*, 37:3 (July 1948), 313–20.
Cavert, Samuel McCrea. 'Hitler and the German Churches', *Christian Century*, 24 May 1933, 683–5.
Cavert, Samuel McCrea, and Henry Pitney Dusen, eds. *The Church Through Half a Century: Essays in Honor of William Adams Brown*. New York and London: Charles Scribner's Sons, 1936.
Central Office for Refugees, The. *Bloomsbury House: The Care of German and Austrian Refugees*. London: Bloomsbury House, 1942.
Christian Council for Refugees from Germany and Central Europe. *Final Report and Survey 1938–1951*. London: Walthamstow Press, Ltd, 1951.
Christian Council for Refugees from Germany and Central Europe. *A Five Year Survey*. London: Bloomsbury House, 1943.
Christian Council for Refugees from Germany and Central Europe. *Reports and Accounts for the Period from October 31st, 1939 to September 30th, 1941*. London: Bloomsbury House, 1941.

Church of England Missionary Council. *The Call to West and East.* London, 1928.
Cohon, Samuel S. 'The Jew and Christian Evangelization', *IRM*, 22:4 (1933), 470–80.
Conning, John S. *The Jew at the Church Door.* New York: Board of National Missions, 1938.
Conning, John S. 'Major Problems and Issues in a Christian Approach to the Jews', *Christians and Jews*, 13–33. New York and London: IMC, 1931.
Conning, John S. 'The Local Church and Its Jewish Neighbors', *Christians and Jews*, 83–6. New York and London: IMC, 1931.
Conning, John S. 'Religion and Irreligion in Israel', *IRM*, 19:3 (1930), 538–49.
Conning, John S. *Our Jewish Neighbors: An Essay in Understanding.* New York: Fleming H. Revell, 1927.
Conning, John S. 'The Jewish Situation in America', *IRM* 16:1 (1927), 64–75.
Dibelius, Otto. *In the Service of the Lord: The Autobiography of Bishop Otto Dibelius*, trans. Mary Ilford. New York, Chicago and San Francisco: Holt, Rinehart & Winston, 1964.
Ehrenström, Nils. 'Movements of International Friendship and Life and Work, 1925–1948', 545–98, *A History of the Ecumenical Movement, 1517–1948*, eds. Ruth Rouse and S.C. Neill. Geneva: WCC, 1954.
Eisen, Max. 'Christian Missions to the Jews in North America and Great Britain', *Jewish Social Studies*, 10:1 (1948), 31–66.
Ellison, H.L. 'The Christian Approach to the Jews: Ambiguities in Terminology', *IRM*, 45:2 (April 1956), 155–60.
Ellison, H.L. 'Church and Israel', *IRM*, 37:1 (1948), 54–6.
Feige, Gregory, trans. *The Church and the Jews: A Memorial Issued by Catholic European Scholars.* Washington and New York: Catholic Association for International Peace and Paulist Press, 1937.
Freudenberg, Adolf, ed. *The Evangelical Church in Germany and the Jewish Question: Selected Documents from the Period of the Church Conflict, 1933–1945.* Geneva: WCC, 1945.
Garvey, A.E. 'The Jewish Problem', *IRM*, 30:2 (1941), 216–24.
Gill, C.H. 'Present Day Emphases in Work for the Jews in Europe and the Near East', *Christians and Jews*, 34–44. New York: IMC, 1931. 34–44.
Gillet, Lev. 'Some Remarks on Dr Parkes' Article', *Theology*, 47 (Oct. 1944), 224–7.
Goodall, Norman. *The Ecumenical Movement: What It Is and What It Does*, 2nd edn. London: Oxford University Press, 1964.
Goodall, Norman. 'The International Missionary Council and The World Council of Churches: Their Present and Future Relationships', *IRM*, 37:1 (1948), 86–92.
Goodall, Norman. 'The Collected Papers of Dr. Mott', *IRM*, 37:1 (1948), 99–106.

Grubb, Kenneth. *Crypts of Power*. London: Hodder & Stoughton, 1971.
Handy, Robert. *We Witness Together: A History of Cooperative Home Missions*. New York: Friendship Press, 1956.
Harling, Otto von. 'The Present Situation in Missions to Jews and Its Challenge', *IRM*, 22:3 (July 1933), 345–52.
Hedenquist, Göte. *The Church and The Jews: A Study Handbook*. London: Edinburgh House Press, 1961.
Hedenquist, Göte. *Twenty Five Years of The International Missionary Council's Committee on the Christian Approach to the Jews*. Upsala: Boktryckeri Aktiebolag, 1957.
Hedenquist, Göte, ed. *The Church and the Jewish People*. London: Edinburgh House Press, 1954.
Herman, Stewart. *The Rebirth of the German Church*. Harper & Brothers, 1946.
Hoffmann, Conrad. *What Now for the Jews: A Challenge to the Christian Conscience*. New York: Friendship Press Inc., 1948.
Hoffmann, Conrad. *The Jews Today: A Call to Christian Action*. New York: IMC, 1941.
Hoffmann, Conrad. 'Modern Jewry and the Christian Church', *IRM*, 23:2 (1934), 189–204.
Hoffmann, Conrad. *A New Approach to an Old Problem: Modern Jewry and the International Committee on the Christian Approach to the Jews*. New York and London: IMC, 1933.
Hoffmann, Conrad. 'Methods of Christian Approach', *Christians and Jews*, 52–60. New York and London, 1931.
Hoffmann, Conrad. *In the Prison Camps of Germany: A Narrative of 'Y' Service Among Prisoners*. New York: Association Press, 1920.
Huber, Max. *The Good Samaritan: Reflections on the Gospel and Work in the Red Cross*. London: Victor Gollancz, 1945.
Huber, Max. 'Red Cross and Neutrality', *International Review of the Red Cross*, No. 209 (1936), 353–363.
International Missionary Council. *The World Mission of Christianity: Messages and Recommendations of the Enlarged Meeting of the International Missionary Council held at Jerusalem, March 24–April 8, 1928*. London and New York: IMC, 1928.
International Student Service. *Nyon Conference on the Jewish Question in Universities, 13–18 April 1931, Die Juden Im Gemeinschaftsleben der Voelker*. Geneva: ISS, 1931.
Jaspers, Karl. *The Question of German Guilt*. New York: Doubleday, 1948.
Karlström, Nils. 'Movements for International Friendship and Life and Work', 509–42, *A History of the Ecumenical Movement*, Vol. 1: 1517–1948, eds., Ruth Rouse and Stephen Charles Neill. Geneva: WCC Publications, 1954.

Keller, Adolf. *Christian Europe Today*. New York and London: Harper & Brothers, 1942.
Keller, Adolf. *Five Minutes To Twelve: A Spiritual Interpretation of the Oxford and Edinburgh Conferences*. Nashville: Cokesbury Press, 1938.
Keller, Adolf. *World Chaos or World Christianity: A Popular Interpretation of Oxford and Edinburgh, 1937*. Chicago, New York: Willett, Clark & Company, 1937.
Keller, Adolf. *Church and State on the European Continent*. London: Epworth Press, 1936.
Kosmala, Hans. *Studies, Essays, and Reviews: Volume III, Jews and Judaism*. Leiden: E.J. Brill, 1978.
Kosmala, Hans. 'What is Judaism', *IRM*, 35:4 (Oct. 1946), 416–21.
Kosmala, Hans. 'The Two Judaisms', *IRM*, 32:4 (Oct. 1943), 420–6.
Kosmala, Hans. 'Judaism and Christianity: The Jewish Point of View', *IRM*, 30:3 (July 1941), 374–88.
Kosmala, Hans. 'Judaism and Christianity: The Summons to the Christian Church', *IRM* 30:4 (Oct. 1941), 521–30.
Kosmala, Hans. 'The Problem of the Hebrew Church', *IRM*, 26:1 (Jan. 1937), 107–18.
Kosmala, Hans and Robert Smith. *The Jew in the Christian World*. London: SCM Press, 1942.
Kraemer, Hendrik. *The Christian Message in a Non-Christian World*. London: Edinburgh House Press, 1938.
Kraemer, Hendrik. 'Christianity and Secularism as a Problem for the Church', *IRM*, 19:2 (Apr. 1930), 195–208.
League of Nations High Commission for Refugees. *Report of the Second Meeting of the Governing Body*. London: Office of the High Commission, 1934.
League of Nations High Commission for Refugees. *Report of the Third Meeting of the Governing Body*. London: Office of the High Commission, 1934.
League of Nations High Commission for Refugees. *Report of the Fourth Meeting of the Governing Body*. London: Office of the High Commission, 1935.
Leiper, Henry Smith. 'From Pulpit to Prison', in *U-Boat to Pulpit*, Martin Niemöller, 186–223. New York: Willett, Clark & Company, 1937; London: William Hodge & Company, 1937.
Leiper, Henry Smith. *Christ's Way and the World's in Church, State, and Society*. New York: Abingdon Press, 1936.
Leiper, Henry Smith. 'Ecumenical Christianity', *The Church Through Half a Century*, eds. Samuel McCrea Cavert and Henry Pitney Van Dusen, 375–91. New York and London: Charles Scribner's Sons, 1936.

Leiper, Henry Smith. *The Church-State Struggle in Germany: A Personal View Based on Two Months' Intimate Contact with the Situation in Europe During August and September, 1934*. London: Friends of Europe, 1935.
Leiper, Henry Smith. *Personal View of the German Churches Under the Revolution: A Confidential Report Based on Intimate Personal Contact with Leaders on Both Sides of the Church and State Controversy in the Third Reich*. New York: UCCLW, 1934.
Leiper, Henry Smith. *German Churches and the Ecumenical Movements*. New York: Central Bureau for European Relief Work, 1933.
Leiper, Henry Smith. 'Antisemitism in Germany', *American Hebrew* (December 1932), 113–19.
Leiper, Henry Smith, with Edward Staples. *S. Parkes Cadman*. Boston: Congregational Christian Historical Society, 1967.
Lowrie, Donald. *The Hunted Children*. New York: W.W. Norton & Co., 1963.
Macfarland, Charles S. *The New Church and the New Germany*. New York: Macmillan Company, 1934.
Mackay, John A. 'The Missionary Legacy to the Church Universal', *IRM*, 37:4 (1948), 369–74.
Mackellar, J.A.C. 'Anti-Semitism', *The Christian Approach to the Jew*, ed. James Black, 189–97. London: Edinburgh House Press, 1927.
Mackie, Robert C. and Charles C. West, Ed. *The Sufficiency of God: Essays on the Ecumenical Hope in Honor of W.A. Visser 't Hooft*. Philadelphia: Westminster Press, 1963.
Mathews, Basil. *The Jew and the World Ferment*. London: Edinburgh House Press, 1934.
Mathews, Basil. *John R. Mott: World Citizen*. New York, London: Harper and Brothers, 1934.
Mathews, Basil. 'What is the Central Objective of the Christian Approach to the Jews', *Christians and Jews*, 61–9. New York and London: IMC, 1931.
Mathews, Basil. *The Clash of World Forces: A Study in Nationalism, Bolshevism and Christianity*. London: Edinburgh House, 1931.
Mathews, Basil. *Roads to the City of God: A World Outlook from Jerusalem*. London: Edinburgh House Press, 1928.
McDougall, David. *In Search of Israel*. Edinburgh: Thomas Nelson and Sons, 1941.
McLeish, Alexander. 'The World Dominion Movement: its Ideals and Activities', *IRM* 23:2 (1934), 215–24.
Mott, John R. 'Nobel Prize Lecture' (13 December 1946), *Nobel Lectures: Peace 1926–1950*, ed. Frederick W. Haberman. Amsterdam: Elsevier Publishing, 1972.

Mott, John R. 'At Edinburgh, Jerusalem and Madras', *IRM*, 27: 3 (1938), 297–320.
Mott, John R. 'The Purpose of the Conference', *Christians and Jews*, 3–5. New York and London: IMC, 1931.
Niemöller, Martin. *Here Stand I*. Chicago: Willet, Clark, & Co., 1937.
NAICCAJ. *Analyses of Questionnaires on Jewish Missions*. New York: IMC, 1932.
Oldham, J.H., ed. *The Oxford Conference Official Report*. Chicago and New York: Willett, Clark & Company, 1937.
Parkes, James. *Voyage of Discoveries*. London: Victor Gollancz, 1969.
Parkes, James. *Antisemitism*. Chicago: Quadrangle Books, 1963.
Parkes, James. *A Reappraisal of the Christian Attitude to Judaism*. Barley: Parkes Library, 1962.
Parkes, James. *Judaism and Christianity*. Chicago: University of Chicago Press, 1948.
Parkes, James. *The Emergence of the Jewish Problem, 1878–1939*. London: RIIA, 1946.
Parkes, James. *The Real Jewish Problem*. London: Peace News, 1945.
Parkes, James. *An Enemy of the People: Antisemitism*. Harmondsworth: Penguin, 1945.
Parkes, James. 'A Christian Looks at the Christian Mission to the Jews', *Theology* 47 (Oct. 1944), 218–24.
Parkes, James. 'Unresolved Frictions', *Liberal Judaism* (May 1944), 18–27.
Parkes, James. 'The Jewish Problem', *The Modern Churchman*, 33 (Oct.–Dec. 1943).
Parkes, James. *Judaism, Christianity and Antisemitism*. London: Gollancz, 1943.
Parkes, James. *The Jewish Question*. Oxford: Clarendon Press, 1941.
Parkes, James. *Anti-Semitism*. London: SCM Press, 1939.
Parkes, James. *The Jewish Problem in the Modern World*. London: Thornton Butterworth Ltd, 1939.
Parkes, James. 'The Fate of the Jews', *The Christian News Letter*, Supp. 6 (6 Dec. 1939).
Parkes, James. *Judaism and Christianity*. Toronto: Committee on Jewish Gentile Relationships, 1938.
Parkes, James. *The Foundations of Antisemitism*. Toronto: Committee on Jewish Gentile Relationships, 1938.
Parkes, James. *The Jew in the Medieval Community: A Study of His Political and Economic Situation*. London: Soncino Press, 1938.
Parkes, James. *The Conflict of the Church and the Synagogue: A Study in the Origins of Antisemitism*. London: Soncino Press, 1934.
Parkes, James. 'The Nature of Antisemitism', *The Church Overseas, An Anglican Review of Missionary Thought and Work*, 6:24 (Oct. 1933).

Parkes, James. *The Jew and His Neighbor: A Study of the Causes of Anti-Semitism*. London: SCM Press, 1930.
Paton, William. 'The Churches in Council: Oxford, Edinburgh, Hangchow', *IRM*, 6:3 (1937), 297–308.
Paton, William. 'Herrnhut', *IRM*, 21:4 (1932), 488–97.
Richter, Julius. 'The Gospel for the Modern Jew from the Standpoint of the German Churches and Missions', *Christians and Jews*, 70–78. New York and London: IMC, 1931.
Riegner, Gerhart M. *Never Despair*. Chicago: Ivan R. Dee, in assoc. with USHMM, 2006.
Rouse, Ruth. *The World's Student Christian Federation: A History of the First 30 Years*. London: SCM Press, 1948.
Rouse, Ruth. 'The Student Christian Movement and Missions', *IRM*, 28:4 (1939), 569–78.
Rouse, Ruth and Stephen Charles Neill. *A History of the Ecumenical Movement, 1517–1948*. Geneva: WCC, 1954.
Ruppin, Arthur. *Jewish Fate and Future*, trans. E.W. Dickes. London: Macmillan, 1940.
Simpson, William W. *The Christian and the Jewish Problem*. London: Epworth Press, 1939.
Simpson, William W. *Youth and Antisemitism*. London: Epworth Press, 1938.
Simpson, William W. and Ruth Weyl. *The Story of the International Council of Christians and Jews*. London: ICCJ, 1987.
Sinclair, Margaret. *William Paton*. London: SCM Press, 1949.
Singer, Charles. *The Christian Approach to Jews*, 3rd Edition. London: George Allen & Unwin Ltd for The British Christian Council for International Friendship, Life and Work, 1938.
Sloan, George L.B. 'The Missionary to the Jews in Palestine Today', *IRM*, 34:4 (1945), 406–11.
Smith, Robert. 'A New Dimension in Evangelism', *IRM* 33:3 (1944), 304–14.
Smith, Robert. 'The New Captivity of the Jews', *IRM*, 30:2 (1941), 225–31.
Söderblom, Nathan. 'The Role of the Church in Promoting Peace', 1930 Nobel Lecture, *Nobel Lectures: Peace 1926–1950*, ed. Frederick W. Haberman. Amsterdam: Elsevier, 1972.
Stone, Jules. *The Numerus Clausus in the Universities of Eastern Europe*. Birmingham: Interuniversity Federation of Great Britain and Ireland, 1927.
Tatlow, Tissington. *The Story of the Student Christian Movement*. London: SCM Press, 1933.
Ten Boom, Willem. 'Zionism', *IRM*, 19:2 (1930), 231–40.

Temple, William. *Nazi Massacres of the Jews & Others*. London: Gollancz, 1943.
Temple, William. *A Conditional Justification of War*. London: Hodder & Stoughton, 1940.
Tomkins, Oliver S. 'The Nature of Oecumenical Cooperation', *IRM*, 34:3 (1945), 301–5.
Visser 't Hooft, W.A. *Memoirs*. Geneva: WCC Publications, 1973.
Visser 't Hooft, W.A., ed. *The New Delhi Report: The Third Assembly of the World Council of Churches, 1961*. New York: Association Press, 1962.
Visser 't Hooft, W.A., ed. *The Evanston Report: The Second Assembly of the World Council of Churches, 1954*. London: SCM, 1955.
Visser 't Hooft, W.A. 'The Genesis of the World Council of Churches', *A History of the Ecumenical Movement, 1517–1948*, ed., Ruth Rouse and Stephen Neill. Geneva: WCC, 1954, 697–731.
Visser 't Hooft, W.A. *The Ecumenical Movement and the Racial Problem*. Paris: UNESCO, 1954.
Visser 't Hooft, W.A., ed. *The First Assembly of the World Council of Churches at Amsterdam, 1948*. New York: Harper & Brothers, 1948.
Visser 't Hooft, W.A., ed. *The World Council of Churches, Its Process of Formation: Minutes and Reports of the Provisional Committee*. Geneva: WCC, 1946.
Visser 't Hooft, W.A. *The Struggle of the Dutch Church: Documents Collected and Edited by W.A. Visser 't Hooft*. Geneva: WCC, 1944.
Visser 't Hooft, W.A. *Report of the World's Student Christian Federation, 1935–1938*. Geneva: WSCF, 1938.
Visser 't Hooft, W.A. *The Story of the World's Student Christian Federation, 1931–1935*. Geneva: WSCF, 1935.
Visser 't Hooft, W.A., and J.H. Oldham. *The Church and Its Function in Society*. London: George Allen & Unwin Ltd, 1937.
Webster, MacDonald. 'The Jewish Problem: Some Newer Aspects', *IRM*, 14:4 (1925), 598–607.
Webster, MacDonald. 'The Need of a New Policy in Jewish Missions', *IRM*, 17:2 (1918), 206–18.
Williams, Lukyn. *A Bird's-Eye View of Christian Apologia until the Renaissance*. Cambridge: Cambridge University Press, 1935.
Williams, Lukyn. 'On Winning Jews to Christ', *IRM*, 20:2 (1931), 202–9.
Williams, Lukyn. *A Manual of Christian Evidences for Jewish People*. Cambridge: W. Heffer, 1911.
World Council of Churches. *Memoranda on Concerns of the Churches*. Geneva: WCC, 1948.

Period journals, newspapers, newsletters

Bulletin of the Christian Institute of Jewish Studies
Christian Century
Christian News Letter
Church of Scotland Jewish Mission Quarterly
ICCAJ News Sheet
ISS Vox Studentium
International Christian Press and Information Service
International Review of Missions
Jewish Chronicle
Jewish Missionary Intelligence
Jewish Telegraphic Agency
WSCF Student World

Secondary sources

Ancel, Jean. 'The "Christian" Regimes of Romania and the Jews, 1940–1942', *HGS* 7:1 (1993), 14–29.

Arad, Yitzhak. 'The Christian Churches and the Persecution of Jews in the Occupied Territories of the USSR', *Judaism and Christianity Under National Socialism*, eds. Otto Dov Kulka and Paul R. Mendes Flohr. Jerusalem: Historical Society of Israel and the Zalman Shazar Center for Jewish History, 1987.

Ariel, Yaakov. 'From Faith to Faith: Conversions and De-Conversions during the Holocaust', *Simon Dubnow Institute Yearbook* 12 (2013), 37–66.

Ariel, Yaakov. *Evangelizing the Chosen People: Missions to Jews in America, 1800–2000*. Chapel Hill and London: University of North Carolina Press, 2000.

Ariel, Yaakov. 'Reply to Lawrence Baron's Response', *HGS* 7:1 (1993), 149–50.

Ariel, Yaakov. 'Jewish Suffering and Christian Salvation: The Evangelical-Fundamentalist Holocaust Memoirs', *HGS*, 6:1, 1991.

Aschheim, Steven E. *Culture and Catastrophe: German and Jewish Confrontations with National Socialism and Other Crises*. New York: New York University Press, 1996.

Bailey, Charles E. 'The Verdict of French Protestantism against Germany in the First World War', *Church History*, Vol. 58, No. 1 (March 1989), 66–82.

Bailey, Charles E. 'The British Protestant Theologians in the First World War: Germanophobia Unleashed', *The Harvard Theological Review*, Vol. 77, No. 2 (Apr. 1984), 195–221.

Balfour, Michael. *Withstanding Hitler in Germany, 1933–1945*. London and New York: Routledge, 1988.
Ban, Joseph Daniel. *The Holocaust: The Response of the Religious Press in the Pacific Northwest to the Antisemitic Policies of the Third Reich*. University of Oregon Press, 1974.
Bank, Jan, with Lieve Gevers. *Churches and Religion in the Second World War*, trans. Brian Doyle. London and Oxford: Bloomsbury, 2016.
Bankier, David. *The Germans and the Final Solution: Public Opinion under Nazism*. Oxford and Cambridge: Blackwell Publishers, 1992.
Bankier, David, and Dan Michman, eds. *Holocaust Historiography in Context*. Jerusalem: Yad Vashem in Association with Berghahn Books, 2008.
Barnes, Kenneth C. *Nazism, Liberalism, & Christianity: Protestant Social Thought in Germany*. Lexington: University Press of Kentucky, 1991.
Barnett, Victoria. 'Ecumenical Protestant Response to the Rise of Nazism, Facism and Antisemitism during the 1920s and 1930s', *Religion, Ethnonationalism, and Antisemitism in the Era of the Two World Wars*, eds. Kevin Spicer and Rebecca Carter Chand, 356–78. Montreal: McGill-Queens University Press, 2022.
Barnett, Victoria. 'The Changing View of the "Bystander" in Holocaust Scholarship: Historical, Ethical, and Political Implications', *Utah Law Review*, No.4:1 (2017), 633–47.
Barnett, Victoria. 'Track Two Diplomacy, 1933–1939: International Responses from Catholics, Jews, and Ecumenical Protestants to Events in Nazi Germany', *Kirchliche Zeitgeschichte*, 27:1 (2014), 76–86.
Barnett, Victoria. 'Fault Lines: An Analysis of the National Conference of Christians and Jews, 1933–1948'. PhD, George Mason University, 2012.
Barnett, Victoria. 'Barmen, the Ecumenical Movement, and the Jews: the Missing Thesis', *Ecumenical Review*, Vol. 61, No. 1, March 2009, 17–23.
Barnett, Victoria. 'Christian and Jewish Interfaith Efforts During the Holocaust: The Ecumenical Context', *American Responses to Kristallnacht*, ed. Maria Mazzenga, 13–29. London: Palgrave Macmillan, 2009.
Barnett, Victoria. 'The Creation of Ethical "Gray Zones" in the German Protestant Church: Reflections on the Historical Quest for Ethical Clarity', *Gray Zones: Ambiguity and Compromise in the Holocaust and Its Aftermath*, eds Jonathan Petropoulas and John K. Roth. Oxford and New York: Berghahn Books, 2005.
Barnett, Victoria. *Bystanders: Conscience and Complicity During the Holocaust*. Westport, CT: Greenwood Press, 1999.
Barnett, Victoria. *For the Soul of the People: Protestant Protest Against Hitler*. Oxford: Oxford University Press, 1992.

Baron, Lawrence. 'Supersessionism Without Contempt: The Holocaust Evangelism of Corrie ten Boom', *Christian Responses to the Holocaust*, ed. Donald Dietrich, 119–31. Syracuse: Syracuse University Press, 2003.
Baron, Lawrence. 'Evangelical Converts, Corrie Ten Boom, and the Holocaust: A Response to Yaakov Ariel', *HGS* 7:1 (1993), 143–8.
Bauer, Yehuda. *Rethinking the Holocaust*. New Haven and London: Yale University Press, 2001.
Bauer, Yehuda. 'The Death Marches, January–May 1945', *Modern Judaism*, 3:1 (1983), 1–21.
Bein, Alex. *The Jewish Question: Biography of a World Problem*, trans. Harry Zohn. New York: Herzl Press, 1990.
Bein, Alex. 'The Jewish Parasite: Notes on the Semantics of the Jewish Problem, with Special Reference to Germany', *Leo Baeck Institute Year Book*, IX, 1964, 3–40.
Bergen, Doris L. 'Religion and the Holocaust', *Lessons and Legacies* IV 41–65. Evanston: Northwestern University Press, 2003.
Bergen, Doris L. *Twisted Cross: The German Christian Movement in the Third Reich*. Chapel Hill and London: University of North Carolina Press, 1996.
Berger, David. *Persecution, Polemic, and Dialogue: Essays in Jewish-Christian Relations*. Boston: Academic Studies Press, 2010.
Besier, Gerhard. '80 Years of the World Council of Churches: Theological, Political and Societal Ambiguities', *Kirchliche Zeitgeschichte*, 30:2 (2017), 294–311.
Besier, Gerhard. *Religion, State and Society in the Transformations of the Twentieth Century*. Berlin: Lit Verlag, 2008.
Besier, Gerhard. *Krieg-Frieden-Abüstung*. Göttingen: Vandenhoeck & Ruprecht, 1982.
Besier, Gerhard and Gerhard Sauter. *Wie Christen ihre Schuld bekennen: Die Stuttgarter Erklärung, 1945*. Göttingen: Vandenhoeck & Ruprecht, 1985.
Bilheimer, Robert. 'The Significance of Amsterdam', *Ecumenical Review* 40:3–4 (Jul.–Oct. 1988), 326–44.
Biliuta, Ionut. '"Christianizing" Transnistria: Romanian Orthodox Clergy as Beneficiaries, Perpetrators, and Rescuers during the Holocaust', *HGS*, 34:1 (2020), 18–44.
Blaschke, Olaf. *Offenders or Victims?: German Jews and the Causes of Modern Catholic Antisemitism*. Lincoln: University of Nebraska Press, 2009.
Blatman, Daniel. *The Death Marches: The Final Phase of Nazi Genocide*, trans. Chaya Galai. Cambridge: Belknap Press of Harvard University Press, 2011.

Borg, Daniel. 'German Protestants and the Ecumenical Movement: The War Guilt Imbroglio, 1919–1926', *Journal of Church and State*, 10:1 (Winter 1968), 51–71.
Boyens, Armin. 'The World Council of Churches and Its Activities on behalf of the Jews in the Nazi Period', 453–69, *Judaism and Christianity Under National Socialism*. Jerusalem: Historical Society of Israel, 1987.
Boyens, Armin. 'The Ecumenical Community and the Holocaust', *Annals of the American Academy of Political and Social Science*, Vol. 450 (Jul. 1980), 140–52.
Boyens, Armin. *Kirchenkampf und Ökumene, 1939–1945: Darstellung und Dokumentation*. Munich: Kaiser 1973.
Boyens, Armin. 'Das Stuttgarter Schuldbekenntnis von 1945', *Vierteljahrshefte für Zeitgeschichte*, 4 (October 1971), 374–97.
Boyens, Armin. *Kirchenkampf und Ökumene, 1933–1939: Darstellung und Dokumentation*. Munich: Kaiser 1969.
Braham, Randolph L. *The Politics of Genocide: The Holocaust in Hungary*, Vols 1, 2. New York: Columbia University Press, 2016, 3rd revised edn.
Braham, Randolph L. 'The Christian Churches of Hungary and the Holocaust', *Yad Vashem Studies* 29 (2001), 241–80.
Braybrooke, Marcus. *Children of One God: A History of the Council of Christians and Jews*. London: Vallentine Mitchell, 1991.
Brichetto, Joanne. 'The Wandering Image: Converting the Wandering Jews', MA, Vanderbilt University, 2005.
Brockway, Allan. 'For Love of the Jews: The International Missionary Council's Committee on the Christian Approach to Jews', PhD, University of Birmingham, 1992.
Brockway, Allan, Paul van Buren, Rolf Rendtorff and Simon Schoon, eds. *The Theology of the Churches and the Jewish People: Statements by the World Council of Churches and its Member Churches*. Geneva: WCC Publications, 1988.
Brown-Fleming, Suzanne. *The Holocaust and Catholic Conscience: Cardinal Aloisius Muench and the Guilt Question in Germany*. University of Notre Dame Press, 2006.
Browning, Christopher. 'From Humanitarian Relief to Holocaust Rescue: Tracy Strong Jr, Vichy Internment Camps, and the Maison des Roches in Le Chambon', *HGS* 30:2 (2016), 211–46.
Browning, Christopher. 'A Final Hitler Decision for the "Final Solution"? The Riegner Telegram Reconsidered', *HGS* 10:1 (1996), 3–10.
Browning, Christopher, with contributions by Jürgen Matthäus. *The Origins of the Final Solution: The Evolution of Nazi Jewish Policy, September 1939–March 1942*. Lincoln and Jerusalem: University of Nebraska Press and Yad Vashem, 2004.

Brudholm, Thomas. 'Surveying a Gap: A Philosophical Perspective on Historians' Responses to Discourses on the "Bystanders"', *Holocaust Studies: A Journal of Culture and History*, 11:3 (Winter 2005), 1–23.
Brustein, William I. *Roots of Hate: Anti-Semitism in Europe Before the Holocaust*. Cambridge: Cambridge University Press, 2003.
Burgess, Greg. *The League of Nations and the Refugees from Nazi Germany*. Bloomsbury Academic, 2016.
Cargas, Harry J. *Problems Unique to the Holocaust*. Lexington: University Press of Kentucky, 1999.
Carmesund, Ulf. 'Refugees or Returnees: European Jews, Palestinian Arabs and the Swedish Theological Institute in Jerusalem around 1948', PhD, Uppsala University, 2010.
Cesarani, David. 'Reporting Anti-Semitism: the *Jewish Chronicle* 1879–1979', *Cultures of Ambivalence and Contempt*, 247–82, eds. S. Jones, T. Kushner and S. Pearce, 247–82. London: Frank Cass, 1998.
Cesarani, David, and Paul A. Levine, eds. *Bystanders to the Holocaust: a Re-evaluation*. London: Frank Cass, 2002.
Chandler, Andrew. *British Christians and the Third Reich: Church, State, and the Judgement of Nations*. Cambridge: Cambridge University Press, 2022.
Chandler, Andrew. *George Bell, Bishop of Chichester: Church, State, and Resistance in the Age of Dictatorship*. Grand Rapids: William B. Erdmans, 2016.
Chandler, Andrew, ed. *The Church and Humanity: the Life and Work of George Bell, 1883–1958*. Farnham: Ashgate, 2012.
Chandler, Andrew, ed. *Brethren in Adversity: George Bell, the Church of England and the Crisis of German Protestantism*. Woodbridge: Boydell Press, 1997.
Chandler, Andrew. 'Lambeth Palace and the Jews of Germany and Austria in 1938', *Leo Baeck Institute Yearbook* (1995), 225–50.
Chandler, Andrew. 'A Question of Fundamental Principles: The Church of England and the Jews of Germany, 1933–1937', *Leo Baeck Institute Yearbook* (1993), 221–62.
Chertok, Haim. *He Also Spoke as a Jew: The Life of the Reverend James Parkes*. London and Portland: Vallentine Mitchell, 2006.
Clark, Christopher. *The Politics of Conversion: Missionary Protestantism and the Jews in Prussia, 1728–1947*. Oxford: Clarendon, 1995.
Clark, Christopher. 'Missionary Politics: Protestant Missions to the Jews in Nineteenth-Century Prussia', *Leo Baeck Yearbook* (1993), 33–50.
Clements, Keith. *Dietrich Bonhoeffer's Ecumenical Quest*. Geneva: WCC, 2015.
Clements, Keith. 'Barmen and the Ecumenical Movement', *Ecumenical Review*, 61:1 (2009), 6–16.

Clements, Keith. *Faith on the Frontier: A Life of J.H. Oldham*. Edinburgh and Geneva: T&T Clark and WCC, 1999.

Clendinnen, Inga. *Reading the Holocaust*. Cambridge: Cambridge University Press, 1999.

Cline, Catherine Ann. 'Ecumenism and Appeasement: The Bishops of the Church of England and the Treaty of Versailles', *The Journal of Modern History*, Vol. 61, No. 4 (Dec. 1989), 693–703.

Cohen, Richard I. 'The "Wandering Jew" from Medieval Legend to Modern Metaphor', *The Art of Being Jewish in Modern Times*, eds Barbara Kirshenblatt-Gimblett and Jonathan Karp, 147–75. University of Pennsylvania Press, 2008.

Cohen, Richard I. 'Jews and Christians in France during World War II: A Methodological Essay', 327–40, *Judaism and Christianity Under the Impact of National Socialism*, eds Otto Dov Kulka and Paul R. Mendes-Flohr. Jerusalem: Historical Society of Israel and the Zalman Shazar Center for Jewish History, 1987.

Cole, Tim. *Traces of the Holocaust: Journeying in and out of the Ghettos*. London, New York: Continuum, 2011.

Confino, Alon. *A World Without Jews: The Nazi Imagination from Persecution to Genocide*. New Haven: Yale University Press, 2014.

Connelly, John. *From Enemy to Brother: The Revolution in Catholic Teaching on the Jews, 1933–1965*. Cambridge: Harvard University Press, 2012.

Conway, J.S. 'How Shall the Nations Repent? The Stuttgart Declaration of Guilt, October 1945', *Journal of Ecclesiastical History*, Vol. 38, No. 4 (October 1987), 596–622.

Conway, J.S. 'Protestant Missions to the Jews, 1810–1980: Ecclesiastical Imperialism or Theological Aberration', *Holocaust and Genocide Studies*, 1:1 (1986), 127–46.

Conway, J.S. *The Nazi Persecution of the Churches: 1933–45*. Toronto: Ryerson Press, 1968.

Crane, Richard Francis. *Passion of Israel: Jacques Maritain, Catholic Conscience, and the Holocaust*. Scranton: University of Scranton Press, 2010.

David, Joel. 'Rebuilding the Soul: Churches and Religion in Bavaria, 1945–1960'. PhD, University of Missouri at Columbia, 2007.

Davies, Alan, ed. *Anti-Semitism and the Foundations of Christianity*. New York: Paulist Press, 1979.

Daughrity, Dyron. *Bishop Stephen Neill: From Edinburgh to South India*. London: Peter Lang, 2008.

Dequeker, Luc. 'Baptism and Conversion in Belgium, 1939–1945', *Belgium and the Holocaust: Jews, Belgians and Germans*, ed. Dan Michman, 235–78. Jerusalem: Yad Vashem, 1998.

Dietrich, Donald J., ed. *Christian Responses to the Holocaust: Moral and Ethical Issues*. Syracuse: Syracuse University Press, 2003.

Dietrich, Donald J. *God and Humanity in Auschwitz: Jewish-Christian Relations and Sanctioned Murder*. New Brunswick: Transaction Publishers, 1995.

Dinnerstein, Leonard. *America and the Survivors of the Holocaust*. New York: Columbia University Press, 1982.

Doerries, Reinhard, and Gerhard Weinberg. *Hitler's Intelligence Chief: Walter Schellenberg*. New York: Enigma Books, 2009.

Ehrenreich, R.M., and Tim Cole. 'The Perpetrator–Bystander–Victim Constellation: Rethinking Genocidal Relations', *Human Organization*, 64:3 (2005), 213–24.

Endelman, Todd M. *Leaving the Jewish Fold: Conversion and Radical Assimilation in Modern Jewish History*. Princeton University Press, 2015.

Endelman, Todd M. 'Comparative Perspectives on Modern Anti-Semitism in the West', *History and Hate: The Dimensions of Anti-Semitism*, ed. David Berger, 95–114. The Jewish Publication Society, 1986.

Enstad, Johannes D. 'Prayers and Patriotism in Nazi-Occupied Russia: The Pskov Orthodox Mission and Religious Revival, 1941–1944', *Slavonic and East European Review*, 94:3 (2016), 468–96.

Ericksen, Robert P. 'Resistance or Complicity? Balancing Assessments of German Churches under Nazism', *Kirchliche Zeitgeschichte*, 26:2 (2015), 246–71.

Ericksen, Robert P. *Complicity in the Holocaust: Churches and Universities in Nazi Germany*. Cambridge: Cambridge University Press, 2012.

Ericksen, Robert P. *Theologians Under Hitler: Gerhard Kittel, Paul Althaus, and Emanuel Hirsch*. New Haven and London: Yale University Press, 1985.

Ericksen, Robert P., and Susannah Heschel. 'The German Churches and the Holocaust', *The Historiography of the Holocaust*, ed. Dan Stone. New York: Palgrave Macmillan, 2004, 296–318.

Ericksen, Robert P., and Susannah Heschel. *German Churches and the Holocaust: Betrayal*. Minneapolis: Fortress Press, 1999.

Ericksen, Robert P., and Susannah Heschel. 'The German Churches Face Hitler: Assessment of the Historiography', *Tel Aviver Jahrbuch für deutsche Geschichte* XXIII (1994), 433–59.

Ettinger, Shmuel. 'The Secular Roots of Modern Antisemitism', *Judaism and Christianity Under National Socialism*. Jerusalem: Historical Society of Israel, 1987, 37–61.

Favez, Jean-Claude. *The Red Cross and the Holocaust*, ed. and trans. John and Beryl Fletcher. Cambridge: Cambridge University Press, 1999.

Feferman, Kiril. 'Save Your Souls: Jewish Conversion and Survival in the Occupied Soviet Territories during the Holocaust', *Modern Judaism*, 39:2, 184–204.

Fein, Helen. *Accounting for Genocide: National Responses and Jewish Victimization during the Holocaust*. Chicago: University of Chicago Press, 1979.
Fleishner, Eva, ed. *Auschwitz: Beginning of a New Era? Reflections on the Holocaust*. New York: KTAV Publishing House, Cathedral Church of St John the Divine, Anti-Defamation League of B'nai B'rith, 1977.
Fogu, Claudio, Wulf Kansteiner and Todd Presner, eds. *Probing the Ethics of Holocaust Culture*. Cambridge, MA: Harvard University Press, 2016.
Friedländer, Saul. *Nazi Germany and the Jews, 1939–1945: The Years of Extermination*. New York. Harper Collins, 2007.
Friedländer, Saul. *Nazi Germany and the Jews: The Years of Persecution, 1933–1939*. New York: Harper Perennial, 1997.
Friedländer, Saul, ed. *Probing the Limits of Representation: Nazism and the 'Final Solution'*. Cambridge, MA: Harvard University Press, 1992.
Friedländer, Saul. *Kurt Gerstein: The Ambiguity of Good*. New York: Knopf, 1969.
Füllenbach, Elias. 'Shock, Renewal, Crisis: Catholic Reflections on the Shoah', *Antisemitism, Christian Ambivalence, and the Holocaust*, ed. Kevin P. Spicer, 201–34. Bloomington: Indiana University Press, 2007.
Garrard, Eva, and Geoffrey Scarre, eds. *Moral Philosophy and the Holocaust*. Farnham: Ashgate Publishing, 2003.
Geras, Norman. *The Contract of Mutual Indifference: Political Philosophy after the Holocaust*, new edn. Manchester: Manchester University Press, 2020.
Gerdmar, Anders. *Roots of Theological Anti-Semitism: German Biblical Interpretation and the Jews, from Herder and Semler to Kittel and Bultmann*. Leiden: Brill, 2009.
Gerlach, Wolfgang. *And the Witnesses Were Silent: The Confessing Church and the Persecution of the Jews*, trans. Victoria Barnett. Lincoln: University of Nebraska Press, 2000.
Grayzel, Solomon. 'Review of *The Church and the Jewish People* by Goete Hedenquist', *Jewish Quarterly Review*, 46:1 (1955), 72–8.
Grieve, Hermann. 'Between Christian Anti-Judaism and National Socialist Antisemitism: The Case of German Catholicism', *Judaism and Christianity Under the Impact of National Socialism*, eds. Otto Dov Kulka and Paul Mendes-Flohr, 169–79. Jerusalem: Historical Society of Israel and Zalman Shazar Center for Jewish History, 1987.
Grochowina, Sylwia, and Katarzyna Kącka. 'Foundations of Nazi Cultural Policy and Institutions Responsible for its Implementation in the Period 1933–1939', *Kultura i Edukacja*, 6 (2014), 173–92.
Gutman, Israel. *Resistance: The Warsaw Ghetto Uprising*. Boston, New York: Houghton Mifflin, 1994.

Gutteridge, Richard. *Open Thy Mouth for the Dumb: The German Evangelical Church and the Jews, 1879–1950*. Oxford: Basil Blackwell, 1976.
Guttstadt, Cory, Thomas Lutz, Bernd Rother and Yessica San Román, eds. *Bystanders, Rescuers or Perpetrators? The Neutral Countries and the Shoah*. Berlin: Metropol, 2016.
Haberman, F.W., ed. *Nobel Lectures, Peace 1926–1950*. Amsterdam: Elsevier, 1972.
Hanebrink, Paul A. *In Defense of Christian Hungary: Religion, Nationalism and Antisemitism, 1890–1944*. Ithaca: Cornell University Press, 2006.
Hardyman, J.T. *Two Minutes from Sloane Square: A Brief History of the Conference of Missionary Societies in Great Britain and Ireland, 1912–1977*. London: CMS, 1977.
Hassing, Arne. 'The Churches of Norway and the Jews, 1933–1945', *Journal of Ecumenical Studies*, 26:3 (1989), 496–522.
Hastings, Derek. *Catholicism and the Roots of Nazism: Religious Identity and National Socialism*. Oxford, New York: Oxford University Press, 2010.
Hayes, Peter. *Why? Explaining the Holocaust*. New York, London: W.W. Norton, 2017.
Hayes, Peter, and John K. Roth, eds. *The Oxford Handbook of Holocaust Studies*. Oxford: Oxford University Press, 2010.
Haynes, Stephen R. *Reluctant Witnesses: Jews and the Christian Imagination*. Louisville: Westminster John Knox Press, 1995.
Herczl, Moshe Y. *Christianity and the Holocaust of Hungarian Jewry*, trans. Joel Lerner. New York: New York University Press, 1993.
Heschel, Susannah. *The Aryan Jesus: Christian Theologians and the Bible in Nazi Germany*. Princeton: Princeton University Press, 2008.
Heschel, Susannah. *Abraham Geiger and the Jewish Jesus*. Chicago: University of Chicago Press, 1998.
Hilberg, Raul. *The Destruction of the European Jews*, Vols 1–3, 3rd edn. New Haven: Yale University Press, 2003.
Hilberg, Raul. *Perpetrators, Victims, Bystanders: The Jewish Catastrophe, 1933–1945*. London: Lime Tree, 1993.
Hochhuth, Rolf. *The Deputy*. New York: Grove Press, 1964.
Hockenos, Matthew D. 'The German Protestant Church and its Judenmission, 1945–1950', *Antisemitism, Christian Ambivalence, and the Holocaust*, ed. Kevin P. Spicer, 173–200. Bloomington: Indiana University Press, 2007.
Hockenos, Matthew D. *A Church Divided: German Protestants Confront the Nazi Past*. Bloomington: Indiana University Press, 2004.
Hogg, William Richey. *Ecumenical Foundations: A History of the International Missionary Council and its Nineteenth Century Background*. New York: Harper and Brothers, 1952.

Isaac, Jules. *Jesus and Israel: A Call for the Necessary Correction of Christian Teaching on the Jews*, trans. Sally Gran, ed. Claire Huchet Bishop. New York: Holt, Rinehart & Winston, 1971.
Isaac, Jules. *The Teaching of Contempt: Christian Roots of Anti-Semitism*, trans. Helen Weaver. New York: McGraw-Hill Book Company, 1965.
Jackson, Eleanor M. *Red Tape and the Gospel: A Study of the Significance of the Ecumenical Missionary Struggle of William Paton, 1880–1943*. Birmingham: Phlogiston Publishing in association with Selly Oak Colleges, 1980.
Jasper, R.C.D. *George Bell: Bishop of Chichester*. London: Oxford University Press, 1967.
Jehle-Wildberger, Marianne. *Adolf Keller: Ecumenist, World Citizen, Philanthropist*, trans. Mark Kyburz with John Peck. Eugene, Oregon: Cascade Books, 2013.
Junginger, Horst. *The Scientification of the 'Jewish Question' in Nazi Germany*. Leiden and Boston: Brill, 2017.
Kampe, Norbert. 'Jews and Antisemites at Universities in Imperial Germany, The Friedrich-Wilhelms-Universität of Berlin: A Case Study on the Students' Jewish Question', *Leo Baeck Institute Year Book XXXII*, 1987, 43–101.
Kapiszewski, Andrzej. 'Controversial Reports on the Situation of Jews in Poland in the Aftermath of World War One', *Studia Judaica*, 7:2 (2004), 257–304.
Karp, Jonathan, and Adam Sutcliffe. *Philosemitism in History*. Cambridge: Cambridge University Press, 2011.
Katz, Steven T. *The Holocaust in Historical Context: The Holocaust and Mass Death before the Modern Age*. New York: Oxford University Press, 1994.
Kershaw, Ian. *Hitler: 1936–1945 Nemesis*. New York and London: W.W. Norton & Co., 2001.
Kershaw, Ian. *The Nazi Dictatorship: Problems and Perspectives of Interpretation*, 3rd ed. London, New York: Edward Arnold, 1993.
Kershaw, Ian. 'The Churches and the Nazi Persecution of the Jews', *Yad Vashem Studies XIX* (1988), 427–37.
Kertzer, David I. *The Pope at War: The Secret History of Pius XII, Mussolini, and Hitler*. New York: Random House, 2022.
Kinnamon, Michael. *Unity as Prophetic Witness: W.A. Visser 't Hooft and the Shaping of Ecumenical Theology*. Minneapolis: Fortress Press, 2017.
Kirby, Diane. 'The Church of England and Religions Division during the Second World War: the Church–State Relations and the Anglo-Soviet Alliance', *Journal of International History*, 4 (2000).
Klemperer, Klemens von. *German Resistance Against Hitler: The Search for Allies Abroad, 1933–1945*. Oxford: Clarendon Press, 1992.

Koblik, Steven. *The Stones Cry Out: Sweden's Response to the Persecution of the Jews, 1933–1945*. New York: Holocaust Library, 1988.
Kraut, Benny. 'Toward the Establishment of the National Conference of Christians and Jews: The Tenuous Road to Religious Goodwill in the 1920s', *American Jewish History*, 77:3 (1988), 388–412.
Kulka, Otto Dov. 'Popular Christian Attitudes in the Third Reich to National Socialist Policies Towards the Jews', *Judaism and Christianity Under the Impact of National Socialism*, 251–67. Jerusalem: Historical Society of Israel, 1987.
Kushner, Tony. *Anglo-Jewry Since 1066: Place, Locality and Memory*. Manchester: Manchester University Press, 2012.
Kushner, Tony. 'Britain, the United States and the Holocaust: In Search of a Historiography', *The Historiography of the Holocaust*, ed. Dan Stone, 253–275. Hampshire and New York: Palgrave Macmillan, 2004.
Kushner, Tony. 'Pissing in the Wind?: The Search for Nuance in the Study of Holocaust Bystanders', *Bystanders to the Holocaust: A Re-evaluation*, eds David Cesarani and Paul Levine, 55–76. London and Portland: Frank Cass Publishers, 2002.
Kushner, Tony. 'The Meaning of Auschwitz: Anglo-American Responses to the Hungarian Jewish Tragedy', *Genocide and Rescue: The Holocaust in Hungary 1944*, ed. David Cesarani, 159–78. London: Berg Publishers, 1997.
Kushner, Tony. *The Holocaust and the Liberal Imagination: A Social and Cultural History*. Oxford: Blackwell Publishing, 1994.
Kushner, Tony. 'Different Worlds: British Perceptions of the Final Solution During the Second World War', *The Final Solution: Origins and Implementation*, ed. D. Cesarani, 246–67. London: Routledge, 1994.
Kushner, Tony. 'James Parkes, the Jews and Conversionism: A Model for Multi-cultural Britain?', *Studies in Church History*, 29 (1992), 451–61.
Kushner, Tony. 'Ambivalence or Antisemitism?: Christian Attitudes and Responses in Britain to the Crisis of European Jewry During the Second World War', *HGS*, 5:2 (1990), 175–89.
Kushner, Tony. *The Persistence of Prejudice: Antisemitism in British Society During the Second World War*. Manchester: Manchester University Press, 1989.
Lang, Berel. *Post-Holocaust: Interpretation, Misinterpretation and the Claims of History*. Bloomington and Indianapolis: Indiana University Press, 2005.
Langmuir, Gavin I. *Toward A Definition of Antisemitism*. Berkeley: University of California Press, 1990.
Langmuir, Gavin I. *History, Religion and Antisemitism*. Berkeley: University of California Press, 1990.
Laqueur, Walter. *The Terrible Secret: Suppression of the Truth about Hitler's 'Final Solution'*. London: Weidenfeld & Nicolson, 1980.

Laqueur, Walter, and Richard Breitman, *Breaking the Silence*. New York: Simon & Schuster, 1986.
Lausten, Martin S. *Jews and Christians in Denmark: From the Middle Ages to Recent Times, 1100–1948*. Leiden: Brill, 2015.
Lawson, Tom. *Debates on the Holocaust*. Manchester: Manchester University Press, 2010.
Lawson, Tom. 'Shaping the Holocaust: The Influence of Christian Discourse on Perceptions of the European Jewish Tragedy', *HGS*, 21:3 (2007), 404–20.
Lawson, Tom. *The Church of England and the Holocaust: Christianity, Memory and Nazism*. Woodbridge: Boydell Press, 2006.
Lawson, Tom. 'Constructing a Christian History of Nazism: Anglicanism and the Memory of the Holocaust, 1945–1949', *History and Memory*, 16:1 (2004), 146–76.
Lawson, Tom. 'The Anglican Understanding of Nazism 1933–1945: Placing the Church of England's Response to the Holocaust in Context', *Twentieth Century British History*, 14:2 (2003), 112–37.
Leustean, Lucian N. *The Ecumenical Movement and the Making of the European Community*. Oxford: Oxford University Press, 2014.
Levenson, Alan T. *Between Philosemitism and Antisemitism: Defenses of Jews and Judaism in Germany, 1871–1932*. Lincoln: University of Nebraska Press, 2004.
Libionka, Dariusz. 'Antisemitism, Anti-Judaism, and the Polish Catholic Clergy during the Second World War, 1939–1945', *Antisemitism and Its Opponents in Modern Poland*, ed. Robert Blobaum, 233–64. Ithaca: Cornell University Press, 2005.
Lipstadt, Deborah. *Beyond Belief: The American Press and the Coming of the Holocaust, 1933–1945*. New York: Touchstone, 1986.
London, Louise. *Whitehall and the Jews, 1933–1948*. Cambridge: Cambridge University Press, 2000.
Longerich, Peter. *Wannsee: The Road to the Final Solution*, trans. Lesley Sharpe and Jeremy Noakes. Oxford: Oxford University Press, 2021.
Longerich, Peter. *Holocaust: The Nazi Persecution and Murder of the Jews*, trans. Shaun Whiteside. Oxford: Oxford University Press, 2010.
Ludlow, Peter W. 'The International Protestant Community in the Second World War', *Journal of Ecclesiastical History*, 29:3 (1978), 311–62.
Ludlow, Peter W. 'The Refugee Problem in the 1930s: The Failures and Successes of Protestant Relief Programmes', *English Historical Review*, 90 (1975), 564–603.
Ludwig, Hartmut. 'Christians Cannot Remain Silent About This Crime: On the Centenary of the Birth of Adolf Freudenberg', *Ecumenical Review*, Vol. 46, No. 4 (1994), 475–85.

Madras, Ronald. *The Catholic Church and Antisemitism: Poland, 1933–1939*. London and New York: Routledge for Vidal Sassoon International Center for the Study of Antisemitism, 1994.

Marcus, Harold. *Legacies of Dachau: The Uses and Abuses of a Concentration Camp, 1933–2001*. Cambridge: Cambridge University Press, 2001.

Marrus, Michael R. 'Holocaust Bystanders and Humanitarian Intervention', *Holocaust Studies: A Journal of Culture and History*, 13:1 (2007), 1–18.

Marrus, Michael R., ed. *The Nazi Holocaust, Part 8: Bystanders to the Holocaust*, Vols 1–3. London, Westport, CT: Meckler Ltd, 1989.

Marrus, Michael R. *The Holocaust in History*. Hanover: New England University Press, 1987.

Marrus. Michael R., and Robert O. Paxton. *Vichy France and the Jews*. Stanford: Stanford University Press, 1995; 2nd edn, 2019.

Mauriello, Christopher E. *Forced Confrontation: The Politics of Dead Bodies in Germany at the End of World War II*. Lanham: Lexington Books, 2016.

May, Larry, and Stacey Hoffman. *Collective Responsibility: Five Decades of Debate in Theoretical and Applied Ethics*. London, Boulder and New York: Rowman & Littlefield, 1991.

Mazzenga, Maria, ed. *American Religious Responses to Kristallnacht*. New York: Palgrave Macmillan, 2009.

Michman, Dan. *Holocaust Historiography Between 1990 to 2021 in Contexts: New Insights, Perceptions, Understanding and Avenues, An Overview and Analysis*. Jerusalem: Yad Vashem, 2022.

Michman, Dan. 'The Jews as a Problem for Modern European Political Logic', *Confronting Antisemitism in Modern Media, the Legal and Political Worlds*, Vol. 5, eds Armin Lange, Kerstin Mayerhofer, Dina Porat and Lawrence H. Schiffmann, 27–43. Berlin: De Gruyter, 2021.

Michman, Dan, ed. *Hiding, Sheltering and Borrowing Identities: Avenues of Rescue During the Holocaust*. Jerusalem: Yad Vashem, 2017.

Michman, Dan. 'Misunderstanding of the Phenomenon of Antisemitism in Some Recent Influential Studies on the Holocaust', *The ISGAP Papers: Antisemitism in Comparative Perspective*, Vol. 2, ed. Charles Asher Small, 235–44. CreateSpace: ISGAP, 2016.

Michman, Dan. *Holocaust Historiography: A Jewish Perspective. Conceptualizations, Terminology, Approaches and Fundamental Issues*. London: Vallentine Mitchell, 2003.

Morgenstern, Matthias, and Alon Segev. *Gerhard Kittels 'Verteidigung': Gerhard Kittel's 'Defense'*. Weisbaden: Berlin University Press, 2019.

Morina, Christina, and Krijn Thijs, eds. *Probing the Limits of Categorization: The Bystander in Holocaust History*. New York, Oxford: Berghahn, 2019.

Nawyn, William. *American Protestantism's Response to Germany's Jews and Refugees, 1933–1941.* Ann Arbor: UMI Research Press, 1981.
Nelson, Burton F. '1934: Pivotal Year of the Church Struggle', *HGS*, 4:3 (1989), 283–97.
Nirenberg, David. *Anti-Judaism: The Western Tradition.* New York: W.W. Norton, 2013.
Paldiel, Mordecai. *Churches and the Holocaust: Unholy Teaching, Good Samaritans and Reconciliation.* New York: Ktav Publishing, 2006.
Pammer, Thomas, ed. *Hoffnungsort Seegasse 16: Hilfaktionen der Schwedischen Israelmission im Nationalsozialismus.* Vienna: Mandelbaum, 2015.
Papen, Patricia von. 'Scholarly Antisemitism During the Third Reich: The Reichsinstitut's Research on the "Jewish Question", 1939-1945'. PhD, Columbia University, 1999.
Paulovicova, Nina. 'Rescue of Jews in the Slovak State, 1939–1945'. PhD, University of Alberta, 2012.
Pawlikowski, John T. 'Historical Memory and Christian–Jewish Relations', *Christ Jesus and the Jewish People Today: New Explorations of Theological Interrelationships,* eds Philip Cunningham, Joseph Sievers, Mary Boys, Hans Hermann Henrix and Jesper Svartvik, 14–30. Grand Rapids: William B. Erdmans, 2011.
Pawlikowski, John T. 'The Church and Judaism: The Thought of James Parkes', *Journal of Ecumenical Studies,* 6:4 (1969).
Pearce, William D. 'The Romanian Orthodox Church during World War II', PhD, University of California Riverside, 2014.
Penkower, Monty N. 'The Bermuda Conference and Its Aftermath: An Allied Quest for "Refuge" during the Holocaust', *The Nazi Holocaust: Bystanders to the Holocaust,* Part 8, Vol. 1, ed. Michael Marrus, 413–31. Berlin: De Gruyter Saur, 1989.
Penkower, Monty N. 'The World Jewish Congress Confronts the International Red Cross during the Holocaust', *Jewish Social Studies,* 41:3/4 (1979), 229–56.
Phayer, Michael. *The Catholic Church and the Holocaust, 1930–1965.* Bloomington: Indiana University Press, 2000.
Pierard, R.V. 'John R. Mott and the Rift in the Ecumenical Movement During World War I', *Journal of Ecumenical Studies* 23/4 (1986), 601–20.
Pierard, R.V. 'Julius Richter and the Scientific Study of Christian Missions in Germany', *Missiology* (1978), 485–506.
Popa, Ion. *The Romanian Orthodox Church and the Holocaust.* Bloomington: Indiana University Press, 2017.
Pulzer, P.G.J. *The Rise of Political Anti-Semitism in Germany and Austria,* 2nd edn. Cambridge: Harvard University Press, 1988.

Rendtorff, Rolf. 'The Effect of the Holocaust on Christian Mission to Jews', SIDIC, XIV:1, 1981.
Reuther, Rosemary Radford. *Faith and Fratricide: The Theological Roots of Anti-Semitism*. Minneapolis: Seabury Press, 1974.
Richmond, Colin. *Campaigner Against Antisemitism: The Reverend James Parkes, 1896–1981*. London: Vallentine Mitchell, 2005.
Rose, Paul Lawrence. *German Question/Jewish Question: Revolutionary Antisemitism in Germany from Kant to Wagner*. Princeton: Princeton University Press, 1990.
Ross, Robert. 'Perverse Witness to the Holocaust: Christian Missions and Missionaries', *Holocaust Studies Annual II* (1986), 126–39.
Ross, Robert. *So It Was True: The American Protestant Press and the Nazi Persecution of the Jews*. Minneapolis: University of Minnesota Press, 1980.
Roth, John K. *Ethics During and After the Holocaust: In the Shadow of Birkenau*. New York: Palgrave Macmillan, 2005.
Rutishauser, Christian. 'The 1947 Seelisberg Conference: The Foundation of the Jewish-Christian Dialogue', *Studies in Christian–Jewish Relations*, Vol. 2, No. 2 (2007), 34–53.
Sadkowski, Konrad. 'Clerical Nationalism and Antisemitism: Catholic Priests, Jews, and Orthodox Christians in the Lublin Region, 1918–1939', *Antisemitism and Its Opponents in Modern Poland*, ed. Robert Blobaum. Ithaca: Cornell University Press, 2005, 171–88.
Sandoz, Yves. 'Max Huber and the Red Cross', *European Journal of International Law*, 18:1 (2007), 171–97.
Saperstein, Marc. 'A Jewish Response to John T. Pawlikowski and Mary C. Boys', *Christ Jesus and the Jewish People Today: New Explorations of Theological Interrelationships*, eds Philip Cunningham, Joseph Sievers, Mary Boys, Hans Hermann Henrix and Jesper Svartvik, 64–76. Wm. B. Eerdmans Publishing Co., 2011.
Saperstein, Marc. 'Christian Doctrine and the Final Solution: The State of the Question', *Remembering for the Future: The Holocaust in an Age of Genocide*, ed. John K. Roth, 814–41. London: Palgrave, 2001.
Schleunes, Karl A., ed. *Legislating the Holocaust: The Bernard Loesener Memoirs and Supporting Documents*. Boulder: Westview Press, 2001.
Schleunes, Karl A. *The Twisted Road to Auschwitz: Nazi Policy Toward German Jews*. Urbana and Chicago: University of Illinois Press, 1970, 1990.
Schmidt, William J. *Architect of Unity: A Biography of Samuel McCrea Cavert*. New York: Friendship Press, 1978.
Schmidt, William J., and Edward Ouellete. *What Kind of Man?: The Life of Henry Smith Leiper*. New York: Friendship Press, 1986.

Schmuhl, Hans-Walter. *The Kaiser Wilhelm Institute for Anthropology, Human Heritage and Eugenics*. New York: Springer Publishing, 2008.
Scholder, Klaus. *A Requiem for Hitler and Other New Perspectives on the German Church Struggle*. London: SCM Press, 1989.
Scholder, Klaus. *The Churches and the Third Reich, Vol. 1, 1918–1934*, trans. John Bowden. Philadelphia: Fortress Press, 1988.
Scholder, Klaus. *The Churches and the Third Reich, Vol. 2, The Year of Disillusionment, 1934 Barmen and Rome*, trans. John Bowden. Philadelphia: Fortress Press, 1988.
Shain, Milton. *A Perfect Storm: Antisemitism in South Africa, 1930–1948*. Cape Town, Johannesburg: Jonathan Ball Publishers, 2015.
Sittser, Gerald L. *A Cautious Patriotism: American Churches and the Second World War*. Chapel Hill: University of North Carolina Press, 1997.
Spicer, Kevin P. *Hitler's Priests: Catholic Clergy and National Socialism*. DeKalb: Northern Illinois University Press, 2008.
Spicer, Kevin P., ed. *Antisemitism, Christian Ambivalence, and the Holocaust*. Bloomington: Indiana University Press, 2007.
Steigmann-Gall, Richard. 'Old Wine in New Bottles', *Antisemitism, Christian Ambivalence, and the Holocaust*, ed. Kevin P. Spicer. Bloomington: Indiana University Press, 2007.
Steigmann-Gall, Richard. *The Holy Reich: Nazi Conceptions of Christianity, 1919–1945*. Cambridge, Mass.: Cambridge University Press, 2003.
Stein, Leon. 'Christians as Holocaust Scholars', *Problems Unique to the Holocaust*, Harry James Cargas, ed. University Press of Kentucky, 1990.
Steinweis, Alan. *Kristallnacht 1938*. Cambridge, MA: Belknap, 2009.
Steinweis, Alan. *Studying the Jew: Scholarly Antisemitism in Nazi Germany*. Cambridge, MA: Harvard University Press, 2006.
Stone, Dan. *The Liberation of the Camps: The End of the Holocaust and Its Aftermath*. New Haven and London: Yale University Press, 2015.
Stone, Dan, ed. *The Holocaust and Historical Methodology*. Oxford and New York: Berghahn Books, 2014.
Stone, Dan., ed. *The Historiography of the Holocaust*. London: Palgrave Macmillan, 2004.
Stone, Dan. 'The Domestication of Violence: Forging a Collective Memory of the Holocaust in Britain', *Patterns of Prejudice*, Vol. 33, No. 2 (1999), 13–29.
Steuer, Kenneth. *Pursuit of an 'Unparalleled Opportunity': The YMCA and Prisoner of War Diplomacy Among Central Power Nations During World War I, 1914–1923*. Columbia University Press, 2008.
Tal, Uriel. 'Modern Lutheranism and the Jews', *Religion, Politics and Ideology in the Third Reich*, 191–203. New York: Routledge.
Tal, Uriel. 'Aspects of Consecration of Politics in the Nazi Era', *Judaism and Christianity Under the Impact of National Socialism*, eds Otto Dov

Kulka and Paul R. Mendes-Flohr. Jerusalem: Historical Society of Israel and Zalman Shazar Center for Jewish History, 1987.

Tal, Uriel. *Christians and Jews in Germany: Religion, Politics, and Ideology in the Second Reich, 1870–1914*, trans. Noah Jonathan Jacobs. Cornell University Press, 1975.

Tal, Uriel. 'Liberal Protestantism and the Jews in the Second Reich, 1870–1914', *Jewish Social Studies*, Vol. 26, No. 1 (Jan. 1964), 23–41.

Ten Cate, Johannes H. 'The Enlargement of the Circle of Perpetrators of the Holocaust', *Jewish Political Studies Review*, 20:3/4 (2008), 51–72.

Toury, Jacob. 'The Jewish Question: A Semantic Approach', *Leo Baeck Institute Year Book XI* (1966), 85–106.

Valman, Nadia, and Tony Kushner, eds. *Philosemitism, Antisemitism and the Jews: Perspectives from the Middle Ages to the Twentieth Century*. Hampshire: Ashgate Publishing Ltd, 2004.

Volkov, Shulamit. 'Antisemitism as a Cultural Code: Reflections on the History and Historiography of Antisemitism in Imperial Germany', *Leo Baeck Institute Year Book XXII* (1978), 25–46.

Weinreich, Max. *Hitler's Professors: The Part of Scholarship in Germany's Crimes Against the Jewish People*. New York: Yiddish Scientific Institute, 1946.

Wistrich, Robert S. *Antisemitism, the Longest Hatred*. New York: Pantheon Books, 1991.

Wyman, David S. *Abandonment of the Jews: America and the Holocaust, 1941–1945*. New York: Pantheon Books, 1984.

Yates, Timothy. *Christian Mission in the Twentieth Century*. Cambridge University Press, 1996.

Zasloff, Tela. *A Rescuer's Story: Pastor Pierre-Charles Toureille in Vichy*. Madison: University of Wisconsin Press, 2004.

Zeilstra, Jurjen A. *Visser 't Hooft, 1900–1985: Living for the Unity of the Church*. Amsterdam University Press, 2020.

Zeilstra, Jurjen A. *European Unity in Ecumenical Thinking, 1937–1948*. Zoetermeer: Uitgeverij Boekencentrum, 1995.

Zimmermann, Moshe. *Wilhelm Marr: The Patriarch of Anti-Semitism*. New York: Oxford University Press, 1986.

Index

Note: 'n.' after page reference indicates number of a note on that page.
Page numbers in *italic* refer to illustrations.

Adversus Judaeos 5
Althaus, Paul 228
American Christian Committee for German Refugees 100
American Jewish Committee (AJC) 40, 264n.84
Ammundsen, Bishop Valdemar 69, 89–92, 104, 111n.80, 112n.83, 112n.85, 120, 130, 137
Anschluss 133–4, *134*, 143, 145, 196, 199, 234
Anthony, A.W. 39–42, 62n.48
anti-Judaism 2–3, 4–5, 8, 25–31, 45–6, 49–54, 57, 77–85, 97–9, 105, 133, 135, 156n.12, 167–70, 172–3, 195–6, 204–5, 237–8, 241–3, 246, 273–7, 296n.47
  see also antisemitism; conversion; evangelisation; Jewish influence; Jewish mentalities and traits; Jewish problem; Jewish provocations; Jewry; Judaism; persecutions
antisemitism 2, 8–9, 18–19, 22n.32, 27, 30–1, 43–6, 50–9, 63n.60, 67–71, 77–83, 93–8, 100–6, 109n.49, 116–23, 124–30, 135–8, 144, 155n.7, 157n.24, 157n.27, 159n.57, 166, 170–1, 183, 186, 188–9, 191–3, 197–9, 202–5, 230, 233–4, 237–8, 240–3, 250–1, 254–5, 268.n169, 270, 273–4, 277–9, 282, 285, 291, 296n.47, 296n.48
  and vicious circle 24, 79, 80–1, 97, 275–6
  see also anti-Judaism; Final Solution; Holocaust; Jewish influence; Jewish mentalities and traits; Jewish problem; Jewish provocations; Nazi campaigns; Nazi ideology; racial antisemitism; racial-identity theory
Arbuthnot, Charles 248, 252
Ariel, Yaakov 22n.32, 157n.27
Aryan laws 7, 69, 70, 75, 77, 85–6, 89–90, 93, 98–102, 105, 114n.121, 133, 135, 137, 153, 275, 281
  see also baptism; non-Aryan Christians; refugees

Aschheim, Steven 276
Asmussen, Hans 111n.80, 132, 223, 229–30, 232–3, 259n.9
Association of Jewish Orthodox Communities 41
atheism 25, 27, 47, 51, 54, 57, 70, 78, 80–1, 88, 98, 275
  see also Bolshevism; communism; Marxism; secularism
Aumônerie des étrangers protestants en France 183, 195
Auschwitz 193, 195
Auschwitz Protocols 192, 194, 213n.103, 214n.107, 217n.152, 283

Baeck, Rabbi Leo 291n.6
Baines, Canon Henry 255
Baky, László 192
Balfour Declaration 26
baptism 7, 35, 98–100, 102, 133, 169, 249
  see also Aryan laws; conversion; evangelisation
Barnett, Victoria 21n.29, 62n.48
Baron, Lawrence 157n.27
Barot, Madeleine 183
Barth, Karl 91, 132, 146, 148–9, 177–8, 190, 209n.46, 214n.107, 218–19, 259n.4
Beeley, Harold 200, 216n.135
  see also ICCAJ; RIIA
Bell, Bishop George 68, 72–5, 85–6, 90, 103–4, 112n.83, 136, 138–41, 144–7, 151–2, 159n.61, 160n.79, 162n.102, 177, 191, 196, 208n.16, 208n.31, 221, 224–30 passim, 244, 261n.43, 262n.49
  see also UCCLW; WCCIF

benevolence 3, 19, 28, 38, 52, 59, 81, 83, 85, 97, 121, 173, 242, 271, 273–4, 277, 279, 286, 289, 290
Bennett, John 175
Bentwich, Norman 136
Bergen-Belsen 218
Bermuda Conference (1943) 189–91, 202–3
Bern Declaration (1926) 14–16, 21n.23
  see also Stockholm conference; UCCLW; war guilt; WCCIF
Bevan, Edwyn 109n.48, 169, 199
Boegner, Marc 103, 112n.83, 146–9, 160n.79, 175, 187, 194, 208n.31, 228, 291.n2
  see also FFPC; Godesberg Declaration; UCCLW; WCCIF
Bolshevism 25, 29, 47, 51, 70
Bonhoeffer, Dietrich 93, 110n.61, 111n.80, 112n.91, 114n.124, 259n.8
Boyens, Armin 280, 283, 285
Bracey, Bertha 140
Braham, Randolph 194, 213n.106
Brethren Council (Bruderrat) 225, 245, 246, 248, 249, 257
  see also DEK; EKD; WCC, founding statement on Jews
Brockway, Rev Allan 22n.33
Brown, William Adams 68, 71–2, 75, 87, 107n.14, 159n.61, 175, 177
Bryce Report 12, 21n.15
Buchenwald 218
Budapest–Warsaw conferences (1927) 27–32, 34, 38, 42, 49, 53, 56–8, 60n.9, 63n.55, 98–9, 124, 185, 199, 257–8, 275
  see also ICCAJ; IMC
Burckhardt, Carl 184, 188

Index

see also Huber; ECCO; ICRC; WCCIF Refugee Office

Cadman, Parkes 68, 75, 100–1
Campbell, Canon John McLeod 199, 204, 216n.145
Carter, Henry 170, 244
Cavert, Samuel 42, 68, 71–2, 75–6, 87, 158n.54, 159n.61, 187–8, 194, 228–9, 234
Central Conference of American Rabbis (CCAR) 38–40, 62n.44, 294n.42
Central Jewish Agency 182
Charles William Eliot Lectures 243
Christian Institute for Jewish Studies (CIJS) 197, 199, 201–2, 204–6
see also Gillet; ICCAJ; Kosmala; Paton
Church of Scotland 27, 33, 35, 168, 171, 188, 202
see also ICCAJ; Macanna; Smith; Webster
Clark, Christopher 8–9, 18–19, 22n.31, 26, 59n.3
Clinchy, Everett 41
Cockburn, Hutchinson 223, 226, 235, 244
Cohon, Rabbi Samuel 23n.35, 58, 83, 289, 294n.42
Comité Inter-Mouvements Auprès Des Évacués (Cimade) 183, 195, 211n.71
see also Barot; ECCO; WCCIF Refugee Office
Commission for Chaplaincy Service to Prisoners of War 143, 233
see also POW; War Prisoners Aid; WCCIF; YMCA
communism 27, 51, 70, 72, 78, 87, 88, 249

Conference of British Missionary Societies (CBMS) 26, 33, 60n.26, 61n.29, 86, 110n.55, 138
Confessing church 91–3, 103, 114n.124, 120, 131–2, 139, 144–5, 150, 152, 157n.22, 162n.98, 186, 220, 224, 229, 232, 252–3, 281
see also Brethren Council; DEK; *Deutsche Christen*; EKD; *Kirchenkampf*; Reich church; UCCLW; WCCIF
confessional theology 232, 286
see also Stuttgart Declaration; Visser 't Hooft
Confino, Alon 296n.47
Connelly, John 156n.12
Conning, John 41, 50–1, 53–5, 57, 65n.91, 65n.92
conversion 2–5, 7–9, 16–17, 19, 22n.32, 23n.33, 26–7, 29, 31–2, 38–42, 46–7, 52, 58, 62n.55, 78, 80, 82–3, 94, 98–9, 106, 109, 117, 119–21, 133, 135, 166, 169, 171, 173, 197, 201, 204, 240, 242–3, 258, 270–4, 276–7, 279, 286–90
and Jewish suffering 54, 101, 119–21, 133, 159n.65, 206, 241–3
see also anti-Judaism; baptism; evangelisation; rights
Conway, John 22n.32, 112n.92
Cooper, E.N. 170
Council of Christians and Jews (CCJ) 170, 197–9, 202, 204, 214n.117, 215n.131, 244–6
Craig, A.C. 221
Crossman, Richard 112n.85

deicide 4, 5, 45, 54, 242, 250, 291
see also anti-Judaism; guilt

Delitzschianum, Institutum Judaicum 33, 53, 118, 131, 134, 196, 199
Deutsche Christen 85–6, 88, 142n.85, 146, 252
  see also Confessing church; DEK; EKD; Godesberg Declaration; *Kirchenkampf*; Reich church; UCCLW; WCCIF
de Vere, Allan 256
Dibelius, Bishop Otto 103, 114n.124, 224–6, 228–9, 233, 252, 261n.46, 262n.59, 287
displaced persons (DPs) 239, 251
Don, A.C. 76
Dulles, Allen 224
Dun, Bishop Angus 247, 248, 251, 253, 254, 256

Ecclesia Militans 284
ecumenical context 9–11, 16–18
ecumenical movement *10*, 14, 16–7, 43, 69, 75, 87, 125, 130, 137–9, 143–4, 146–7, 150, 154, 173, 176–8, 181, 195, 221, 231–2, 235, 273, 284
ecumenical Protestant 2, 18, 31, 76, 148, 180, 230–2, 272
ecumenical term 17–18, 125, 128
ecumenical unity 10, 14–16, 55, 71, 76, 85, 89–90, 94, 125, 139, 143, 145, 147, 154, 174–5, 177–8, 218, 230, 232, 240, 280–2, 284, 287
ecumenism 11, 14, 16, 69, 125, 128, 145, 148, 150, 153, 174, 176–7, 179–80, 190, 219, 231, 281–2, 284
  see also supranationality; supraraciality; *Una Sancta*
Eden, Anthony 259n.8

Ehrenström, Nils 90–1, 152
Eidem, Archbishop Erling 160n.79
Emergency Committee of Christian Organisations (ECCO) 142, 174–5, 179–84, 187, 253
  see also Burckhardt; Huber; ICRC; Mackie; Visser 't Hooft; WCCIF Refugee Office
Emerson, Sir Herbert 139, 183, 189–90
emancipation (Jews) 25–6, 29, 31, 57, 99, 118, 172
  see also rights
Endelman, Todd 278, 292n.19
Endre, László 192
Ericksen, Robert 287
Eternal Jew 206, 290
European Central Bureau for Inter-Church Aid (ECB) 68, 181, 210n.61
European Student Relief (ESR) 36, 43–4, 211n.71
  see also Hoffmann; ISS; Parkes
euthanasia 220
Evangelical Church in Germany (EKD) 226–33, 254–6, 248–9, 250, 257, 261n.43, 266n.117
  see also Brethren Council; Confessing church; DEK; Stuttgart Declaration; WCC; WCCIF
evangelisation 2–3, 5, 9–10, 16, 25–31, 32–7, *37*, 38–43, 46–7, 48, 51–3, 55, 62n.44, 82–3, *84*, 94, 97–9, 109n.49, 131, *132*, 166–8, 171–2, 180, 195–7, 198–204, 205–6, 233–40, 241–3, 244, 246, 249, 252–4, 256, 258, 272, 274–5, 277–9, 286–7
and Jewish opposition 38–43, 62n.55, 82–3, 109n.49, 288–90, 294n.42

Index 331

and reparation 3, 28, 31, 233, 238, 240–1, 245–6, 248, 287, 289
  see also anti-Judaism; baptism; conversion; rights
Evian Conference (1938) 134, 135

Federal Council of Churches (FCC) 33, 38–42, 60n.28, 65n.92, 67–8, 75–6, 105–6, 107n.14, 130, 235
  Goodwill Committee 39–42, 62n.44, 62n.48
  see also Anthony; Cadman; Cavert; CCAR; Clinchy; Leiper; Macfarland
Fein, Helen 287
Final Solution 2, 17, 290
  see also Holocaust; Jewish problem; Nazi campaigns
Foreign Missions Conference of North America 41, 47
Forgács, Gyula 99
Freehof, Rabbi Solomon 58, 294n.42
Freeman, Kathleen 170
French Federation of Protestant Churches (FFPC) 13–14, 27, 72, 211n.71, 228, 241–4, 246–8, 253, 256–7
  see also Boegner; Maury; Stockholm conference; war guilt; WCC founding statement on Jews
French–German Armistice (1940) 183, 185
Freudenberg, Adolf 139, 140, 142, 185, 188, 191–2, 195, 209n.51, 214n.112, 223–4, 226, 227, 235, 264n.92
  see also WCCIF Refugee Office

Fricke, Otto 223–4, 247–8, 252–3, 264n.92, 268n.160
Füllenbach, Elias 156n.12

Garvie, A.E. 169, 179
Geras, Norman 288
Gerlach, Wolfgang 162n.105
German Evangelical Church (DEK) 11–16, 67–76, 85–94, 99, 102, 108n.30, 110n.62, 125, 144–53, 155n.2, 194, 218–22, 223–33, 281–2, 287
  see also Brethren Council; Confessing church; *Deutsche Christen*; EKD; *Kirchenkampf*; Reich church; UCCLW; war guilt; WCCIF
German Regulation of Name Changes Law (1938) 153, 164n.128
  see also antisemitism; Aryan laws; persecutions
Gerstein, Kurt 186
Gerstenmaier, Eugen 150, 223, 226, 228–9, 260n.22
Gestapo 133
Gill, C.H. 51, 140
Gillet, Lev 200, 202, 215n.134
Godesberg Declaration (1939) 146–54, 162n.105, 163n.120, 282
  see also Deutsche Christen; Heckel; Lutheran Bishop Statement; Reich church; WCCIF
Goebbels, Joseph 105
Goldstein, Rabbi Herbert 41, 294n.42
Golterman, W.F. 255
Grubb, Kenneth 131–2, 140, 155n.1, 158n.39, 252, 255, 268n.157
Grüber, Heinrich 140, 182, 159n.67

guilt 11–16, 54, 68–9, 108n.30, 113n.106, 120, 127–8, 218–33, 242, 245–7, 250–1, 257, 259n.9, 270, 280, 281–2, 286
  and reparation 233–40
  see also deicide; war guilt

Harling, Otto von 53–6, 118, 233
Hartenstein, Karl 253
Hauge, Reidar 229
Heckel, Bishop Theodor 93, 103, 110n.50, 112n.89, 112n.90, 112n.92, 114n.124, 144–5, 149–53
  see also Godesberg Declaration; Reich church; UCCLW; WCCIF
Hedenquist, Göte 160n.79, 234–5, 247, 252, 263n.65, 264n.86, 264n.92
Heering, G.J. 255–6
Heinemann, Gustav 233
Henriod, H.L. 46, 68–9, 71–3, 75, 87, 89, 101, 112n.83, 130, 132, 136–8, 140, 145, 158n.54, 159n.61, 210n.51
  see also UCCLW; WA
Herman, Stewart 224–6, 227, 228–9, 260n.25
Heschel, Susannah 266n.117
High Commission for Refugees (HCR) 3, 94, 99–101, 135–7, 139, 167, 182–3, 189–90
  see also Emerson; Kotschnig; Kullmann; McDonald
Himmler, Heinrich 95
Hitler, Adolf 2, 5, 8, 16, 19, 58–9, 67, 76–7, 80–3, 85, 87–8, 91, 94, 98, 120, 134, 139, 142, 162n.98, 199–200, 219, 225, 237, 241, 249, 253, 267n.129, 270, 275–6, 281, 283, 290

Hockenos, Matthew 266n.117
Hoffmann, Conrad 24, 36–8, 43, 46–7, 49, 52–3, 65n.92, 78–9, 79, 80–5, 84, 94–8, 99–103, 104–6, 114n.121, 117–18, 120, 129–30, 131, 133–5, 134, 138–43, 140, 148, 165–6, 179–80, 196, 198, 201–3, 217n.152, 233–40, 242–4, 247, 249–53, 257, 275–6, 279, 286–7
  see also ESR; ISS; ICCAJ; IMC; WCC; YMCA
Holocaust 6–8, 17–18, 116, 278, 287, 290
  bystanders xvi, 6–7, 8, 17, 21–22n.29, 278, 286–8, 290
  corpses xv, 186
  death marches xv–xvi, 218
  deportations 154, 182, 184–7, 192–4, 200, 211n.73
  exterminations 1, 7, 154, 166, 185–9, 191–2, 200–2, 216n.135, 217n.152, 222, 237–8, 240, 258, 270–2, 278, 283, 287–8, 292n.24
  ghettos 172, 184, 192, 200, 202, 204
  Hungarian Jewry 135, 191–5
  Jewish Reservation 154, 164n.131, 182–5, 200
  perpetrators 6, 288
  survivors 204, 233, 238, 239, 242–3, 250, 255
  victims 6–7, 100–1, 122, 136, 166, 222, 285, 288
Home Missions Council (HMC) 33, 41, 56, 57, 60n.28, 65n.91, 65n.92, 91
Horton, Walter 126, 128, 158n.54, 235
Huber, Max 143, 180–1, 184, 264n.92

see also Burckhardt; ECCO; ICRC; Visser 't Hooft; WCCIF Refugee Office
humanitarian concerns 6, 36–8, 43, 47, 154, 156n.18, 168, 195n.6, 202

imperium in imperio 30, 70
International Christian Committee for German Refugees (ICCR) 137–9, 160n.79
International Christian Press and Information Service (ICPIS) 178–9, 193–4, 230
International Committee of the Red Cross (ICRC) 143, 180–5, 187–9, 194, 212n.84, 223
see also Burckhardt; ECCO; Huber; WCCIF
International Committee on the Christian Approach to the Jews (ICCAJ) 1–4, 9–10, *10*, 11, 16–19, 22n.31, 22n.32, 22n.33, 24, 32–8, *37*, 41–2, 46–7, *48*, 49–59, 60n.26, 60n.28, 62n.44, 64n.75, 65n.91, 65n.92, 71, 75, *79*, 78–85, *84*, 86, 94, 96–106, 108n.48, 109n.49, 110n.55, 116–124, 126, 128, 130–43, *132*, *134*, *140*, 155n.1, 156n.12, 159n.61, 159n.66, 159n.67, 160n.79, 165–73, 180, 195–206, *201*, 207n.8, 214n.118, 215n.133, 216n.135, 233–40, 244, 247–58, 263n.65, 263n.77, 264n.86, 264n.92, 270–9, 280, 285–7, 288–90
see also anti-Judaism; antisemitism; baptism; benevolence; conversion; evangelisation; guilt; Hoffmann; IMC; Jewish influence; Jewish mentalities; Jewish problem; Jewish provocations; Jewry; Judaism; nationalism; Nazism; non-Aryan Christians; racial antisemitism; racial-identity theory; refugees; reparation; rights
International Hebrew Christian Alliance 27, 110n.55, 136
International Missionary Council (IMC) 1, *10*, 9–11, 26–7, 32–3, 42, 47, 51, 55, 236, 256
see also Budapest–Warsaw conferences; ICCAJ; Mott
International Student Service (ISS) *10*, 43–4, 63n.58, 76–7, 94–5, 113n.97
see also Kotschnig; Parkes
internees 143, 181, 183, 186, 192, 195, 203
see also refugees; WCCIF Refugee Office
Israel (biblical) 119–22, 154, 196, 205, 246, 249, 253
Israel (modern state) 248, 250–2, 254–5, 258
see also Palestine; Zionism

Jewish influence 3, 19, 25, 29, 50–2, 54, 57, 70, 72, 78, 81–2, 87, 105–6, 173, 276–7, 290
Jewish mentalities and traits 3, 27, 30, 45–6, 49–52, 59, 60n.20, 70, 97, 113n.106, 118, 249, 275
Jewish problem (Jewish question) 1–5, 7–9, 16–17, 20n.7, 25–31, 34, 44, 49, 51, 54, 57–8, 75, 77, 88, 94–5, 97, 118–19, 132, 139, 149, 165–6, 169–70, 173, 185, 188, 192, 194–7, 205, 237, 245–6, 248, 257, 271–2, 274–7, 284, 286, 290–1, 296n.48

Jewish problem (Jewish question) (*cont.*)
  and 'Disappearance of Jew' 79, 79–81, 83, 275–7
  and solution 2, 8, 16, 17, 31, 36, 51, 55, 59, 81–2, 135, 173, 195, 201, 204, 237, 270–1, 274, 279, 290
  and threat of Jewishness 76–85, 106, 238, 275–7, 290, 296n.47
  see also anti-Judaism; antisemitism; conversion; Final Solution; Jewish influence; Jewish mentalities and traits; Jewish provocations; Jewry (modern); racial antisemitism; racial-identity theory
Jewish provocations 3, 24, 30, 45–6, 49–52, 59–1, 54, 60n.20, 70–2, 74, 79, 80–1, 97, 113n.106, 118, 121, 155n.10, 275
Jewry (modern) 78–82, 97–8, 106, 120–1, 129–30
  equation with Nazism 80, 120–1, 129–30, 133, 156n.22, 169n.66, 173, 204
Joint Commission on Goodwill 38–41, 62n.44
  see also CCAR; FCC, Goodwill Committee
Joint Distribution Committee (JDC) 183, 200, 211n.71, 215n.133
Judaism 4–5, 25, 29–30, 42, 51, 57, 58–9, 78–9, 96–7, 102, 119, 120, 149, 151, 162n.105, 165, 167, 198–9, 204–6, 242–3, 270, 275, 277–8, 288–9
Junginger, Horst 64n.75

Kapler, Hermann 14, 67–9, 73–5, 85, 282

Keller, Adolf 68–71, 87, 107n.10, 108n.30, 112n.83, 132, 137, 138, 210n.57
Kirchenkampf 232, 280, 285
  see also Brethren Council; Confessing church; *Deutsche Christen*; DEK; EKD; Reich church; UCCLW; WCCIF
Kittel, Gerhard 49, 64n.75, 132
Köberle, Adolf 132
Koechlin, Alphons 145, 162n.102, 226, 228, 229, 264n.92, 291n.2
Koenig, Pierre 228
Kohnstamm, Philip 116–17, 121, 132
Kosmala, Hans 118, 131–2, 134, 140, 196–7, 199–200, 202, 204–5
Kotschnig, Walter 43, 76–7, 108n.30, 136–7
Kraemer, Hendrik 179–80, 228, 241
Kraut, Benny 38–40, 62n.44, 62n.48
Kristallnacht 138, 145, 153, 282
Krummacher, Friedrich W. 93, 103, 112n.90, 112n.92, 145, 150
Kullmann, Gustave 139, 167
Kushner, Tony xi, 6, 296n.47

Laffon, General Émile 228
Lang, Archbishop Cosmo 76–7, 125, 150
League of Nations (LON) 3, 15, 28, 63n.60, 94, 169, 178, 181, 182
Leiper, Henry 68, 75, 85, 87, 89–93, 103, 107n.14, 112n.83, 130, 140–1, 150, 156n.20, 158n.54, 177, 236
Lieb, Fritz 132

Index 335

Lilje, Hanns 114n.124, 144–5, 232–3
Lipstadt, Deborah 217n.152
Lowrie, Donald 185–6, 211n.73
  see also Holocaust, deportations; Pétain; Nîmes Committee
Lutheran Bishop Statement (1939) 151–3, 163–4n.120, 282

Maas, Hermann 132
Macanna, Clephane 160n.79, 173
McDonald, James G. 94, 101, 114n.119, 114n.121, 135–7
Macfarland, Charles 87–9, 110n.61, 110n.62
Mackay, John 256
Mackie, Robert 175, 179, 221
Maclennan, Kenneth 179
Marahrens, Bishop August 144–5, 151–3, 162n.98, 163n.120, 262n.53
Marshall, Louis 40, 294n.42
Martin, Hugh 179
Marxism 70, 88
Mathews, Basil 51, 158n.54
Matthäus, Jürgen 164n.131, 211n.67
Mattuck, Rabbi Israel 170, 199, 294n.42
Maury, Pierre 228–9, 248–50
Mays, B.E. 255
Meiser, Bishop Hans 162n.98, 163n.120, 228–9, 233
Michelfelder, S.C. 226, 228–9, 261n.40
Michman, Dan 296n.48
Ministry of Information (MOI) 140, 176, 179, 182
Minorities Treaties 43–4, 63n.60
Montefiore, Claude 62n.55, 294n.42
moral suasion 274, 277

Morrison, Charles Clayton 120, 130
Mott, John R. 11–13, 27–8, 32–4, 36–8, 39–43 *passim*, 46–7, 55, 58, 64n.73, 76, 98, 108n.30, 126, 131, 159n.61, 256
  see also ICCAJ; IMC; Nobel Peace Laureates; WCC; WCCIF; WSCF; YMCA
Müller, Reich Bishop Ludwig 85–6, 88, 90, 112n.92

National Conference of Jews and Christians (NCJC) 41–2, 46, 62n.44, 62n.48
nationalism 25, 29, 43–5, 49, 51, 77, 97, 120–1, 129, 133, 251, 275
National Socialist Party (Nazi Party) 69, 71, 76–7, 93, 103, 145–6, 150, 155n.7, 231
Nazi campaigns 4, 6–7, 18–19, 67, 69, 72, 75, 77, 79, 82, 90, 95, 101–2, 105, 120, 134, 143, 145–6, 153–4, 166, 168, 180, 186–8, 191–3, 202, 218, 222, 238, 242–3, 271–2, 274, 281, 284–6, 288
  see also antisemitism; Final Solution; Holocaust; Jewish problem; persecutions
Nazi ideology 44, 45, 59, 69, 72, 80, 82, 85, 105–6, 119, 151, 153, 275, 277–9, 290–1
  see also antisemitism; Jewish problem; Holocaust
Nazi Party members 86, 93, 112n.92, 145, 150
Nazi research institutes 105–6, 115n.132, 162n.105
Nazism 2, 7, 16, 44, 67, 69–70, 100–1, 119, 120–1, 130, 152, 222, 224–5, 229, 230, 231, 274

Nazism (*cont.*)
  and equation with Jews 80,
    120–1, 129–30, 133, 156n.22,
    169n.66, 173, 204
Neill, Bishop Stephen 241, 243,
    256, 264–5n.94, 271
Nes, Rev J. van 53–4
neutrality 6, 12, 13, 43, 44, 55,
    143, 181–2, 184, 187, 191,
    286
  and policy 174–6, 181, 191
  and silence 173–9, 180–95,
    281–3, 285–6, 293n.33
  political and spiritual 174–6, 181
  see also ECCO; Huber; ICRC;
    MOI; Temple; Visser 't Hooft;
    WCCIF Refugee Office
Newell, Herbert 244–6, 248, 251
Newman, Rabbi Louis Israel 82–3,
    292n.13, 294n.42
New York Board of Rabbis 41
Niemöller, Martin 120, 130, 132,
    144, 156n.20, 223, 225–6,
    228, 231–3, 256, 262n.49,
    262n.53, 262n.59, 287, 291
Niesel, Wilhelm 233, 248–50, 257,
    267n.129
Nîmes Committee 185, 211n.71
  see also Lowrie
Nirenberg, David 296n.47
Nobel Peace Laureates 4, 11, 15,
    125, 180, 281
non-Aryan Christians 18, 86,
    100–1, 133–9, 140–8, 153–4,
    159n.63, 166, 180, 181–4,
    195, 239, 254, 273–4, 277,
    283
  see also Aryan laws; baptism;
    Confessing church; HCR;
    ICCAJ; ICCR; Kotschnig;
    McDonald; Parkes; refugees;
    UCCLW; WCCIF
numerus clausus 43–5, 63n.60

Oesterreicher, Fr Johannes 118,
    156n.12
Oldham, Joseph A. 71–2, 92,
    102–5, 125–6, 158n.44,
    159n.61, 162n.102, 177
Orthodox churches 17, 22n.30,
    125, 148, 215n.134, 225, 290
Oud Wassenaar Declaration (1919)
    13
  see also war guilt

Palestine 26, 30, 60n.9, 97–8,
    99–100, 116–17, 131, 165,
    168–9, 203–4, 234, 249,
    250–2, 255, 264n.92,
    267n.147
  see also Israel (modern state);
    refugees; Zionism
Paris Peace Conference (1919)
    63n.60
Parkes, James 23n.34, 43–7, 52–3,
    63n.63, 76–8, 94–7, 104–5,
    113n.97, 113n.98, 136,
    153–4, 170, 197–9, 204–6,
    207n.16, 214n.120, 215n.130,
    243–4, 246–7
  see also antisemitism; Aryan
    laws; CCJ; conversion; HCR;
    Hoffmann; ICCAJ; ISS;
    Jewish problem; Kotschnig;
    Mattuck; McDonald;
    refugees; RIIA; SCM;
    Simpson; SJC; Temple
Paton, William 71–2, 103, 117,
    126–42 *passim*, 146–51,
    157n.24, 158n.54, 159n.61,
    163n.120, 166–71, 175, 177,
    179–80, 189–91, 196–206,
    207n.8, 283
  see also Godesberg Declaration;
    ICCAJ; IMC; WCCIF
Pernow, Birger 131, 160n.79, 234,
    264n.86

Index

persecutions 7, 18–19, 31, 53, 68, 72, 75, 80–2, 105, 118–22, 125, 138, 220, 222, 240–1, 245, 275–8, 280, 283–5, 289
Pétain, Marshal Philippe 185
Prenter, Dr Regin 253
Presbyterian Board of National Missions (USA) 131, 138, 202–3, 236
Pressel, Wilhelm 225
Prisoners of War (POW) 36, 143, 180–1, 189, 202, 222, 233
propaganda (roles) 41, 42, 67, 69–70, 94, 96, 105, 122, 148, 171, 176, 205, 275, 284

race (Jews as a) 30, 31, 45, 58–9, 73, 77, 86, 88–9, 94, 100, 104, 118, 120, 122, 149, 151, 190, 204, 248–9, 275
race and nation (Christian universalism) 127–30
  see also supranationality; supraraciality
racial and national pride 30, 57–8, 97, 100, 121, 127–9, 275
racial antisemitism 9, 79, 80, 82–3, 97–8, 116, 120–9, 273, 277–8, 296n.48
  see also anti-Judaism; antisemitism; Jewish problem
racial-identity theory 25, 30, 57–9, 81, 97, 100, 106, 113, 118, 129, 173, 275
racism 59, 122–3, 126–9, 278
Ravasz, Bishop László 135
refugees 3, 8, 94, 98–102, 133–43, 134, 147–8, 154, 159n.63, 165–9, 180–95, 200–04, 201, 207n.8, 211n.71, 215n.133, 239, 244, 252, 273–4, 277, 283

and conversionary opportunity 165–7, 169, 195, 202–3
  see also Anschluss; Aryan laws; Barot; ECCO; Freudenberg; HCR; Hoffmann; ICCR; ICRC; ISS; internees; Kotschnig; McDonald; Nazi campaigns; Parkes; Toureille; UCCLW; WCCIF
Reich church 91–3, 103, 114n.124, 144–5, 149, 150, 153, 162n.98, 282
  see also Confessing church; DEK; *Deutsche Christen*; Godesberg Declaration; Heckel; *Kirchenkampf*; Krummacher; UCCLW; WCCIF
Reisner, Erwin 131–4, 159n.63, 159n.66, 159n.67
  see also Anschluss; ICCAJ
Rengstorf, Karl Heinrich 49, 64n.75, 233, 264n.92, 271
res judicata 14, 21n.22
Richter, Julius 49–50, 54–6, 132
Riegner, Gerhart 187–8, 191, 193, 283
Riga 48, 185
rights 25, 29, 43, 94, 102–3, 123, 127, 144, 153, 250–2, 282–3
  and evangelisation 167–8, 171–3
Röhm, Ernst 95
Roosevelt, Franklin D. 134, 194
Rouse, Ruth 86–7, 110n.56
Royal Institute of International Affairs (RIIA)169, 182, 200
Rupp, E.G. 262n.49

Schleunes, Karl v, xi, 114n.120
Schmidt, K.L. 132
Schönfeld, Hans 71, 90, 107n.14, 150, 223–4, 227, 210n.51, 264n.94

Schreiber, A.W. 88, 110n.61
secularism 47, 49–51, 54, 97, 117–18, 121, 129, 173, 275
Siegmund-Schultze, Friedrich 137
Simpson, William 160n.79, 197–8, 214n.117, 214n.118, 243–5, 249, 253
Smend, Rudolf 233
Smith, Robert 132, 166–8, 171–3, 197, 200, 202–6, 235, 271, 289
Snoek, Johan 270, 285
Society of Jews and Christians (SJC) 170, 199, 215n.131
  see also Mattuck; Parkes
Söderblom, Archbishop Nathan 12–16, 125, 180
  see also Bern Declaration; Nobel Peace Laureates; Stockholm conference; UCCLW; war guilt
solidarity 34, 81, 144, 178, 219, 231, 241, 253, 257
Staerk, Willy 120, 156–7n.22
Stapel, Wilhelm 77
Stockholm conference (1925) *10*, 14, 16, 26, 67–8, 125
  see also Bern Declaration; Söderblom; UCCLW; war guilt; WCCIF
Strauss, Roger 41, 294n.42
Strong, Tracy 211n.73
Student Christian Movement (SCM) 9, 10, 27, 36, 43, 78, 94–5, 179
Sturm, Colonel Marcel 228
Stuttgart Declaration of Guilt (1945) 223–6, 227, 228–33, 234, 248, 257
  see also confessional theology; EKD; guilt; Herman; Visser 't Hooft; war guilt; WCC; WCCIF

supersessionism 4–5, 28, 119, 149, 157n.27, 196, 253, 272, 279, 291
supranationality 10–17, 55, 89–90, 92, 125, 127, 146, 175, 232, 281
suprarraciality, 89, 125, 127
Swedish Mission to Israel 131–2, 234–5
  see also Hedenquist; ICCAJ; Kosmala; Pernow; Reisner
Swiss Committee for non-Aryan Refugees 139
Swiss Protestant Federation of Churches 27
sympathy 36–8, 71–3, 75–6, 91–2, 104, 123–4, 145, 165, 203, 256, 278, 289

Tal, Uriel 156n.22, 270–1, 277–8, 283
Tatlow, Tissington 76, 113n.97
Temple, Archbishop William 72, 146–51, 159n.61, 175–7, 179, 182, 191, 194, 198, 208n.31, 209n.43, 215n.130, 219–20
  see also Godesberg Declaration; neutrality; MOI; Paton; Visser 't Hooft; WCCIF
ten Boom, Willem 116–17, 120–1, 130–2, 157n.27, 159n.63
Thadden, Reinold von 144
Theresienstadt 188
Tomkins, Oliver 243, 247, 291n.2
Toureille, Pierre 183, 210n.64
Treaty of Trianon (1920) 43, 63n.60
Treaty of Versailles (1919) 12–14, 108n.30, 219
Treysa conference (1945) 223, 226
Tübingen 49, 132

Index

unanimity 2, 16, 28, 58, 99, 104, 117, 122, 130, 140–2, 174, 226, 229, 234, 240, 256, 258, 272
Una Sancta 17, 104, 125, 148, 280
Universal Christian Council for Life and Work (UCCLW) *10*, 10–11, 15–17, 68–9, 71–5, 85–94, 98, 101–4, 116, 120, 123–30, 136–8, 142–5, 177, 219, 280–2, 285–6
  as Christian mouthpiece 16, 125, 285
  Chamby (1936) 103–4, 114n.124, 137, 144, 282
  Fanø (1934) 90–4, 102, 112n.85, 120, 130, 144, 282
  Novi Sad (1933) 85–90, 92, 282
  Oxford (1937) 102–4, 116, 123–30, 138, 144–5, 151, 219, 282
  see also Bell; Bern Declaration; Leiper; Söderblom; Stockholm conference; war guilt; WCCIF
universalisation (of Jews) 2, 5, 9, 25–6, 28, 49, 57, 82, 95–6, 105, 121, 272, 274, 276, 279, 290
universalism (Christian) 1, 3, 19, 89, 98, 126–8, 151, 171–2, 175, 220, 256, 281
  see also supranationality; supraraciality; *Una Sancta*

Vidler, Alec 169, 205
Visser 't Hooft, Willem Adolf 70–2, 87, 130–1, 138–43, 146–52, 159n.67, 173–80, 182, 186, 189–95, 196, 198, 209n.46, 209n.51, 214n.107, 219–23, 224, 226, 228–9, 231–2, 236, 244, 247, 283–5, 287
  see also Godesberg Declaration; neutrality; Stuttgart Declaration; UCCLW; WCC; WCCIF
Vogt, Paul 214n.107

Waetjen, Eduard 223, 260n.22
Wandering Jew 239–40, 264n.88
war guilt
  and (WWI) 11–16, 68–9, 108n.30, 218, 222, 232
  and (WWII) 218–32, 246, 257, 259n.9, 280–1
War Prisoners Aid 187, 202
Warsaw ghetto 184, 186, 200, 202
Waxman, Rabbi Meyer 58, 294n.42
Webster, Macdonald 26–7, 29, 35, 51, 61n.37, 78, 237, 272
Westphal, Rev Charles 251, 253, 268n.162
Wise, Rabbi Stephen 188
World Alliance for Promoting International Friendship through the Churches (WA) *10*, 10, 13–14, 69, 89–90, 93–4, 130, 137, 142, 181
World Conference on Faith and Order (WCFO) 9, *10*, 11, 130, 145
World Council of Churches (WCC) 1, 3–4, *10*, 10–11, 15–18, 116, 155n.1, 179, 206, 231, 270–1, 280, 283, 285–7, 291n.2
  and founding statement on Jews (1948) 1, 3, 16, 108n.20, 231–3, 237, 241, 244, 247–58, 265n.108, 280, 286
  and preliminary materials 241–47, 248–9, 256–7

World Council of Churches in Formation (WCCIF) *10*, 15–17, 22, 30, 60n.26, 130–1, 143–54, 169, 173–80, 195–6, 202–3, 204n.46, 218–23, 224–8, 227, 229–33, 234–7, 239–40, 244–7
and Refugee Office 138–9, 140–3, 147–8, 180–95
see also Bermuda Conference; Confessing church; DEK; *Deutsche Christen;* ECCO; EKD; Godesberg Declaration; ICCAJ; ICRC; IMC; Lutheran Bishop Statement; neutrality; Reich church; Stuttgart Declaration; UCCLW; war guilt; WCC; WJC
World Jewish Congress (WJC) 182, 187–91
see also Bermuda Conference; Riegner; WCCIF
World Missionary Conference 9–11, *10*, 34
World Student Christian Federation (WSCF) *10*, 10–12, 27, 36, 43–4, 70, 142, 175, 181

Wurm, Bishop Theophil 153, 163n.20, 220–1, 223, 225–6, 228–9, 231–2, 245, 261n.43, 262n.53, 266n.117

Yates, Timothy 34
YMCA *10*, 10–11, 27, 35, 36, 60n.28, 61n.29, 65n.92, 142–3, 181, 185–7, 210n.61, 211n.71
see also Lowry; Nîmes Committee; War Prisoner Aid
YWCA *10*, 10, 35, 61n.29, 181, 210n.61

Zionism 25, 29, 49, 79, 97, 99–100, 121, 133, 157n.27, 159n.63, 203, 234, 237–8, 241, 244, 250–1, 275
see also Israel (modern state); Palestine
Zoellner, Wilhelm 103, 144, 162n.98
see also Reich church

Milton Keynes UK
Ingram Content Group UK Ltd.
UKHW021257191124
2962UKWH00006B/39